LABOUR MARKET INSTITUTIONS AND PRODUCTIVITY

This book explains the role of formal labour market institutions in keeping the labour utilisation in Central and Eastern Europe above the level characteristic for Western European states. It provides an innovative and enriching take on labour utilisation at large and how various formal labour market institutions can affect the ongoing trend in labour utilisation in a way that is not covered by the extant literature. The impact of labour market institutions on labour market outcomes is analysed throughout 12 chapters, both from a cross-country perspective and in detailed case-studies, by 21 labour market experts from various CEE countries. Most chapters are based on empirical methods yet are presented in an easy-to-follow way in order to make the book also accessible for a non-scientific audience. The volume explores three key questions:

- How can labour utilisation be increased by labour market institutions?
- Which CEE countries managed to create a labour market institutional framework beneficial for labour utilisation?
- How should the labour market institutions in CEE countries be reformed in order to increase labour utilisation?

The book argues that the legacy of transition reforms and a centrally planned past is still relevant in explaining common patterns among CEE countries and concludes that increasing the stock of skills accumulated by the employed and improving utilisation of these skills seems to be the first-best solution to increase labour utilisation.

The book will be of interest to post-graduate researchers and academics in the fields of labour economics, regional economics, and macroeconomics as well as scholars interested in adopting an institutional analysis approach. Additionally, due to the broader policy implications of the topic, the book will appeal to policymakers and experts interested in labour economics.

Beata Woźniak-Jęchorek is an associate professor at the Institute of Economics at Poznań University of Economics and Business in Poland.

Michał Pilc is an assistant professor at the Institute of Economics at Poznań University of Economics and Business in Poland.

ROUTLEDGE STUDIES IN LABOUR ECONOMICS

THE POLITICAL ECONOMY OF EMPLOYMENT RELATIONS
Alternative Theory and Practice
Aslihan Aykac

THE ECONOMICS OF TRADE UNIONS
A Study of a Research Field and Its Findings
Hristos Doucouliagos, Richard B. Freeman and Patrice Laroche

YOUNG PEOPLE AND THE LABOUR MARKET
A Comparative Perspective
Floro Caroleo, Olga Demidova, Enrico Marelli and Marcello Signorelli

WOMEN'S ECONOMIC EMPOWERMENT IN TURKEY
Edited by Onur Burak Çelik and Meltem İnce Yenilmez

A COMPARATIVE PERSPECTIVE OF WOMEN'S ECONOMIC EMPOWERMENT
Edited by Meltem İnce Yenilmez and Onur Burak Çelik

MEDITERRANEAN MIGRATION AND THE LABOUR MARKETS
Policies for Growth and Social Development in the Mediterranean Area
Edited by Salvatore Capasso and Eugenia Ferragina

THE DIGITAL TRANSFORMATION OF LABOR
Automation, the Gig Economy and Welfare
Edited by Anthony Larsson and Robin Teigland

LABOUR MARKET INSTITUTIONS AND PRODUCTIVITY
Labour Utilisation in Central and Eastern Europe
Edited by Beata Woźniak-Jęchorek and Michał Pilc

For a full list of titles in this series, please visit: www.routledge.com/Routledge-Studies-in-Labour-Economics/book-series/RSLE

LABOUR MARKET INSTITUTIONS AND PRODUCTIVITY

Labour Utilisation in Central and Eastern Europe

Edited by Beata Woźniak-Jęchorek and Michał Pilc

Routledge
Taylor & Francis Group
LONDON AND NEW YORK

First published 2021
by Routledge
2 Park Square, Milton Park, Abingdon, Oxon OX14 4RN

and by Routledge
605 Third Avenue, New York, NY 10017

First issued in paperback 2022

Routledge is an imprint of the Taylor & Francis Group, an informa business

British Library Cataloguing-in-Publication Data
A catalogue record for this book is available from the British Library

Library of Congress Cataloging-in-Publication Data
Names: Woźniak-Jęchorek, Beata, editor. | Pilc, Michał, editor.
Title: Labour market institutions and productivity : labour utilisation in Central and Eastern Europe / edited by Beata Woźniak-Jęchorek and Michał Pilc.
Other titles: Labor market institutions and productivity
Description: 1 Edition. | New York : Routledge, 2020. | Series: Routledge studies in labour economics | Includes bibliographical references and index.
Identifiers: LCCN 2020026870 (print) | LCCN 2020026871 (ebook)
Subjects: LCSH: Labor market—Europe, Eastern. | Labor market—Europe, Central. | Labor policy—Europe, Eastern | Labor policy—Europe, Central. | Manpower policy—Europe, Eastern. | Manpower policy—Europe, Central. | Europe, Eastern—Economic conditions—1989- | Europe, Central—Economic conditions.
Classification: LCC HD5764.7.A6 L2773 2020 (print) | LCC HD5764.7.A6 (ebook) | DDC 331.120943—dc23
LC record available at https://lccn.loc.gov/2020026870
LC ebook record available at https://lccn.loc.gov/2020026871

ISBN: 978-0-367-56423-0 (pbk)
ISBN: 978-0-367-44428-0 (hbk)
ISBN: 978-1-003-00965-8 (ebk)

DOI: 10.4324/9781003009658

Typeset in Times New Roman
by Apex Covantage, LLC

CONTENTS

List of figures vii
List of tables x
List of contributors xiii
Foreword xix
JESUS FERREIRO

Introduction **1**
BEATA WOŹNIAK-JĘCHOREK AND MICHAŁ PILC

PART I
Labour market institutions and labour utilisation across the CEE region **7**

1 Labour market regulation and labour utilisation in CEE countries **9**
BEATA WOŹNIAK-JĘCHOREK AND SŁAWOMIR KUŹMAR

2 Institutional determinants of firm-sponsored training of young employees **34**
DOMINIK BUTTLER

3 Skills utilisation – analysis across countries and occupations. Western European and post-socialist countries comparison **59**
MAGDALENA ANDRAŁOJĆ AND KEA TIJDENS

4 Unemployment benefits in CEE countries. Does their limited scope match societal preferences? **90**
MONIKA BANASZEWSKA AND MICHAŁ PILC

5 **Part-time employment in Central and Eastern Europe: a cross-country analysis** 116
KAMILA FIALOVÁ

PART II
Labour market reforms and utilisation: learning from countries' experiences 141

6 **Structures, institutions, and agency: the drivers of the expansion of precarious employment in Poland** 143
ADAM MROZOWICKI

7 **Skills utilisation and gender: Estonian case study** 164
MARYNA TVERDOSTUP

8 **Utilisation of returning migrants' skills and labour: the case of Lithuania** 188
EGIDIJUS BARCEVIČIUS, LUKA KLIMAVIČIŪTĖ, AND LUKAS PUKELIS

9 **The economic effects of the minimum wage in Slovenia** 212
SUZANA LAPORŠEK AND MATIJA VODOPIVEC

10 **The role of old-age pension systems as labour market institutions: the Czech Republic and Poland compared** 237
PAWEŁ ŁUCZAK AND MICHAŁ POLAKOWSKI

11 **How active labour market policy helps the most disadvantaged: evidence from the Czech Republic** 260
ONDŘEJ HORA AND TOMÁŠ SIROVÁTKA

12 **Eroding collective bargaining in CEE countries as a counterproductive factor in the process of labour utilisation: the cases of Bulgaria and Poland** 284
JAN CZARZASTY AND VASSIL KIROV

Conclusions 309
BEATA WOŹNIAK-JĘCHOREK AND MICHAŁ PILC

Index 313

FIGURES

1.1 Number of reforms adopted by CEE countries vs. EU-15 mean between 2000–2017 (by selected policy domain and direction) 16
1.2 Employment Protection Legislation for regular and temporary contracts in CEE vs. mean in EU-15 countries 18
1.3 Employment Protection Legislation in Europe in 2013 19
1.4 Job security rules in CEE vs. EU- 15 mean between 2000–2017 20
2.1 Training incidence among young employees and trade unions strength 48
2.2 Training incidence among young employees and labour market policy spending 49
2.3 Training incidence among young employees and features of education systems 50
2.4 Training incidence among young employees and employment protection legislation 51
2.5 Training incidence among young employees and economic conditions 51
3.1 The occupational matrix in Belarus 73
3.2 The occupational matrix in the Czech Republic 73
3.3 The occupational matrix in Hungary 74
3.4 The occupational matrix in Poland 74
3.5 The occupational matrix in Romania 75
3.6 The occupational matrix in the Russian Federation 75
3.7 The occupational matrix in Slovakia 76
3.8 The occupational matrix in Ukraine 76
3.9 The occupational matrix in Belgium 77
3.10 The occupational matrix in Denmark 77
3.11 The occupational matrix in Germany 78
3.12 The occupational matrix in Italy 78
3.13 The occupational matrix in the Netherlands 79
3.14 The occupational matrix in Spain 79
3.15 The occupational matrix in Sweden 80

3.16 The occupational matrix in the United Kingdom 80
3.17 Subjective qualification mismatch across analysed countries in 2008–2018 82
3.18 Qualification mismatch by type of country and the group of occupation in 2008–2018 83
4.1 Spending on unemployment benefits in CEE countries vs. mean and median spending in EU-15 countries in the years 1995–2017 (as % of GDP) 96
4.2 The median values of the minimum and the maximum unemployment benefit duration in CEE countries vs. EU-15 in the years 2002–2016 (in days) 97
4.3 Net replacement rate in unemployment in CEE countries vs. mean and median in EU-15 countries in the years 2001–2017 (as %) 98
4.4 Pseudo-coverage rates of unemployment benefits in CEE countries vs. mean and median in EU-15 countries in the years 2007–2016 (as %) 99
5.1 Total and involuntary PT employment in Europe (% of total employment), 2018 121
5.2 Part-time employment in CEE countries (% of total employment), 1996–2018 123
6.1 Basic characteristics of the Polish labour market 146
7.1 Labour market dynamics 168
8.1 Emigration, immigration, and return migration (number of people), Lithuania 2004–2018 190
8.2 Labour productivity in selected CEE countries, annual growth rate (%) 2004–2018 192
8.3 Hours worked per capita in selected CEE countries, annual growth rate (%) 2004–2018 193
8.4 Number of articles on return migration scraped from the main news portals 202
9.1 The ratio between the minimum and average gross wages and cumulative indices of real minimum and real average gross wage growth, 1995–2018 217
9.2 The minimum wage real growth and real GDP growth in Slovenia, 1996–2018, in % 218
9.3 Number and share of FTEs receiving a wage set at the minimum wage, yearly averages, 2005–2015 219
9.4. Hourly minimum wage in euros and PPS and nominal and real developments in minimum wage between 2018 and 2019 in % 220
9.5 The minimum wage as the percentage of average wages of workers employed full time in the EU Member States, 2007–2015 221

9.6 Change of value added compared to previous year (in %) and number and share of FTEs receiving a wage set at the minimum wage by selected industry affiliations, 2006–2015 224
9.7 Wage distribution – non-agricultural workers in dependent employment, 2008–2013 225
10.1 Employment rate of older men and women (55–64) between 1998 and 2018, percentage points 244
10.2 Average effective age of retirement between 1999 and 2018 249
10.3 The number of newly granted old-age pensions, in thousands 251
11.1 Presence of training programs' participants and people in the control group in PES register in 750 days after the start of the program 273
11.2 Presence of subsidised workplaces' participants and people in the control group in PES register in 750 days after the start of the program 274
11.3 Presence of public works' participants and people in the control group in PES register in 750 days after the start of the program 274

TABLES

1.1	Labour utilisation in CEE vs. mean in EU-15 countries	21
1.2	Labour utilisation and job security regulation – descriptive statistics	24
1.3	Canonical correlation analysis in CEE and EU-15 countries – summary	25
1.4	The standardised canonical coefficients (weights) in CEE and EU-15 countries	25
2.1	The operationalisation of institutional variables and their sources	42
2.2	Descriptive statistics, micro-level variables	44
2.3	Descriptive statistics, macro-level variables	45
2.4	Micro-level determinants of firm-sponsored training, 2010. Marginal effects, multilevel random intercept logit model	46
2.5	The share of young employees (aged 35 or less) who participated in training in 2010	47
2.6	Impact of the institutional variables on firm-sponsored training incidence, results of the two-level random intercept model	52
2.7	The composition of micro-level characteristics in a comparative perspective (percentages except for education measured in years)	54
3.1	The number of respondents in each country (years 2008–2018)	62
3.2	The number of respondents in each occupation in the years 2008–2018	63
3.3	The occupational matrix	65
3.4	Low-paid occupations in the analysed countries	66
3.5	High-paid occupations in the analysed countries	68
3.6	Mixed occupations in the analysed countries	69
3.7	Pay satisfaction (mean) in particular occupational groups by country	84
4.1	The percentage of answers (weighted) to the survey questions concerning unemployment benefits	103
4.2	Estimation results for the CEE countries	104
4.3	Estimation results for the EU-15 countries	106

5.1	Part-time employment in CEE countries, 2018	122
5.2	Relationship between part-time and full-time employment, inactivity and total employment (as a share of the population): coefficients of correlation with part-time employment, 1995–2018	125
5.3	Business cycle effects on the part-time employment rate and the involuntary part-time employment rate: total working population aged 15–64	129
5.4	Business cycle effects on the part-time employment rate in CEE: demographic sub-groups	131
5.5	Part-time employment determinants: results of empirical estimations	132
6.1	The forms of paid work in Poland and their occurrence	147
6.2	The current and desired type of work situation among young Poles (in %)	152
7.1	Definitions and empirical measures of the main variables	171
7.2	Summary statistics by gender	176
7.3	Gender gaps in SUW – total sample	177
7.4	Gelbach decomposition of gender gaps in SUW	179
7.5	Gender-specific returns to SUW	180
8.1	Descriptive statistics of the sample, LFS data for the period 2013–2018	197
8.2	Work-related regression results	199
8.3	OLS regression results regrading wages	200
8.4	LDA topic modelling algorithm, 1 topic, 20 words	203
8.5	The number of articles mentioning specific institution, programme, or concept	204
9.1	Employment probability among individuals employed in March 2009, using static firm-level minimum wage shock values from 2009	226
9.2	Regressions of employment based on firm-level data using static minimum wage shock – firms with more than 10 workers, using shock calculated based on predicted wages, 2010–2015	229
9.3	Summary of key regression coefficients and marginal effects using static minimum wage shock – firms with more than 10 workers, using shock calculated based on predicted wages, 2010–2015	231
10.1	The scale of attractiveness of early retirement and late retirement	240
10.2	Change in employment rates of older workers by educational level between 2000 and 2017, percentage points	244
10.3	Preferences for early retirement of older workers in selected European countries, percentage points	246

10.4	Logistic regression predicting likelihood of looking for early retirement based on subjective health, CASP index, gender, BMI, and living with a partner	247
11.1	Brief description of main ALMP tools in the Czech Republic	266
11.2	Development of number of program participants in public works, subsidised workplaces and training (total for years 2011–2018)	268
11.3	Share of chosen groups in ALMP programs and indexes of targeting	269
11.4	Stated reasons to leave PES register for program participants and control groups	271
12.1	Labour productivity per person employed and hour worked	287
12.2	Total R&D personnel and researchers by sectors of performance, as a percentage of the total labour force and total employment	288
12.3	Exports of high-technology products as a share of total exports	289
12.4	Main economic indicators for Bulgaria and Poland	290
12.5	Single-employer collective agreements in Bulgaria registered annually	293
12.6	Trade union density in Poland (%): survey data	298
12.7	Single-employer collective agreements in Poland registered annually	299
12.8	Emigration and immigration in Bulgaria and Poland	303

CONTRIBUTORS

Editors

Beata Woźniak-Jęchorek is an associate professor at the Institute of Economics at Poznań University of Economics and Business in Poland. Her theoretical and empirical works cover labour economics and institutional problems of labour markets and have appeared in several journals and two books published by Routledge Taylor & Francis Group. Her last book, *Institutional Determinants of the Polish Labour Market. A Theoretical and Empirical Study*, was awarded by The Polish Academy of Science as being the best book in 2016 on the labour market in Poland. She has also received the BISE Bank Award for the best Ph.D. thesis. In 2020, she has been granted a scholarship of Polish National Agency for Academic Exchange for a one-year stay at the Northwestern University. Her current project aims to identify the challenges in labour market institutions in the age of Industry 4.0.

Michał Pilc is an assistant professor at the Institute of Economics at Poznań University of Economics and Business in Poland. His research concentrates on labour economics and especially on the political economy of labour market institutions. His publications appeared in several journals including *Economic and Industrial Democracy*, *Communist and Post-Communist Studies*, and *Post-Communist Economies*. He has been granted the START scholarship from the Foundation for Polish Science. He also received the Dekaban Liddle Fellowship (as a junior fellow), which is granted in a collaboration between the University of Glasgow, the University of Warsaw, and the Piast Institute.

Contributors

Magdalena Andrałojć is an assistant professor at Poznań University of Economics and Business in Poland. She conducts research in the field of labour market, wages, and the social and economic value of work. She has participated in many international projects concerning labour market and human resources management financed by Eurofound Work Organisation, by EU Commission in VI Framework Programme, and the Polish government. She was granted EPUNET Research Visits at CEPS/INSTEAD, Luxembourg, and a Marie Curie Fellowship, at Aalborg University, Denmark. She is a coach with ICF accreditation ACC.

Monika Banaszewska is an assistant professor at Poznań University of Economics and Business, Institute of Finance, Department of Public Finance. She received a Ph.D. degree in 2014. She teaches public finance, local government finance, and taxation. She had a few research stays at University of Kassel (Germany). She also obtained a research grant from DAAD. Her research interests focus on fiscal federalism, fiscal policy, and political economy. She has authored several papers in these fields and has presented her research results at a number of national and international conferences.

Egidijus Barcevičius is an associated professor at Vilnius University and Research Director at Public Policy and Management Institute (PPMI). During the last ten years he has contributed to several studies on migration, the labour market, and digital transformation in Lithuania and other EU countries. He has led several research projects supported by the Lithuanian Research Council. They include: 'Friends or foes? Integration of return migrants into the labour market and society of Lithuania' and 'Vicious cycle? Analysing return and repeated migration of Lithuanians'. He is also engaged in applied, policy-oriented research and provides evidence-based advice to national and international institutions.

Dominik Buttler works as an assistant professor in the Department of Labour and Social Policy at Poznań University of Economics and Business, Poland. His research interests include labour economics and economics of education, with a particular focus on the school-to-work transition.

Jan Czarzasty is an assistant professor in the Institute of Philosophy, Sociology and Economic Sociology, Warsaw School of Economics (SGH). He is the head of the Economic Sociology Unit; expert of the Institute of Public Affairs (ISP) in Warsaw, correspondent of the European Foundation for the Improvement of Living and Working Conditions (Eurofound) in Dublin, collaborator of the European Trade Union Institute (ETUI); independent expert working for social partners both at the national and cross-national level; research fellow at the Central European Labour Studies Institute (CELSI) in Bratislava; assistant-chief editor of the *Warsaw Forum of Economic Sociology*; reviewer for the *British Journal of Industrial Relations*, *Competition and Change*, *Employee Relations*, *Transfer*, *Social Policy & Administration*. His last publications appeared in several journals including *European Journal of Industrial Relations*, *Employee Relations*, and *Transfer: European Review of Labour and Research*.

Kamila Fialová is a senior researcher in the Department of Economic Sociology at the Institute of Sociology of the Czech Academy of Sciences. She holds a

Ph.D. in economics from the Institute of Economic Studies, Charles University in Prague. She also studied demography at the Faculty of Science at Charles University. In the past she worked as a macroeconomic analyst at the Czech Republic Government Office, in the Chief Economist Unit of Komeční banka (Société Générale Group), and was also several times hired as a short-term consultant by the World Bank. Her specialisation covers macroeconomic and labour market research, and her main academic interest is the labour market institutional environment, informal employment, part-time work, poverty, and well-being. Her academic experience includes publishing of research articles, teaching, conference presentations, and acting as a referee for several renowned academic journals.

Ondřej Hora is an assistant professor at the Faculty of Social Studies of Masaryk University, the Czech Republic, and a researcher at the Research Institute of Labour and Social Affairs. His main interests are social policy, employment policy, and evaluation research. His latest research was about the position of young people on the labour market. It was published in the books *Effective Interventions for Unemployed Young People in Europe* (Routledge), *Local Matters: How Neighbourhoods and Services Affect Social Inclusion and Exclusion of Young People in European Cities,* and *Youth Unemployment and Job Insecurity in Europe: Problems, Risk Factors and Policies.*

Luka Klimavičiūtė is a researcher at Public Policy and Management Institute (PPMI) who works on issues related to migration, employment, and technology in the public sector. Luka is well versed in quantitative methods, including work with survey data, regression analysis, and randomised control trials for the European Commission as well as Oxford's Migration Observatory. In 2018, she helped implement the second wave of the COLLEEM Survey of 40,000 respondents for the Joint Research Centre (JRC). Additionally, she is involved in the CEE Youth comparative study of young migrants from Poland and Lithuania in the context of Brexit. Before joining PPMI, Luka consulted for various organisations, including the World Bank and Migration Policy Institute.

Vassil Kirov is an associate professor at the Bulgarian Academy of Sciences and Associate Researcher at the European Trade Union Institute (ETUI). His research interests are in the sociology of work and organisations, employment relations, and digitalisation. Vassil Kirov has been a researcher in large EU-funded research projects (SMALL, WORKS, WALQING, ENLIVEN, BEYOND4.0) and has worked as an external expert for the European Commission, the International Labour Organisation, the European Foundation for Working and Living Conditions, and CEDEFOP. Vassil Kirov has been a Member of the European Commission High-Level Expert Group on the Impact of the Digital Transformation on EU Labour Markets. Currently he is a visiting professor at Sciences Po, France. He has published several books and articles in international scientific journals. Among his last publications are the co-edited books published by Palgrave and Routledge.

Sławomir Kuźmar is an assistant professor at the Institute of Economics at Poznań University of Economics and Business in Poland. In 2016 he received a Ph.D. in economics from the Faculty of Economics, Poznań University of Economics and Business. His research interests include institutional analysis of the labour market, political analysis, and regional development studies. He is an author of a number of scientific papers and has participated in several national research programs and projects.

Suzana Laporšek is an assistant professor at University of Primorska, Faculty of Management, Slovenia. In 2014 she received a Ph.D. in economics from the Faculty of Economics, University of Ljubljana (with a doctoral thesis 'Minimum Wage Effects in Slovenia: Empirical Analysis with Microdata'). At the Faculty of Management, she lectures in the field of finance. Her research interests include finance and labour market analyses, with special interest in the evaluation of the labour market policy effects. She is an author of a number of scientific papers and has participated in several national and international research programmes and projects.

Paweł Łuczak works at the Department of Labour and Social Policy, Institute of Socio-Economics, Poznań University of Economics and Business. His main areas of research include long-term-care policy, housing issues, and comparative social policy. He is currently the principal investigator in the research project that aims at incorporating the housing dimension into comparative social policy research on long-term-care policy (funded by National Centre for Science Poland). He has written several papers in English (the latest paper has been published in *Social Policy & Administration*) and Polish (including papers for the Commissioner of Human Rights in Poland and the Bureau of Research of the Polish parliament).

Adam Mrozowicki is a sociologist, an associate professor in social sciences (economic sociology) at the Institute of Sociology at University of Wrocław in Poland. His academic interests lie in the areas of the sociology of work, economic sociology, comparative employment relations, precarity, critical social realism, and biographical methods. He authored *Coping with Social Change. Life Strategies of Workers in Poland's New Capitalism* (Leuven University Press, 2011) as well as more than 60 articles and book chapters, of which the most focused on the analysis of subjectivity and social agency of disadvantaged sections of the Polish and Central and East European societies. His most recent research within the DFGNCN-funded project PREWORK (www.prework.uni.wroc.pl) concerns social consciousness, life strategies, and civic activism of young precarious workers in Poland and Germany.

Michał Polakowski works at the Department of Labour and Social Policy, Institute of Socio-Economics, Poznań University of Economics and Business. His main interests focus on comparative political economy of pension reforms, labour market institutions, childcare policy, EU governance, and social investment. He is the author of publications on pension reforms, social investment, and childcare policies. He earned his Ph.D. from Maastricht University, the Netherlands. Recently he finished a project 'Crises and Reforms Of Old-Age Pension Systems – a Comparative Analysis' sponsored by National Centre for Science Poland (agreement UMO-2016/20/S/HS5/00452).

Lukas Pukelis works as a lead data scientist at Public Policy and Management Institute (PPMI). After defending his Ph.D. in political science at Tartu University (Estonia), he started focusing on applying Big Data approaches and novel natural language processing techniques in social sciences. His main area of research is developing ways to leverage unstructured text data from the web to produce valuable insights and new indicators.

Tomáš Sirovátka is Professor of Social Policy at the Faculty of Social Studies, Masaryk University, and the head of Brno Research Centre of Research Institute of Labour and Social Affairs. He publishes in international journals like *Journal of European Social Policy, Social Policy and Administration, International Journal of Social Welfare, International Journal of Sociology and Social Policy,* and *Journal of Comparative Policy Analysis*. He co-edited *The Governance of Active Welfare States in Europe* (2011), *Innovation in Social Services* (2014), *Effective Interventions for Unemployed Young People in Europe. Social Innovation or Paradigm Shift?* (2018) and *Youth Unemployment and Job Insecurity in Europe: Problems, Risk Factors and Policies* (2019) and has contributed to many comparative books on labour market policies.

Kea Tijdens (Ph.D.) is a retired research coordinator at the University of Amsterdam and professor of sociology of women's work at Erasmus University Rotterdam. Since 2000 she has been also a scientific coordinator of the worldwide WageIndicator web survey on work and wages. She has published on wage setting, industrial relations, working time, and segregation in *European Journal of Industrial Relations*, *International Journal of Manpower*, *IZA Journal of Labour Economics*, *Journal of Official Statistics*, *Human Resources for Health*, and *World Development*. She has received FP6, FP7, and H2020 EU grants, as well as several Social Dialogue grants from the EU.

Maryna Tverdostup is a post-doctoral researcher at the University of Innsbruck, Department of Public Finance, and at the University of Tartu, School of Economics and Business Administration. She holds a Ph.D. from the University of Tartu (November 2018). Currently she is working at the Special Research Unit SFB F63 'Credence Goods, Incentives and Behaviour' at the University of Innsbruck. She is also a part of InWeGe *'Income, Wealth and Gender'* project, funded by European Union's Rights, Equality and Citizenship

Programme (2014–2020). Her research interests include economics of gender and migration, applied micro-econometrics, and experimental and behavioural economics.

Matija Vodopivec is an assistant professor at University of Primorska, Faculty of Management, Slovenia. He received a Ph.D. in economics from the Faculty of Economics, University of Ljubljana, in June 2019 (with a doctoral thesis 'The Effects of Employment Protection Legislation on Worker Flows and Productivity in Slovenia'). His professional experience includes working as an external consultant for a OECD labour market policy review in Slovenia, two ECB research projects on wage and labour adjustment dynamics in the Euro area, and an EU-funded project on reform strategies for social protection in Slovenia. His current research interests include the relationship between labour market outcomes and health, as well as the effect of employment protection legislation on worker and job flows in Slovenia.

FOREWORD

Since Milton Friedman set out the existence of a natural rate of unemployment, determined by structural and institutional elements, the study of the impact of labour market institutions on labour market results has gained relevance not only in the research agenda of the academic economists but also in the strategies of economic policy of public authorities and international organisations.

Mainstream economics accepts the existence of a long-term equilibrium rate of unemployment, the Non-Accelerating Inflation Rate of Unemployment (NAIRU). According to this view, in the long term the levels of employment and unemployment depend on the prevailing labour market institutions (trade unions, collective bargaining, unemployment benefits, employment protection legislation, pension systems, minimum wages, active labour market policies, etc.).

As far as these labour institutions get away the decisions concerning both wage-setting process and the conditions for hiring and firing a worker from what happens in an ideal world of perfect competition, it is claimed that those institutions introduce rigidities and distortions in the working of labour markets. These institutions would lead to an excessive real wage (well above the marginal productivity of labour) and, consequently, to a level of employment below that of the market-clearing equilibrium and to unemployment.

It must be emphasised that labour market institutions would also have a negative impact on economic activity in the short term and in the long term. On the one hand, adverse labour market institutions exacerbate the response of labour markets to business cycle fluctuations (demand-side shocks), thus increasing the volatility of economic activity. On the other, by reducing the long-term employment and raising the structural rate of unemployment (an impact that can be amplified by the existence of hysteresis effects), they can also have a negative impact on the level and growth of potential output.

Fuelled by these approaches and the recommendation made by international organisations, many developed and emerging economies, among them the transition economies of Central and Eastern Europe (CEE), have introduced reforms in their labour markets, with the aim of making them more flexible. In the case of the CEE countries, these reforms had two objectives: in the short term, to alleviate the negative impact on labour markets of the restructuring processes of their productive structure; in the long term, to accelerate the economic growth, helping these economies to catch up with their Western partners.

Despite the spread of the reforms making the labour market more flexible, the empirical evidence has been unable to reach a conclusive response to the questions concerning which institutions do have a significant impact on labour marker results or to the sign, direction, and size of these effects. Indeed, the confirmation of the existence of indirect negative consequences (labour segmentation, rising inequality, disincentives to capital and human accumulation, disincentives to innovation, etc.), cast serious doubts about the net long-term effects on the labour market and economic activity.

The uncertainty on the effects of labour market institutions necessitates conducting case studies that allow assessing the real impact generated by certain institutions on the labour market and economic activity in specific countries. This approach implies to accept the fact that the impact of some (if not all) labour market institutions may differ depending on the particular economic, social, and political features existing in the countries where they operate. In other words, a certain labour market institution, and, therefore, a similar reform in that institution, may have different consequences in different countries.

It is, therefore, evident that this book is relevant and timely. As mentioned, CEE countries face a set of structural problems that generate the risk to be subdued to a middle-income trap, impeding them the desired convergence with the most advanced European partners. To solve this problem, it must be known whether their current labour market institutions favour their processes of growth and development or, on the contrary, hamper them. If there exists a consensus on the necessary reform of some labour institutions, public authorities and social agents must have a correct idea on the short and long-term impact of this kind of reform, which requires an appropriate benchmarking based on the knowledge of the working of the labour market institutions in countries with similar characteristics.

Professor Jesus Ferreiro
Department of Applied Economics V
University of the Basque Country UPV/EHU
Bilbao, Spain

INTRODUCTION

Beata Woźniak-Jęchorek and Michał Pilc

This book focuses on the institutional determinants of labour utilisation in Central and Eastern European (CEE) countries. The common goal of the economic transition in this part of Europe was to reach the level of economic development characteristic of the Western European states. Despite the nearly 30-year period of positive changes that aim has not been achieved yet. In actuality, the societies of CEE countries face the problem of a middle-income trap and a risk of freezing the difference in the achieved welfare between them and Western European countries in the long run. Crucial in overcoming this problem is the utilisation of the available labour resource close to its potential level, which in the last three decades has been shrinking due to emigration to Western European countries and the ageing of European society. In this context the question arises how labour utilisation can be increased by labour market institutions and whether these institutions help utilise the labour resource in CEE close to its potential.

Thus, the aim of the book is to assess whether formal labour market institutions facilitate keeping the labour utilisation in CEE countries above the level characteristic for Western European states. The labour market institutions are understood in the book as a 'system of laws, norms, or conventions resulting from a collective choice and providing constraints or incentives that alter individual choices over labour and pay'. That system consists of active labour market policy, collective bargaining, employment protection legislation, minimum wage, pension system, policies to increase gender quality and inclusion, unemployment benefits, and union density, among others. The geographical scope of the study is the group of Central and Eastern European countries that have become members of the European Union: Bulgaria, Croatia, the Czech Republic, Estonia, Hungary, Latvia, Lithuania, Poland, Romania, Slovakia, and Slovenia. Thus, many Balkan countries will be excluded from the analysis mostly because they do not enjoy freedom of movement within the common EU market but also due to the missing data on labour market institutions. The book concentrates predominantly on the current differences in labour market institutional framework among countries. However, in order to better understand the determinants of these differences, particular chapters will describe also the trajectories of changes in labour market institutions from the early years of the transition period. Thus, the time scope of the study covers in fact the period from the 1990s till today.

OECD treats labour utilisation as a synonym to hours worked per capita and concludes that together with labour productivity it determines the level of GDP per capita. In that sense labour utilisation is a statistical indicator of the quantity of employed labour which can be precisely measured; however, it does not inform whether that quantity maximises society's utility. In fact, the OECD definition equates people with other means of production and presupposes that the time they spend working could not be decreased (assuming constant labour productivity) if their welfare was to remain stable. Thus, it is not surprising that definitions of labour utilisation, which to a various extent incorporate the qualitative aspect of labour, are not uncommon in the literature. For that reason, a broader definition of labour utilisation will be employed in this book which is understood as a contribution of human labour to GDP. This definition, apart from a quantitative aspect of labour, allows us to also incorporate the utilisation of the population's skills in the economy. So, in order to maximise labour utilisation not only the number of hours worked per capita should be equal to its potential level but also employees should be matched to job offers according to the most productive use of their skills. Throughout the book such indicators as labour force participation rate, employment rate, and the number of hours worked per capita will be used to measure the quantitative aspect of labour utilisation. To capture the qualitative aspect, it will be assessed to what extent the skills of the employed are utilised, or it will be approximated by labour productivity.

There is a broad consensus in the literature that labour market outcomes are determined by a labour market institutional framework. This framework in CEE countries – in order to adjust to the dynamic changes taking place in the labour market – was thoroughly rebuilt at the beginning of the transition period and significantly revised in later years. It resulted in the heterogeneity of institutional arrangements among CEE countries despite their common socialist legacy. In this book, we will employ that heterogeneity to assess which elements of the labour market institutional framework are beneficial for labour utilisation in CEE and which could be still improved.

The structure of the book

The book is divided into two parts according to the geographical scope and the applied methods: cross-country analyses and case studies. The first part (consisting of the first five chapters) has the broad ambition to show the different types of labour market institutions determining the labour utilisation across all CEE countries. In this part, the authors will identify how a particular institution needs to be constructed in order to keep labour utilisation at a high level and will compare the indicators characterising that institution between CEE and Western European (EU-15) states. The second part (comprising seven chapters) of the book also tries to identify how labour market institutions need to be constructed in order to keep labour utilisation at a high level but applies the case study perspective to that end. Even though in that part the authors focus their attention on particular countries and institutions, they include a brief comparison of the selected case to other CEE countries and Western European states.

In Chapter 1 Beata Woźniak-Jęchorek and Sławomir Kuźmar explore the nature of the relation between labour market regulations and quantitative aspects of labour utilisation in both CEE and EU-15 countries. Their analysis focuses especially on job security rules, which refer to the regulations governing the initiation and termination of employment contracts. They test the hypothesis that more strict regulation in terms of job security correlates with lower employment and productivity. In the first part of their empirical analysis they identify the main changes in labour market regulations using two types of data (from descriptive and indicator-based databases) in the CEE region and compare these trends with their counterparts in EU-15 countries. Then, to show the impact of employment protection regulations on labour utilisation in CEE and EU-15, they survey the canonical correlation between the job security indicators and labour utilisation measures between 2000–2013.

In Chapter 2 Dominik Buttler tries to verify which institutional factors can explain a cross-country variation in firm-sponsored training among young workers in Europe. In particular he tests the impact of four institutional characteristics: the strength of trade unions, the generosity of labour market policy, the features of education systems, and the level of employment protection. The focus is on the data from 23 countries representing five transition regimes: employment centred (e.g. Germany), universalistic (e.g. Sweden), liberal (e.g. Ireland), subprotective (e.g. Spain), and post-socialist (e.g. CEE countries). In the empirical part of the chapter, Buttler uses a two-level random intercept logit model to study the micro- and macro-level (mostly institutional) determinants of firm-sponsored training incidence. His analysis is based predominantly on the European Social Survey 2010, OECD, and ILOSTAT.

In Chapter 3 Magdalena Andrałojć and Kea Tijdens incorporate wage growth and wage level indicators to elaborate on an occupational matrix for different occupations, which illustrates skills utilisation on the labour market in Western European and post-socialist countries. In particular, they check how the skills mismatch translates to skills underutilisation in selected Western European and post-socialist countries. Their analysis is based on the WageIndicator web survey on work and wages from 2008 till 2018. Looking for similarities and differences in occupational structure between countries and regions, they also indicate probable migration movement.

In Chapter 4 Monika Banaszewska and Michał Pilc identify the main changes in the unemployment benefits schemes in CEE countries that have been introduced during the last three decades and compare these schemes with their counterparts in EU-15 states. The chapter concentrates also on the differences in the societal preferences between CEE and EU-15 countries concerning the governments' responsibility to provide a decent standard of living for the unemployed and identifies the main factors that determine these differences. The study is based on a broad set of data sources comprising Eurostat and OECD, as well as US Social

Security Administration (2019), Mutual Information System on Social Protection (2019) databases and, predominantly, the Role of Government survey (2018).

In Chapter 5 Kamila Fialová explores the part-time employment phenomenon in CEE countries as a form of non-standard employment relationships that has been rapidly expanding in Europe over the recent decades. In particular, she examines the relationship between part-time work and labour utilisation and tries to evaluate whether a potential expansion of part-time employment may facilitate growth in labour utilisation in CEE countries compared to the situation in the Western Europe (WE) region. The chapter describes also the main patterns of part-time work and the differences between the two regions. The analysis based on panel data identifies the main determinants of part-time employment and the key factors that limit its utilisation in the CEE region.

In Chapter 6, Adam Mrozowicki puts forward an interesting explanation of the drivers of the expansion of precarious employment. He focuses on the situation in Poland, in which precarisation of work – at least with respect to the expansion of temporary contracts – has been the most advanced in Central and Eastern Europe. In particular, in this chapter three drivers of precarisation are analysed: (a) socio-economic structures typical of the Polish variety of capitalism, (b) the three pillars of socio-economic institutions underlying precarity, including legal regulations, normative expectations, and cultural-cognitive schemes, and (c) agential responses of workers aimed at surviving, managing, or possibly resisting precarisation. Particular attention is paid to two former factors – institutions and workers' agency – which are held responsible for the perpetuation of precarity.

In Chapter 7, Maryna Tverdostup focuses on gender disproportions in skills utilisation in Estonia, the country with the highest gender wage gap in Europe. The empirical analysis is based on the survey data from the Program of International Assessment of Adult Competencies (PIAAC), which allows employing a direct measure of labour utilisation – on-the-job use of information-processing and generic skills. The major focus of the analysis is understanding which factors drive the gender gap in skills use at work. The chapter disentangles three major sets of these factors: demographic, human capital, and job related by using a multivariate OLS regression approach and Gelbach decomposition.

In Chapter 8, Egidijus Barcevičius, Luka Klimavičiūtė, and Lukas Pukelis analyse the situation of the returning migrants in the Lithuanian labour market and the effect of return migration on labour productivity and utilisation. The authors argue that during the last few years emigration from Lithuania has slowed down, and a significant number of emigrants have returned after the first wave of migration in 2004. To explore the status of return migrants in the Lithuanian labour market, the implications of return migration for labour utilisation and the role that different institutions play in facilitating labour market integration of the returnees, this chapter concentrates on two sources of data. Firstly, the authors use Lithuanian Labour Force Survey data for 2013–2018 to analyse the recent returnees. Secondly, they experiment with emerging big-data type tools and machine-based automatic text processing to analyse articles on return migration in the main news portals for 2004–2018.

In Chapter 9, Suzana Laporšek and Matija Vodopivec discuss the developments of minimum-wage policy in Slovenia and compare Slovenian minimum-wage policy to other EU countries. In particular, they examine the effects of Slovenia's dramatic 22.9% minimum-wage increase in March 2010 on a variety of economic outcomes including the wage distribution, the employment probability of individual workers, and firm performance. An in-depth study of the 2010 minimum-wage increase is relevant not only because of the magnitude of the increase but also because it provides an interesting case study of the effects of such an increase on labour utilisation immediately following a deep recession.

In Chapter 10 Paweł Łuczak and Michał Polakowski look at diverse pension designs in the Czech Republic and Poland and try to assess whether old-age pension systems facilitate keeping labour utilisation of older people at the high level in these countries. A pension system is framed here as a formal labour market institution that either facilitates an early withdrawal from the labour market or prolongs the employment of older people. The selection of the Czech Republic and Poland for the study is justified by substantial heterogeneity of institutional arrangements concerning pension systems, as they represent two divergent policy paths concerning pension reforms that were taken in CEE during the transition period.

In Chapter 11 Ondřej Hora and Tomáš Sirovátka assess how the public employment services are successful in integrating the long-term and repeatedly unemployed into the labour market in the Czech Republic. The analysis concentrates on the times after the crisis (2014–2016) and the key active labour market policy (ALMP) instruments (vocational training, subsidised jobs and public works) which are the most widespread types of ALMP programs in the Czech Republic. The analysis is based on administration data from the Public Employment Services. The measurement of the impact is done using a quasi-experimental evaluation based on matching or propensity scores in combination with exact matching. In turn, assessment of the implementation of ALMPs' conditions is based on a secondary analysis of various policy documents, implementation studies, and statistics.

Finally, in Chapter 12 Jan Czarzasty and Vassil Kirov investigate the impact of wage bargaining decentralisation and its ultimate deterioration (in a significant part caused by weakness of trade unions) on labour utilisation in two cases – Bulgaria and Poland. They argue that the general collapse of collective bargaining triggered by deliberate political choices in the beginning of transformation and further deepened by the weakness of both trade unions and employer organisations in each country, has not only pushed pay determination to the enterprise level but also has left the process largely in the hands of individual employers. The pursuit of low-wage competitive advantage in both countries has had visible consequences in the international division of labour by driving sizeable shares of the domestic workforce abroad (to EU-15), thus leaving widening gaps in national labour markets which have been filled by incoming migration from non-EU countries.

Part I

LABOUR MARKET INSTITUTIONS AND LABOUR UTILISATION ACROSS THE CEE REGION

1

LABOUR MARKET REGULATION AND LABOUR UTILISATION IN CEE COUNTRIES

Beata Woźniak-Jęchorek and Sławomir Kuźmar

Introduction

The debates about labour market regulation are often heated, reflecting ideological differences about the role of government intervention on the market. The opinion that labour regulations are needed to circumvent the weak bargaining power of employees in employment relationships, inadequate insurance against the risk of unemployment, to moderate effects of downswings in aggregate demand, and to enhance investments in human capital is characteristic for an institutionalist approach. From this perspective, institutions can reduce inequality and cut transaction costs, thereby enhancing productivity. The other 'distortionist' view underlines the advantage of the market process and argues that strict protection legislation increases the dualism of the labour market by favouring regular workers, increases effective labour costs, discourages hiring, and impedes adjustment to economic shocks (Freeman, 1993; Masso & Eamets, 2004). In the distortionist approach, institutions impede economic efficiency and can have perverse equity effects. These two visions differ significantly in their theoretical starting points, research methods, limitations, and even what constitutes evidence. The institutionalist research often downplays the value of sound empirical analysis that challenges its assumptions. In turn, the distortionist approach tends to be ahistorical, clinically measuring the impacts of institutions without appreciating that they have evolved through a social and political process as a part of a given society's social contract (Betcherman, 2015, p. 126).

Labour market regulations are usually understood as the rules determining, *inter alia*, what types of employment contracts are permissible, setting boundaries for wages and benefits, hours, and working conditions, and proscribing certain employment practices. However, regulations providing social protection for workers can be understood more broadly as an important part of the institutional framework around the labour market, including also rules for trade unions and collective bargaining, unemployment insurance, active labour market programmes, minimum wages, and equity legislation.

Generally, the labour regulations were designed for wage and salary work and presume widespread compliance, either voluntarily or through the enforcement capacity of the state (or trade unions). These assumptions are more difficult to maintain in CEE countries than in Western ones. In the case of Central and Eastern Europe, employment forms are more diverse, with large shares of workers in non-wage activities such as self-employment and family enterprise work. Even many wage employees are in the informal sector. Furthermore, the power of trade unions in this part of Europe is much weaker due to low unionisation. Therefore, setting an appropriate level of labour market regulation is dependent on country- or region-specific domain and made complicated by the fact that formal rules may differ due to various factors, e.g. the size of a country and the market, national social policies, social, cultural, historical, and legal traditions.

The nature of employment, coupled with limited administrative and enforcement capacities, raises questions about how labour markets are regulated in CEE countries, especially in the domain of job security rules, and how these regulations affect the labour utilisation. This question is an important part of the vigorous and continuously growing discussion on the role of labour market regulations for labour market flexibility and performance but also for its dualism and segmentation.

The particularly challenging issue in this research is measuring labour market regulations, which are inherently qualitative and multi-dimensional. To describe reforms carried out in the labour market, we can use two types of databases: descriptive[1] or indicator based.[2] Descriptive databases collect information on enacted reforms on the basis of pre-defined criteria with the aim of providing an exhaustive description of the main policy measures taken. These databases are useful especially when analysing the reform process and reform strategy characteristics. In turn, indicator-based databases aim at quantifying the level or stringency associated with the existing stock of regulations and institutions. While indicator-based databases permit a very effective synthesis of information for comparisons over time and across countries, which make them suited for statistical analysis on macro data, they do not provide information at the level of the specific policy measures (Turrini, Koltay, Pierini, Goffard, & Kiss, 2015, pp. 3–4).

Taking this into consideration, the first goal of this chapter is to identify the main changes in labour market regulations using two types of data (from descriptive and indicator-based databases) in the CEE region and to compare these trends with their counterparts in EU-15 countries. The second aim is to assess the correlation between job security rules (also known as employment protection legislation)[3] and quantitative aspects of labour utilisation in these two parts of Europe – CEE and EU-15 countries. It will help to assess whether labour market regulations in terms of job security facilitate keeping the labour utilisation in CEE countries above the level characteristic for Western European states.

In our analysis we have focused especially on job security rules, which refer to the regulations governing the initiation and termination of employment contracts. The employment protection rules determine the degree of job security by restricting the ability of employers to hire workers on an explicitly non-permanent basis or by making dismissal costly. The stringency of these rules can range from protective (restrictions on non-permanent contracts and limited employer dismissal rights) to flexible (unrestricted, non-permanent contracting and minimal limits on dismissal).

This chapter aims to make two contributions to the existing literature. First, particular attention is paid to extend research findings in the context of CEE countries; the evidence available for these countries is much more limited. Second, our research attempts to bridge two segmented bodies of literature, one established on a descriptive database and the other on an indicator-based database which have dominated research and policy debate in this field.

In our study we follow the hypothesis that more regulation in terms of job security correlates with lower employment and productivity. In this perspective, employment protection rules have been identified as an institution and mobility barrier into the core labour market (Bentolila, Dolado, & Jimeno, 2012; Rueda, 2005; Saint-Paul, 1996). To answer the identified research questions, qualitative and empirical analysis including canonical correlation analysis will be used.

Our results indicate that CEE and EU-15 countries differ significantly in terms of employment protection regulations and labour utilisation. These differences are especially evident in the case of different quantitative aspects of labour utilisation. For example the mean level of GDP per person employed in CEE countries in 2017 amounted to 63% of the mean EU-15 level. Similarly, hour productivity in CEE countries was only little more than half the level of the EU-15. What is also interesting is the great heterogeneity observed not only between these two groups of countries, but also within the CEE group itself. This difference includes both job protection regulation and labour utilisation. Our analysis indicates that the labour markets in Lithuania, Estonia, and the Czech Republic were the most protected, while the regulations in Hungary and Slovakia were the least protected or 'freest'. Simultaneously, empirical investigation of the relation between the employment protection regulations and quantitative aspects of labour utilisation indicate that less strict job protection regulation coexists with higher levels of labour utilisation, albeit extracted values of canonical correlations between the sets of studied variables as groups seems to be a little higher in the case of CEE countries than in the EU-15 group.

The chapter is structured as follows: we begin with short background sections on the impact of employment protection rules for labour utilisation; in the next section, we present the main trends of labour market reforms in 2000–2017 from a descriptive perspective in both regions – CEE and EU-15 countries – on average; then, we focus on indicator-based data concerning job security rules such as Employment Protection Legislation (EPL) index from the OECD database, the Hiring and Firing Regulations (HFR) index, the Hours Regulations (HR) index, and the Mandated Cost of Workers Dismissal (MCWD) index – the three subcomponents of Labour Market Regulations index developed by Fraser Institute; in the subsequent section, to show the impact of employment protection regulations on labour utilisation, we will survey the relation between these job security indicators and labour utilisation measures in CEE countries between 2000–2013 and compare the results with their counterparts in EU-15 countries; the final section concludes and underlines our main findings.

Theoretical background

The challenge in establishing labour market rules is to avoid the extremes of over- and under-regulation. Two perspectives are found here. The first perspective suggests that strict employment protection policies can benefit workers, especially the most vulnerable, without heavy costs to employers (Betcherman, 2019). In this context, according to economic theory, labour markets require regulations for the same reasons that all markets do – to mitigate market failures, like imperfect information, and to protect buyers (employers) and sellers (employees). Employment protection legislation comprises both a 'transfer' component (e.g. severance payments from the employer to employee) and a 'deadweight loss' component (e.g. procedural costs, dispute settlement processes) protecting *ipso facto* the most vulnerable on the market. Strict employment protection, especially concerning procedural requirements, also reduces the likelihood of jobs being destroyed in the event of economic shocks. Additionally, from the point-of-view of the workers' well-being, the strong regulations can be important in promoting job quality (Fenwick, Howe, Marshall, & Landau, 2007), encouraging investment in job training (Almeida & Aterido, 2008), discouraging absenteeism, and improving worker effort through the sense of a higher attachment to a firm (Jimeno & Toharia, 1996) or worker job satisfaction (Wilczyńska, Batorski, & Torrent-Sellens, 2016).

A more sceptical view sees more regulation as leading to a decrease in employment, consumption, productivity, and competitiveness and hurting the very workers the regulations are intended to benefit (ILO, 2003; Boeri, Cahuc, & Zylberberg, 2015; Betcherman, 2019). In this perspective, on the one hand, restrictions on firing workers (strong job security rules) result in a less flexible labour market with smaller flows between jobs and between employment and non-employment, reduce the speed at which employment adjusts to shocks, and increase the incidence of long-term unemployment (Bertola, 1990; Hamermesh, 1993; Hopenhayn & Rogerson, 1993; OECD, 2004; Boeri & Van Ours, 2008; Deakin, Malmberg, & Sarkar, 2014). Over-regulation creates also obstacles specially to labour reallocation to more productive activities,[4] which is an important driver of trade factor productivity growth (Melitz & Ottaviano, 2008). On the other hand, flexible market conditions' reducing the costs and risk of changing jobs make labour mobility across sectors possible to promptly respond to market fluctuations, increase the responsiveness of wages to changing economic conditions, and provide the right incentive mechanisms for both employers and employees (Boeri, 2005; Martin & Scarpetta, 2012; Damiani, Pompei, & Ricci, 2016). The ability to use temporary work contracts increases labour market flexibility, as it allows the employers to adjust their operations more effectively by replacing temporarily absent employees or filling seasonal work positions by temporary employees, meeting business-cycle fluctuations and short spikes in demand (OECD, 2002). However, at the same time the growing share of temporary employment can hamper productivity growth (because investment in the workforce is discouraged) and fail to increase employment levels (because secure employment is substituted with temporary jobs).

Additionally, the combination of strong protection against dismissal for those on open-ended contracts and loose enforcement of protection for temporary or other non-standard contracts induces labour market segmentation (Boeri & Garibaldi, 2007; Boeri, 2011; Eichhorst, Marx, & Wehner, 2017). We meet two phenomena here. On the one hand, stricter employment protection legislation regulating permanent contracts increases the likelihood of a temporary contract's being used. And on the other hand, strong job security for permanent contracts widens the gap between the job tenure of permanent and temporary workers and between their respective wage levels (European Commission, 2017). However, empirical evidence supporting the conjecture that deregulating employment protection (easing dismissal protections) especially for the possibility of permanent workers' reducing segmentation and 'insider–outsider divides' is still sparse (Kahn, 2010; see Rubery & Piasna, 2016 for an overview; Eichhorst et al., 2017). There is also strong evidence that temporary contracts, in particular, depress worker health and well-being (De Cuyper et al., 2008; Mani, Mullainathan, Shafir, & Zhao, 2013; Benach et al., 2014).

Generally, in empirical studies, the effects on job security legislation outcomes are still an open question. Job security regulations can potentially affect employment, unemployment, earnings, productivity, and other outcomes, but the estimated effects of labour market regulations on macroeconomic outcomes are inconclusive – sometimes positive or negative – but in many cases extremely modest (among others: Grubb & Wells, 1993; Scarpetta, 1996; Nickell, 1997; Elmeskov, Martin, & Scarpetta, 1998; Nickell & Layard, 1999; Glyn, Baker, Howell, & Schmitt, 2004; Howell, Baker, Glyn, & Schmitt, 2007; ILO, 2012, 2015; World Bank, 2013; Avdagic & Salardi, 2013; IMF, 2015; Adascalitei & Pignatti Morano, 2015). The lack of statistically significant effects has been related to model specification, data treatment, and the difficulties in precisely measuring the legal and effective stringency of labour legislation (IMF, 2015).

Research also shows that job security rules have different effects on formal and informal employment (Acemoglu, 2001; Albrecht, Navarro, & Vroman, 2006; Meghir, Narita, & Robin, 2015; Almeida & Carneiro, 2009; Almeida & Aterido, 2011; ILO, 2014) and do not have the same effects on all types of workers. According to predictions of conventional dual-sector theories, more costly job security rules would shift production from the formal to the informal sector. And the effects are most favourable for workers covered by these protections – typically, prime-working-age males and better-educated workers are overrepresented in this group, while youth, women, and less-skilled workers in uncovered jobs gain no benefit from these protections (Lazear, 1990; Nickell, 1997; Bertola, Blau, & Kahn, 2002; Kahn, 2007; Pagés & Montenegro, 2007).

How to assess labour market regulation changes in EU countries

The discussion in the opening section shows that two sources of measuring labour market regulation data exist: descriptive and indicator-based databases. For our analysis we have chosen the descriptive LABREF database, which records measures in labour market and welfare policy introduced in EU member states between 2000–2017. This database shows the changes in labour market regulation in nine policy domains (active labour market policy [ALMP], early withdrawal, job protection [EPL], labour taxation, other welfare-related benefits, unemployment benefits, wage setting, working time, and immigration/mobility) and is helpful to understand the main trends in labour market reforms in Europe. The second source of data for our analysis will be two indicator-based databases which are widely used in policy-oriented research on the role of labour market institutions and share the same characteristic: they aim at capturing labour market institutions in general and at describing them with one number. We will focus here on the Employment Protection Legislation (EPL) index[5] as the main measure of *de jure* job security regulation that has been published by OECD. This index makes it possible to quantify the overall strictness of employment protection legislation capturing the most important features of regulation, both for regular and temporary contracts and for collective dismissals. It was aimed at describing in depth one specific labour market institution – job security rules.

Then we will identify the main changes in the Hiring and Firing Regulations (HFR) index,[6] the Working Regulations (WR) index,[7] and the Mandated Costs of Worker Dismissal (MCWD) index[8] – three subcomponents of the Labour Market Regulations (LMR) index[9] developed by the Fraser Institute in the framework of the Economic Freedom around the World database. This second indicator-based database is partly based on data produced by the World Bank Employing Workers Indicator – a series of indicators developed by the World Bank, measuring some specific aspects of labour regulations, the survey conducted among employers published by the World Economic Forum. Using these different, specific indicators, we can classify the countries on these which are rather promoting labour market flexibility or preferably ensuring employment protection.

Insights from the descriptive database

By analysing labour market reform in CEE and EU-15 countries across the descriptive LABREF database, we have observed that even countries with similar institutional settings (characterised by similar transition history and market maturity) have not followed the analogous reform patterns from the 2000s. The specific scope and direction of reforms in each country depend primarily on the priority given to each labour market problem, the features of legislation that can best contribute to achieving the reform objectives, the need to address other issues to effectively and feasibly ensure the reform path, and the wide differences in national legislation systems and the need to preserve their internal coherence.

Figure 1.1 shows the evolution of the total number of reforms under each policy domain in CEE vs. the mean in EU-15 countries, classified by direction (the number of reforms increasing/decreasing underlying policy settings in 2000–2017). The bars shaded in dark refer to the total number of reforms in the various domains in a given period that took place in a given CEE country and, additionally, the mean in EU-15 that contributed to increasing the underlying policy settings (e.g. increasing the tax burden, the generosity of benefits, or the stringency of regulation). Correspondingly, the lightly shaded bars, on the negative portion of the vertical axis, report the number of reforms underlying policy setting that took place in a given domain.

A first look at Figure 1.1 reveals that the frequency of policy interventions varies considerably across policy domains. On average, most reforms were undertaken in the active labour market policy, and other welfare-related benefits, while early withdrawal, wage setting, and immigration/mobility reforms are relatively infrequent.

A second look at the graphs reveals that there are considerable differences across countries and policy domain regarding the direction of measures. In some policy domains, reforms normally take place in one direction only. For instance, while most reforms strengthened ALMPs, a large majority of reforms contributed to the reduction of labour taxation or the stringency of regulations concerning working time and the measures increasing the generosity of benefits or easing entitlement conditions (other welfare-related benefits). In contrast, in other domains such as job protection there is a more balanced distribution of reforms in terms of direction of their effects on underlying policy settings over the analysed period.

When looking at the distribution of reforms across CEE countries and comparing them to the mean in the EU-15, two observations stand out. First, although reform activity is relatively broad based and takes place in some extent in all countries, reforms do not always occur simultaneously in all countries. In particular, Lithuania and Latvia had more intense reform activity (with 193 and 191 regulation changes, respectively), while Slovenia and Estonia were on the opposite side (with only 101 and 132 regulation changes, respectively). In comparison with the EU-15, where the average number of reform changes in 2000–2017 was 191.9, it turns out that reform activism was more intense in countries with a longer record of EU membership. Obviously, a larger number of reforms in a given country, in a given period, does not necessarily imply that more extensive or effective policy actions have been put in place.

A second observation is that the distribution of reforms across domains is not the same for each CEE country. For instance, Lithuania was the most active in the domains of job protection, unemployment benefits, other welfare-related benefits, and immigration/mobility, while Romania was most active in working time, job protection, and wage setting areas. In the EU-15, on average, the most reforms have been made in unemployment benefits, active labour market policies, and immigration/mobility. These differences reflect the fact that the distribution

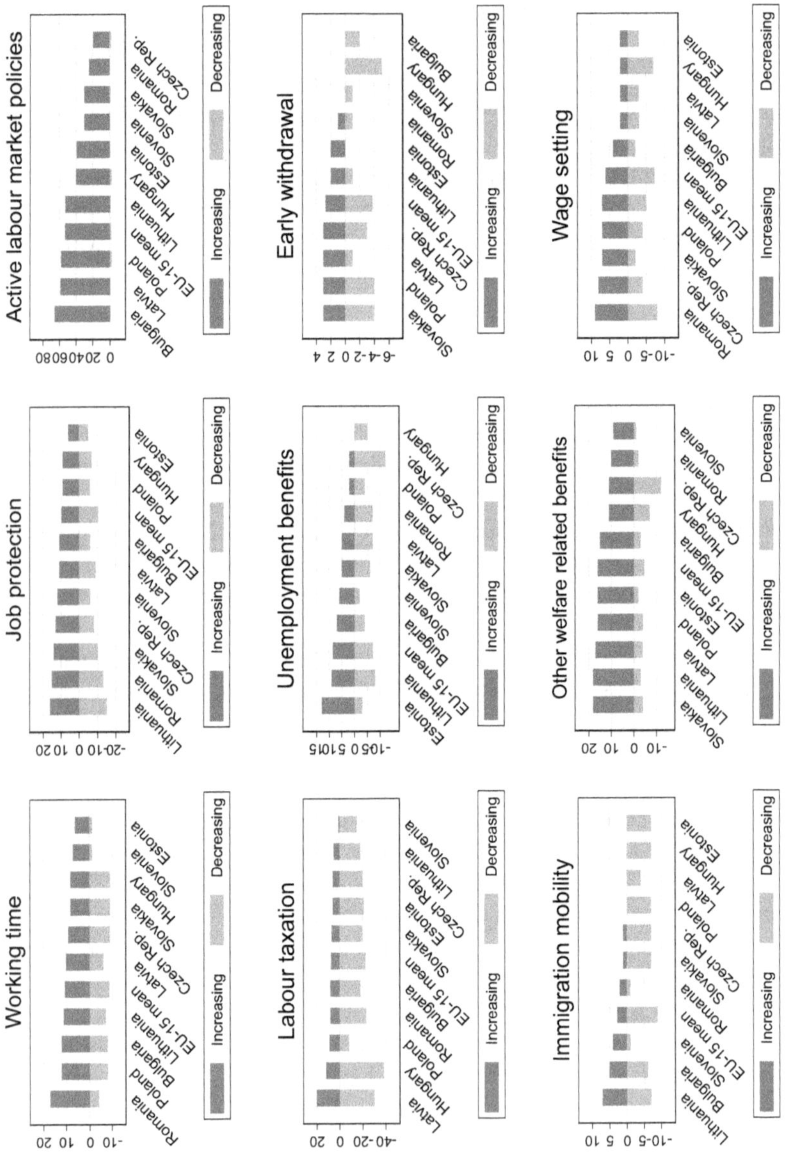

Figure 1.1 Number of reforms adopted by CEE countries vs. EU-15 mean between 2000–2017 (by selected policy domain and direction)

Source: Own elaboration based on LABREF database.

of reforms across domains and countries echoes the interplay between shocks and the main features of existing institutions. As Turrini et al. (2015, p. 28) state, the reform stance depends on the labour market conditions in an expected way, with high unemployment being associated with reforms lowering the tax burden on labour and raising the generosity of unemployment benefits and that of active labour market policies. It confirms the role of social expectation and desire towards the reforms, even if they generate social costs (Alesina, Algan, Cahuc, & Giuliano, 2015; Boeri, Conde-Ruiz, & Galasso, 2012; Emmenegger, 2014; Gallego & Marx, 2017; Lucifora & Moriconi, 2015; Vindigni, Scotti, & Tealdi, 2015).

Finally, it is worth pointing out that reform measures are far from being homogenous objects. Some of the problems are linked to the inevitable risk of missing information and non-obvious classification for the policy field or direction. Therefore, it is difficult to find evidence for reform activism and the level of employment protection measured by indicators from indicator-based databases.

Insights from the indicator-based database

Regarding the indicator-based data concerning EPL in CEE versus the mean in EU-15 countries, it is worth noting that indicators on OECD employment protection legislation have limits and should be interpreted with caution.[10] However, the methodology of calculating the EPL index was being improved over time (OECD, 1999, 2004; Venn, 2009) and is commonly employed in the literature (Skedinger, 2010, pp. 25–26; Venn, 2009, p. 6). We have decided to base the research predominantly on the first version[11] of the EPL index, which covers the largest time series (from the 1990s to 2013).

The first remark from Figure 1.2 is that until 2009 employment protection legislation indicators for individual regular contracts remained broadly stable in the EU-15. At the same time the regulation of fixed-term contracts in the EU-15 was noticeably loosened. These ‘partial’ labour market reforms have been held responsible for increasing the gap between highly protected permanent workers and poorly protected temporary workers (Boeri & Garibaldi, 2007). In CEE countries, we have observed more important changes in regulations for both regular (a decrease of 17% in Latvia in 1997 and of 32% in Slovenia in 2000/2001) and temporary contracts (an increase in Latvia, Poland, Lithuania, and Slovakia). On average EPL for regular contracts decreased in the CEE countries by 17%, and in the case of temporary contracts, increased nearly twice. In the EU-15 EPL decreased by 14% and 37% for regular and temporary contracts, respectively. What is also interesting is that the employment protection legislation for temporary contracts in some CEE countries has increased earlier in many cases than in the EU-15 (as an example – an increase of 42% in Lithuania in 1998 or sixfold increase in Poland in 2001/2002).

In the EU-15, in-depth reforms of employment protection legislation for temporary contracts have been undertaken since 2008. The main goal of these reforms

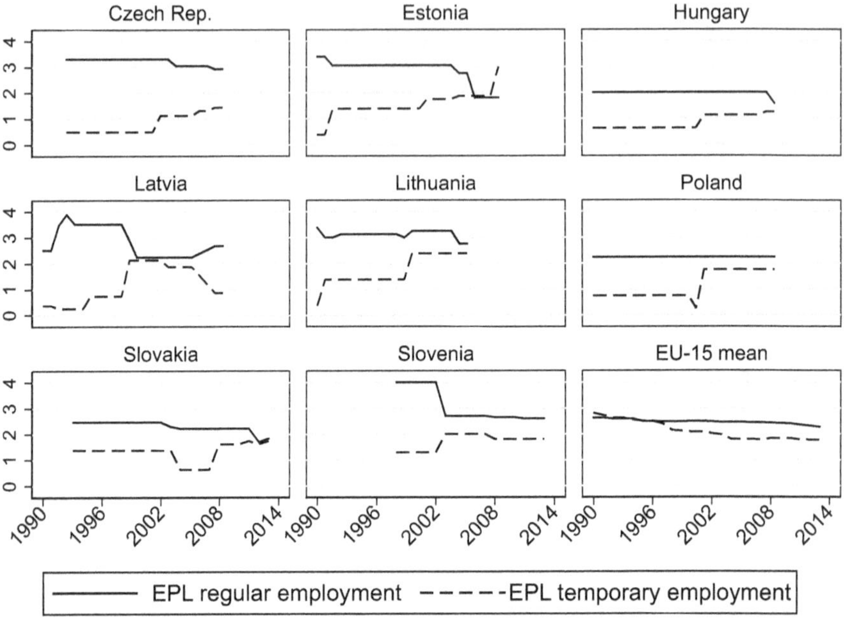

Figure 1.2 Employment Protection Legislation for regular and temporary contracts in CEE vs. mean in EU-15 countries

Source: Own elaboration based on OECD database and Pilc (2019) Database.

Notes: No EPL data for Bulgaria and Romania. The OECD compiles its Employment Protection Legislation Index for most of its member countries (the OECD) from 21 elements of legislation. The latest update of this index covers legislation in force in 2013 (or 2014 or 2015 for a limited number of countries as, for instance, Lithuania). Score from 0 to 6 with higher scores representing stricter regulation.

has been to discourage their excessive use, including through higher non-wage costs (European Commission, 2017). As a consequence, the employment protection legislation indicators for open-ended contracts either have remained constant or have markedly decreased (Figure 1.2). In CEE countries, the incidence of measures reducing EPL for temporary contracts appears to be particularly strong in Latvia. In other countries, we have rather observed a convergence of changes in both EPL index based on the large extent of reforms that have weakened permanent worker protection against dismissal (by, among others, limiting the scope for reinstatement in the case of unfair dismissal, capping back pay, cutting levels of severance pay, and extending the duration of the trial period) and the increase of protection of temporary workers.

However, in 2013 the great heterogeneity of job protection between European countries (Figure 1.3) can still be observed. As a consequence of implemented reforms, the most protected in CEE countries were labour markets in Lithuania, Estonia, and the Czech Rep., and the 'most flexible' was Hungarian and Slovak employment legislation.

In the EU-15, France and Portugal have had the most strictness employment regulations, while Great Britain and Ireland was classified at the opposite side with the lowest employment protection legislation. Partly, this heterogeneity is obviously the effect of differences in initial economic and labour market conditions but also in the level of political freedom, political stability, incidence of law violations, size of the shadow economy, progress in privatisation and restructuring of companies, and fiscal revenues. Some research suggests also that it is due to the lack of full information about the consequences of these reforms in the long run (Saint-Paul, 1996, p. 300).

In order to verify the trends in employment protection regulations with more contemporary data, we have decided to use the subjective measure of the Hiring and Firing Regulations (HFR) index, the Working Regulations (WR) index, and the Mandated Costs of Worker Dismissal (MCWD) index. In contrast to EPL, HFR is a *de facto* measure of employee protection but not differentiating between employment types. In turn, WR and MCWD are important measures in capturing the degree of flexibility of the labour market.

Comparing CEE countries, in the analysed period, the most protected labour market in terms of HFR (characterised by the lowest values of indicator) were observed in Slovenia and Slovakia; in WR, Estonia and Hungary; and in MCWD regulations, the Czech Rep., Hungary, Latvia, and Slovakia, with the value equal to 7.8. Therefore, the subjective HFR index based on employer survey confirm the same picture of the labour market as depicted by the EPL index and classified Lithuania and Slovenia among the most protected countries in Central and Eastern Europe.

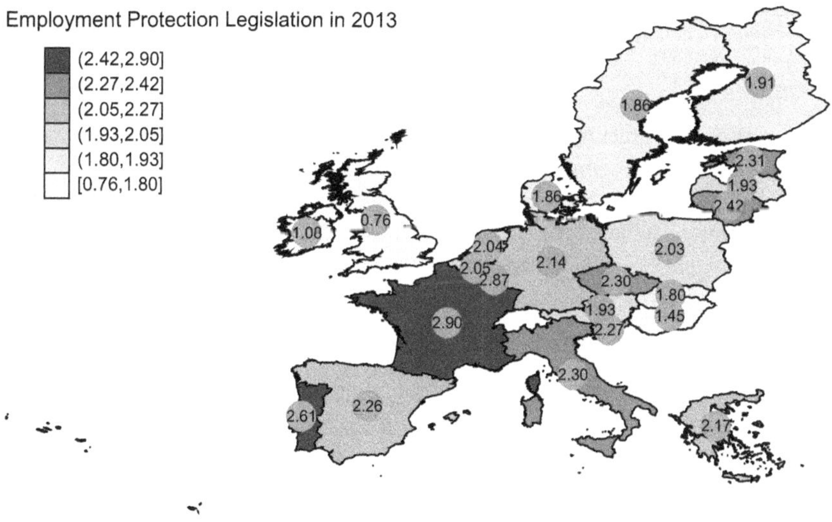

Figure 1.3 Employment Protection Legislation in Europe in 2013

Source: Own elaboration based on OECD database.

Notes: The OECD EPL index is a synthetic indicator of regulation strictness on dismissals and the use of temporary contracts.

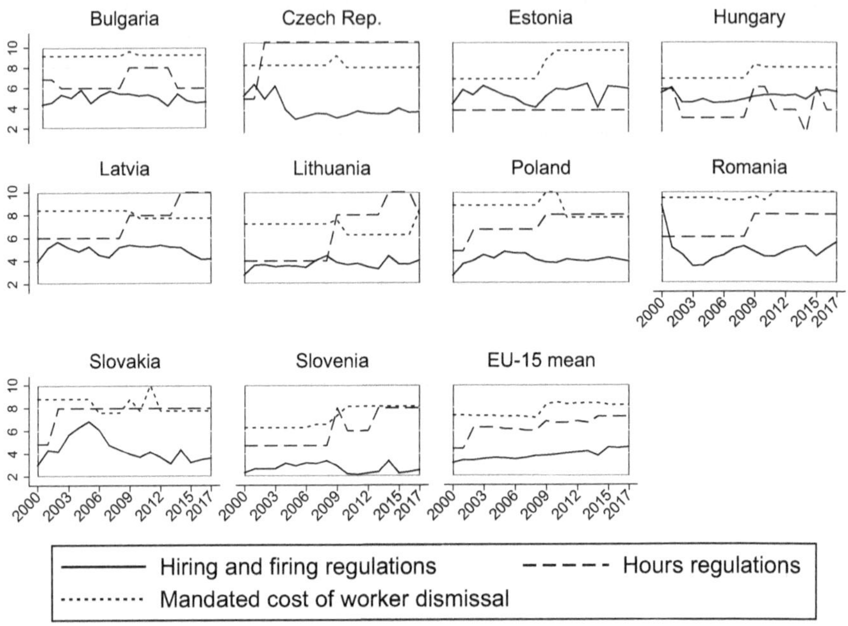

Figure 1.4 Job security rules in CEE vs. EU- 15 mean between 2000–2017

Source: Own elaboration based on Fraser Institute database.

Notes: Each subcomponent of the LMR index is placed on a scale from 0 to 10 and focuses on regulatory restraints that limit the freedom of exchange in the labour market. A higher score means less employment protection.

In terms of convergence with the EU-15, Poland, Slovakia, Slovenia, and Lithuania are following the same path in WR and MCWD regulations as the EU-15, providing still growing protection especially in terms of working hours and the cost of worker dismissal. What seems to be especially evident is the important difference between HFR and two other indicators, present in both the CEE and EU-15 countries.

Labour utilisation in CEE countries

This section looks at the evolution of quantitative aspects of labour utilisation in CEE countries and the EU-15. As was mentioned in the introduction of this book, OECD treats labour utilisation as a synonym to hours worked per capita and concludes that, together with labour productivity, it determines the level of GDP per capita. Therefore, throughout this chapter we will use such indicators as GDP per person employed, GDP per hour worked, labour force participation rate, and employment to population rate, as well as the number of hours worked per capita and the number of hours worked per person employed to measure the quantitative aspect of labour utilisation (Table 1.1).

Table 1.1 Labour utilisation in CEE vs. mean in EU-15 countries

Country	*Year*	*GDP_pc*	*GDP_ppe*	*GDP_phw*	*HW_pc*	*HW_ppw*	*EPL*	*LFPR*
Bulgaria	1995	9 208	22 000	13	716	1 711		
	2000	8 632	21 771	13	650	1 640	50.4	60.7
	2010	14 659	30 646	19	787	1 645	59.8	66.7
	2017	18 181	36 492	22	819	1 643	66.9	71.3
	t1 = 1995	197	166	173	114	96	133	117
Czech Republic	1993	17 197	35 422	19	902	1 857	69.0	72.1
	2000	20 646	43 646	23	897	1 896	65.2	71.6
	2010	27 555	57 304	32	865	1 800	65.0	70.2
	2017	31 798	62 985	35	901	1 784	73.6	75.9
	t1 = 1993	185	178	185	100	96	107	105
Estonia	1990	9 970	21 562				69.0	73.9
	2000	14 857	35 569	19	797	1 909	60.6	71.1
	2010	21 552	52 427	29	744	1 810	61.2	73.8
	2017	28 430	58 304	33	874	1 792	74.1	78.8
	t1 = 1990	285	270	175	110	94	107	107
Hungary	1992	14 188	32 417	16	902	2 061	58.0	64.4
	2000	17 263	41 603	20	844	2 033	56.0	59.9
	2010	21 535	54 254	31	705	1 777	55.0	61.9
	2017	25 817	55 699	32	807	1 741	68.2	71.2
	t1 = 1992	182	172	203	89	85	118	110
Latvia	1995	7 969	21 290					
	2000	10 750	27 555	16	692	1 775	57.3	67.0
	2010	17 561	43 663	25	699	1 738	58.5	73.0
	2017	24 092	52 785	31	774	1 695	70.1	77.0
	t1 = 1995	302	248	201	112	95	122	115
Lithuania	1995	8 922	21 831	14	616	1 508		
	2000	11 623	29 071	18	644	1 610	58.8	70.5
	2010	20 091	49 910	30	661	1 643	57.6	70.2
	2017	28 288	58 960	37	772	1 608	70.4	75.9
	t1 = 1995	317	270	253	125	107	120	108
Poland	1993	9 797	26 222	14	722	1 933	58.9	68.8
	2000	14 245	37 539	20	707	1 863	55.0	65.8
	2010	20 789	52 096	28	732	1 834	58.9	65.3
	2017	26 131	61 539	34	771	1 815	66.1	69.6
	t1 = 1993	267	235	250	107	94	112	101
Romania	1995	10 127	19 772	11	934	1 823		
	2000	10 123	21 084	11	890	1 853	63.0	68.4
	2010	16 966	37 518	20	841	1 861	60.2	64.9
	2017	22 762	51 565	28	799	1 811	63.9	67.3
	t1 = 1995	225	261	262	86	99	101	98

(*Continued*)

Table 1.1 Continued

Country	*Year*	*GDP_pc*	*GDP_ppe*	*GDP_phw*	*HW_pc*	*HW_ppw*	*EPL*	*LFPR*
Slovakia	1995	13 077	33 285	18	728	1 853	60.2	69.3
	2000	15 449	41 205	23	681	1 816	56.8	69.9
	2010	24 785	62 025	34	721	1 805	58.8	68.7
	2017	29 902	68 550	40	748	1 714	66.2	72.1
	t1 = 1995	229	206	223	103	92	110	104
Slovenia	1995	17 838.2	38 457.0	21.9	814.2	1 755.4		
	2000	21 974	47 806	28	786	1 710	62.8	67.5
	2010	27 736	59 065	35	789	1 680	66.2	71.5
	2017	30 333	63 437	39	775	1 622	69.3	74.2
	t1 = 1995	170	165	179	95	92	110	110
EU-15	1990	29 001	65 578	39	736	1 689	63.0	67.9
mean	2000	37 267	79 451	49	765	1 658	65.6	70.5
	2010	40 881	85 189	54	748	1 591	66.2	73.0
	2017	43 802	89 950	58	753	1 580	68.2	74.4
	t1 = 1990	151	137	146	102	94	108	110

Source: Own elaboration based on OECD database.

Notes: GDP_pc – GDP per capita; GDP_ppe – GDP per person employed; GDP_phw – GDP per hour worked; HW_pc – hours worked per capita, HW_ppe – hours worked per person employed, EPR – Employment to population ratio; LFPR – Labour force participation rate.

For the full sample 1995–2017,[12] average GDP growth per capita was generally higher in the CEE countries than in the reference group of the EU-15 countries from Western Europe. However, developments differed markedly across the CEE countries during this period. The Baltic states experienced very large growth, while the Czech Rep., Hungary, and Slovenia have gained much less.

The other indicators also indicate the substantial heterogeneity across the countries. Bulgaria and the Baltic states stand out for very high rates of hours worked per capita, while Hungary, Romania, and Slovenia have recorded a decrease in labour utilisation. In other countries the growth of hours worked per capita was less brisk. This somewhat heterogeneous pattern across the CEE countries is also noticed in Dombi (2013a, 2013b).

In almost all CEE states, the employment recovery in the 2000s was accompanied by sluggish or even falling hours worked per employed. While employment surpassed its 90s level everywhere (in CEE and EU-15 countries), developments in hours worked per employed continued to decrease (except Lithuania). This reflects a general trend to work fewer hours. Different factors may explain this declining trend in average hours worked per worker, including the rising importance of services, a sector where part-time workers are over-represented,[13] and the effect of technological change.

The relationship between employment protection indicators and labour utilisation measures

To obtain a more detailed picture of the role of employment protection regulations for the labour utilisation levels, we have decided to look at the relationship between particular indicators of these regulations such as the EPL index (for regular and temporary contracts, version 1) as well as the Hiring and Firing Regulations (HFR) index, the Hours Regulations (HR) index, and the Mandated Cost of Worker Dismissals (MCWD) index. Being aware that each of the available institutional indicators from the indicator-based database produce a different outlook of regulations, we believe that it is still possible to use them for some specific analysis and needs. As Aleksynska and Cazes (2016, p. 23) show, the cross-country comparisons within a particular year, and based on disaggregated components, can in many instances provide interesting insights on phenomena measured by these components.

In order to verify the level of labour utilisation we have decided to use indicators presented in Table 1.1. Due to availability of data our countries sample exclude Bulgaria and Romania as non-OECD countries, and the time periods covered for each country are not identical, but the period ranges in general from the 2000 to 2013.[14] Table 1.2 reports the basic descriptive statistics of data used in the empirical investigation.

To study the relation between the employment protection regulations (EPR) and labour quantitative aspects of utilisation (LU) the canonical correlation analysis was used. This analysis was executed in order to test if there was any difference between the indicators that were related to EPR from one side and LU from the other side. Basically, this method provides a simultaneous analysis of a dependent variable set and a set of independent variables. In general, it determines whether two sets of variables are independent of each other in a linear sense. This is done by finding a composite for the multiple dependent variables and a composite for the multiple independent variables. Then these composites are correlated simultaneously in order to obtain a canonical function. This process continues until all the correlations between the two sets are included. In effect this analysis permits the assessment of the strength of the overall relationships between the linear composites (canonical variates[15]), for the independent and dependent variables as well as the relative contribution of each variable to the canonical functions (relationships) that are extracted (Hair, Black, Babin, & Anderson, 2013, p. 17). The relative contribution of each variable can be evaluated by the canonical loadings and cross loadings which reflect the variance that the observed variable shares with the canonical variate and can be interpreted like a factor loading in assessing the relative contribution of each variable to each canonical function. The larger the coefficient, the more important it is in deriving the canonical variate (Dattalo, 2014, p. 12)

The canonical correlation analysis was performed separately for CEE and EU-15 country groups for the standardised sets of EPR sub-indices[16] and LU

Table 1.2 Labour utilisation and job security regulation – descriptive statistics

Variable	*Obs*	*Mean*	*Std. Dev.*	*Min*	*Max*
CEE mean					
GDP_ppe	180	47461.7	11130.8	21084.0	68549.9
GDP_phw	180	26.9	6.5	11.4	40.0
HW_pc	180	774.6	67.0	619.3	924.2
HW_ppw	180	1768.5	101.2	1558.0	2032.8
EPR	180	61.9	4.9	49.7	74.1
LFPR	180	68.7	4.2	59.6	78.8
HFR	180	4.4	1.0	2.1	8.8
HR	180	6.6	2.1	2.0	10.0
MCWD	180	8.1	1.0	6.3	10.0
EPL_re	93	2.5	0.5	1.6	3.5
EPL_te	93	1.6	0.9	0.0	4.0
EU-15 mean					
GDP_ppe	270	84703.4	15802.9	53198.0	142984.2
GDP_phw	270	53.3	11.6	30.2	83.9
HW_pc	270	757.6	99.7	625.0	1119.3
HW_ppw	270	1609.4	164.1	1360.4	2044.0
EPR	270	66.6	6.3	48.8	77.9
LFPR	270	72.6	5.2	60.3	82.5
HFR	270	3.8	1.4	1.3	8.5
HR	265	6.4	1.9	2.0	10.0
MCWD	265	7.8	2.2	1.0	10.0
EPL_re	203	2.4	0.7	1.1	4.6
EPL_te	203	1.9	1.1	0.3	2.8

Source: Own elaboration based on OECD and Fraser Institute database.

Notes: Obs. – total number of observation of particular measure, Std. Dev, – mean standard deviation; Abbreviations concerning labour utilisation as in Table 1.1.; HRR – Hiring and firing regulations; HR – Hours regulations; MCWD – Mandated cost of worker dismissal; EPL_re – EPL regular employment; EPL_te – EPL temporary employment

indicators. Canonical variates of EPR indicators and LU were tested in hierarchal form. The values of the canonical correlations with its significance levels in CEE as well as EU-15 countries were presented in Table 1.3, whereas in Table 1.4 we discuss the standardised canonical coefficients (weights) which present the relative contribution of each particular indicator to each canonical function.[17] The standardised canonical coefficients are interpreted in a manner analogous to interpreting standardised regression coefficients.

Obtained results showed that the sets of variables related to EPR and LU as groups are significantly related to each other, and a strong correlation exists between them in both groups of studied countries; however, this relation seems to be a little higher in the case of CEE countries than in the EU-15 group. In the case of CEE countries, the first pair of canonical variates (functions 1 to 5, root 1) with

Table 1.3 Canonical correlation analysis in CEE and EU-15 countries – summary

Canonical roots	*Canonical R*	*Canonical R^2*	*Wilks' lambda*	*F*	*DF*	*p*
CEE						
1	0.902	0.814	0.062	11.043	30	0.000*
2	0.642	0.412	0.333	5.434	20	0.000*
3	0.525	0.276	0.566	4.512	12	0.000*
4	0.405	0.164	0.781	3.712	6	0.002*
5	0.256	0.065	0.935	3.009	2	0.055
EU-15						
1	0.842	0.709	0.068	24.436	30	0.000*
2	0.773	0.598	0.237	17.446	20	0.000*
3	0.514	0.264	0.603	9.028	12	0.000*
4	0.383	0.147	0.819	6.810	6	0.000*
5	0.199	0.040	0.961	4.063	2	0.002*

Source: Own elaboration.

Notes: Asterisks denote 0.01 significance level.

Table 1.4 The standardised canonical coefficients (weights) in CEE and EU-15 countries

Indicators	*Canonical weights*				
	Root 1	*Root 2*	*Root 3*	*Root 4*	*Root 5*
CEE					
GDP_ppw	7.980*	8.231	8.310	1.033	2.232
GDP_phw	11.997*	12.637	9.497	0.230	2.493
HW_pc	0.591*	1.732*	1.956*	2.914*	1.849
HW_ppe	2.933*	0.639	2.346	1.687	2.340
EPR	0.531*	1.735*	3.594*	2.702*	3.456
LFPR	0.266*	0.100	2.568*	0.211	0.487
HFR	0.243*	0.745*	0.319	0.545	0.982
HR	0.117*	0.651*	0.517*	0.001	0.505
MCWD	0.059	1.173*	1.467*	0.836	1.216
EPL_re	1.252*	0.320*	0.323	0.615*	0.336
EPL_te	0.690*	0.041	0.143	0.722*	0.502
EU-15					
GDP_ppe	0.064	4.703*	13.780*	5.804	0.879
GDP_ phw	2.115*	4.920*	16.395*	7.987	0.788
HW_pc	0.792*	0.195*	0.342*	0.242	0.249
HW_ppe	1.287*	0.914*	4.884*	2.510	0.792
EPR	0.740*	0.554*	1.388*	1.741	0.997
LFPR	0.497*	0.703*	0.856*	1.927	0.470
HRR	0.467*	0.333*	0.561*	0.827*	0.230
HR	0.236*	0.009	0.601*	0.342	1.211*
MCWD	0.539*	0.092*	0.678*	0.377*	0.099
EPL_re	0.538*	0.032*	0.696*	0.577	0.502
EPL_te	0.245*	0.776*	0.067	0.550	0.773

Source: Own elaboration.

Notes: Asterisks denote 0.05 significance level. Abbreviations as in Table 1.2.

a maximum canonical correlation of 0.902 was extracted. It was statistically significant with a p-value of less than 0.05. Based on the residual variance, the other variates were tested in step-down order. Second, third, fourth, and fifth canonical variates had canonical correlations of 0.642, 0.525, 0.405, and 0.256, respectively. All these pairs of canonical covariates were significant. For the EU-15 countries, the obtained canonical correlation values for subsequent roots (1 to 5) were as follows: 0.842, 0.773, 0.514, 0.383, 0.199. these results indicate that between the sets of EPR sub-indices and LU indicators a strong, positive correlation exists, which means that less strict job protection regulation coexist with higher levels of labour utilisation.

Considering the relative contribution of each particular EPR sub-indexes in CEE countries to each canonical function, it can be noticed that the highest values of statistically significant, standardised canonical coefficients were observed for indicators such as: EPL for regular and temporary employment, Mandated Cost of Worker Dismissal (MCWD), and Hiring and Firing Regulations (HFR), whereas Hours Regulations (HR) were of the least significance in the creation of a meaningful relationship between the analysed groups of variables. In the set of labour utilisation measures the highest coefficients were observed in the case of GDP per hour worked, GDP per person employed, and hours worked per person employed.

Assessing the values and significance of job security and labour utilisation sub-indexes in the EU-15, it can be spotted that the highest values of canonical weights were observed for indicators such as MCWD, EPL for regular employment, and HFR. In the set of labour utilisation measures the highest coefficients were observed in case of GDP per hour worked, hours worked per person employed and hours worked per capita.

While assessing the correlation between different macroeconomic values, it must be borne in mind that the existence of a correlation neither proves the real causal link nor allows defining the direction of the analysed correlation, i.e. whether or not particular labour market institutions contribute to higher levels of labour utilisation, or perhaps the higher level of labour utilisation is the determinant of more dynamic changes in institutional framework in a given country.

Conclusion

The first goal of this chapter was to identify the main changes in labour market regulations using two types of data (from descriptive and indicator-based databases) in the CEE region and to compare these trends with their counterparts in EU-15 countries. From a descriptive perspective, the chapter empirically analyses both the number of labour market reforms carried out in 2000–2017 and the direction taken by policy settings as a result of reform activity. The analysis shows that reform activism was more intense in countries with a longer record of EU membership than in the CEE. Active labour market policies and unemployment benefits were made more generous especially in these countries (see also: Turrini et al., 2015). Within the job protection regulations, it reveals a large frequency of reforms in Lithuania and Slovakia, with measures pointing in both directions (increasing and decreasing). At the same time, relative to the EPL index, Lithuania is assessed as the freest country, with Slovakia and Hungary following, in Central and Eastern Europe. Regarding permanent and fixed-term contracts, the raising of EPL restrictiveness for temporary contracts was observed in these countries. Generally, the incidence of measures relaxing conditions for permanent contracts and the measures tightening conditions for fixed-term contracts was observed in both parts of Europe (except Latvia). It may reflect, in a number of cases, a gradual adjustment to past reforms relaxing conditions for temporary contracts and creating employment segmentation. Deregulation of permanent employment was seen as the way to tackle this segmentation and a visibly unfair distribution of job security and market risks and limits of transition possibilities to permanent jobs. Under such a regime, it is believed that permanent contracts would be less permanent, although the reliance on temporary contracts would also decline (Eichhorst et al., 2017, p. 15).

To confirm the general trends in employment protection reforms with more recent data, we have also analysed the specific indicators of labour market regulations such as Hiring and Firing Regulations (HFR), Hours Regulations (HR), and Mandated Costs of Worker Dismissal (MCWD). Pronounced differences exist across countries. Hiring and firing regulations are less unconstrained in Estonia, Hungary, and Romania than in other CEE and EU-15 countries. Hours Regulations are less restricted in Estonia, Hungary, and Bulgaria, while MCWD are smaller in Romania, Bulgaria, and Estonia than the average of the EU-15. It confirms that CEE countries do not represent a homogenous group with one model of labour market institutions.

The second aim was to assess the correlation between employment protection legislation and quantitative aspects of labour utilisation in these two parts of Europe – CEE and EU-15 countries. The empirical analysis based on the data from OECD and the Fraser Institute confirms that less strict job protection regulation coexists with higher levels of labour utilisation, albeit extracted values of canonical correlations were higher in the case of CEE countries than in the EU-15 group.

However, it also should be noted that the interpretation of the role of EPR strictness for labour utilisation involves two main problems. First, in many researches it appears that state regulations are not always followed in the private sector (Masso & Eamets, 2004), and there is a lot of evidence of violations of these regulations in enterprises in CEE countries (Muszyński, 2016; Goraus-Tanska & Lewandowski, 2016). Secondly, it is important for EPL strictness to measure which proportion of the workforce is actually covered by the regulations. In CEE countries, the other atypical forms of work (civil, self-employment) are more widespread than in the EU-15, which may reflect in the poor enforcement of legislation and the inability to depict labour market regulations by existing indicators.

Acknowledgements

The theoretical and descriptive part of the study conducted by Beata Woźniak-Jęchorek was supported by Regional Initiative for Excellence programme of the Minister of Science and Higher Education of Poland, years 2019–2022, grant no. 004/RIF/2018/19, financing 3.000.000 PLN.

The empirical part of the research conducted by Sławomir Kuźmar was supported by the Polish National Science Centre Grant number 2014/13/N/HS4/02061, titled *Determinants of regional labour productivity in Poland over the period 1995–2013*.

Notes

1 The examples of descriptive database are the ILO database, which provides synthetic information on measures adopted in the fields of minimum wages, maternity protection, and working time along with referrals to relevant regulations; the NATLEX database, providing a comprehensive record of abstracts of legislation and relevant information of national labour, social security, and related human rights laws for more than 190 countries; the OECD Job Strategy, which contains information on reforms in seven main policy areas grouped in two sub-periods (1995–1999 and 2000–2004); the Social Reforms Database developed by FRDB-IZA, which provides information on reforms starting from the 1980s in four broad policy areas: EPL, public pension systems, non-employment benefits, and migration policies; and finally, the LABREF database, which records labour market and welfare policy measures introduced in EU member states.

2 The examples of indicator-based database are the Employment Protection Legislation (EPL) indicators developed by the OECD; the ILO EPLex indicator, which are aimed at describing in-depth employment protection legislation; the Labour Market Regulation (LMR) index developed by the Fraser Institute in the framework of the Economic Freedom around the World database; the World Bank Doing Business database, which provides a number of indicators concerning labour market regulations for 85 countries in the early 2000s; the Labour Market Efficiency (LME) index produced by the World Economic Forum, which is a part of the broader Global Competitiveness Index; and finally, the Global Labour Survey (GLS) database conducted in 2004 at Harvard Law School, which seeks to measure *de facto* labour practices around the world, covering aspects of labour institutions such as employment regulations, employee benefits, and wage setting and builds indices of labour practices in ten broad areas for 33 countries.

3 In this chapter we will use three terms interchangeably: 'job security rules/regulations', 'employment protection rules/regulations', and 'employment protection legislation'.

4 In the case of slowing labour reallocation, strict job security rules can limit the potential efficiency gains from the movement of workers from low- to high-productivity sectors and firms. At the same time, higher productivity can result where firms benefit from the experience of longer-tenure workers or when they adjust to lower flexibility by investing more in capital or in the training of the existing workforce.

5 Grubb and Wells (1993) developed an employment regulation indicator that became the basis for the OECD employment protection legislation (EPL) index, which is now available for the period 1985–2013.

6 Hiring and Firing Regulations is based on the survey question: 'Hiring and firing of workers is . . . 1 = impeded by regulations, 7 = flexibly determined by employers' and

coming from the Global Competitiveness Report developed by the World Economic Forum (Aleksynska & Cazes, 2016).

7 This subcomponent is based on the World Bank's Doing Business, Rigidity of Hours index, which is described as follows: 'the rigidity of hours index has 5 components: (i) whether there are restrictions on night work; (ii) whether there are restrictions on weekly holiday work; (iii) whether the work-week can consist of 5.5 days; (iv) whether the work-week can extend to 50 hours or more (including overtime) for 2 months a year to respond to a seasonal increase in production; and (v) whether paid annual vacation is 21 working days or fewer. For questions (i) and (ii), when restrictions other than premiums apply, a score of 1 is given. If the only restriction is a premium for night work and weekly holiday work, a score of 0, 0.33, 0.66, or 1 is given according to the quartile in which the economy's premium falls. If there are no restrictions, the economy receives a score of 0. For questions (iii), (iv) and (v), when the answer is "no", a score of 1 is assigned; otherwise a score of 0 is assigned'. Countries with less rigid work rules receive better scores in this component. This component was previously named 'Mandated cost of hiring a worker'. Because of the pressure from ILO, this indicator was dropped from Doing Business. In order to maintain as much consistency over time as possible, the data have been revised back to 2002, with these data replacing the previous values. Source World Bank, Doing Business (various issues).

8 This subcomponent is based on the World Bank's Ease of Doing Business data on the cost of the advance notice requirements, severance payments, and penalties due when dismissing a redundant worker. The formula used to calculate the 0-to-10 ratings was as follows: $(V_{max} - V_i)/(V_{max} - V_{min})$ multiplied by 10. V_i represents the dismissal cost (measured in weeks of wages). The values for V_{max} and V_{min} were set at 108 weeks (1.5 standard deviations above average) and 0 weeks, respectively. Countries with values outside of the V_{max} and V_{min} range received ratings of either 0 or 10 accordingly. Source: World Bank, Doing Business (various issues).

9 LMR is the combination of separate indicators on minimum wage, flexibility in hiring and firing, level of collective bargaining, unemployment insurance, and the use of military conscription. This indicator therefore covers labour market institutions that are the subject of analysis in other chapters of this book.

10 Not all changes in employment protection legislation modify the OECD indicators. A change may be insufficient to modify the scoring given to a particular characteristic of government regulation. Alternatively, specific aspects of the legislation may not be considered in the calculation of the index (e.g. the length and uncertainty of judicial procedures in case of unfair dismissal or treatment of the self-employed). Moreover, the indicators do not fully capture certain aspects relating to the enforcement of employment protection legislation. A third common criticism concerns the inevitable degree of subjectivity affecting the codification of national legal features into a composite index (Venn, 2009). Since codification may at times provide a misleading interpretation of national rules and procedures or ignore relevant non-legislative data, the OECD index should be handled with care or possibly integrated with an up-to-date and more comprehensive EU-28 database.

11 Version 1 of the strictness of employment protection against individual and collective dismissals for workers with a regular contract incorporates eight data items concerning regulations for individual dismissals. It is therefore identical to the version 1 of the indicator of strictness of employment protection against individual dismissal (regular contracts; OECD, 2019).

12 In some cases, the time series have varied depending on the availability of data.

13 The research shows that the rise of part-time employment contributes to the overall decline in the average hours worked. More on part-time employment in Chapter 5.

14 This is mainly due to the availability of EPL data, which ends in 2013.

15 A pair of canonical variates is called a canonical root.
16 In order to provide data comparability, EPL indexes were converted and normalised to a range from 0 to 6, with higher scores representing less strict regulation.
17 More detailed information concerning the canonical loadings and cross loadings is available on request.

References

Acemoglu, D. (2001). Good jobs versus bad jobs. *Journal of Labor Economics*, *19*(1), 1–21.

Adascalitei, D., & Pignatti Morano, C. (2015, October). *Labour market reforms since the crisis: Drivers and consequences* (Research Department Working Paper No. 5). Geneva: International Labour Office.

Albrecht, J., Navarro, L., & Vroman, S. (2006). *The effects of labor market policies in an economy with an informal sector* (IZA Discussion Paper No. 2141). Bonn: Institute for the Study of Labor (IZA).

Aleksynska, M., & Cazes, S. (2016). Composite indicators of labour market regulations in a comparative perspective. *IZA Journal of Labor Economics*, *5*(3), 1–33. ISSN: 2193–8997, Heidelberg: Springer.

Alesina, A., Algan, Y., Cahuc, P., & Giuliano, P. (2015). Family values and the regulation of labor. *Journal of the European Economic Association*, *13*(4), 599–630.

Almeida, R. K., & Aterido, R. (2008, October). *The incentives to invest in job training: Do strict labor codes influence this decision?* (Social Protection Discussion Papers No. 46189). Washington, DC: The World Bank.

Almeida, R. K., & Aterido, R. (2011). On-the-job training and rigidity of employment protection in the developing world: Evidence from differential enforcement. *Labour Economics*, *18*(S1), S71–S82.

Almeida, R. K., & Carneiro, P. (2009). Enforcement of labor regulation and firm performance. *Journal of Comparative Economics*, *37*(1), 28–46.

Avdagic, S., & Salardi, P. (2013). Tenuous link: Labour market institutions and unemployment in advanced and new market economies. *Socio-Economic Review*, *11*(4), 739–769.

Benach, J., Vives, A., Amable, M., Vanroelen, C., Tarafa, G., & Muntaner, C. (2014). Precarious employment: Understanding an emerging social determinant of health. *Annual Review of Public Health*, *35*(1), 229–253.

Bentolila, S., Dolado, J. J., & Jimeno, J. F. (2012). Reforming an insider-outsider labor market: The Spanish experience. *IZA Journal of European Labour Studies*, *1*(1), 1–29.

Bertola, G. (1990). Job security, employment and wages. *European Economic Review*, *34*, 851–886.

Bertola, G., Blau, F. D., & Kahn, L. M. (2002). *Labor market institutions and demographic employment patterns* (Working Paper Series No. 9043). Cambridge, MA: National Bureau of Economic Research.

Betcherman, G. (2015). Labor market regulations: What do we know about their impacts in developing countries? *The World Bank Research Observer*, *30*(1), 124–153.

Betcherman, G. (2019). Designing labor market regulations in developing countries. *IZA World of Labor*, *57*(2), 1–11, doi: 10.15185/izawol.57.v2

Boeri, T. (2005, May). *Reforming labor and product markets: Some lessons from two decades of experiments in Europe* (IMF Working Papers No. WP/05/97), 1–27.Washington, DC: International Monetary Fund.

Boeri, T. (2011). Institutional reforms and dualism in European labor markets. In D. Card & O. Ashenfelter (Eds.), *Handbook of labor economics*. Amsterdam: Elsevier.

Boeri, T., Cahuc, P., & Zylberberg, A. (2015). *The costs of flexibility-enhancing structural reforms: A literature review* (OECD Economics Department Working Papers No. 1264). Paris: OECD Publishing.

Boeri, T., Conde-Ruiz, J. I., & Galasso, V. (2012). The political economy of flexicurity. *Journal of the European Economic Association, 10*(4), 684–715.

Boeri, T., & Garibaldi, P. (2007). Two tier reforms of employment protection: A honeymoon effect? *Economic Journal, 117*(521), F357–F385.

Boeri, T., & Van Ours, J. (2008). *The economics of imperfect labor markets*. Princeton and Oxford: Princeton University Press.

Damiani, M., Pompei, F., & Ricci, A. (2016). Temporary employment protection and productivity growth in EU economies. *International Labour Review, 155*(4), 587–622.

Dattalo, P. (2014). *A demonstration of canonical correlation analysis with orthogonal rotation to facilitate interpretation*. Unpublished manuscript, School of Social Work, Virginia Commonwealth University, Richmond, VA.

De Cuyper, N., de Jong, J., De Witte, H., Isaksson, K., Rigotti, T., & Schalk, R. (2008). Literature review of theory and research on the psychological impact of temporary employment: Towards a conceptual model. *International Journal Management Reviews, 10*(1), 25–51.

Deakin, S., Malmberg, J., & Sarkar, P. (2014). How do labour laws affect unemployment and the labour share of national income? The experience of six OECD countries, 1970–2010. *International Labour Review, 153*(1), 1–27.

Dombi, Á. (2013a). Economic growth and development in Central and Eastern Europe after the transformation. *Public Finance Quarterly, 58*(4), 452–468.

Dombi, Á. (2013b). The sources of economic growth and relative backwardness in the Central Eastern European countries between 1995 and 2007. *Post-Communist Economies, 25*(4), 425–447.

Eichhorst, W., Marx, P., & Wehner, C. (2017). Labor market reforms in Europe: Towards more flexicure labor markets? *Journal for Labour Market Research, 51*(3), 1–17, doi: 10.1186/s12651-017-0231-7

Elmeskov, J., Martin, J. P., & Scarpetta, S. (1998). Key lessons for labour market reforms: Evidence from OECD countries' experience. *Swedish Economic Policy Review, 5*, 205–252.

Emmenegger, P. (2014). *The power to dismiss: Trade unions and the regulation of job security in Western Europe*. Oxford: Oxford University Press.

European Commission. (2017). *Labour market and wage developments in Europe*. Annual Review 2017, Directorate-General for Employment, Social Affairs and Inclusion.

Fenwick, C., Howe, J., Marshall, S., & Landau, I. (2007). *Labour and labour-related laws in micro and small enterprises: Innovative regulatory approaches* (Small Enterprise Programme, SEED Working Paper No. 81). Geneva, Switzerland: ILO.

Freeman, R. B. (1993). *Labor market institutions and policies: Help or hindrance to economic development?* Proceedings of the World Bank Annual Conference on Development Economics 1992. Washington, DC: The World Bank.

Gallego, A., & Marx, P. (2017). Multi-dimensional preferences for labour market reforms: A conjoint experiment. *Journal of European Public Policy, 24*(7), 1027–1047.

Glyn, A., Baker, D., Howell, D., & Schmitt, J. (2004). *Labor market institutions and unemployment: A critical review of the cross-country evidence* (Department of Economics Discussion Paper No. 168). University of Oxford.

Goraus-Tanska, K., & Lewandowski, P. (2016). *Minimum wage violation in Central and Eastern Europe* (IZA Discussion Papers, No. 10098). Bonn: Institute for the Study of Labor (IZA).

Grubb, D., & Wells, W. (1993). *Employment regulation and patterns of work in EC countries* (Economic Studies 21). Paris: OECD.

Hair, J. F., Black, W. C., Babin, B. J., & Anderson, R. E. (2013). *Multivariate data analysis* (8th ed.). Upper Saddle River, NJ: Prentice Hall.

Hamermesh, D. S. (1993). *Labor demand*. Princeton: Princeton University Press.

Hopenhayn, H., & Rogerson, R. (1993). Job turnover and policy evaluation: A general equilibrium analysis. *Journal of Political Economics*, *101*(5), 915–938.

Howell, D. R., Baker, D., Glyn, A., & Schmitt, J. (2007). Are protective labor market institutions at the root of unemployment? A critical review of the evidence. *Capitalism and Society*, *2*(1), 1–71.

ILO. (2003). *Flexibilizing employment: An Overview*. Geneva, Switzerland: International Labour Office.

ILO. (2012). *World of work report 2012: Better jobs for a better economy*. Geneva, Switzerland: International Labour Organization and International Institute for Labour Studies.

ILO. (2014). *Transitioning from the informal to the formal economy* (Report V(1)). Geneva, Switzerland: International Labour Office.

ILO. (2015). Labour regulation and employment patterns. In *World employment and social outlook: The changing nature of jobs*. Geneva, Switzerland: International Labour Office.

IMF. (2015, April). Where are we headed? Perspectives on potential output. In *World economic outlook: Short- and long-term factors*. Washington, DC: International Monetary Fund.

Jimeno, J. F., & Toharia, L. (1996). Effort, absenteeism, and fixed term employment contracts. *Revista Española de Economía*, *13*, 105–119.

Kahn, L. M. (2007). The impact of employment protection mandates on demographic temporary employment patterns: International microeconomic evidence. *Quarterly Journal of Economics*, *117*(521), 333–356.

Kahn, L. M. (2010). Employment protection reforms, employment and the incidence of temporary jobs in Europe: 1996–2001. *Labour Economics*, *17*(1), 1–15.

Lazear, E. P. (1990). Job security provisions and employment. *Quarterly Journal of Economics*, *58*(4), 757–782.

Lucifora, C., & Moriconi, S. (2015). Political instability and labour market institutions. *European Journal of Political Economy*, *39*, 201–221.

Mani, A., Mullainathan, S., Shafir, E., & Zhao, J. Y. (2013). Poverty impedes cognitive function. *Science*, *341*(6149), 976–980.

Martin, J. P., & Scarpetta, S. (2012). Setting it right: Employment protection. Labour reallocation and productivity. *De Economist*, *160*, 89–116.

Masso, J., & Eamets, R. (2004). *Labour market flexibility and employment protection regulation in the Baltic states* (IZA Discussion Papers No. 1147). Bonn: Institute for the Study of Labor (IZA).

Meghir, C., Narita, R., & Robin, J. M. (2015). Wages and informality in developing countries. *American Economic Review*, *105*(4), 1509–1546. doi: 10.1257/aer.20121110

Melitz, M. J., & Ottaviano, G. I. P. (2008). Market size, trade, and productivity. *Review of Economic Studies*, *75*, 295–316.

Muszyński, K. (2016). Factors behind the growth of civil law contracts as employment contracts in Poland – A study of labour law violations. *Prakseologia*, *158*, 323–359.

Nickell, S. (1997). Unemployment and labor market rigidities: Europe versus North America. *Journal of Economic Perspective*, *11*(3), 55–74.

Nickell, S., & Layard, R. (1999). Labour market institutions and economic performance. *Handbook of Labour Economics*, *3*, 3029–3084, Amsterdam: Elsevier.

OECD. (1999). *OECD employment outlook 1999*. Paris: OECD Publishing.

OECD. (2002). *OECD employment outlook 2002*. Paris: OECD Publishing.

OECD. (2004). *OECD employment outlook 2004*. Paris: OECD Publishing.

OECD. (2019). Retrieved from https://stats.oecd.org/Index.aspx?DataSetCode=EPL_OV

Pagés, C., & Montenegro, C. E. (2007). Job security and the age-composition of employment: Evidence from Chile. *Estudios de Economia*, *34*(2), 109–139.

Pilc, M. (2019). *The database of labour market institutions and its determinants*. Database collected as a part of the project titled "The analysis of the determinants of labour market institutions" financed by the National Science Centre in Poland (Grant No. 2015/17/D/HS4/00319).

Rubery, J., & Piasna, A. (2016). *Labour market segmentation and the EU reform agenda: Developing alternatives to the mainstream* (ETUI Research Paper No. 10). Brussels: European Trade Union Institute.

Rueda, D. (2005). Insider-outsider politics in industrialized democracies: The challenge to social democratic parties. *American Political Science Review*, *99*(1), 61–74.

Saint-Paul, G. (1996). Exploring the political economy of labour markets institutions. *Economic Policy*, *11*(23), 263–315.

Scarpetta, S. (1996). Assessing the role of labour market policies and institutional settings on unemployment: A cross-country study. *OECD Economic Studies*, *26*, 43–98.

Skedinger, P. (2010). *Employment protection legislation: Evolution, effects, winners and losers*. Cheltenham: Edward Elgar.

Turrini, A., Koltay, G., Pierini, F., Goffard, C., & Kiss, A. (2015). A decade of labour market reforms in the EU: Insights from the LABREF database. *IZA Journal of Labor Policy*, *4*(12).

Venn, D. (2009). *Legislation, collective bargaining and enforcement: Updating the OECD employment protection indicators* (OECD Social, Employment and Migration Working Papers No. 89). Paris: OECD Publishing.

Vindigni, A., Scotti, S., & Tealdi, C. (2015). Uncertainty and the politics of employment protection. *Journal of Labor Economics*, *33*(1), 209–267.

Wilczyńska, A., Batorski, D., & Torrent-Sellens, J. (2016). Employment flexibility and job security as determinants of job satisfaction: The case of Polish knowledge workers. *Social Indicators Research*, *126*(2), 633–656.

World Bank. (2013). *World development report 2013: Jobs*. Washington, DC: World Bank Publications.

2

INSTITUTIONAL DETERMINANTS OF FIRM-SPONSORED TRAINING OF YOUNG EMPLOYEES

Dominik Buttler

Introduction

The principle of maximising labour utilisation assumes that not only the number of hours worked per capita is equal to its potential level but also employees are matched to job offers according to the most productive use of their skills. This principle presents a static framework in which neither employers nor employees invest in human capital. This chapter aims to fill this gap by studying the institutional determinants of firm-sponsored training delivered to young employees.

In the theoretical part of the chapter, the notions of school-to-work transition and transition regimes will be used. These theoretical concepts allow us to identify the set of institutional features influencing the supply of firm-sponsored training. The opportunities for skill development are one of the most recognisable dimension of employment quality, which is another key concept in this chapter.

In the chapter the data from 23 countries representing five transition regimes will be analysed: employment centred (e.g. Germany), universalistic (e.g. Sweden), liberal (e.g. Ireland), sub-protective (e.g. Spain) and post-socialist. This last type, least recognised in the literature, is represented by eight countries: Bulgaria, the Czech Republic, Estonia, Hungary, Lithuania, Poland, Slovenia, and Slovakia. In the empirical part of the chapter a two-level random intercept logit model will be used to study the micro- and macro-level (mostly institutional) determinants of firm-sponsored training incidence. The set of micro-level variables comes from the fifth round of the European Social Survey (ESS, 2010). That wave of the study conducted in 2010 contains the unique rotating module covering the topic of employment quality ('Family Work and Well-being'). The macro-level variables characterising mainly the institutional features come from internationally comparative databases including OECD and ILOSTAT.

The analysis performed in this chapter revealed that the cross-country variation in firm-sponsored training incidence is substantial. In general, firms in countries representing post-socialist regimes invest relatively little in human capital. Part of this variation can be explained by the differences in institutional features. More training delivered by companies coincides with a generous, active labour market policy, strong trade unions, and vocationally oriented education systems. The supply of firm-sponsored training is also higher in developed and well-functioning economies. Finally, in comparison to their peers from Western Europe, young individuals in CEE countries have longer unemployment experiences and are more frequently employed in sectors investing little in human capital. These factors reduce the probability of receiving a firm-sponsored training.

The remainder of this chapter is organised as follows. The second part summarises the theoretical framework. The third part identifies the institutional features that will be analysed and summarises their expected impact on firm-sponsored training incidence. In the fourth part the empirical strategy will be outlined. The fifth part discusses the results and the last part concludes.

Main analytical concepts

Opportunities for skill development as a dimension of employment quality

The central part of this chapter is the notion of employment quality formulated by Duncan Gallie, which consists of five dimensions: skill use at work, the level of autonomy at work (task discretion), the opportunities for skill development, job security, and the level of work–family balance (Gallie, 2007a, p. 6). It might be surprising that a seemingly important dimension of employment quality – the level of salary – is not a part of the list. As was emphasised by Gallie: 'this is partly a definitional issue, with the notion of "job" focusing primarily on the intrinsic characteristics of work experience in contrast to "conditions of employment" which are concerned with the extrinsic features of work' (Gallie, 2007a, p. 6).

For similar reasons employment quality is less frequently proxied by measures of job- or life-satisfaction – they are not the intrinsic job characteristics but rather their outcomes. The impact of employment quality on subjective well-being measures can be moderated by various characteristics. For example, the relationship between job security and life satisfaction is moderated by perceived employability (Green, 2011). Hence, we can imagine the cases when employment of low quality is only weakly correlated with job of life satisfaction. Out of five aspects of employment quality, this chapter focuses on one – the opportunities of skill development. This notion will be used to analyse the cross-country variation in firm-delivered training incidence.

Employment and transition regimes

The concept of employment quality is useful for comparative analyses since it is embedded in the framework of employment regimes (Gallie, 2007a, 2007b). There are three ideal types of such regimes: inclusive, dualist, and market. In the inclusive regime, strong and organised trade unions act in favour of a high level of employment. As a result, a relatively 'tight labour market will strengthen employees' power at the workplace level, will be conducive to greater participation at work and will broaden concern about the quality of work' (Gallie, 2007a, p. 18). In the inclusive regimes, the level of unemployment protection is high with developed passive and active labour market policies.

The dualist employment regimes are similar, however, with stronger division between core and peripheral segments of the labour market. As a result, 'the nature of employment regulation will tend to reflect this providing strong employment protection, good employment conditions, and generous welfare support for the core workforce, but much poorer conditions for those on non-standard contracts' (Gallie, 2007a, p. 19).

Finally, in market regimes the position of the organised labour is relatively weak, and the main coordinating mechanism is the labour market. The employment quality and work conditions depend on the bargaining process at the company level. Less recognised types concern Mediterranean (sometimes referred to as sub-protective regimes) and transitional countries (representing post-socialist regimes). The concept of employment regimes overlaps in many areas with other similar typologies like production regimes, flexicurity regimes, welfare regimes, transition regimes.

Transition regimes

The last of the concepts – the transition regime – refers to the notion of school-to-work transition which can be defined as a 'sequence of educational, labour-market and related transitions that take place between the first significant branching point within educational careers and the point when – and if – young people become relatively established in their labour-market careers' (Raffe, 2014, p. 177). In such a framework school-to-work transition comprises 'relatively enduring features of [each] country's institutional and structural arrangements which shape transition processes and outcomes' (Smyth, Gangl, Raffe, Hannan, & McCoy, 2001, p. 19). Raffe (2008) mentions various institutional factors shaping the national transition patterns: labour market structure (degree of flexibility and regulation, dominant national form of labour market organisation), labour market policy and other relevant policies (youth programmes, career education and guidance), features of the educational system (standardisation, stratification, educational orientation, institutional linkages), the broader economic environment and family and cultural factors (Raffe, 2008, pp. 284–287).

The typology of transition regimes can be linked to welfare or employment regimes' typologies; however, it requires taking into account specific contextual factors, in particular, the characteristics of an education system and its links to labour market arrangements. The typology constructed by Walther (2006) distinguishes four ideal types of transition regimes: universalistic (corresponding to the inclusive employment regime), liberal (market employment regime), employment-centred (dualist employment regime) and sub-protective.

The universalistic transition regime shares many institutional features with Nordic countries. The schooling system is comprehensive and offers a vast majority of graduates access to higher education. The education and training are standardised according to the national frameworks, but there is also room for individual learning paths. Counselling is institutionalised and developed at all stages of transition into employment. The labour market policy measures towards young people are focused on fostering personal development. The level of social security is high, with the universal access to social assistance (eligibility is based on citizenship).

The liberal transition regime is typical for Anglo-Saxon countries. The schooling system offers mostly general education. The post-compulsory tracks offer diverse options including vocational paths. Moreover, the level of unemployment benefits is low and conditional on job search activities, while the labour market policy measures aim at fast employment. The low levels of employment protection and graduate qualification result in high vertical and horizontal mobility as well as dynamic flows between labour market states.

In the employment-centred transition regime fitting the cases of Germany or Switzerland, the educational system is highly tracked and selective. In the schooling system the vocational education is highly developed. The vocational programs are either school or firm based in the form of a so-called dual-apprenticeship system. Additionally, the labour market has a dual structure with the core offering protected and regulated employment and peripheries comprising precarious jobs. The level of social security reflects the dual structure of the labour market. Unemployment benefits are usually conditional on previous work experiences.

The sub-protective regime typical for many Mediterranean countries offers mostly general programs. Vocational education is less developed and mostly school based. Like in the employment-centred regime, the labour market is segmented with core and peripheral jobs. A high level of employment protection combined with a low level of labour force qualification makes the transition into employment in the core segment of the labour market long. The access of young individuals to social benefits is limited. Therefore, higher education, besides its main role, offers a 'shelter' during this long 'queuing phase' (Walther, 2006, pp. 126–129). Both employment and transition regimes literature were developed in the context of developed countries and offer a modest theoretical framework for understanding the institutional characteristics of CEE countries. As emphasised by Walther (2006): 'tentatively, "post-socialist" regimes can be characterized by their shift away from a socialist heritage, with universalistic and employment-centred aspects, towards either a more employment-centred or an increasingly sub-protective present' (Walther, 2006, p. 124).

Although in SWT literature the cluster of post-socialist countries is least researched, there are studies summarising their common features as well as analyses recognising the heterogeneity of this group. Naturally, the legacy of a centrally planned economy and the economic transition is emphasised. The SWT system before 1989 is described as offering a stable and secure transition but limited choice (Pohl & Walther, 2007). In centrally planned economies the collaboration of (usually state-owned) firms and vocational schools was tight, resulting in a developed vocational education with combined school- and work-based programmes (Noelke & Horn, 2014). Such a system, however, based more on state coercion than voluntary cooperation of institutions (e.g. trade unions, organisations of employers), was fragile to neo-liberal changes which started after 1989. According to Robert (2014) this was particularly the case of former Soviet Union states. In the course of transformation to capitalism in most post-socialist countries, the vocational training system collapsed, resulting in the shift towards a comprehensive education and school-based vocational education. Such trends were complemented by the rapid rise in tertiary education enrolment (Zamfir, Militaru, Mocanu, & Lungu, 2020). It can be explained by the processes of deindustrialisation, employment insecurity, and rising competition in the transition period, which increased the demand for general education. Only in some post-socialist economies, e.g. Slovenia, Slovakia, the Czech Republic, and to some extend in Poland, the vocational track remained a popular educational path (Robert, 2014). However, only in a few countries (e.g. Hungary, Slovenia) the vocational education is based on dual schemes (Zamfir et al., 2020). The common experience of the transformation was also the liberalisation of the labour market. Both the employment protection and trade union density declined, however, at a different pace. The labour market legislation is relatively flexible in Hungary and Poland (where in addition the share of non-standard employment is very high) and more restrictive in Slovenia and Lithuania. In systems where the links between education and the labour market are weak, which is the case of most CEE countries, the school-to-work transition can be supported by (particularly active) labour market policy measures (Hadjivassiliou, Tassinari, Eichhorst, & Wozny, 2016; Zamfir et al., 2020). The level of labour market policy spending is generally low in post-socialist states. However, in terms of activation there are large discrepancies within the cluster with countries representing the features of liberal (e.g. Poland and Slovakia), sub-protective (Bulgaria, Romania) or even universalistic (Slovenia) models (see Pohl & Walther, 2007, p. 548). To sum up, despite their heterogeneity, the countries representing the post-socialist cluster have mainly comprehensive education systems with underdeveloped vocational programmes. The linkages between the education system and the labour market are usually weak (the vocational education is usually school based). The relatively low level of employment protection prevails; however the traces of labour market dualism can be also observed (the protected core is complemented by low quality non-standard jobs; Hadjivassiliou et al., 2016).

Institutional determinants of firm-sponsored training

Features of education systems

The institutional features of education systems are characterised along several dimensions. Allmendinger (1989) has identified two of them, the standardisation of educational provisions and the stratification of educational opportunity. The first attribute of the educational system concerns the nationwide standards of education quality. Two forms of this dimension were further distinguished. The standardisation of input refers to the degree of freedom the schools have with respect to what and how they teach. In highly standardised educational systems (with respect to input) the quality and content of training provided by schools is regulated at the national level. The standardisation of output refers to the way the educational performance of students is verified. In highly standardised educational systems (with respect to output) the competences of graduates are tested through centralised exit examinations. The stratification of educational opportunity characterises the selectivity of the tracking system in education. A high level of stratification of educational opportunity describes the education systems in which the students are selected into tracks at an early age, where the tracks differ in terms of curricula and the mobility between tracks is limited. Another attribute of the educational system refers to its vocational orientation (Shavit & Muller, 2000). The vocationally oriented education systems are not only those where the proportion of students choosing the vocational track is high but also where the teaching process of occupation-specific skills includes practical training at the workplace (so-called dual apprenticeship system).

The relationship between the features of education systems and training incidence can be explained with the use of the notions of organisational and qualification spaces (Maurice, Sellier, & Silvestre, 1986). These spaces: 'define different logics that govern the recruitment, training, deployment, and mobility of workers' (Raffe, 2011, p. 319). Qualification spaces correspond to vocationally oriented, stratified, and standardised education systems which equip individuals with occupation-specific skills and work as efficient sorting devices. The education–job match is relatively strong, which reduces the demand for on-the-job training. Organisational spaces coincide with low levels of vocational orientation, stratification, and standardisation. Under such circumstances the majority of graduates do not have specific skills, and the links between qualifications and firms are weaker. This leads companies to invest more in employee training. The relationship between training and features of education systems will be similar when we refer to the signalling theory (Breen, 2005). Vocationally oriented, highly stratified, and standardised education systems send more informative signals about graduates' skills. It increases the education–job match and keeps the demand for further training low. The opposite relationship will concern general education systems. However, not only the features but also the quality of the education system should explain the cross-national differences in training provision. This is because the costs of training better-educated individuals are lower, which increases the firms' return to human capital investment. Therefore, the supply of skilled individuals (e.g. with a tertiary education degree) should increase the incidence of training, since the companies will be more likely to fill the training vacancies for skilled jobs (Brunello, 2001, p. 3).

Industrial relations and employment protection

Trade unions increase the incentives for training through influencing the wage structure. When this structure is flatter (wages are more compressed), the firms' return to training is higher due to the positive differences between the wage rate and the productivity gains. Trade unions can also negotiate with firms to increase the amount of employees' investment via training and, generally, their activities aim at reducing the worker flows, which decreases the risk of losing trained employees (Acemoglu & Pischke, 1999; Vogtenhuber, 2015).

The hypothetical impact of the employment protection on training incidence is equivocal. Due to the fact that the higher level of protection increases the costs of layoffs, workers are selected more carefully, and highly skilled individuals are employed more often. The better skills– or education–job match lessens the incentives for employees' training. However, hiring highly skilled workers encourages employers to deliver more training since its efficiency is higher (the same argument as with respect to the quality of education). Moreover, in the case of skill shortages, higher costs of layoffs make firms invest in employees' training rather than look for new hires.

Labour market policies

The explanation of the hypothetical impact of active labour market policy (utilising such measures as, e.g. training schemes, subsidised employment, apprenticeship programs) and passive labour market policy (unemployment benefits) also concerns the concept of match quality. In countries with generous ALMP unemployed are on average better prepared for a particular job; hence less on-the-job training is required. The generous PLMP gives the unemployed the opportunity to look for the job they are qualified for and not for any job (Tatsiramos, 2014; Tatsiramos & Ours, 2014). This increases the skills– or education–job match and reduces the demand for training.

The review of empirical results

The analysis of Brunello (2001) conducted for 13 Western European countries (European Community Household Panel) confirmed that the training incidence is positively correlated with trade union density, the strength of employment protection, the supply of educated labour, as well as negatively correlated with the level of stratification. Interestingly, the other study using the same dataset (although covering a different time period – 1995–2001) – indicated the negative relationship between training incidence and employment protection (Bassanini, Booth, Brunello, De Paola, & Leuven, 2005). The positive relationship between union density and training was also confirmed by Dieckhoff, Jungblut, and O'Connell (2007), who used the ECHP dataset for seven Western European countries, and – at the micro-level – by Booth, Francesconi, and Zoega (2003). Their analysis with the use of British Household Panel Study data indicated that union-covered workers were, relative to other employees, more likely to receive training. The study of Vogtenhuber (2015) concerning the cases of 14 European countries (including such CEE states as Bulgaria, Estonia, Croatia, Lithuania, Slovakia) with the use of Adult Education Survey data confirmed the negative relationship between stratification and training incidence, as well as the positive impact of the supply of educated workers and education quality.

Expected impact of institutional determinants on firm-sponsored training incidence

This chapter aims to verify the impact of some institutions on the incidence of training (financed by firms) among young workers. Based on the review presented in the previous section, the following hypotheses are tested:

H1: The incidence of training is higher in countries with stronger trade unions.

H2: The incidence of training is lower in countries with more generous active or passive labour market policies.

H3: The incidence of training is lower in countries with vocationally oriented or stratified or standardised education systems.

Although both theoretical predictions and empirical evidence underline the equivocal influence of employment protection legislation on the incidence of training, in case of high return to human capital investment caused by the stricter selection of workers and high costs of layoffs, greater employment protection should rather coincide with a high incidence of training. It allows to propose the last hypothesis:

H4: The incidence of training is higher in countries with stronger employment protection.

The empirical strategy

Data and variables

Institutional variables and other macro-level variables

The set of institutional variables and their construction is summarised in Table 2.1.

In the empirical part of the chapter, the models will also control for two other non-institutional macro-level variables whose impact on the training incidence was confirmed in the literature: GDP per capita and unemployment rate. Due to the data constraints, two features of education systems – institutional linkages and standardisation of input – are not taken into account.

Table 2.1 The operationalisation of institutional variables and their sources

Variable	*Operationalisation*
Trade unions strength	
Trade union density	Share of workers who are trade union members (OECD, ILOSTAT)
Collective bargaining coverage	Share of workers to whom collective bargaining agreements apply (OECD, ILOSTAT)
Labour market policy	
Active labour market policy	Spending on active labour market programmes as a share of GDP, standardised by unemployed rate, OECD
Passive labour market policy	Spending on passive labour market programmes as a share of GDP, standardised by unemployed rate, OECD
Education system	
Standardisation of output	Standardisation of output index constructed by Bol and van de Werfhorst (2013): a dummy variable indicating whether in a country there is a curriculum based on a central exit exam. Data source: Eurydice (2004), Woessmann (2005)
Stratification (tracking)	A set of tracking subindices: (1) the age of first selection, (2) the share of schools using any form of students' selection, (3) the number of tracks that are available for 15-year-olds. Indices constructed with the use of data from 2009, OECD (2010).
Vocational orientation	A share of vocational students in the upper secondary education (OECD)
Employment protection	The second version of the index of employment protection legislation (OECD). The synthetic index compiled from 21 items covering different aspects of employment protection regulations as they were in force on January 1 of each year. The scale range is 0 to 6, where 6 corresponds with the stronger EPL. Separate EPL indices are constructed for temporary and regular contracts.

Source: Own elaboration.

Training incidence and other micro-level variables

The set of micro-level variables comes from the European Social Survey (ESS, 2010). This is the source of high-quality comparative data covering the majority of European countries. Since 2002 the survey is being conducted biennially. The number of participating countries ranges from 22 (2002) to 31 (2008). A great number of topics are covered repeatedly, and they are complemented by rotating thematic modules. One of the rotating modules – Work, Family, and Wellbeing – added to the main survey in years 2004 and 2010 covers the topic of employment quality, including the incidence and financing of employees' training (Gallie, Dieckhoff, Russel, Steiber, & Tahlin, 2010). Given the fact that the variables characterising education systems come from the years 2005–2009, in the analysis only the data from the 2010 wave of ESS are used. Besides its high quality, there are at least two reasons to use this dataset. First, contrary to other surveys used so far (e.g. Brunello, 2001; Vogtenhuber, 2015), it allows us to identify precisely the training financed by the employer. Second, its geographical scope is relatively vast and covers a great number of states representing the post-socialist cluster. In this study the data from 23 European countries will be analysed, including 8 from CEE. It must be emphasised that the study concerns the world from nearly a decade ago, when most of the economies analysed in this chapter were influenced by the economic crisis of 2007. The Great Recession affected the economic conditions of states analysed in this study; however, in this regard only few countries differ substantially when years 2010 and 2020 are compared. In 2010 the unemployment rate in the Baltic states (represented in this analysis by Estonia and Lithuania) was particularly large and in Mediterranean countries remained still relatively low. The labour market effects of the crisis appeared there a few years later and – particularly in Greece – have persisted till now. The crisis affected the wealth of countries proxied by GDP per capita, but the rank of countries analysed in this chapter with respect to that index remained relative stable. Most importantly, the institutional context which is the main focus of the study did not change much.

The dependent variable is extracted from the ESS question which reads: 'During the last twelve months, have you taken any course or attended any lecture or conference to improve your knowledge or skills for work?' Moreover, respondents who answered 'yes' to that question were asked: 'How much of this training or education was paid for by your employer or firm?' Based on the answers the dummy variable was constructed, such that: 1 indicates participation in training which was sponsored by a company at least in some part, and 0 indicates no training or training paid fully by a worker.

The list of independent variables collected at the individual level includes the set of personal characteristics: years of education, the type of contract (limited or unlimited duration), whether a person was unemployed over the last five-year period, self-assessed health status, ethnic minority member status (whether someone was born in a foreign country or both parents come from a foreign country), age, and sex. These regressors are complemented by firm characteristics: firm size, sector (public vs. private) and industry (based on NACE rev. 2 classification).

Sample and methods

The final sample consists of individuals who were employees (thus, the self-employed were excluded from the analysis). Due to the construction of the ESS survey, the group of family business workers could not be taken into account. Only young individuals (aged 15–35) were selected into the analysis, since it is expected that the impact of education systems' features will be particularly strong within this group. The final sample consists of 5792 individuals from 23 countries. The descriptive statistics of micro-level and macro-level variables are presented in Tables 2.2 and 2.3, respectively.

The analysis is performed with the use of the two-level random intercept logit model where individuals are nested in countries. The model can be formulated as follows:

$$y_{ij}^{*} = \alpha + \boldsymbol{I}_{j}^{'}\beta + \boldsymbol{X}_{ij}^{'}\gamma + u_{ij} + e_{j} \qquad (2.1)$$

Table 2.2 Descriptive statistics, micro-level variables

	mean	*min*	*max*
Personal characteristics			
firm-sponsored training (1 – yes, 0 – no)	0.35	0	1
age	28.36	15	35
female (1 – yes, 0 – no)	0.49	0	1
migrant (1 – yes, 0 – no)	0.13	0	1
years of education	14.01	0	29
limited duration contract (1 – yes, 0 – no)	0.27	0	1
self-reported bad health (1 – yes, 0 – no)	0.013	0	1
not unemployed in last 5 yrs	0.72	0	1
unemployed less than 12m in last 5 yrs	0.21	0	1
unemployed more than 12 m last 5 yrs	0.07	0	1
Firm characteristics			
public sector	0.26	0	1
firm size (under 10 employees)	0.27	0	1
firm size (10–99 employees)	0.45	0	1
firm size (100–499 employees)	0.16	0	1
firm size (above 500 employees)	0.12	0	1
NACE sectors			
C: manufacturing	0.16	0	1
F: construction	0.07	0	1
G: trade	0.14	0	1
H: transport	0.06	0	1
I: accommodation & food	0.07	0	1
M: prof. & tech. activities	0.06	0	1
P: education	0.07	0	1
Q: health & social work	0.11	0	1
other sectors	0.26	0	1

Source: Own elaboration based on (ESS, 2010).

Table 2.3 Descriptive statistics, macro-level variables

	Number of obs.	*Mean*	*Min*	*Max*
Trade union strength				
union density	23	28.16	8.1	70.30
collective bargaining coverage	23	55.25	10.1	98.00
Labour market policy				
active labour market policy	23	6.19	0.80	18.37
passive labour market policy	23	11.36	1.63	32.51
Education system				
standardisation of output	23	0.74	0.00	1.00
stratification				
age of first selection	23	14.04	10.00	16.00
share of students in selective schools	23	0.33	0.01	0.88
number of tracks available for 15 yrs old	23	2.65	1.00	7.00
share of students in vocational schools	23	48.16	5.00	73.00
Employment protection				
employment protection, regular contracts	23	2.31	1.26	4.13
employment protection, temporary contracts	23	1.63	0.38	3.63
GDP per capita (US dollars)	23	35 358	6 843	87 770
Unemployment rate (15+)	23	10.00	3.52	19.86

Source: Own elaboration based on OECD and ILOSTAT data.

The symbol y^*_{ij} denotes a latent continuous variable that underlines the observed dependent variable y_{ij}. The latter is a binary variable indicating whether an individual *i* from the country *j* received a firm-sponsored training or not. The relationship between the observed and the latent variable is such that:

$$y_{ij} = \begin{cases} 1 \; if \; y^*_{ij} \geq 0 \\ 0 \; if \; y^*_{ij} < 0 \end{cases} \tag{2.2}$$

The sets of individual- and country-level independent variables are denoted as $\boldsymbol{X}_{ij}$ and $\boldsymbol{I}_j$ respectively. The terms u_{ij} and e_j denote individual- and country-level residuals. Due to the fact that the number of analysed countries is relatively small ($N = 23$) the full set of institutional variables should not be analysed in one model. This could lead to biased estimates (see, e.g., Stegmueller, 2013). Therefore, the stepwise procedure is applied. First, the models with a full set of micro-level regressors but only one institutional macro-level variable at a time will be estimated. In the next step this exercise will be repeated but with additional controls, country-level GDP per capita, and unemployment rate, respectively. Eventually, three groups of institutional effects will be estimated (from models without macro-level controls, from models with GDP control and from models with unemployment rate control). Such a strategy serves as a robustness check of estimated institutional effects and at least partly reduces the risk of country-level omitted variable bias. The multilevel setting allows us to estimate the corrected standard errors which otherwise could be underestimated due to the clustering at the country level.

Results

Micro-level determinants

The micro-level determinants of firm-sponsored training in principle behave according to expectations (see Table 2.4). In accordance with the human capital theory the investment in workers with a higher stock of accumulated human

Table 2.4 Micro-level determinants of firm-sponsored training, 2010. Marginal effects, multilevel random intercept logit model

	Marginal effects	*Standard errors*
Personal characteristics		
age	0.005	(0.007)
female (1 – yes, 0 – no)	−0.319***	(0.067)
migrant (1 – yes, 0 – no)	−0.501***	(0.098)
years of education	0.121***	(0.011)
limited duration contract (1 – yes, 0 – no)	−0.371***	(0.078)
self-reported bad health (1 – yes, 0 – no)	0.125	(0.256)
not unemployed in last 5 yrs	ref.	ref.
unemployed less than 12m in last 5 yrs	−0.172**	(0.080)
unemployed more than 12 m last 5 yrs	−0.491***	(0.137)
Firm characteristics		
public sector (1 – yes, 0 – no)	0.278***	(0.067)
firm size (under 10 employees)	ref.	ref.
firm size (10–99 employees)	0.208***	(0.080)
firm size (100–499 employees)	0.530***	(0.100)
firm size (above 500 employees)	0.739***	(0.112)
NACE sector		
C: manufacturing	ref.	ref.
F: construction	0.273*	(0.148)
G: trade	0.181	(0.138)
H: transport	0.410***	(0.150)
I: accommodation & food	−0.489***	(0.187)
M: prof. & tech. activities	0.548***	(0.149)
P: education	0.837***	(0.152)
Q: health & social work	0.816***	(0.137)
other sectors	0.495***	(0.104)
Number or respondents	5792	

Source: Own elaboration.

Notes: Asterisks denote significance levels: *** – 0.01, ** – 0.05 and * – 0.1.

capital is more effective. This would explain why the more educated receive more training – contrary to workers with unemployment experiences.

The evidence that ethnic minority members and women are less likely to receive training could suggest a sort of labour market exclusion. However, it could be also caused by other mechanisms – for example, these groups are more likely to quit jobs, which makes investing in them less profitable. Firm-sponsored training is more likely in the public sector, in larger companies, and in some industries – particularly in innovative sectors, such as: health and social work, education, professional and technical activities.

Macro-level determinants

Training incidence and institutional features – correlation analysis

Table 2.5 shows that the cross-country variation in firm-sponsored training incidence is substantial. In general, there are clear differences between countries representing universalistic (Norway, Sweden, Finland) or employment-centred

Table 2.5 The share of young employees (aged 35 or less) who participated in training in 2010

Country	*Paid by employer*	*Paid by others*	*Number of respondents*
Denmark (DK)	0.59	0.06	190
The Netherlands (NL)	0.57	0.08	261
Finland (FI)	0.56	0.18	224
Sweden (SE)	0.54	0.08	217
Norway (NO)	0.54	0.08	271
Switzerland (CH)	0.48	0.13	249
Belgium (BE)	0.47	0.11	255
Great Britain (GB)	0.44	0.08	349
Slovenia (SI)	0.40	0.11	202
Germany (DE)	0.39	0.11	390
France (FR)	0.37	0.06	241
Estonia (EE)	0.34	0.19	231
Slovakia (SK)	0.30	0.07	172
Hungary (HU)	0.30	0.08	227
Spain (ES)	0.27	0.13	276
Israel (IL)	0.26	0.07	317
Poland (PL)	0.25	0.12	310
Lithuania (LT)	0.23	0.09	104
The Czech Republic (CZ)	0.20	0.05	329
Ireland (IE)	0.18	0.08	310
Bulgaria (BG)	0.12	0.03	169
Portugal (PT)	0.12	0.07	205
Greece (GR)	0.06	0.08	293
Average share	0.35	0.09	5792

Source: Own elaboration based on (ESS, 2010).

regimes (Germany, Netherlands) and sub-protective (Greece, Portugal, Spain) or post-socialistic regimes (Bulgaria, the Czech Republic, Lithuania).

Countries representing these two latter regimes, with the exception of Slovenia and Estonia, score below the European average in terms of enterprise-sponsored training. Estonia and Slovenia seem to be outliers among post-socialist states as well as Bulgaria, which, however, is localised in the low end of the training distribution. What can be also seen in the table is that the low supply of training delivered by companies is not traded off by training financed from other sources (private or public). On the contrary, the correlation between these two types of instruction is positive ($r = 0.29$). It further deepens the divide between the low end and high end of training distribution in Europe. At first glance, the training incidence seems to be also correlated with economic conditions – more instruction is delivered in richer countries.

The more nuanced picture can be seen in figures showing the relationship between institutional variables and training incidence.

Figure 2.1 presents a relatively strong and positive relationship between training incidence and two characteristics describing the strength of labour unions: trade union density and collective bargaining coverage. This is in accordance with theoretical consideration outlined before. It must be noted, however, that the former relationship is mostly driven by the group of countries representing the universalistic regime (Norway, Finland, Sweden) as well as Denmark and Belgium. With respect to union density, the group of post-socialist countries appears homogenous, except for Slovenia as an outlier, with substantially higher share of trade union membership. Training incidence is slightly less correlated with collective bargaining coverage. However, most of the countries in the sample contribute to this relationship. The outlier position of Slovenia with respect to other post-socialist countries is even more pronounced here. The case of Bulgaria with the lowest level of bargaining coverage is also noticeable. Countries representing a sub-protective employment regime (Greece, Portugal, Spain) constitute a

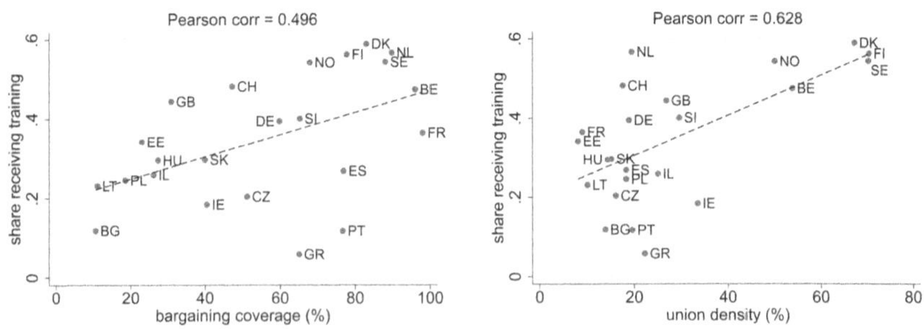

Figure 2.1 Training incidence among young employees and trade unions strength

Source: Own elaboration based on ESS micro-level data merged with ILOSTAT macro-level data.

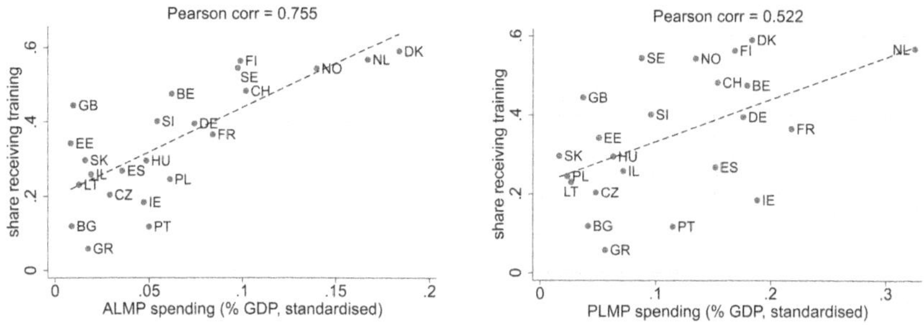

Figure 2.2 Training incidence among young employees and labour market policy spending

Source: Own elaboration based on ESS micro-level data merged with OECD macro-level data.

particular group with a relatively high level of bargaining coverage but a low share of young individuals receiving training.

Contrary to the expectations both active and passive labour market policy spending is strongly and positively correlated with the share of young individuals receiving firm-sponsored training (see Figure 2.2). However, this result at least with respect to ALMP spending can be explained with the reference to human capital theory. ALMP measures increase the stock of human capital of job candidates. The investment in employees with higher levels of human capital brings higher returns encouraging firms to deliver more training.

It is also possible that enterprise-supplied training is publicly subsidised as a part of ALMP. Given the nature of the data, it is not possible to verify whether such an effect exists. The positive correlation between training incidence and PLMP spending is more difficult to explain. This relationship may well be spurious given the fact that PLMP and ALMP are highly correlated. In the next part of the chapter a more sophisticated method will be used to shed more light on this relationship. As far as the group of post-socialist countries is concerned, it looks relatively homogenous with regard to labour market policy spending. However, some patterns mentioned earlier can also be observed – Slovenia is the country with the most generous labour market policy, whereas Bulgaria's score is one of the lowest.

The next group of institutional determinants concerns educational policy. Three out of four features of the education system show hardly any relationship with training incidence (see Figure 2.3). Furthermore, the characteristics of the education system measuring the level of standardisation, which is not presented in the figures since it is proxied by the binary variable (indicating whether in a country there exists a curriculum-based central exit exam), is also uncorrelated with training incidence.

Only vocational orientation seems associated with the share of young workers receiving firm-sponsored training. The direction of this relationship is, however, positive – contrary to the expectations. Also, in this case the reasoning utilising the human capital theory can be applied – if vocational education equips graduates

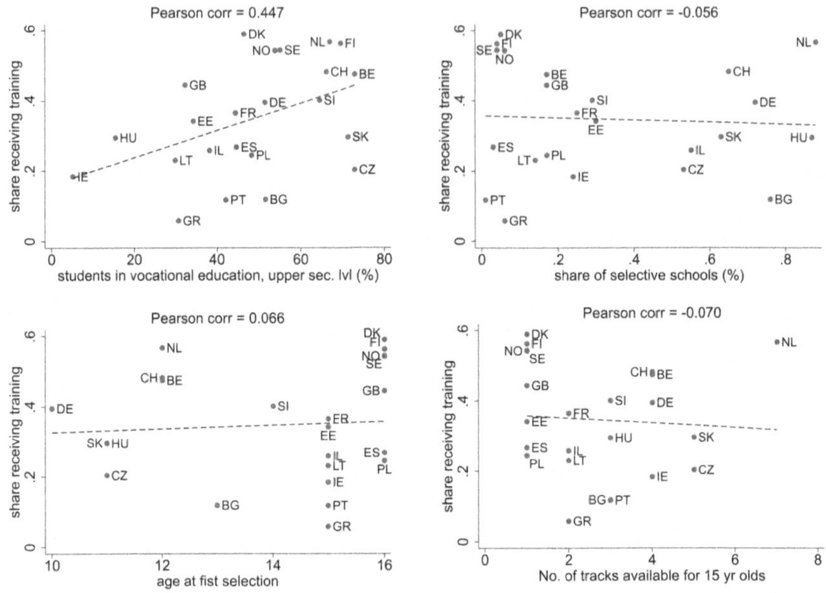

Figure 2.3 Training incidence among young employees and features of education systems
Source: Own elaboration based on ESS micro-level data merged with OECD macro-level data.

with industry- or job- specific human capital, the personnel investment through training can be more profitable. The group of post-socialist countries reveals vast diversity with respect to vocational orientation of the education system. In the analysed period, the share of students in vocational education ranged from very high in the Czech Republic, Slovakia, and Slovenia through moderate in Bulgaria and Poland to low in Lithuania and Hungary.

The relationship between training incidence and employment protection legislation is much weaker and apparent only with respect to regular contract jobs (see Figure 2.4). The negative correlation does not support the formulated hypothesis but is consistent with the expectation that stronger employment protection results in a stricter selection of candidates who demand less training as employees. It should be noted, however, that the observed relationship would turn positive after excluding the cases of Greece, Portugal, and the Czech Republic.

The analysis of post-socialist country cases reveals two outliers – the Czech Republic and Bulgaria with particularly high and particularly low levels of protection respectively.

The last group of figures show that firm-sponsored training incidence is strongly correlated with economic condition characteristics – GDP per capita (positively) and unemployment rate (negatively; see Figure 2.5).

These macro-level variables are also associated with some institutions under scrutiny, e.g. ALMP and PLMP spending. Therefore, the next section presents the

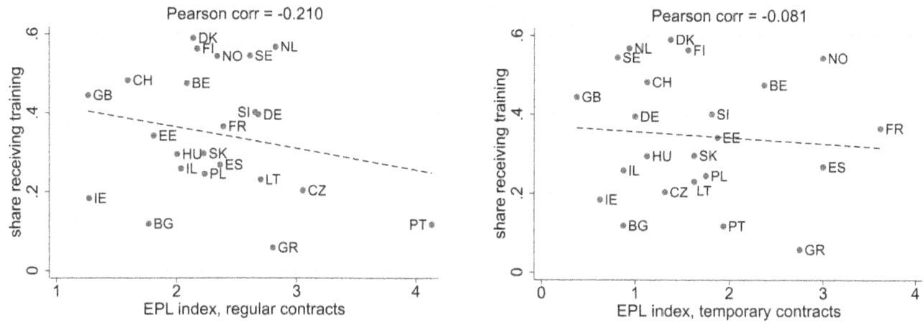

Figure 2.4 Training incidence among young employees and employment protection legislation

Source: Own elaboration based on ESS micro-level data merged with OECD and ILOSTAT macro-level data.

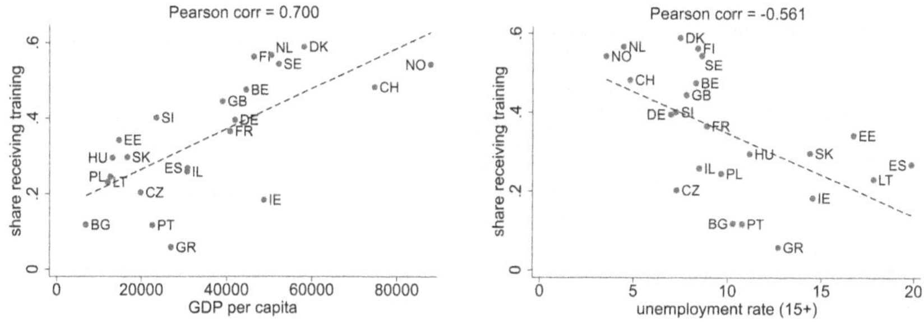

Figure 2.5 Training incidence among young employees and economic conditions

Source: Own elaboration based on ESS micro-level data merged with World Bank macro-level data.

results of training incidence determinants estimated with the use of a two-level random intercept logit model.

Training incidence and institutional features – regression analysis

More in-depth analysis of institutional features' impact on training incidence is possible with the use of a two-level random intercept logit model. The estimated coefficients come from three groups of regression models (described in section 'Sample and Methods'): (1) where only one institutional variable at a time was included, (2) where one institutional variable was included jointly with another macro-level variable – GDP per capita and (3) where one institutional variable was included jointly with another macro-level variable – unemployment rate. The results of these analyses are presented in Table 2.6.

Table 2.6 Impact of the institutional variables on firm-sponsored training incidence, results of the two-level random intercept model

	Marginal effect (1)	*Marginal Effect (2)*	*Marginal Effect (3)*
Trade union strength			
union density	0.022***	0.001	0.016**
	(0.007)	(0.007)	(0.07)
bargaining coverage	0.012***	0.003	0.008
	(0.005)	(0.005)	(0.05)
Labour market policy			
active labour market policy	0.110***	0.074**	0.091***
	(0.023)	(0.033)	(0.029)
passive labour market policy	0.047***	0.011	0.030*
	(0.019)	(0.020)	(0.018)
Education system			
central examination	0.145	0.369	0.016
	(0.370)	(0.273)	(0.309)
age of first selection	0.008	−0.034	0.054
	(0.081)	(0.061)	(0.068)
No. of tracks available for 15-yr-olds	−0.029	−0.019	−0.095
	(0.099)	(0.073)	(0.082)
share of students in selective schools	−0.009	0.334	−0.382
	(0.562)	(0.421)	(0.470)
share of students in vocational schools	0.020**	0.014**	0.011
	(0.008)	(0.006)	(0.008)
Employment protection			
employment prot., regular contracts	−0.256	−0.099	−0.294
	(0.266)	(0.205)	(0.217)
employment prot., temporary contracts	−0.098	−0.142	0.003
	(0.195)	(0.143)	(0.165)
GDP per capita (in 10 000 USD)	0.251***	–	–
	(0.059)		
Unemployment rate (15+)	−0.104***	–	
	(0.032)		

Source: Own elaboration based on the ESS micro-level data merged with OECD, World Bank, and ILOSTAT macro-level data.

Notes: Asterisks denote significance levels: *** –0.01, ** –0.05 and * –0.1. Standard errors are presented in parentheses. Marginal effects, based on the estimate of the two-level random intercept logit model (see equation 2.1), measure the impact of the macro-level variables on the firm-sponsored training probability. The set of micro-level variables, treated here as controls, was the same as in Table (2.4). The estimates for these variables ($N = 5792$) are not presented for the sake of clarity. The coefficients in column (1) come from the set of eleven separate models where only one macro-level institutional variable (among the listed above) was included in the model at a time. Coefficients in column (2) and (3) come from the same model specifications with additional controls for GDP per capita and unemployment rate respectively. The estimated effects of GDP per capita and unemployment rate presented in column (1) come from models without any institutional variables as controls.

The presented estimates confirm the findings from the previous section. Only some effects, however, are robust. The positive impact of ALMP spending remains positive and statistically significant across three different specifications (without macro-level variables and with GDP and unemployment rate controls), unlike the PLMP spending proxy, which loses its significance once macro-level controls are introduced. Moreover, in the specification where both ALMP and PLMP proxies are included (not reported here), only the former remains statistically significant. It suggests that the positive relationship between PLMP and training incidence presented in Figure 2.2 might be spurious. Out of the two proxies for labour unions' strength, the union density is more robust, but it also loses its predictive power once GDP per capita is controlled for. The only education system feature predicting the firm-sponsored training incidence is the vocational orientation. The estimated positive effect also loses significance in one model specification (where the unemployment rate is controlled for). The most robust characteristics allowing to explain the cross-country variation in enterprise-delivered training are both variables describing economic conditions – GDP per capita (positive impact) and the unemployment rate (negative impact). These two variables were statistically significant in all model specifications.

Training incidence and country-level characteristics: the international comparison

The cross-country variation in training incidence can be explained not only through macro-level variables but also through various composition of micro-level determinants analysed in the previous section. The results presented in Table 2.4 show that the probability of receiving firm-sponsored training is higher for better-educated individuals and for those working in the public sector and larger companies. Less likely to receive training are individuals working on limited duration contracts, women, members of ethnic minorities, and those who experienced unemployment in the past. There is also a significant cross-industrial variation in training incidence. A particularly high level of human capital investment concerns employees in such industries as education (P) and human health and social work activities (Q). Low levels of investment are associated with manufacturing (C) and wholesale and retail trade sectors (G). The cross-country differences in the distribution of these characteristics, presented in Table 2.7, can explain the international variation of firm-sponsored training incidence.

A relatively high share of employees receiving training in Estonia, Hungary and Slovakia (with comparison to other CEE countries) can be associated with the fact that a small fraction of workers is hired on limited-duration contracts in those countries. The school-to-work transition in the post-socialist cluster seems more turbulent than in countries representing universal, liberal, and employment-centred regimes, which is reflected by a large share of workers who experienced unemployment. Within this group the lowest level of early job insecurity concerns the cases of the Czech Republic and Slovakia – countries representing

Table 2.7 The composition of micro-level characteristics in a comparative perspective (percentages except for education measured in years)

	universal	*liberal*	*sub-protective*	*emp-centred*	*BG*	*CZ*	*EE*	*HU*	*LT*	*PL*	*SI*	*SK*
with limited contract	$22.5_{a,c,g}$	$28.7_{a,f}$	37.6_{b}	$25.4_{a,c,f}$	$17.8_{a,c,g}$	$17.3_{c,g}$	$16.5_{c,d,g}$	$17.2_{c,e,g}$	$13.5_{a,c,g}$	46.5_{b}	$35.6_{b,f}$	12.8_{g}
unemployed in the past	$25.4_{a,b,d}$	$23.5_{a,c}$	$32.9_{b,d,e}$	21.7_{a}	$34.9_{b,c,d,e}$	$23.1_{a,b}$	$36.4_{d,e}$	40.1_{e}	$32.7_{a,b,d,e}$	$38.1_{e,f}$	$30.2_{a,b,d,e}$	$27.3_{a,b,d,e}$
education (in years)	$14.56_{a,c,d}$	15.06_{a}	13.80_{b}	$13.87_{b,e}$	13.32_{b}	13.38_{b}	$14.21_{a,b}$	$13.85_{b,c,e}$	$13.83_{b,d,e}$	$14.56_{a,e,f}$	$13.59_{b,f}$	$14.13_{a,b}$
in large firms	$25.6_{c,d}$	35.8_{a}	13.8_{b}	33.6_{a}	$17.2_{b,c,d}$	$23.7_{c,d}$	$16.9_{b,c}$	37.4_{a}	$17.3_{b,c,d}$	$27.7_{a,c}$	40.6_{a}	$32.0_{a,d}$
in public sector	$28.9_{a,c}$	$28.1_{a,c}$	17.2_{b}	$28.6_{a,c}$	$16.6_{a,b}$	$21.9_{a,b}$	$24.2_{a,b,c}$	$24.2_{a,b,c}$	$20.2_{a,b,c}$	$23.5_{a,b,c}$	35.6_{c}	$26.2_{a,b,c}$
Nace Rev. 2 sectors												
manufacturing (C)	$12.1_{a,d,g,h}$	9.6_{a}	$14.5_{a,b,c}$	$14.3_{a,b}$	$24.3_{b,c,e}$	$22.5_{c,e}$	$18.2_{b,c,d,e}$	25.6_{e}	$26.9_{c,e,f}$	$17.7_{b,c,e,g}$	$20.8_{b,c,e,h}$	$27.9_{e,i}$
trade (G)	$14.5_{a,d,e,f}$	$17.3_{a,d,e}$	$13.4_{a,d,e,f}$	$13.6_{a,d,e,f}$	$20.1_{a,b}$	$18.8_{a,c}$	$8.2_{d,f}$	$13.7_{a,d,e,f}$	$8.7_{a,d,e,f}$	$20.6_{b,c,e}$	7.4_{f}	$9.3_{a,d,e,f}$
education (P)	6.9_{a}	8.5_{a}	6.6_{a}	7.8_{a}	2.4_{a}	5.8_{a}	9.5_{a}	5.3_{a}	3.8_{a}	6.1_{a}	5.0_{a}	5.2_{a}
health (Q)	$13.8_{a,c}$	14.4_{a}	5.2_{b}	15.2_{a}	$4.7_{b,c}$	4.9_{b}	4.3_{b}	3.5_{b}	$5.8_{a,b}$	5.8_{b}	0.0	$9.9_{a,b}$
Number of respondents	712	659	774	1345	169	329	231	227	104	310	202	172

Source: Own elaboration.

Notes: universal regime (Finland, Sweden, Norway), liberal regime (Ireland, GB), sub-protective regime (Portugal, Spain, Greece), employment centred regime (Belgium, Switzerland, Germany, Netherlands, Denmark). Except for education, displayed indices show percentages. APA-style formatting shows significant differences in fraction (mean) tests (at 0.05 significance level). If two values are significantly different, all subscript letters are different. If the difference is not significant at least one subscript letters is repeated (e.g. with respect to employment in manufacturing, the difference between Bulgaria and the liberal cluster is statistically significant but between Bulgaria and the employment-centred cluster is not).

vocationally oriented education systems. It is well proved that vocational orientation is associated with lower levels of youth unemployment (Bol & Van de Werfhorst, 2013; Breen, 2005; Levels, van der Velden, & Stasio, 2014; Wolbers, 2007). This mechanism could explain the positive relationship between vocational orientation and training incidence – vocational orientation contributes to smoother school-to-work transitions and greater accumulation of human capital. This in turn increases the probability of receiving firm-sponsored training.

Many cross-country differences with respect to years of education are not statistically significant. However, the lowest value of this statistic in the Bulgarian sample is noticeable and consistent with a very low share of young individuals receiving training in this country. The comparison of Bulgaria and Slovenia with respect to employment in large companies (employing more than 100 workers) and in the public sector can also explain the differences in firm-sponsored training incidence between these two post-socialist countries. On top of that, one-fifth of young workers in Bulgaria are employed in the trade industry, which invests relatively little in employee training. The share of workers active in this sector in Estonia and Slovenia is significantly lower. Contrary to countries representing universal and liberal regimes, CEE economies offer a great number of jobs in manufacturing – another sector in which companies invest little in human capital.

Conclusion

One of the facets of the labour utilisation principle is that workers are matched to job offers according to the most productive use of their skills. This static framework can be developed by allowing firms to influence the education– and skills–job match through professional training. The analysis performed in this chapter aimed to verify whether differences in the institutional context can explain the cross-country variation with respect to employee training delivered by companies. Thereby, this study was focused on the indirect impact of institutions on labour utilisation.

The cross-country variation in firm-sponsored training incidence is substantial. In general, there are clear differences between countries representing universalistic (Norway, Sweden, Finland) or employment-centred regimes (Belgium, Switzerland, Germany, Netherlands, Denmark) and sub-protective (Greece, Portugal, Spain) or post-socialistic regimes. In countries representing the two last clusters, the level of firm-sponsored training incidence is relatively low. However, the group of post-socialist countries is far from being homogenous. Out of eight countries under scrutiny, five seem to constitute a group which is similar in many respects: Poland, the Czech Republic, Hungary, Slovakia, and Lithuania. On top of that, there are three notable outliers – Bulgaria (with a particularly low level of personnel investment), Estonia and Slovenia (which score around the European average).

A part of this cross-country variation can be explained by the differences in institutional features. More training is delivered in countries with a more generous active labour market policy as well as – however these effects are less robust – with stronger trade unions and more vocationally oriented education systems.

The results suggest that the professional training delivered by the state (in the form of vocational programmes or active labour market policy measures) does not crowd out the involvement of employers in this sphere. On the contrary, the human capital investment of the state seems to be multiplied by the investments made by companies. It can be treated as a positive externality of state intervention, which justifies its role as a supplier of the professional training. Besides institutional factors, economic conditions also strongly influence the supply of employee training. The richer the country and the lower the unemployment rate, the higher the level of human capital investment is. These effects also have implications for the role of the state. In times of economic downturn companies tend to reduce their involvement in employee training. In such circumstances more training can be delivered by the state (e.g. through active labour market policy measures) to foster labour market utilisation.

Besides the macro-level factors, the composition effects also help to understand cross-country variation in training incidence. In most post-socialist countries, a relatively large fraction of young workers has unemployment experiences. This significantly reduces their chances to receive firm-sponsored training. The process of labour market entry can be supported by various institutions. One of the most recognised solutions is the developed vocational education – an area largely neglected in most post-socialist countries in the transition period. Finally, some variation in firm-sponsored training incidence can be explained by the differences in industrial composition. In particular, the CEE countries have a high share of employment in manufacturing – the industry which invests relatively little in personnel training. To some extent a low level of training delivered by firms in post-communist countries reflects their position in the global (or European) value chain.

References

Acemoglu, D., & Pischke, J.-S. (1999). Beyond Becker: Training in imperfect labour markets. *The Economic Journal*, *109*(453), 112–142. doi:10.1111/1468-0297.00405

Allmendinger, J. (1989). Educational systems and labor market outcomes. *European Sociological Review*, *5*(3), 231–250.

Bassanini, A., Booth, A., Brunello, G., De Paola, M., & Leuven, E. (2005). *Workplace training in Europe* (IZA Discussion Paper No. 1640). Retrieved from https://econpapers.repec.org/paper/izaizadps/dp1640.htm

Bol, T., & van de Werfhorst, H. G. (2013). Educational systems and the trade-off between labor market allocation and equality of educational opportunity. *Comparative Education Review*, *57*(2), 285–308. doi:10.1086/669122

Booth, A. L., Francesconi, M., & Zoega, G. (2003). Unions, work-related training, and wages: Evidence for British men. *Industrial and Labor Relations Review*, *57*(1), 68–91. doi:10.2307/3590982

Breen, R. (2005). Explaining cross-national variation in youth unemployment market and institutional factors. *European Sociological Review*, *21*(2), 125–134. doi:10.1093/esr/jci008

Brunello, G. (2001). *On the complementarity between education and training in Europe* (IZA Discussion Paper No. 309). Retrieved from https://ideas.repec.org/p/iza/izadps/dp309.html

Dieckhoff, M., Jungblut, J.-M., & O'Connell, P. J. (2007). Job-related training in Europe. Do Institutions Matter? In D. Gallie (Ed.), *Employment regimes and the quality of work*. Oxford: Oxford University Press, pp. 77–104.

ESS Round 5: European Social Survey Round 5 Data. (2010). *NSD – Norwegian Centre for Research Data, Norway – Data archive and distributor of ESS data for ESS ERIC* (Data file 3.4 ed.). doi:10.21338/NSD-ESS5-2010

Eurydice. (2004). *European glossary on education: Examinations, qualifications and titles* (Vol. 1, 2nd ed.). Brussels: Eurydice.

Gallie, D. (2007a). *Employment regimes and the quality of work*. Oxford: Oxford University Press.

Gallie, D. (2007b). Production regimes and the quality of employment in Europe. *Annual Review of Sociology*, *33*, 85–104.

Gallie, D., Dieckhoff, M., Russel, H., Steiber, N., & Tahlin, M. (2010). *Round 5 family, work and well-being – final module template*. Retrieved from www.europeansocialsurvey.org/data/demo_module_family.html

Green, F. (2011). Unpacking the misery multiplier: How employability modifies the impacts of unemployment and job insecurity on life satisfaction and mental health. *Journal of Health Economics*, *30*(2), 265–276. doi:10.1016/j.jhealeco.2010.12.005

Hadjivassiliou, K., Tassinari, A., Eichhorst, W., & Wozny, F. (2016). *Assessing the performance of school-to-work transition regimes in the EU* (IZA Discussion Papers No. 10301).

Levels, M., van der Velden, R., & Stasio, V. D. (2014). From school to fitting work: How education-to-job matching of European school leavers is related to educational system characteristics. *Acta Sociologica*, *57*(4), 341–361. doi:10.1177/0001699314552807

Maurice, M., Sellier, F., & Silvestre, J.-J. (1986). *The social foundations of industrial power*. Cambridge, MA: MIT Press.

Noelke, C., & Horn, D. (2014). Social transformation and the transition from vocational education to work in Hungary: A differences-in-differences approach. *European Sociological Review*, *30*(4), 431–443. doi:10.1093/esr/jcu048

OECD. (2010). *PISA 2009 results: What makes a school successful?* (Vol. 4). Paris: OECD.

Pohl, A., & Walther, A. (2007). Activating the disadvantaged: Variations in addressing youth transitions across Europe. *International Journal of Lifelong Education*, *26*(5), 533–553. doi:10.1080/02601370701559631

Raffe, D. (2008). The concept of transition system. *Journal of Education and Work*, *21*(4), 277–296.

Raffe, D. (2011). Cross-national differences in education-work transitions. In M. London (Ed.), *The Oxford handbook of lifelong learning* (pp. 312–328). New York: Oxford University Press.

Raffe, D. (2014). Explaining national differences in education-work transitions. *European Societies*, *16*(2), 175–193. doi:10.1080/14616696.2013.821619

Robert, P. (2014). Job mismatch in early career of graduates under post-communism. *International Journal of Manpower*, *35*(4), 500–513. doi:10.1108/IJM-05-2013-0113

Shavit, Y., & Muller, W. (2000). Vocational secondary education. *European Societies*, *2*(1), 29–50. doi:10.1080/146166900360710

Smyth, E., Gangl, M., Raffe, D., Hannan, D., & McCoy, S. (2001). *Comparative analysis of transitions from education to work in Europe* (ESRI Final Report to the European Commission). Dublin: Economic and Social Research Institute.

Stegmueller, D. (2013). How many countries for multilevel modeling? A comparison of frequentist and Bayesian approaches. *American Journal of Political Science*, *57*(3), 748–761. doi:10.1111/ajps.12001

Tatsiramos, K. (2014). Unemployment benefits and job match quality. *IZA World of Labor*. Bonn: Institute for the Study of Labor. doi:10.15185/izawol.44

Tatsiramos, K., & Van Ours, J. (2014). Labor market effects of unemployment insurance design. *Journal of Economic Surveys*, *28*(2), 284–311. doi:10.1111/joes.12005

Vogtenhuber, S. (2015). Explaining country variation in employee training: An institutional analysis of education systems and their influence on training and its returns. *European Sociological Review*, *31*(1), 77–90. doi:10.1093/esr/jcu083

Walther, A. (2006). Regimes of youth transitions choice, flexibility and security in young people's experiences across different European contexts. *Young*, *14*(2), 119–139. doi:10.1177/1103308806062737

Wolbers, M. H. J. (2007). Patterns of labour market entry. A comparative perspective on school-to-work transitions in 11 European countries. *Acta Sociologica*, *50*(3), 189–210. https://doi.org/10.1177/0001699307080924

Woessmann, L. (2005). The effect heterogeneity of central examinations: Evidence from TIMSS, TIMSS-repeat and PISA. *Education Economics*, *13*(2), 143–169.

Zamfir, A.-M., Militaru, E., Mocanu, C., & Lungu, E. O. (2020). School-to-work transition of higher education graduates in four European countries. *Compare: A Journal of Comparative and International Education*, *50*(1), 36–52. doi:10.1080/03057925.2018.1493572

3

SKILLS UTILISATION – ANALYSIS ACROSS COUNTRIES AND OCCUPATIONS. WESTERN EUROPEAN AND POST-SOCIALIST COUNTRIES COMPARISON

Magdalena Andrałojć and Kea Tijdens

Introduction

After 30 years of economic transition in post-socialist countries, qualifications and skills mismatch is still the most important issue affecting the labour markets in this part of Europe. The same applies to the Western European countries. Although the unemployment in EU-15 states is generally low, there is still a problem with structural unemployment, i.e. a mismatch between supply and demand for a specific type or level of qualifications (Kocór, 2017). It has a negative impact on productivity, the individuals' job engagement, and pay satisfaction.

The supply of occupations is an effect of people's decisions concerning their career development and the possibilities given by the educational system. One of the commonly used predictors of skills mismatch is the wage level and wage growth in various occupations. The OECD argues that 'the analysis of wage dynamics, usually referred to as "wage pressure", is one of the most powerful tool[s] available to measure the tightening of the labour market in specific occupations and, as such, to detect skills imbalances' (OECD, 2017, p. 32).

Following this statement, the main aim of this chapter is, on the one hand, to prepare an occupational matrix for each analysed country incorporating wage growth and wage level indicators and compare these matrixes between selected Western European and post-socialist countries and on the other hand to look for similarities and differences in the skills use on these markets. In particular, we analysed how the skills mismatch translates to skills underutilisation on these markets. We also believe that such analysis can help us understand the migration processes between European countries. The assumption here is that the people whose occupation is classified as low paid and surplus in the origin country and, at the same time, high paid and shortage in the country of destination might be the most willing to migrate. The study is conducted for 16 Western European and post-socialist countries for the period 2008–2016.

Our main conclusion is that the occupational matrix differs between countries. However, there are some regularities as far as the skills utilisation is concerned. Namely, there are a lot of similarities between post-socialist countries that visibly distinguish this group from the Western European countries. It indicates that in terms of labour utilisation, the process of convergence between post-socialist countries and Western European countries is still not fully completed, despite the open borders within the EU.

The chapter is organised as follows. In the first part we review the literature concerning skills utilisation, which is a broad concept and can be explained differently. We show the main definitions and methods of analysis derived from the literature. The second part of the chapter is dedicated to the construction and analysis of the occupational matrix, which illustrate the skills utilisation in the analysed countries. Using two indicators, namely the wage level and wage growth, we have divided the analysed 47 occupational groups into four large categories: (1) high paid and shortage, (2) high paid and surplus, (3) low paid and shortage, and (4) low paid and surplus. In the third and fourth sections we analyse the subjective measures of qualification match and pay satisfaction in these four groups of the matrix. The first conjecture here is that the biggest over-qualification and the lowest satisfaction would be in surplus and low-paid jobs. This group mainly deals with the 'wage penalty' phenomenon widely described in the literature. The second conjecture is that under-qualification and high satisfaction would be in high-paid shortage professions. Thus, we try to show the skills mismatch in two dimensions. The first dimension is objective and is given by a classification of each occupation into one of the four cells of the matrix using the data on wages. The second one is given by subjective qualification mismatch within the occupational matrix.

Skills mismatch – a literature review

If a workplace does not match an employee's qualifications, the acquired human capital cannot be utilised entirely and therefore converted into expected returns because such an employee is not optimally productive (Kracke, Reichelt, & Vicari, 2017, p. 6). To analyse the qualification mismatch, and labour utilisation in general, the US National Commission on Employment and Unemployment Statistics proposed in 1978 the Labour Utilisation Framework (LUF), developed later on by ILO (ILO, 2008; Sullivan & Hauser, 1978).[1] LUF indicated four forms of underutilisation: unemployment, inadequate utilisation by hours of work (insufficient hours), inadequate utilisation by the level of income (a wage that is not adequate to meet basic needs), and a mismatch of education and occupation (inadequate use of skills; Sullivan & Hauser, 1978, p. 26). The data for the United States in 1960–1976 showed that the biggest growth of inadequate utilisation was in the fourth group, i.e. the mismatch of education and occupation (Sullivan & Hauser, 1978, p. 45).

Starting from the publication of LUF, the discussion concerning skills utilisation has been increasingly lively. The recent literature distinguishes between qualification mismatch (vertical mismatch) and the field of study mismatch (horizontal mismatch; Montt, 2017; Quintini, 2011a; Sloane, 2003). Indicators of qualification mismatch measure the alignment of a worker's formal qualification level to the required level in her or his job. When workers' educational level is above the requirements, we talk about 'over-qualification', and when it is below, we talk about 'under-qualification'. Indicators of a mismatch concerning the field of study measure the alignment between a worker's specialisation (the field of study) and the field in which the worker is employed (OECD, 2018, p. 23).

Empirical evidence derived from the literature shows that all forms of mismatch (i.e. the vertical and the horizontal one) can have negative consequences for both workers and the entire economy (OECD, 2018, p. 23; Romero & Salinas-Jimanez, 2018). The literature highlights that, on average, the over-qualified and field of study-mismatched workers suffer a wage penalty when compared to well-matched workers with the same level of formal qualifications (Brynin & Longhi, 2009; Hartog & Sattinger, 2013; Kracke et al., 2017, p. 6; Levels, Van der Velden, & Allen, 2014; McGuinness & Pouliakas, 2017; OECD, 2018, p. 3; Quintini, 2011a, 2011b; Wolbers, 2003). Furthermore, the field-of-study mismatch explains a lower level of satisfaction at work (Béduwé & Giret, 2011; OECD, 2018, p. 3), and it generates a higher job turnover, as unsatisfied workers tend to move often in a search for a better job match.

It is important to notice that the demand for specific qualifications varies by occupation, because human capital is mostly specific (Kracke et al., 2017, p. 6). However, in the literature we can find a lot of studies concerning qualification mismatch, but most of them are done by industry (e.g. De Pedraza, Tijdens, & Visintin, 2016; Roosaar, Masso, & Varblane, 2019) or highly aggregated occupational groups e.g. high-, medium-, and low-skilled occupational groups (OECD, 2018). Taking into account that an occupation reflects a special sort of skills and the required level of education (as it is presented in the ISCO classification[2]), it is worth conducting an analysis concerning skills utilisation by focusing on the demand and supply for particular occupations[3] (e.g. 4-digit level of ISCO classification).

Occupational matrix

Methods and the theoretical framework

To construct an occupational matrix, we use data from the WageIndicator web survey on work and wages from 2008 till 2018 for 16 European countries. WageIndicator is a self-administered, voluntary, multi-country, continuous survey posted at the national WageIndicator websites (for a detailed description see Tijdens, Van Zijl, Hughie-Williams, Van Klaveren, & Steinmetz, 2010).

The analysed countries have been divided into two groups: Western European and post-socialist. The analysed post-socialist countries are Belarus (BY), the Czech Republic (CZ), Hungary (HU), Poland (PL), Romania (RO), Russia (RU), Slovakia (SL), and Ukraine (UA). Western European countries included in the analysis are the following: Belgium (BE), Denmark (DK), Germany (DE), Italy (IT), the Netherlands (NL), Spain (ES), Sweden (SE), and the United Kingdom (UK).[4] Thus, the geographical scope of the study is different than in other chapters in the book and reflects the geographical scope covered by the WageIndicator survey. We have not decided to exclude Belarus, Ukraine, and Russia from the analysis mainly because (as the obtained results indicate) in terms of skills utilisation they share many similarities with other post-socialist countries from Central and Eastern Europe. As a result, we analysed 1,901,936 questionnaires from 16 countries. The number of analysed questionnaires, sorted by country, is shown in Table 3.1.

In order to make our analysis more comprehensible, we computed the homogeneous (as far as the type of work, tasks, and qualification is concerned) 47 occupational groups, which were the same for all 16 countries and covered the entire occupational structure from the ISCO-08 classification. However, we have decided to exclude occupations with less than 20 observations in one country. Consequently, the size of our sample decreased to 1,405,299 observations. The full list of analysed occupations with the ISCO-08 coding and the number of questionnaires in each occupation in the years 2008–2018 is presented in Table 3.2.

Table 3.1 The number of respondents in each country (years 2008–2018)

Regions	*Country*	*Number of respondents (in thousands)*
Western European Countries	Belgium (BE)	173 954
	Denmark (DK)	7 726
	Germany (DE)	355 919
	Italy (IT)	26 892
	The Netherlands (NL)	753 660
	Spain (ES)	83 521
	Sweden (SE)	13 833
	The United Kingdom (UK)	66 972
Post-Socialist Countries	Belarus (BY)	155 249
	The Czech Republic (CZ)	60 962
	Hungary (HU)	10 328
	Poland (PL)	9 235
	Romania (RO)	4 395
	The Russian Federation (RU)	44 476
	Slovakia (SL)	13 634
	Ukraine (UA)	121 180

Source: Own elaboration based on the WageIndicator data 2008–2018 (Tijdens et al., 2010).

Table 3.2 The number of respondents in each occupation in the years 2008–2018

Occupation number	*ISCO code*	*Occupation name*	*The number of respondents*
1	0	Armed forces occupations	4 406
2	6	Skilled agricultural, forestry, and fishery workers	10 689
3	9	Elementary occupations	57 949
4	11	Chief executives, senior officials, and legislators	19 183
5	25	Information and communications technology professionals	67 841
6	31	Science and engineering associate professionals	63 016
7	32	Health associate professionals	38 396
8	35	Information and communications technicians	26 638
9	52	Sales workers	72 922
10	53	Personal care workers	26 528
11	54	Protective services workers	16 683
12	71	Building and related trades workers, excluding electricians	36 538
13	72	Metal, machinery, and related trades workers	46 502
14	73	Handicraft and printing workers	8 684
15	74	Electrical and electronics trades workers	28 918
16	75	Food processing, wood working, garment, and other craft and related trades workers	21 744
17	81	Stationary plant and machine operators	29 243
18	82	Assemblers	5 713
19	221	Medical doctors	8 172
20	222	Nursing and midwifery professionals	12 308
21	235	Other teaching professionals	10 409
22	241	Finance professionals	20 904
23	242	Administration professionals	19 430
24	243	Sales, marketing, and public relations professionals	25 487
25	261	Legal professionals	12 713
26	264	Authors, journalists, and linguists	12 056
27	265	Creative and performing artists	3 254
28	342	Sports and fitness workers	7 092
29	511	Travel attendants, conductors, and guides	3 737
30	513	Waiters and bartenders	16 688
31	514	Hairdressers, beauticians, and related workers	5 333
32	2631	Economists	7 076
33	2632	Sociologists, anthropologists, and related professionals	4 316
34	2634	Psychologists	3 585
35	3411	Legal and related associate professionals	4 040
36	881, 882, 883	Drivers (locomotive, car, truck, bus)	26 314

(*Continued*)

Table 3.2 Continued

Occupation number	*ISCO code*	*Occupation name*	*The number of respondents*
37	211, 212, 213, 214, 215, 231	Science and engineering professionals (apart from architects), University teachers	86 424
38	232, 233, 234	Techers (vocational, secondary, primary school)	23 522
39	3434, 512	Cooks and Chefs	16 606
40	3435, 3433	Managers	90 269
41	14, 13, 12	Business and administrative associate professionals (without secretaries)	101 179
42	331, 332, 333, 335	Architects, planners, surveyors, and designers	24 793
43	2161, 2166, 3432	Social work and counselling professionals and associated professions	12 442
44	2635, 3412	Other health professionals	14 661
45	3413, 2636	Secretaries	42 050
46	223, 224, 225, 226	Mobile plant operators	7 836
47	334, 412	Clerical support workers (without secretaries)	201 010
		Total	1 405 299

Source: The same as for Table 3.1.

To a large extent, people's decisions concerning their career development (e.g. investment in education) are made on the perceived earnings or the chance to be promoted in a chosen occupation (Galiakberova, 2019, p. 415). Thus, we analysed occupations from two perspectives: the level of received wages and the wage dynamics.

The OECD Skills for Jobs database defines skills as either hard to find (in shortage) or easy to find (in surplus) (OECD, 2018, p. 6). In this context, we have decided to use the terms 'shortage' and 'surplus' occupations in our analysis. They were identified on the basis of the dynamics of the wage level: surplus was those for which wage growth was lower than the average wage growth in a country, and shortage was those for which wage growth was higher than the average wage growth. This classification is based on the interplay between labour supply and demand, i.e. we assumed that occupations more (less) valuable to employers should have a better (worse) wage dynamic.[5] Thus, the analysis led us to build the occupational matrix for each country, consisting of four groups of occupations: (1) high paid and shortage, (2) high paid and surplus, (3) low paid and shortage, and (4) low-paid and surplus (see Table 3.3). This matrix has been the basis for further investigation in the subsequent sections where we allocated the occupation in particular countries to these four groups and tried to answer the question of how this allocation translates to the skills underutilisation and pay satisfaction.

Table 3.3 The occupational matrix

	Low-paid occupations	*High-paid occupations*
Shortage occupations	The wage median for occupation is lower than a wage median for a country. The wage dynamics for occupation is higher than the country's average.	The wage median for occupation is higher than a wage median for a country. The wage dynamics for occupation is higher than the country's average.
Surplus occupations	The wage median for occupation is lower than a wage median for a country. The wage dynamics for occupation is lower than the country's average.	The wage median for occupation is higher than a wage median for a country. The wage dynamics for occupation is lower than the country's average.

Source: Own elaboration.

Cross-country similarities and differences in the occupational matrix

The study covered 47 occupations in 16 countries, which means that we have analysed 752 combinations (country and occupation). Most occupations – in Western and in post-socialist countries – were classified as shortage and low paid (such type of occupation appeared in Western European states 113 times and in post-socialist countries 130 times). The next group was low paid and surplus, then high paid and shortage, and at the end high paid and surplus.

Due to the significant amount of analysed occupations, the main results are presented in three tables. Table 3.4 shows the occupations that in most countries were low paid, Table 3.5 covers the occupations that were classified as high paid, while Table 3.6 presents the occupations that were classified differently in the countries.

Table 3.4 presents the occupations which were classified in most Western European and post-socialist countries as low paid. Among these, it is particularly worth paying attention to the occupations that among the post-socialist countries were in surplus while among the Western European states were in shortage. Such a difference may indicate that population's skills associated with these occupations as not being fully utilised in the post-socialist countries and may also help predict the migration flows from Eastern to Western Europe. Such a situation appeared for the following occupations: elementary occupations which were in surplus in the Czech Republic, Romania, Russia, Slovakia, and Ukraine, while being in shortage in Belgium and Germany; health associate professionals (in surplus in Belarus, the Czech Republic, Russia, Slovakia, and Ukraine, but in shortage in Denmark,

Table 3.4 Low-paid occupations in the analysed countries

No	*Occupation*	*Western European countries*				*Post-Socialist countries*			
		surplus low paid	*shortage low paid*	*surplus high paid*	*shortage high paid*	*surplus low paid*	*shortage low paid*	*surplus high paid*	*shortage high paid*
2	Skilled agricultural, forestry, and fishery workers	DK DE NL ES	BE IT SE UK	0	0	RU	BY CZ HU PL SK UA	0	0
3	Elementary occupations	DK IT NL ES SE	BE DE	0	0	CZ RO RU SK UA	BY HU PL	0	0
7	Health associate professionals	BE IT ES UK	DE NL SE	DK	0	BY CZ RU SK UA	HU PL RO	0	0
9	Sales workers	BE DK DE SE	IT NL ES UK	0	0	CZ PL RO RU SK UA	BY HU	0	0
10	Personal care workers	BE DK	DE IT NL ES SE UK	0	0	0	BY CZ HU PL RO RU SK UA	0	0
11	Protective services workers	BE DK IT NL	DE ES SE UK	0	0	BY CZ PL RO UA	HU RU SK	0	0
12	Building and related trades workers, excluding electricians	DE NL ES SE	BE DK IT UK	0	0	CZ RO RU	HU PL SK	BY UA	0
14	Handicraft and printing workers	DE NL ES UK	BE DK IT SE	0	0	RO	CZ HU PL RU SK UA	0	BY
16	Food processing, wood working, garment, and other craft and related trades workers	BE DK IT NL ES SE UK	DE	0	0	PL RU SK	BY CZ HU RO UA	0	0

17	Stationary plant and machine operators	BE DE NL ES	DK IT SE UK	0	0	CZ RU SK	BY HU PL RO	UA	0
18	Assemblers	BE	DK IT NL ES SE UK	0	DE	CZ	HU PL RO RU SK	0	BY UA
30	Waiters and bartenders	DK DE IT ES	BE NL UK	0	0	BY PL SK	CZ HU RO RU UA	0	0
36	Drivers (locomotive, car, truck, bus)	DK DE ES	BE IT NL SE UK	0	0	HU PL RU	CZ RO SK	UA	BY
39	Cooks and Chefs	DK ES	BE DE IT NL SE UK	0	0	BY CZ PL RO SK	HU RU UA	0	0
45	Secretaries	DE SE UK	BE DK IT	DK	NL	UA	BY CZ HU PL RO RU SK	0	0
46	Mobile plant operators	BE DK DE IT NL UK	ES	0	0	PL	BY CZ HU SK	RO	RU UA
47	Clerical support workers (without secretaries)	DK DE UK	BE IT NL ES SE	0	0	CZ RU SK UA	BY HU PL RO	0	0

Source: The same as for Table 3.1.

Table 3.5 High-paid occupations in the analysed countries

No	Occupation	Western European countries				Post-Socialist countries			
		surplus low paid	*shortage low paid*	*surplus high paid*	*shortage high paid*	*surplus low paid*	*shortage low paid*	*surplus high paid*	*shortage high paid*
4	Chief executives, senior officials, and legislators	0	0	DE	BE DK IT NL ES SE UK	0	0	BY RO	CZ HU PL RU SK UA
5	Information and communications technology professionals	0	0	BE DK DE NL SE	IT ES UK	0	0	BY SK	CZ HU PL RO RU UA
6	Science and engineering associate professionals	IT	0	BE	DK DE NL ES SE UK	0	PL	BY HU	CZ RO RU SK UA
19	Medical doctors	0	0	BE DK DE NL ES UK	IT SE	0	RU UA	BY RO	CZ HU PL SK
22	Finance professionals	0	0	DK DE NL ES UK	BE IT ES	0	0	PL RU	BY CZ HU RO SK UA
23	Administration professionals	0	0	BE DK NL SE	DE IT ES UK	0	BY UA	CZ RU	HU PL RO SK
24	Sales, marketing, and public relations professionals	0	0	BE DK NL UK	DE IT ES SE	PL	BY	HU RU	CZ RO SK UA
25	Legal professionals	0	0	DK DE NL	BE IT ES SE UK	0	SK	HU RU	BY CZ RO PL UA
32	Economists	0	0	DK DE NL ES	BE SE UK	0	0	CZ HU PL SK	BY RO RU UA
37	Science and engineering professionals (apart from architects), University teachers	0	0	DK DE NL	BE IT ES SE UK	BY	0	PL	CZ HU RO RU SK UA
38	Techers (vocational, secondary, primary school)	0	SE	DE NL ES	BE DK IT UK	0	CZ RU	BY HU	PL RO SK UA
40	Managers	0	0	DK DE NL	BE IT ES SE UK	0	0	BY RO UA	CZ HU PL RU SK
41	Business and administrative associate professionals (without secretaries)	SE	UK	BE DK DE	IT NL ES	UA	PL	RU	BY CZ HU RO SK

Source: The same as for Table 3.1.

Table 3.6 Mixed occupations in the analysed countries

No	*Occupation*	*Western European countries*				*Post-Socialist countries*			
		surplus low paid	*shortage low paid*	*surplus high paid*	*shortage high paid*	*surplus, low paid*	*shortage low paid*	*surplus high paid*	*shortage high paid*
1	Armed forces occupations	SE	ES	IT NL	BE UK	BY	HU	CZ PL RO UA	RU SK
8	Information and communications technicians	BE DK NL ES UK	IT SE	DK	0	BY	0	HU RO UA	CZ PL RU SK
13	Metal, machinery, and related trades workers	DK IT NL ES	BE DE SE UK	0	0	PL	CZ RU SK	BY RO UA	HU
15	Electrical and electronics trades workers	IT ES SE	BE DE NL	0	DK UK	BY	CZ RU SK	HU PL RO UA	0
20	Nursing and midwifery professionals	0	DE SE	BE DK IT ES	NL UK	0	BY CZ HU PL RU UA	BY	0
21	Other teaching professionals	UK	ES SE	DK	BE DE IT NL	PL	BY CZ RO RU UA	SK	HU
26	Authors, journalists, and linguists	IT	SE	BE DK NL ES	DE UK	BY HU	PL RO RU	CZ SK	UA
27	Creative and performing artists	DE NL	IT SE	DK	BE ES UK	PL	CZ HU RO RU	BY UA	SK
28	Sports and fitness workers	DK ES	BE IT NL UK	0	0	CZ PL	HU RU	BY SK	UA
29	Travel attendants, conductors, and guides	BE DK	DE IT NL ES SE UK	0	0	BY	RO RU UA	CZ HU PL	0
31	Hairdressers, beauticians, and related workers	NL	BE DK DE ES UK	0	0	BY RO SK	CZ RU	HU UA	0

(*Continued*)

Table 3.6 Continued

No	*Occupation*	*Western European countries*				*Post-Socialist countries*			
		surplus low paid	*shortage low paid*	*surplus high paid*	*shortage high paid*	*surplus, low paid*	*shortage low paid*	*surplus high paid*	*shortage high paid*
33	Sociologists, anthropologists, and related professionals	0	SE	BE DK IT ES	DE NL UK	BY SK	0	CZ PL RU UA	HU
34	Psychologists	ES	IT UK	DK NL	BE DE SE	PL RU SK	RO UA	BY	CZ HU
35	Legal and related associate professionals	BE DE NL	0	SE	DK IT ES UK	BY CZ RU UA	PL SK	0	0
42	Architects, planners, surveyors, and designers	NL ES	BE IT SE UK	DE	DK	BY PL	CZ	RO SK UA	HU RU
43	Social work and counselling professionals and associated professions	0	BE DE IT ES SE	0	DK NL UK	BY HU UA	CZ PL RU SK	0	0
44	Other health professionals	DE ES	SE	UK	BE DK IT NL	BY RU	CZ PL RO SK UA	HU	0

Source: The same as for Table 3.1.

the Netherlands, and Sweden); sales workers (in surplus in the Czech Republic, Poland, Romania, Russia, Slovakia, Ukraine, while being in shortage in Italy, the Netherlands, Spain, the United Kingdom); building workers (in surplus the Czech Republic, Romania, Russia, Belgium and in shortage in Germany, Italy, the United Kingdom); food processing, wood working, garment, and other craft and related trades workers (in surplus in Poland, Russia, and Slovakia, while being in shortage in Germany); waitress and bartenders (in surplus in Belarus, Poland, Slovakia, and in shortage in Belgium, the Netherlands, the United Kingdom); cooks and chefs (in surplus in most post-socialist states and in shortage in most Western European countries); clerical support workers (in surplus in the Czech Republic, Russia, Slovakia, Ukraine and in shortage in Belgium, Italy, the Netherlands, Spain, Sweden). If the pay is low but the wage dynamics are high, it indicates that the utilisation of skills associated with such an occupation is rising, and the motivation to migrate should be lower. This is the case for skilled agricultural, forestry, and fishery workers in almost all post-socialist countries (except for Romania) or personal care workers.

The occupations classified in most Western European countries and post-socialist countries as high paid are presented in Table 3.5. It can be assumed that the demand for qualifications associated with these occupations is high and these qualifications are utilised effectively in the economy. In consequence, employees working in these occupations should be less inclined to migrate. Among these occupations are information and communications technology professionals,[6] medical doctors, finance professionals, science and engineering professionals, or managers. However, it worth noticing that among occupations listed in Table 3.5 we can find some countries where such occupations are low paid, e.g. medical doctors in Russia and Ukraine, administration professionals in Belarus and Ukraine, legal professionals in Slovakia, teachers in Russia and in the Czech Republic, or sales marketing and PR professionals in Poland. In such cases there might be some economic motivation to move to another country, especially where the wages are high (OECD, 2018, p. 7). However, it should be remembered that such occupations are usually restricted to people that are well qualified (i.e. they needed many years to obtain the appropriate education level). People who invested a lot to get the education are less willing to change the occupation when they migrate. Thus, we predict the migration flows of well-qualified employees should be lesser than in the case of low-paid occupations analysed earlier, all other things being equal. It also means that in these post-socialist countries where such occupations are in surplus, there is a higher risk that they will remain ineffectively utilised over a long period than in similar cases among the low-paid occupations.

A very interesting group of occupations are the mixed occupations presented in Table 3.6. Mixed occupations are classified in different parts of the occupational matrix in particular countries. There are some high-paid shortage occupations in post-socialist countries and at the same time low-paid surplus in Western countries: e.g. information and communications technicians. In such cases the economic motivation to migrate probably would be the lowest. At the same time the utilisation of skills associated with these occupations is probably much higher in post-socialist countries, which gives them some comparative advantage over the states where there is a surplus.

There are also some occupations that are low paid and in surplus in post-socialist countries and high paid and in shortage in Western European countries. We expect that in these cases the economic motivation to emigrate from the post-socialist countries would be probably the highest. In result, the skills under-utilisations associated with these occupations may be short-lived due to the process of migration. Among such occupations are the following: electrical and electronics trade workers (possible migration from Belarus to Denmark or the United Kingdom); other teaching professionals (mainly from Poland to Belgium, Germany, Italy, the Netherlands); authors, journalists, and linguists (mainly from Belarus and Hungary to Germany and the UK); other health professionals (possible migration from Belarus and Russia to Belgium, Denmark, Italy, the Netherlands); sociologists, anthropologists, and related professionals (mainly from Belarus and Slovakia to Germany, the Netherlands, the United Kingdom); legal and related associate professionals (mainly from Belarus, the Czech Republic, Russia, Ukraine to Denmark, Italy, Spain, the United Kingdom); social work and counselling professionals and associated professionals (mainly from Belarus, Hungary, Ukraine to Denmark, the Netherlands, the United Kingdom).

Similarly, there are some occupations that are low paid in post-socialist countries and high paid in Western European countries and classified as shortage in both groups of countries (e.g. nursing and midwifery professionals or other health professionals). In this case, the motivation to migrate is probably also strong (see more about the health professions' migration: McAleese, Clyne, Matthews, Brugha, & Humphries, 2016).

The occupational matrix in particular countries

We have decided to present results for particular countries in figures. Figures 3.1 to 3.16 present these results for all analysed countries in relative terms, i.e. how much particular occupations deviated from the 0 level, representing 'median' for wage levels and 'mean' for wage dynamics. The numbers in the first column of Tables 3.4 to 3.6 were used to represent occupations on Figures 3.1 to 3.16.

On the left side of the figures there are occupations which are paid less. In many countries in this group we can find: elementary occupations (no 3), personal care workers (no 10), waiters and bartenders (no 30), hairdressers, beauticians, and related occupations (no 31), social workers, counselling professionals and associated professions (no 43). On the right side of the figures there are occupations which are paid the most. In many countries they consist of chief executives, senior officials, and legislators (no 4), information and communications technology professionals (no 5), medical doctors[7] (no 19), legal professionals (no 25), economists (no 32), legal and related associate professionals (no 35), and managers[8] (no 40). Thus, in this dimension we do not observe substantial differences between the analysed countries.

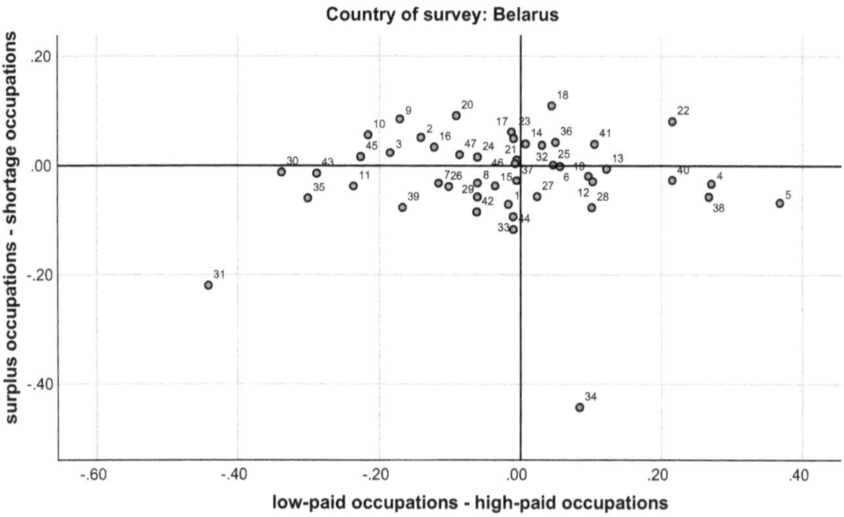

Figure 3.1 The occupational matrix in Belarus

Source: Own elaboration based on WageIndicator data 2008–2018 (Tijdens et al., 2010).

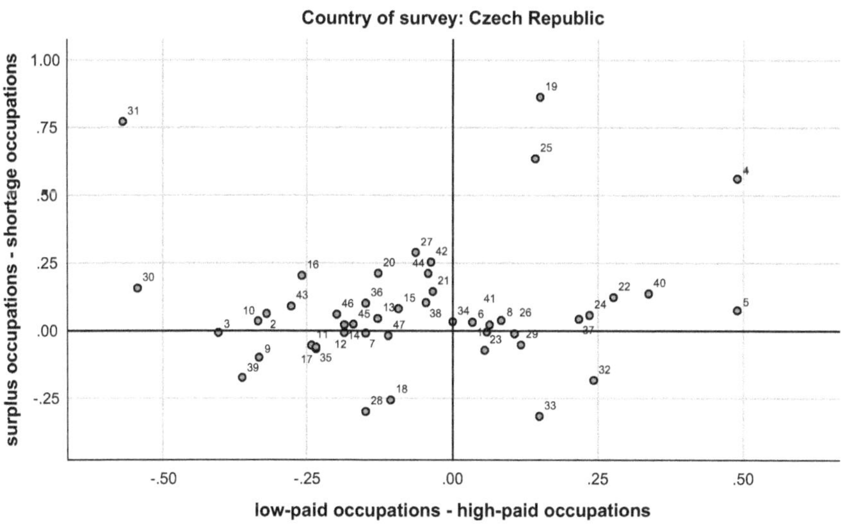

Figure 3.2 The occupational matrix in the Czech Republic

Source: The same as for Figure 3.1.

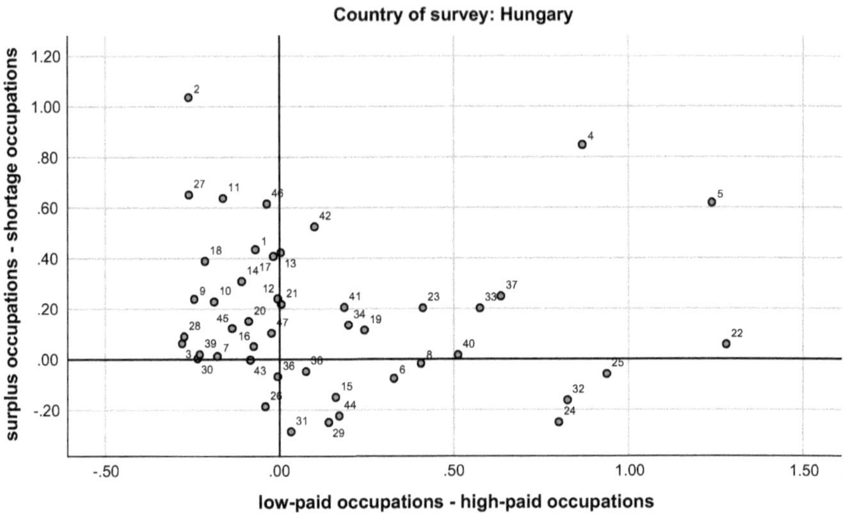

Figure 3.3 The occupational matrix in Hungary

Source: The same as for Figure 3.1.

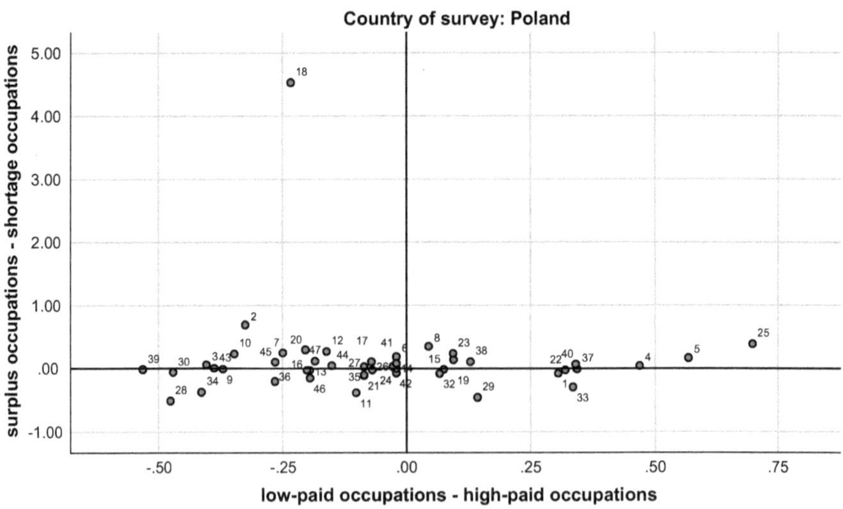

Figure 3.4 The occupational matrix in Poland

Source: The same as for Figure 3.1.

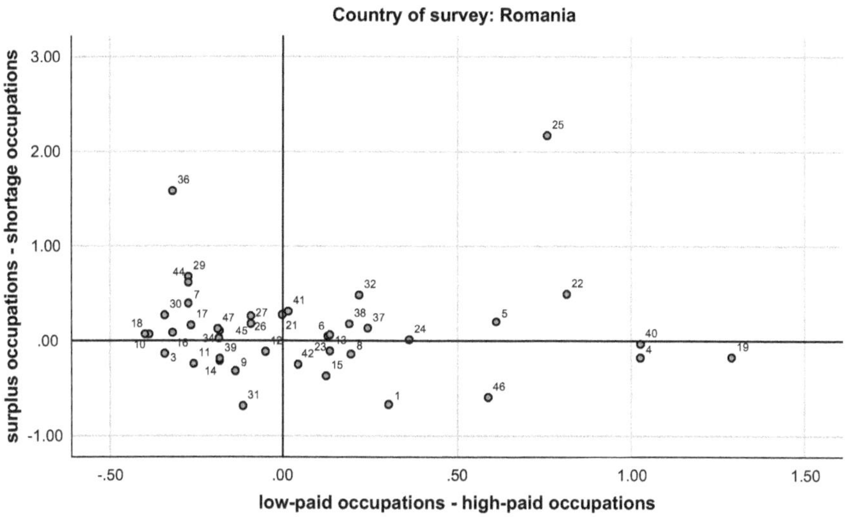

Figure 3.5 The occupational matrix in Romania

Source: The same as for Figure 3.1.

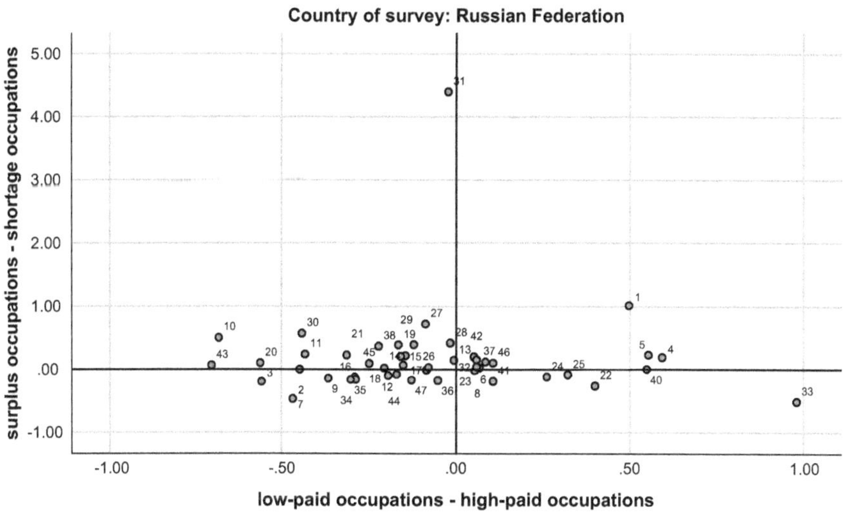

Figure 3.6 The occupational matrix in the Russian Federation

Source: The same as for Figure 3.1.

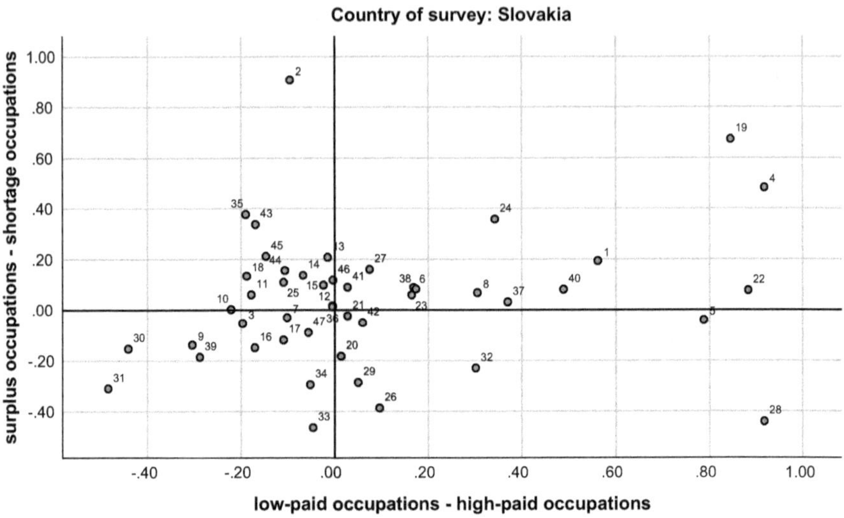

Figure 3.7 The occupational matrix in Slovakia

Source: The same as for Figure 3.1.

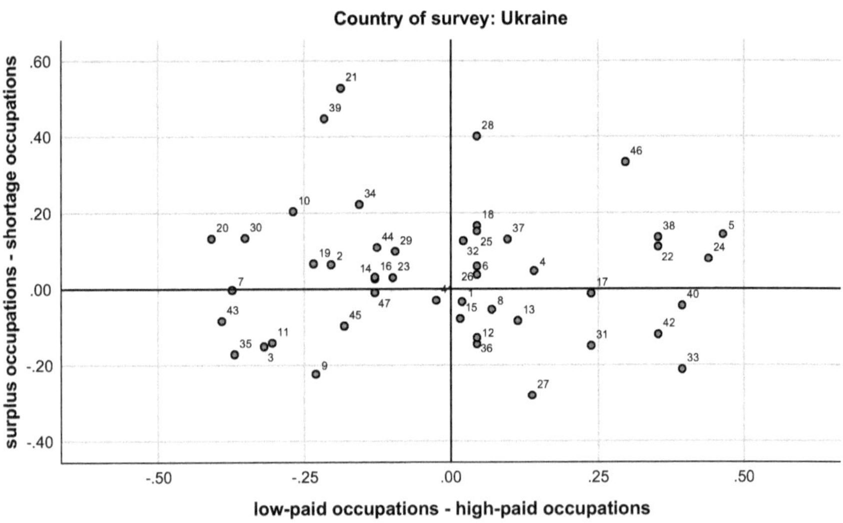

Figure 3.8 The occupational matrix in Ukraine

Source: The same as for Figure 3.1.

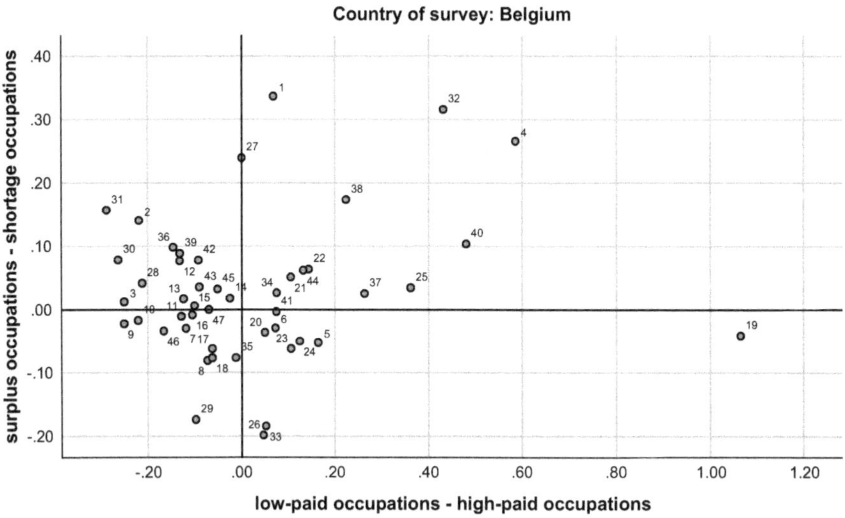

Figure 3.9 The occupational matrix in Belgium

Source: The same as for Figure 3.1.

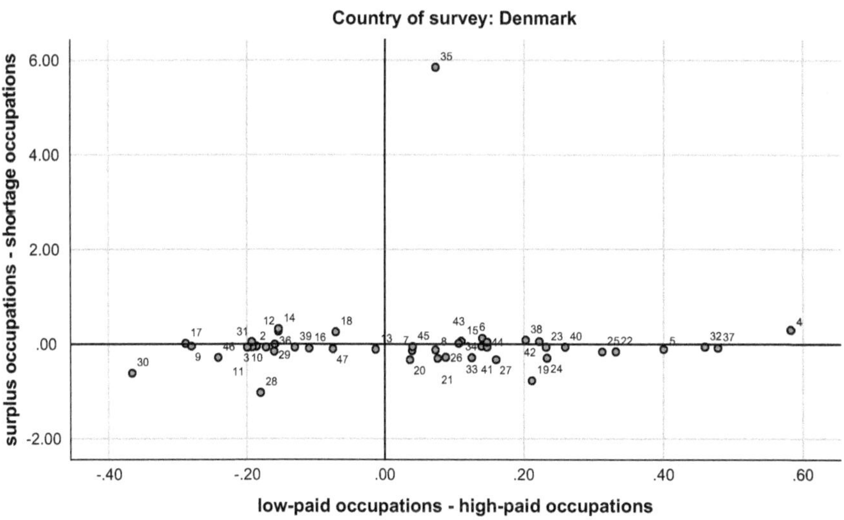

Figure 3.10 The occupational matrix in Denmark

Source: The same as for Figure 3.1.

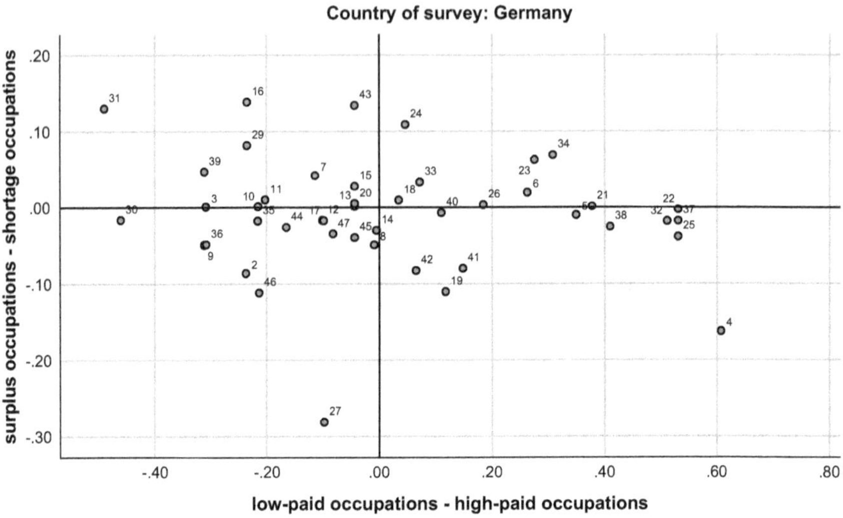

Figure 3.11 The occupational matrix in Germany

Source: The same as for Figure 3.1.

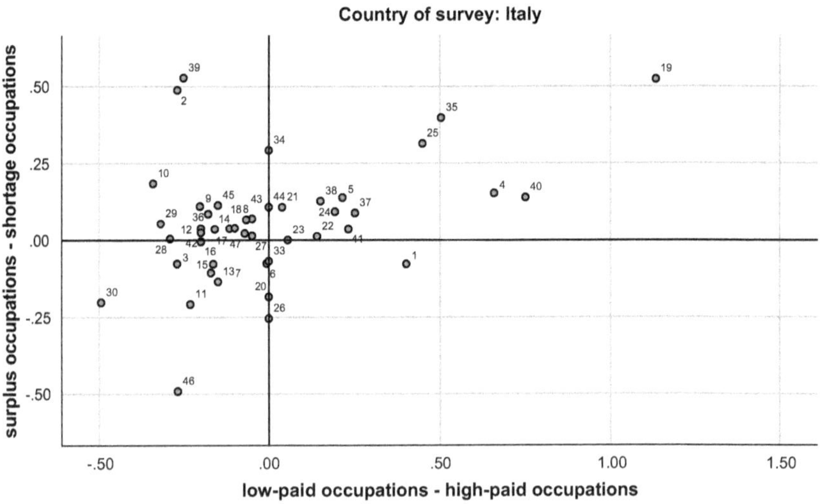

Figure 3.12 The occupational matrix in Italy

Source: The same as for Figure 3.1.

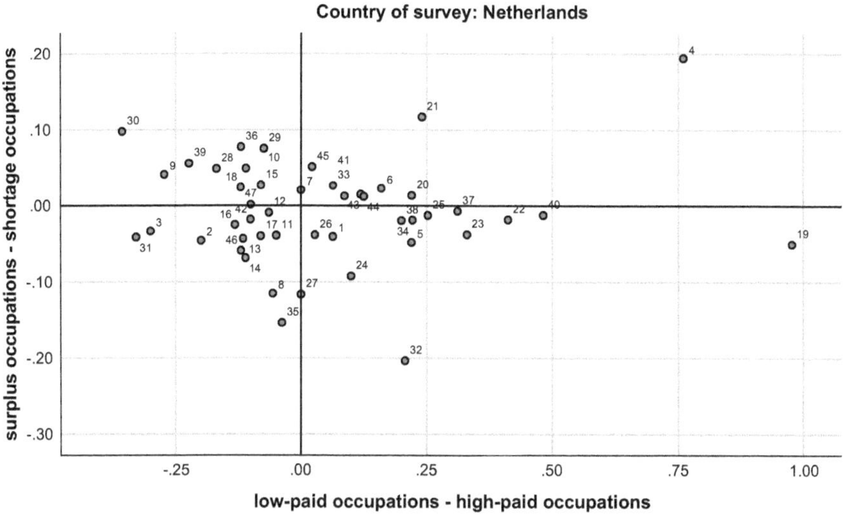

Figure 3.13 The occupational matrix in the Netherlands

Source: The same as for Figure 3.1.

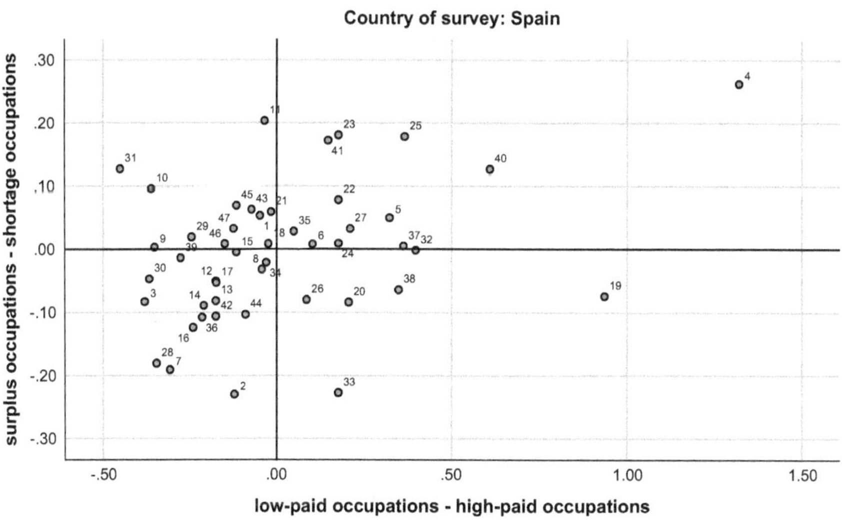

Figure 3.14 The occupational matrix in Spain

Source: The same as for Figure 3.1.

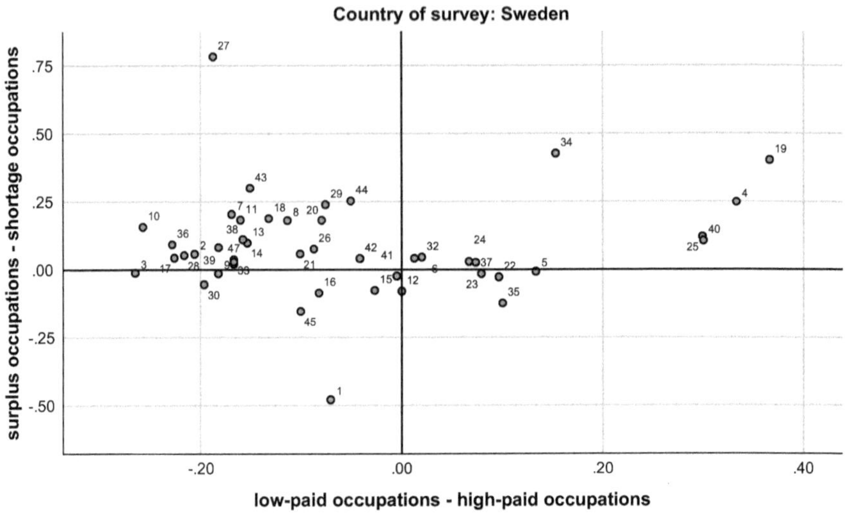

Figure 3.15 The occupational matrix in Sweden

Source: The same as for Figure 3.1.

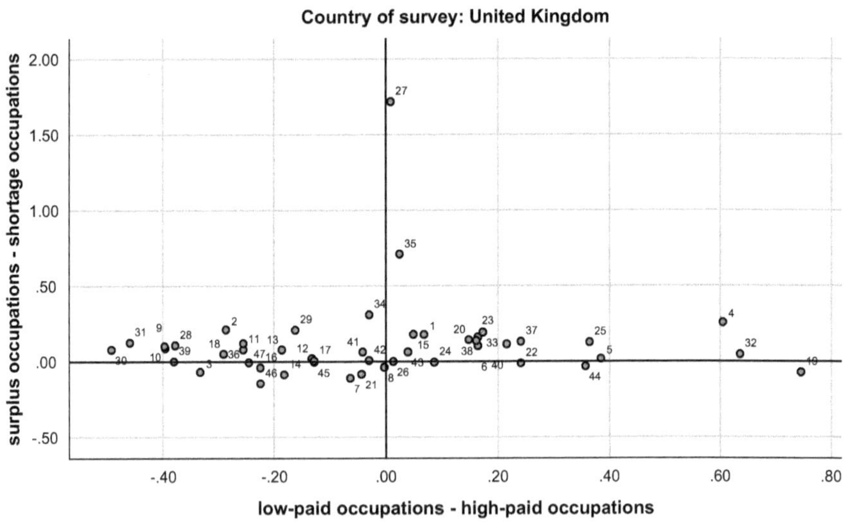

Figure 3.16 The occupational matrix in the United Kingdom

Source: The same as for Figure 3.1.

At the same time, occupations with the highest wage dynamics – shortage occupations (presented at the top of particular figures) – were different in each country. The only occupations that appeared often are chief executives, senior officials, and legislators (no 4). Apart from that we observed very high dynamics for armed forces occupations (no 1) in Belgium; skilled agricultural, forestry, and fishery workers (no 2) in Hungary, Slovakia, and Italy; assemblers (no 18) in Poland; hairdressers, medical doctors (no 19) in the Czech Republic, Slovakia, and Italy; other teaching professionals (no 21) in Ukraine; legal professionals (no 25) in the Czech Republic and Romania; artists (no 27) in Sweden and the United Kingdom; beauticians and related workers (no 31) in the Czech Republic and Russia; legal and related associate professionals (no 35) in Denmark and the United Kingdom; drivers (no 36) in Romania; cooks and chefs (no 39) in Italy.

Occupations with the lowest wage dynamics – surplus occupations (at the bottoms of the figures) – were also different in each country. The examples include armed forces occupations (no 1) in Sweden and Romania; skilled agricultural, forestry, and fishery workers (no 2) in Spain; assemblers (no 18) in the Czech Republic; authors, journalists, and linguists (no 26) in Belgium; artists (no 27) in Ukraine and Germany; sports and fitness workers (no 28) in the Czech Republic and Slovakia; travel attendants, conductors, and guides (no 29) in Belgium; hairdressers, beauticians, and related workers (no 31) in Belarus and Romania; economists (no 32) in the Netherlands; sociologists, anthropologists, and related professionals (no 33) in Spain, the Czech Republic, Slovakia, Russia, Belgium; psychologists (no 34) in Belarus; mobile plant operators (no 46) in Romania and Italy. It indicates that the convergence process between the labour markets in European countries is far from being finished and suggests that similar qualifications are utilised in each European country to a different degree.

The conducted analysis of the occupational matrix allows us to conjecture that qualifications associated with occupations that are in surplus are probably not effectively utilised in the analysed countries. At the same time, we expect that this underutilisation may be only partly decreased by the process of migration. The decision to emigrate may be especially tempting for employees working in low-paid, surplus occupations in post-socialist countries, when these occupations are deficient and high paid in Western European countries. However, the emigration may be less tempting in other cases. Thus, we expect that in many occupations, both in post-socialist countries and Western European states, the skills underutilisation remains a significant problem. Therefore, the next two sections concentrate on analysing this issue in detail.

Qualification mismatch in relation to the occupational matrix

To fully explore the qualification mismatch, we need two sorts of information: the level of worker education and the educational requirements for the job. To face the problem of missing data about educational requirements, three methods concerning gathering information are presented in the literature (Tijdens et al., 2018, p. 997). The most popular among them is the so-called subjective method, where workers are asked to indicate the educational attainment required for their job and the skill mismatch measure is thus based on the workers' self-assessment. We have also followed this approach and supplemented our study based on wages (presented in the previous section) by analysing the data on workers' self-reported qualificational mismatch that are the part of the WageIndicator survey. Employing the survey data helps us also limit the problem that formal qualifications mismatch and skills mismatch are not necessarily the same phenomenon (Kracke et al., 2017, p. 6). Employees can be formally well matched but mismatched regarding their actual skills (and vice versa). In this perspective, the analysis based on workers' self-assessment of the qualificational mismatch can be regarded as even more accurate than studies based solely on the data concerning the level and the field of education of employees.

In our study 67.8% of respondents declared that their qualifications match the requirements, 32.2% declared that the qualifications are mismatched – with shares of over-qualified 24.4%, and under-qualified 7.8%.[9] Interestingly, the highest share of mismatched workers was in Ukraine (40.3%), Russia (40%), Slovakia (39.5%), and Belarus (37.4%), while the lowest was in Poland (5.9%), Germany (20.2%), Sweden (22.2%), and Denmark (23.3%). In general, in post-socialist countries 30.5% of respondents declared that they are over-qualified, while in West European countries it was 20.9%. Figure 3.17 gives more details.

When we take a closer look at particular occupations, the highest over-qualification (above 50% of respondents declaring over-qualification) has been recorded for the following: waitresses and bartenders (Slovakia 66%, Ukraine 62%, Russia 59%, the United Kingdom 56%, the Netherlands 53%, and Belarus

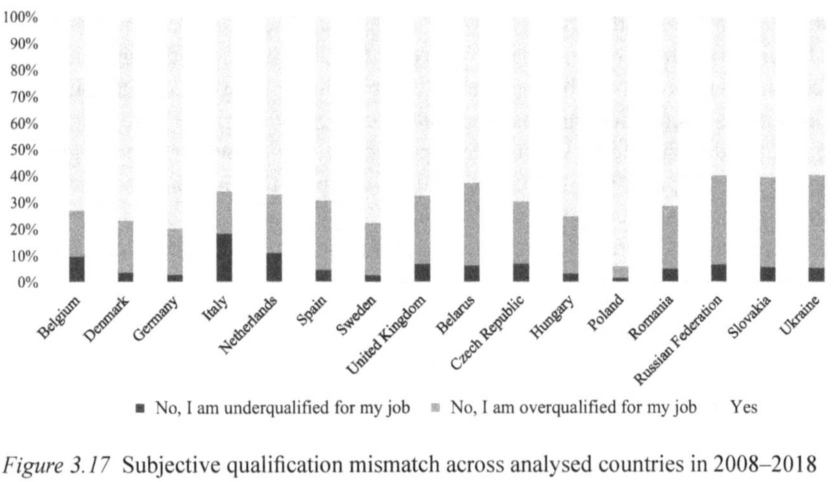

Figure 3.17 Subjective qualification mismatch across analysed countries in 2008–2018

Source: The same as for Figure 3.1.

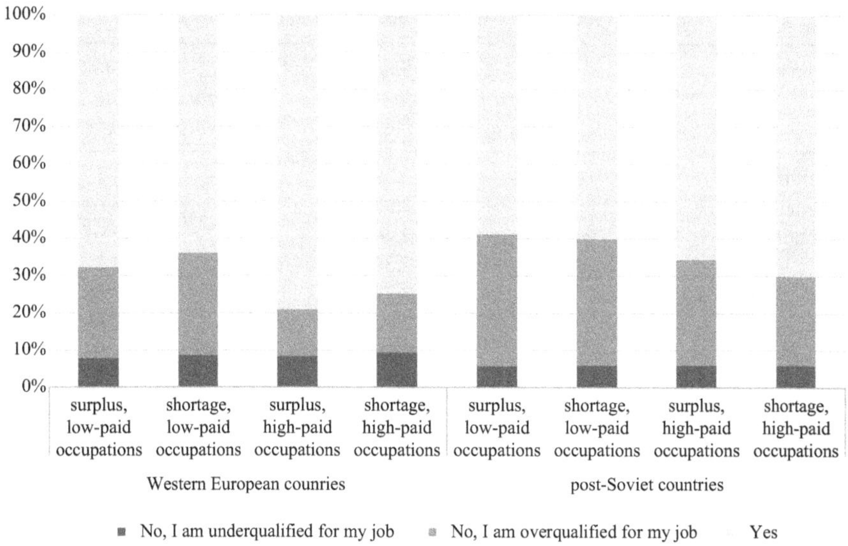

Figure 3.18 Qualification mismatch by type of country and the group of occupation in 2008–2018

Source: The same as for Figure 3.1.

52%); secretaries (Russia 63%, Ukraine 61%, Belarus 55%); sales workers (the United Kingdom 62%, Ukraine 57%, Slovakia 55%, Romania 53%); elementary occupations (Slovakia 57%, the Czech Republic 55%, Russia 55%, Ukraine 52%); assemblers (Slovakia 51%); agricultural workers, forestry, and fishery workers (Slovakia 53%); sociologists, anthropologists, and related professionals (Slovakia 62%); stationary plant and machine operators (Slovakia 54%). As it can be noticed most of the highly over-qualified people work in low-paid occupations in post-socialist countries. In this context it is not surprising that such people are more prone to emigrate, even if after the migration they remain more over-qualified than native workers (Visintin, Tijdens, & van Klaveren, 2015).

Considering the four groups identified in the occupational matrix the largest over-qualification was declared by workers in the low-paid, surplus occupations, notably 29.3% (see Figure 3.18). It indicates that this group deals with the 'wage penalty' phenomenon to a large extent. Not surprisingly, under-qualification is the largest in the shortage, high-paid occupations – in this group of occupations the under-qualification problem was declared by 7.9% of respondents.

Pay satisfaction in relation to the occupational matrix

The level of wage and the degree of working according to one's qualifications should also have a significant impact on pay satisfaction. In the WageIndicator survey respondents could also assess their pay satisfaction on a scale from

Table 3.7 Pay satisfaction (mean) in particular occupational groups by country

Country	*Surplus, low-paid occupations*	*Shortage, low-paid occupations*	*Surplus, high-paid occupations*	*Shortage, high-paid occupations*
Belgium	2.75_{a}	2.72_{a}	2.95_{b}	3.12_{c}
Denmark	2.67_{a}	$2.98_{a,b}$	2.94_{b}	$3.03_{b,c}$
Germany	2.59_{a}	2.49_{b}	3.05_{c}	2.91_{d}
Italy	2.42_{a}	2.39_{a}	$2.57_{a,b}$	2.70_{b}
The Netherlands	2.66_{a}	2.72_{b}	3.14_{c}	2.98_{d}
Spain	2.29_{a}	2.32_{a}	2.72_{b}	2.69_{b}
Sweden	2.80_{a}	2.50_{b}	2.97_{c}	3.03_{c}
The United Kingdom	2.32_{a}	2.35_{a}	2.65_{b}	2.70_{b}
Belarus	2.23_{a}	2.12_{b}	2.37_{c}	2.34_{c}
The Czech Republic	2.78_{a}	2.70_{b}	3.11_{c}	3.15_{c}
Hungary	1.86_{a}	2.11_{b}	2.42_{c}	2.64_{d}
Poland	$2.57_{a,b}$	2.51_{a}	$2.74_{b,c}$	2.75_{c}
Romania	2.41_{a}	2.51_{a}	2.79_{a}	2.71_{a}
Russia	2.23_{a}	2.09_{b}	2.54_{c}	2.56_{c}
Slovakia	2.42_{a}	2.37_{a}	2.72_{b}	2.77_{b}
Ukraine	2.15_{a}	1.91_{b}	2.21_{c}	2.23_{c}
Western European countries	2.59_{a}	2.60_{a}	3.06_{b}	2.91_{c}
Post-Socialist countries	2.35_{a}	2.25_{b}	2.41_{c}	2.67_{d}
ALL	2.53_{a}	2.54_{a}	2.93_{b}	2.83_{c}

Source: The same as for Table 3.1.

Notes: Subscripts show whether the values in particular rows are significantly different (at the 0.05 significance level). If two values are significantly different, all their subscript letters are different. If the difference is not significant, at least one subscript letter is repeated. For instance, for Belgium the difference in mean pay satisfaction between surplus, low-paid occupations and shortage, low-paid occupations are not statistically significant.

1 (highly dissatisfied) to 5 (highly satisfied). Table 3.7 shows the average job satisfaction in the analysed countries for the occupation groups identified with the occupational matrix.

It may be noticed that the pay satisfaction is generally low. Only in few cases (for highly paid occupations) does it exceed the level of 3.0. These occupations with high pay satisfaction were armed forces occupations (the highest was in Belgium, the Netherlands, the United Kingdom, the Czech Republic, and Slovakia); finance professionals (the highest was in the Czech Republic, Belgium, the Netherlands); legal professionals (especially in Belgium and Germany); economists (once more especially in Belgium, the Czech Republic, Germany, and the Netherlands); science and engineering professionals, university teachers (Belgium, Germany, and the Netherlands); chief executives, senior officials, and legislators (in Belgium, Germany, the Netherlands, Sweden, the Czech Republic, Slovakia); managers (Belgium, the Netherlands, Sweden, the Czech Republic);

information and communications technology professionals (Denmark, the Czech Republic, Romania); information and communications technicians (the Czech Republic, Denmark).

The occupations with low pay satisfaction (the average below 2.0) were personal care workers (the lowest level was in Russia, Belarus, Ukraine, Hungary); protective services workers (Russia and Ukraine); skilled agricultural, forestry, and fishery workers (Belarus, Russia, and Ukraine); other teaching professionals (once more the lowest satisfaction was in Belarus, Hungary, Ukraine); elementary occupations (especially in Belarus, Russia, and Ukraine); hairdressers, beauticians, and related workers (quite surprisingly in Belarus, Germany, and the United Kingdom); legal and related associate professionals (Ukraine, Russia and, surprisingly, Spain); drivers (Belarus, Russia, Ukraine); social work and counselling professionals and associated professions (Belarus, Hungary, Russia, Ukraine, Poland); health associate professionals (Belarus, Hungary, Russia, Ukraine).

There was also a group of occupations in which the pay satisfaction was high in one country and very low in another country, e.g.: medical doctors (very high in Belgium, the Netherlands, the United Kingdom, and very low in Belarus, Russia, Ukraine); nursing and midwifery professionals (very high in Spain and very low in Belarus, Hungary, Russia, Ukraine); creative and performing artists (very high in Germany and very low in Belarus); sports and fitness workers (very high in the Czech Republic and very low in Belarus and Russia); travel attendants, conductors, and guides (very high in Belgium and the Czech Republic but very low in Ukraine); psychologists (very high in the Netherlands but very low in Belarus and Ukraine); and teachers (very high in Belgium, but very low was in Belarus, Ukraine, and Russia).

In the context of the analysis presented in this section, two main observations are particularly relevant. Firstly, in all four occupational groups the pay satisfaction is lower in post-socialist countries than in Western European states. Secondly, most occupations with high pay satisfaction belong to the high-paid occupations with good qualification match, while people who work in low-paid occupations and are over-qualified for their jobs declare also low pay satisfaction. It shows that the previously identified differences based on the absolute levels of wages and their dynamics (that were analysed with the occupational matrix) are also reflected in the subjective evaluations of respondents' income situations.

Conclusion

Despite the uncertainty that is inherent in any attempt to predict future skill needs, the analysis of past trends in skill imbalances helps us assess the share of workers whose skills are not utilised effectively, predict the possible migration flows, and recommend reforms in the system of education. This chapter presents an analysis of 47 occupational groups in 16 European countries in the years 2008–2016 that is based on the WageIndicator survey that consists of almost 2 million questionnaires. To that end we have used the occupational matrix that allowed us to identify four groups of occupations: (1) high paid and shortage, (2) high paid and surplus, (3) low paid and shortage, and (4) low paid and surplus. This analysis was inspired by the following questions: Which occupations are allocated in particular groups and how does this allocation differ between countries? How is the allocation of occupations into the four groups related to the qualification mismatch and skills utilisation? Do the surplus and the low-paid occupations coincide with low pay satisfaction?

Our main conclusion is that the occupational matrix differs between countries. However, there are some regularities as far as skills utilisation is concerned. The most striking is the percentage of workers who declare that they are working below their qualifications, which still remains significantly higher in post-socialist countries (30.5%) than in the Western European countries (20.9%). It indicates that, in terms of labour utilisation, the process of convergence between post-socialist countries and Western European states is still not fully completed.

Moreover, the analysis of qualification mismatch with the occupational matrix showed that the over-qualification is higher in the group of low-paid occupations, especially those that are in surplus. Over-qualification is connected with the 'wage penalty' phenomenon, which is associated with the lowest pay satisfaction among all the identified occupational groups and with skills underutilisation. We also predict that workers employed in such occupations are the most prone to emigrate. At the opposite side there are high-paid, shortage occupations. Workers employed in these occupations often report that they are not qualified enough to perform them (even though in most cases they have a higher education). However they are generally very satisfied with their wages. We also conjecture that they are the least prone to emigrate.

It is also characteristic that among the low-paid, surplus group there are occupations that are mostly based on routine tasks, while in the high-paid, shortage group there are occupations that demand non-routine cognitive skills. Thus, these results corroborate other studies indicating that in the contemporary labour market there is an increasing demand for high-level cognitive skills and a decrease in the demand for routine or physical abilities (OECD, 2018, p. 7). As a result, jobs facing a high risk of automation are, on average, in surplus, and occupations in critical shortage are those facing the lowest risk of being automated (OECD, 2018, p. 4). Taking into account that people often start to develop their occupational skills and think about their future career developments when they are teenagers or even children, the obtained results give a strong incentive to focus on the educational systems in the post-socialist countries in order to adjust them to the needs of the modern labour market better.

Acknowledgment

This study was financed by the National Science Centre, Poland, project no 2013/09/D/HS4/02701.

Notes

1 The framework was originally suggested by Philip Hauser as a mean to operationalise the measurement of visible and invisible underemployment defined in the 'Resolution concerning measurement and analysis of underemployment and underutilisation of manpower' adopted by the Eleventh International Conference of Labour Statisticians (October 1966). It was subsequently applied in a number of South-East Asian countries (ILO, 1982) and later also for the United States (Sullivan & Hauser, 1978).

2 ISCO – The International Standard Classification of Occupations is one of the main international classifications for which ILO is responsible. It organises jobs into a clearly defined set of groups according to skills and education level needed to do the tasks and duties in the job. The last version of this classification is known as ISCO-08. The classification structure is available on the ILO webpage (ISCO, 2008).

3 Interesting analyses at this disaggregated level for the Czech Republic were done by Tijdens, Beblavý, and Thum-Thysen (2018). They analysed the 'granulated' skill mismatch for 279 occupations.

4 All these countries are different as far as the labour market is concerned. The comprehensive and interesting analysis of labour market developments in transition countries after 1989 was done by Cazes and Nesporova (2003).

5 A similar approach can be also noticed in the OECD methodology, where wage dynamics is one of the indicators that has been used to rank occupations in shortage or in surplus within each country (OECD, 2018, p. 6). In the OECD report, besides the wage growth, other indicators were also analysed: employment growth, hours worked growth, unemployment rate, and change in under-qualification. We are aware that there is no perfect indicator of shortage or surplus occupation, but the results presented in this chapter indicate that the wage growth remains a good approximation.

6 On average, across the OECD shortages are the strongest in the field of computers and electronics (i.e. the knowledge of computer hardware and software, programming and applications; OECD, 2018, p. 7).

7 Interesting comparative analyses of 16 health professions in 20 countries was done by Tijdens, de Vires, and Steinmetz (2013). The highest median wage was observed for medical doctors and the lowest for personal care workers (similar to our results).

8 More about the demand for managers see: Keefe (2015).

9 It is similar to the level characteristic for the OECD countries, with the exception of the share of under-qualified workers, which is higher. Across the OECD, approximately 35% of workers are mismatched by qualifications, with shares of over- and under-qualified workers being, on average, roughly the same (17% and 19% respectively; OECD, 2018, pp. 4, 24).

References

Béduwé, C., & Giret, J. (2011). Mismatch of vocational graduates: What penalty on French labour market. *Journal of Vocational Behaviour*, *78*(1), 68–79.Brynin, M., & Longhi, S. (2009). Overqualification: Major or minor miss-match? *Economics of Education Review*, *28*(1), 114–121.

Cazes, S., & Nesporova, A. (2003). *Labour markets in transition: Balancing flexibility and security in Central and Eastern Europe*. Geneva, Switzerland: International Labour Office.

De Pedraza, P., Tijdens, K. G., & Visintin, S. (2016). *The role of the short-term employed in the matching process before and after the crisis: Empirical evidence from the Netherlands* (Amsterdam Institute for Advanced Labour Studies Working Paper No. 165). Amsterdam: University of Amsterdam. doi:10.13140/RG.2.2.20599.83361

Galiakberova, A. A. (2019). Conceptual analysis of education role in economics: The human capital theory. *Journal of History Culture and Art Research*, *8*(3), 410–421. doi:10.7596/taksad.v8i3.2256

Hartog, J., & Sattinger, M. (2013). Nash bargaining and the wage consequences of educational mismatches. *Labour Economics*, *23*(C), 50–56. doi:10.1016/j.labeco.2013.03.002

ILO. (1982). *Report III*. Thirteenth International Conference of Labour Statisticians (ICLS). Geneva: International Labour Organistaion.

ILO. (2008). *Working group on labour underutilisation, beyond unemployment: Measurement of other forms of labour underutilisation*. 18th International Conference of Labour Statisticians, Geneva: International Labour Organisation. Retrieved from www.ilo.org/wcmsp5/groups/public/dgreports/stat/documents/meetingdocument/wcms_100652.pdf

ISCO. (2008). *Resolution concerning updating the international standard classification of occupations*. Geneva: International Labour Organisation. Retrieved from www.ilo.org/public/english/bureau/stat/isco/docs/resol08.pdf

Keefe, J. (2015). The demand for human resource managers: An occupational perspective. *Advances in Industrial and Labour Relations*, *21*, 57–86. doi:10.1108/S0742-618620140000021003

Kocór, M. (2017). Skills shortages and mismatches on the Polish labour market and public policy recommendations. *Zarządzanie Publiczne, 4*(42), 38–52. doi:10.15678/ZP.2017.42.4.03

Kracke, N., Reichelt, M., & Vicari, B. (2017). *Wage losses due to overqualification: The role of formal degrees and occupational skills* (Institute for Employment Research of the Federal Employment Agency Discussion Paper No. 10/2017, pp. 1–30).

Levels, M., Van der Velden, R., & Allen, J. (2014). Educational mismatches and skills: New empirical tests of old hypotheses. *Oxford Economic Papers*, *66*(4), 959–982.

McAleese, S., Clyne, B., Matthews, A., Brugha, R., & Humphries, N. (2016). Gone for good? An online survey of emigrant health professionals using Facebook as a recruitment tool. *Human Resources for Health, 14*(34), 135–144. doi: 10.1186/s12960-016-0130-y

McGuinness, S., & Pouliakas, K. (2017). Deconstructing theories of overeducation in Europe: A wage decomposition approach, skill mismatch. *Labour Markets Research in Labour Economics*, *45*, 81–127. doi:10.1108/S0147-912120170000045003

Montt, G. (2017). Field-of-study mismatch and overqualification: Labour market correlates and their wage penalty. *IZA Journal of Labour Economics*, *6*(2), 1–20. doi:10.1186/s40172-016-0052-x

OECD. (2017). *Getting skills right: Skills for jobs indicators*. Paris: OECD Publishing. doi:10.1787/9789264277878-en

OECD. (2018). *Skills for jobs*. Paris: OECD Publishing. Retrieved from www.oecdskillsforjobsdatabase.org/methodology.php

Quintini, G. (2011a). *Over-qualified or under-skilled: A review of existing literature* (OECD Social, Employment and Migration Working Paper). Paris: OECD Publishing. doi:10.1787/5kg58j9d7b6d-en

Quintini, G. (2011b). *Right for the job: Over-qualified or under-skilled?* (OECD Social, Employment and Migration Working Papers No. 120). Paris: OECD Publishing. doi:10.1787/1815199X

Romero, L. M., & Salinas-Jimanez, M. M. (2018). Skills use in the workplace and its effects on wages and on job satisfaction: An application to the Spanish case. *Personnel Review*, *47*(2), 494–516. doi:10.1108/PR-03-2017-0088

Roosaar, L., Masso, J., & Varblane, U. (2019). Age-related productivity decrease in high-waged and low-waged employees. *International Journal of Manpower, 40*(6), 1151–1170. doi:10.1108/IJM-03-2018-0086

Sloane, P. (2003). Much ado about nothing? What does the overeducation literature really tell us. In F. Büchel, A. de Grip, & A. Mertens (Eds.), *Overeducation in Europe: Current issues in theory and policy* (pp. 11–45). Cheltenham: Edward Elgar Publishing.

Sullivan, T. A., & Hauser, P. M. (1978). *The labour utilization framework: Assumptions, data and policy implications.* Washington, DC: National Commission on Employment and Unemployment Statistics.

Tijdens, K., Beblavý, M., & Thum-Thysen, A. (2018). Skill mismatch comparing educational requirements vs attainments by occupation. *International Journal of Manpower, 39*(8), 996–1009. doi:10.1108/IJM-10-2018-0328

Tijdens, K., de Vires, D. H., & Steinmetz, S. (2013). Health workforce remuneration: Comparing wage levels, ranking, and dispersion of 16 occupational groups in 20 countries. *Human Resources for Health, 11*(11), 1–15. doi:10.1186/1478-4491-11-11

Tijdens, K., Van Zijl, S., Hughie-Williams, M., Van Klaveren, M., & Steinmetz, S. (2010). *Codebook and explanatory note on the WageIndicator dataset, a worldwide, continuous, multilingual web- survey on work and wages with paper supplements* (Amsterdam Institute for Advanced Labour Studies Working Paper No. 10-102). Amsterdam: University of Amsterdam.

Visintin, S., Tijdens, K., & van Klaveren, M. (2015). Skill mismatch among migrant workers: Evidence from a large multi-country dataset. *IZA Journal of Migration, 4*(14), 1–34. doi:10.1186/s40176-015-0040-0

Wolbers, M. (2003). Job mismatches and their labour market effects among school-leavers in Europe. *European Sociological Review, 19*, 249–266.

4

UNEMPLOYMENT BENEFITS IN CEE COUNTRIES. DOES THEIR LIMITED SCOPE MATCH SOCIETAL PREFERENCES?

Monika Banaszewska and Michał Pilc

Introduction

The literature agrees that the impact of unemployment benefits on labour utilisation is significant. However, the size and even direction of that impact is ambiguous and depends both on the details of the unemployment benefits scheme and characteristics of the labour market.

The question concerning the role of unemployment benefits for labour utilisation can be especially important for the Central and Eastern European (CEE) countries which adopted fairly generous unemployment benefits schemes in the beginning of the transition period but were soon forced to reduce them (often substantially) in order to keep their budget discipline (Lehmann & Muravyev, 2012, p. 241; Vanhuysee, 2006, p. 74). In this context, it is worth identifying the main changes in the unemployment benefits schemes in CEE that were introduced during the last three decades and to compare these schemes with their counterparts in EU-15 countries. It will help to assess whether the unemployment benefits systems help to maintain the labour utilisation in CEE countries above the level characteristic of the Western European states.

Moreover, even though governments can usually freely design the details of the unemployment benefits scheme, the possibility to increase (or decrease) public expenditure on that scheme may be limited by preferences of particular groups of labour market participants. Thus, the second aim of this chapter is to analyse the differences in the societal preferences between CEE and EU-15 countries concerning the governments' responsibility to provide a decent standard of living for the unemployed and to identify the main factors that determine these differences.

The study is based on a broad set of data sources comprising Eurostat and OECD, as well as US Social Security Administration (2019) and Mutual Information System on Social Protection (2019) databases. The comparative analysis in the first part of the chapter encompasses 11 CEE countries and 15 Western European states and concentrates predominantly on the first two decades of the 21st century. As for the last decade of the 20th century, we provide the descriptive overview of main trends in both groups of countries. In order to analyse the societal preferences, the Role of Government survey (ISSP Research Group, 2018) has been employed. We focus on the most recent wave that was conducted around 2016. It has allowed us to include in the study seven countries from CEE and seven states from EU-15.

Our results indicate that CEE and EU-15 countries differ significantly not only as far as the unemployment benefits system generosity is concerned but also in terms of the set of individuals' characteristics that have an impact on societal preferences concerning the government's responsibility to provide a decent standard of living for the unemployed. The former difference is important, because (despite the conflicting theoretical transmission channels) the main standpoint of the empirical literature is that generous unemployment benefits exert a detrimental impact on labour market outcomes. Thus, we can tentatively conclude that the substantially less generous unemployment benefit schemes in CEE can be considered an advantage of CEE countries over EU-15 states in terms of labour utilisation. However, the identified differences between CEE and EU-15 countries in individuals' preferences concerning the unemployment benefits system suggest that this advantage may be not a steady state. In fact, we expect that the more similar, in terms of accumulated wealth and political maturity, the CEE countries to the EU-15 states became, the more similar the generosity of unemployment benefits systems in these two groups of countries would be.

The chapter is organised as follows: The next section reviews the literature concerning the influence of unemployment benefits generosity on labour utilisation and compares the unemployment benefits in CEE countries to their counterparts in EU-15 states. The third section describes the differences in the impact of individuals' characteristics on their preferences concerning the unemployment benefits system among the analysed groups of countries and tries to identify the sources of these differences. The last section concludes.

Unemployment benefits in CEE and EU-15 and their impact on labour utilisation

How the unemployment benefits system is constructed

The struggle to make a living after losing a job belongs to the major social risks for which private insurance coverage is negligible (Chiu & Karni, 1998). Therefore, the unemployment benefit scheme accounts for the standard ingredient of social protection systems. Eligibility criteria differ significantly between insurance and assistance schemes (under contribution and welfare principle, respectively). In the former case money is distributed among the unemployed with sufficient contribution (employment) spell. The spending on unemployment insurance allowances is, by default, financed from employees and/or employers contributions. When employment insurance duration is exhausted, an individual who remains jobless (and passes a means test), qualifies for unemployment assistance. The latter system is also addressed at individuals who are initially not eligible for the insurance benefit. Sometimes unemployment assistance takes the form of a fixed-rate supplement for the poorest among the eligible unemployed (Atkinson & Micklewright, 1991, pp. 1688–1693; Boeri & Van Ours, 2008, pp. 225–226; Stovicek & Turrini, 2012, p. 5).

The impact of unemployment benefit on labour utilisation

The elevated unemployment rate faced by industrialised countries since the 1970s has drawn scholarly attention to the question of efficiency implications of labour market institutions. Among them, unemployment benefits are perceived as alleged culprits responsible for the worsened labour market situation (Blanchard, Bean, & Münchau, 2006; Blanchard & Wolfers, 2000; Howell & Rehm, 2009; Nickell, Nunziata, & Ochel, 2005). This discussion has been facilitated by the developments in the implicit contract (Baily, 1977; Feldstein, 1976) and especially the job-search theory (Lippman & McCall, 1976; Mortensen, 1986; Rogerson, Shimer, & Wright, 2005).

There are a few channels through which unemployment benefits may adversely affect the labour market (Allard, 2005; Boeri & Van Ours, 2008, pp. 230–237; Holmlund, 1998; Nickell, 1997; Oesch, 2010; Tatsiramos & Van Ours, 2014):

- i The participation effect. Because of the unemployment benefit scheme, individuals gain access to an additional non-labour income source. Consequently, the unemployment benefit leads to a higher reservation wage than in the laissez-faire situation. Moreover, under a plausible assumption that the leisure time is a normal good, a reservation wage increases with the value of unemployment benefit. All in all, the participation effect manifests in lower labour supply, since job seekers receiving governmental transfers have higher wage expectations;
- ii The job search effect (moral hazard problem for job seekers). A job seeker decides upon the optimal time spent on job search, which competes with leisure. The more generous is the flow of money from the government, the more discouraged is an unemployed person from active job seeking. Thus, unemployment benefit results in lower probability of job finding and hence longer unemployment spells.
- iii Moral hazard problem on workers. The perspective of receiving allowance reduces the effort of the employed who are less concerned about being fired. It translates into lower labour productivity.
- iv The wage effect. The unemployment benefit strengthens the bargaining position of workers as their fallback option (unemployment) becomes more

valuable. The level of wages increases with the generosity of unemployment benefit, because the latter creates a floor in a negotiation process. In addition, employers are forced to offer better remuneration; otherwise their employees are more likely to shirk their responsibilities and have lower productivity.

v The taxation effect. Generous unemployment benefits may require higher labour taxation, which increases labour costs and, in turn, reduces both labour supply and demand. A higher tax wedge diminishes the return from employment, and this discourages from undertaking a new job (decreasing labour supply) and hiring new employees (decreasing labour demand).

However, the literature indicates also that the disincentive effect of unemployment benefits can be (partly) mitigated thanks to their proper construction *inter alia* by establishing demanding eligibility criteria and merging passive support with labour activation programmes (European Commission, 2006; Grubb, 2001). The optimal construction of unemployment benefits includes a replacement rate that diminishes over time. Decent support at the onset of unemployment preserves living standards and enables one to focus entirely on the job search. Then the pressure to find a new job strengthens, because the transfer decreases as the time passes (Boeri & Van Ours, 2008, p. 226). Even without this mechanism, the adverse effect on exit rates lessens along with approaching benefit expiration. It is because the closer the benefit expiration is, the lower the value of unemployment is, and, accordingly, the reservation wage (Tatsiramos & Van Ours, 2014, p. 290).

Furthermore, the impact on the length of unemployment spell and exit rate does not exhaust the list of potential consequences of unemployment benefits. One should take into account also the post-employment outcomes (job match quality) such as wage level, employment stability, and the probability of full-time employment. Unemployment benefits may reduce the job mismatch by enabling unemployed workers to find a job that maximises their productivity and, hence, cause higher labour utilisation in the long run. Moreover, under the existence of unemployment benefit, low-paid vacancies of low productivity that provide implicit insurance against revenue loss are less likely to be filled. It incentivises employers to create job positions of high productivity (Acemoglu & Shimer, 2000).

The access to unemployment benefit is critically important for liquidity-constrained individuals who otherwise would be forced to accept low-quality job offers. The unemployment benefit serves thereby as a correction in the incomplete credit and insurance market, due to which households are incapable of perfect consumption smoothing. The liquidity effect may improve social welfare, even though it manifests itself in longer unemployment spells (Chetty, 2008).

In addition, generous support for the unemployed may motivate people to work longer if a sufficient employment record is a prerequisite to get access to this social scheme. By the same token, ineligible job seekers pursue a more intense job search. Therefore, the entitlement (eligibility effect) may cause higher labour supply (Boeri & Van Ours, 2008, p. 238). The incentive to increase labour supply strengthens under a scheme in which benefits are calculated on the basis of previous earnings.

The countervailing theoretical effects of unemployment benefit on labour utilisation have spurred an extensive empirical literature. Initially, it consisted mostly of cross-country (macro) analyses exploiting aggregated data. Nowadays, this strand of literature consists almost entirely of micro analyses utilising beneficiaries' records in a specific country or region (for reviews, please see Holmlund, 1998, 2014; Schmieder & von Wachter, 2016; Tatsiramos & Van Ours, 2014). Due to severe endogeneity concerns,[1] the empirical verification of unemployment benefit incentive effects requires a credible identification strategy. With time, more and more micro-analyses exploited the quasi-experimental designs: the difference-in-differences approach, based on changes in the unemployment benefit scheme over time (e.g. Lalive & Zweimüller, 2004; Van Ours & Vodopivec, 2008), and the regression discontinuity design, based on the discontinuities in the construction of unemployment benefit (e.g. Fackler, Stegmaier, & Weigt, 2019; Schmieder, von Wachter, & Bender, 2012a).

The bottom-line result that emerges from the empirical literature is that unemployment exit rate decreases, and the length of the unemployment period increases with the replacement rate and benefit duration (e.g., Boeri & Van Ours, 2008, pp. 238–245; Le Barbanchon, 2016; Schmieder et al., 2012a, 2012b). On the contrary, there is no clear-cut evidence that transfers to the unemployed improve their job match quality. For instance, a positive effect is documented by: Centeno and Novo (2009), Tatsiramos (2009); a positive result only for specific sub-groups is reported by: Caliendo, Tatsiramos, and Uhlendorff (2013); while no effect is document by: Card, Chetty, and Weber (2007), Lalive (2007), and Fackler et al. (2019). The combination of these results leads to the conclusion that, by and large, unemployment benefits have a detrimental effect on labour utilisation.

How to measure the unemployment benefit generosity

The discussion in the previous section shows that the strength of transmission from unemployment benefits to labour market outcomes rests critically on unemployment benefit generosity, which can be roughly approximated with the aggregated expenditures on that scheme in relation to GDP. However, it is worth analysing its particular components, because not only they can vary substantially between countries, but they can also have a different impact on labour utilisation.

Four core properties characterise unemployment benefit generosity: level, duration, coverage, and strictness (Layard, Nickell, & Jackman, 2005, p. xxvii).[2] For the sake of intertemporal and international comparability, the level of benefits is commonly expressed in the form of their ratio to previous earnings. The gross (net) replacement rate compares benefits to previous earnings before (after) taxation. The (potential) duration of benefits means a maximum time span within which an eligible person receives governmental transfers. Typically, the unemployment benefit duration in a specific country is not uniform but varies depending on job seeker's personal characteristics (age, employment/contribution period) or labour market conditions (regional unemployment rate). The ratio of benefit recipients to the unemployed population informs about the coverage of support. It is called the pseudo-coverage rate, as the former and the latter groups do not necessarily overlap. The strictness of unemployment benefits is a multidimensional concept. The access to unemployment benefits is often dependent on a sufficient contribution period and a valid reason for quitting a job. Moreover, job seekers who do not show sufficient search effort[3] are ordinarily punished with an unemployment benefit reduction or even its removal. Finally, the quantitative assessment of strictness poses a particular challenge. It requires a detailed and thorough analysis of labour market legislation and then a convincing quantification of the gathered material. Given these constraints, the aggregate indices of unemployment benefit strictness regard a limited group of countries (mostly developed Western countries) or cover a limited time span, typically a single year (Allard, 2005; Hasselpflug, 2005; Immervoll & Knotz, 2018; Langenbucher, 2015; Venn, 2012). Thus, in this chapter, we do not analyse this aspect of unemployment benefit generosity.

The evolution of unemployment benefit schemes in CEE and EU-15

The transition of Central and Eastern European countries from a centrally planned to a market economy revealed a large scale of labour force misallocation and its low productivity (Boeri & Keese, 1992; Douarin & Mickiewicz, 2017, pp. 205–218; Freeman, 1994). Initially, CEE countries offered fairly generous unemployment benefits to deal with the consequences of unemployment, which was inevitable under the market economy. However, they were soon forced to reduce them in order to keep the budget discipline during the largely unanticipated initial recession, which was one of the consequences of the introduced reforms (Lehmann & Muravyev, 2012, p. 241; Vanhuysee, 2006, p. 74). The numerous revisions in CEE countries at the beginning of the 1990s included the shortening of benefit duration and the tightening of benefit eligibility criteria.[4] After these adjustments, transition countries, in comparison to Western European welfare states, provided the unemployed with benefits of lower relative value, shorter duration, and under longer required employment record (OECD, 1992, pp. 249, 258, 259).[5]

The tightening of unemployment benefit schemes in CEE mirrored the imposing of stricter conditions and sanctions on claimants in many EU-15 countries (for more details, please see Allard, 2005; Knotz, 2018). The retrenchment of unemployment

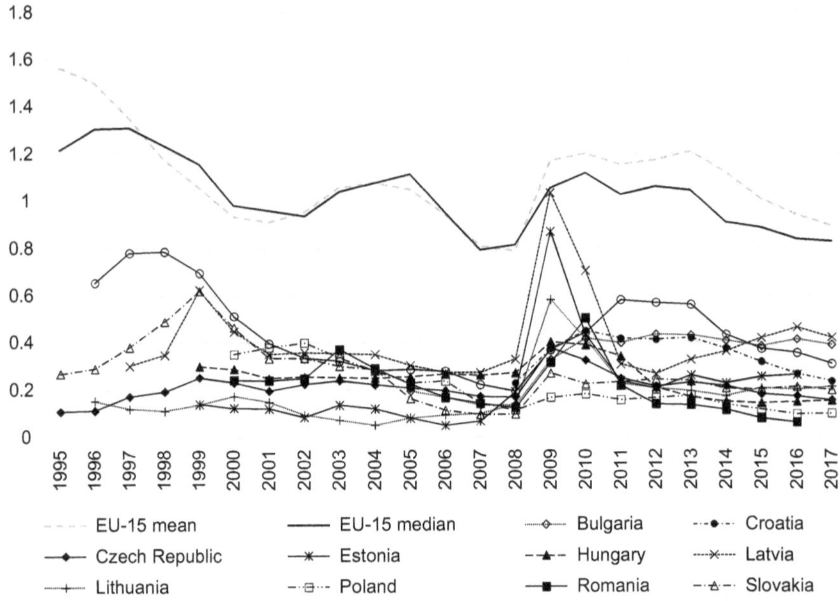

Figure 4.1 Spending on unemployment benefits in CEE countries vs. mean and median spending in EU-15 countries in the years 1995–2017 (as % of GDP)

Source: Own elaboration on the basis of Eurostat.

Notes: This ratio includes periodic cash payments in the form of full and partial unemployment benefits.

benefits in the 'old' EU conformed with the OECD (1994) and the Commission of the European Communities (1997) recommendations.[6] Still, however, in the whole period 1995–2017 the level of spending on unemployment benefits in CEE states was markedly lower than in EU-15 countries (see Figure 4.1).[7] The only exceptions were two Baltic countries (Estonia and Latvia) in 2009, when their economies were hit hard by the global financial and economic crisis. Overall, CEE countries are largely homogenous in terms of fiscal manifestation of the unemployment benefit schemes.

The question arises whether the discrepancy with regard to the unemployment benefits expenditures-to-GDP ratio between EU-15 and CEE stems from a difference in a particular characteristic of these benefits (e.g. the replacement rate) or rather results from the compound effect of various characteristics. In order to address this question, we analyse the variation of unemployment benefit duration, net replacement rates, and pseudo-coverage rates over time and across (groups of) countries.

To start with, in the majority of EU-15 social welfare systems unemployment insurance is supplemented with unemployment assistance, while among CEE

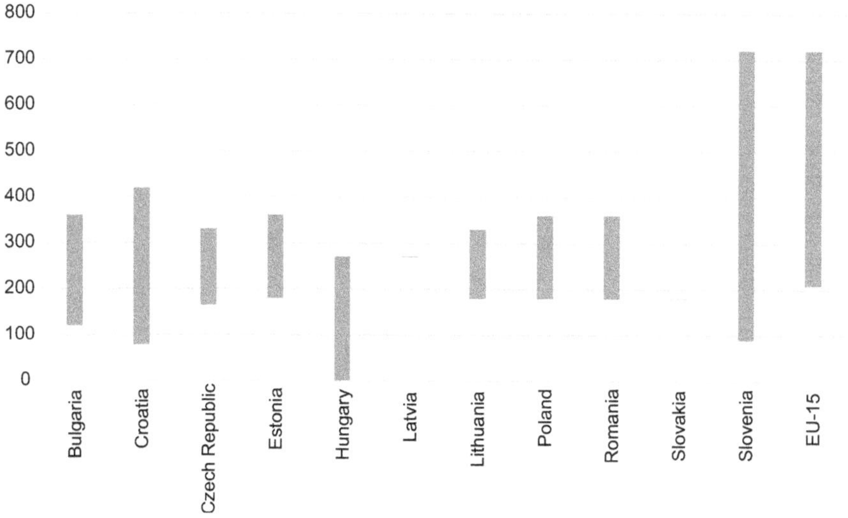

Figure 4.2 The median values of the minimum and the maximum unemployment benefit duration in CEE countries vs. EU-15 in the years 2002–2016 (in days)

Source: Own elaboration.

Notes: The bottom and top of the range are medians of the minimum and maximum duration of unemployment benefits out of 2002, 2004, 2006, 2008, 2010, 2012, 2014, and 2016 values. We consider unemployment insurance schemes only. We do not take into account the extensions of benefit duration for the unemployed participating in vocational training and these aimed to bridge the gap between employment and obtaining pension rights. The calculations for EU-15 exclude Belgium, in which unemployment benefit is, as a rule, unlimited. In case of discrepancies between US SSA and MISSOC databases, the values reported in MISSOC database were chosen.

states an unemployment assistance scheme exists only in Estonia and was in force for some time in Hungary and Slovenia.[8]

As far as the unemployment benefit duration is concerned, there were intermittent changes in this respect in CEE and EU-15 countries in the 21st century. Consequently, without losing much information, we present the scope of unemployment duration on the basis of median values of lower and upper ranges over the period 2002–2016. Figure 4.2 clearly shows that the unemployed in CEE countries enjoyed transfers for much shorter time than their counterparts in EU-15 states. The strictest policy in that respect was conducted by Hungary, where the duration was a linear function of contribution period with a cap. Among the CEE countries, the widest range of unemployment duration existed in Slovenia, with the upper range (25 months for the insured aged over 55) at the level of EU-15 median upper range.

Net replacement rates in unemployment are depicted in Figure 4.3. Again, unemployment benefit schemes in CEE states are found to be less generous than in EU-15 countries throughout the whole analysed period. Whereas unemployment

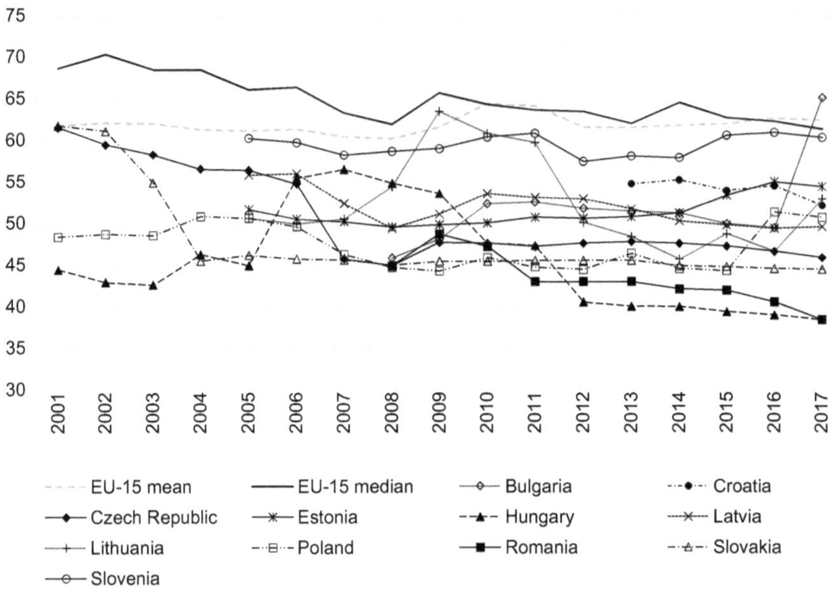

Figure 4.3 Net replacement rate in unemployment in CEE countries vs. mean and median in EU-15 countries in the years 2001–2017 (as %)

Source: Own elaboration on the basis of OECD database.

Notes: Net replacement rate in unemployment measures the proportion of previous in-work income that is maintained during the unemployment after paying taxes. The presented values are calculated on the basis of the average out of 18 cases: three periods (after 2 months, 1 year and 2 years), 6 family types (single/couple, without/with children, jobless partner/partner with earnings at the average country's level) for a job seeker whose previous earnings were at the average country's level. We do not include housing benefits.

benefits in all CEE countries accounted for 38.5 to 65.2 percent of previous earnings, the average value for EU-15 countries did not fall below 60 percent in any of the analysed years.

Furthermore, the coverage of unemployment benefits didn't exceed either median or mean for EU-15 in the years 2007–2016 in any CEE country. In comparison to other indicators the pseudo-coverage rate in CEE exhibited also fairly small variation over time.[9]

Thus, for every considered dimension of the unemployment benefit scheme all CEE countries were found to be less generous than the level characteristic of EU-15 states. Against the backdrop of empirical literature, it implies that unemployment benefits in CEE are less distortionary and constitute a comparative advantage towards the goal of high labour utilisation.

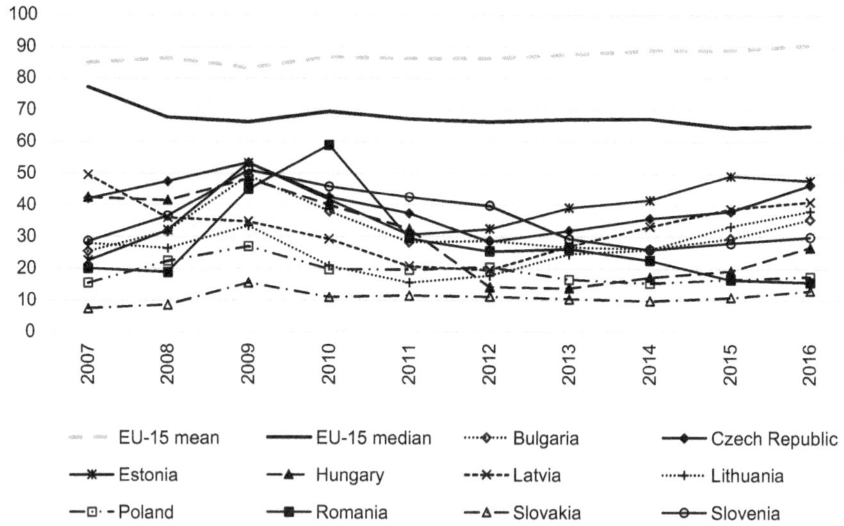

Figure 4.4 Pseudo-coverage rates of unemployment benefits in CEE countries vs. mean and median in EU-15 countries in the years 2007–2016 (as %)

Source: Own elaboration on the basis of OECD database.

Notes: The pseudo-coverage rate is the ratio of benefit recipients to the unemployed population. The former and the latter groups do not necessarily overlap. Thus, the pseudo-coverage rate may exceed 100%, as it happened in the case of Austria, Finland, France, Germany, Ireland. EU-15 mean (median) was calculated without Greece. The data for Croatia is not available either.

Societal expectations concerning unemployment benefits

The theory and hypotheses

Although the determinants of the unemployment benefits generosity (and, more broadly, labour market institutional framework) have been already analysed in the literature, none of the existing theoretical approaches is able to exhaustively explain both its variation over time and across countries. On the one hand, most studies embedded in the political economics approach are based on a strong assumption that agents are able to assess the long-term consequences of particular policies for their economic security with mathematical precision (Anesi & de Donder, 2013; Boeri, Conde-Ruiz, & Galasso, 2012; Di Gioacchino, Sabani, & Tedeschi, 2014). On the other hand, many studies rooted in the political science have analysed the determinants of labour market institutional framework employing the perspective of legal traditions, social Catholicism, varieties of capitalism, or the power resources thesis (Botero, Djankov, La Porta, Lopez-de-Silanes, & Shleifer, 2004; Emmenegger, 2014; Gordon, 2015; Thelen, 2014). Although predictions based on these theories – especially the power resources thesis – are largely consistent with the observed heterogeneity of institutional arrangements, these perspectives offer in fact a partial explanation. Their basic units of analysis are interest groups, not particular individuals. Moreover, they lack solid microeconomic underpinnings which explain individual decisions to support these groups.

Thus, both of these strands of literature tend to rely on relatively simple assumptions about individuals' preferences and actions, often neglecting the heterogeneity of these preferences among countries and particular individuals. As far as the unemployment benefits scheme is concerned, such heterogeneity between the EU-15 and CEE countries may arise from the diversity of these countries' wealth and the level of economic insecurity[10] experienced by individuals. The latter is important, because there is a large body of evidence confirming that when individuals feel economically insecure, they support state interventionism and redistribution (Blekesaune, 2007; Häusermann, Kurer, & Schwander, 2015; Marx, 2015, 2016; Pilc, 2018; Rueda, 2008; Singer, 2013). The higher average level of economic security experienced by individuals in EU-15 countries, in comparison to CEE states, results from the higher level of job security, greater total value of assets accumulated by households, better access to formal credit, and a more generous social policy (Anderson & Pontusson, 2007; EBRD, 2011, pp. 44–59; ISSP Research Group, 2017; Ivlevs, 2014; Osberg & Sharpe, 2014). Due to these differences, it may be expected that in EU-15 countries the risk of experiencing an out-of-work period has a significant adverse impact on the perceived economic security among the smaller groups of individuals than in CEE countries. These considerations allow us to propose the first research hypothesis.

> H1: Both in EU-15 and CEE countries the public support for the generous unemployment benefits scheme is higher in socio-economic groups that experience economic difficulties; however, these groups in CEE are significantly larger than in EU-15.

Moreover, when the economically deprived group of individuals is small, a rational economic agent should expect to receive more in the form of redistribution from other members of the society than in a situation when the deprived group is larger and the group of better-off potential donators is less numerous. For this reason, we expect that the differences in expectations concerning the unemployment benefits scheme generosity in the groups experiencing economic difficulties and other members of the society should be more noticeable in EU-15 than in CEE countries. Furthermore, we also expect that this mechanism will be strengthened by the relative deprivation effect. The theory of relative deprivation indicates that it is not the absolute level of deprivation but rather its comparison with the situation of other individuals or groups that matters when individuals assess their economic situation and formulate economic policy preferences (Marx, 2016; Runciman, 1966; Walker & Smith, 2002). Thus, the smaller the group of economically deprived individuals in comparison to the better-off subpopulation is, the greater the difference in expectations concerning the unemployment scheme generosity between these two groups should be. Therefore, the individuals experiencing economic difficulties in EU-15 countries should have even more reasons to expect generous unemployment benefits schemes than their more numerous counterparts in CEE states. It allows us to propose the second hypothesis.

H2: Individual characteristics associated with the economic deprivation that significantly affect the individuals' support for the unemployment benefits system in EU-15 have a greater explanatory power than in CEE.

Furthermore, we expect that the differences between CEE and EU-15 states in terms of the societal preferences towards the generosity of unemployment benefits may arise also from the differences in the political systems in these regions. Voters in CEE countries generally endorse a greater role of the government more strongly, but at the same time they are more critical of their welfare states' efficiency and effectiveness (Roosma, 2016, pp. 50–53; Rose, 2009, pp. 17–18). As a result, and in consistency with the valence theory of voting[11] (Hobolt, Tilley, & Banducci, 2013; Marx, 2015, p. 46), political systems in CEE are characterised by more frequent entrances of new parties and the demise of the established ones (Deegan-Krause & Haughton, 2018; Hagopian, 2007, p. 586; Haughton & Deegan-Krause, 2015). What is more, political parties in Central and Eastern Europe have weaker organisational structures than in Western democracies (Rohrschneider & Whitefield, 2012, p. 174). Thus, even large CEE parties have much weaker bonds with the particular interest groups than parties in EU-15 (Rohrschneider & Whitefield, 2012, pp. 138–156). It means that political parties in CEE can incorporate various societal preferences into their programmes more easily and to a greater degree than parties in EU-15, which gives them more flexibility (Rohrschneider & Whitefield, 2012, p. 176). In consequence, assigning particular parties to the left or right wing is less reliable in Central and Eastern Europe than in EU-15. Moreover, due to the greater flexibility of CEE parties and the greater discrepancy between expectations towards the state policy and its deliverables in CEE, we also expect that the trust towards the civil servants should have a lesser impact in CEE on formulating the policy expectations than has been found in EU-15 (Di Gioacchino et al., 2014). These considerations allow us to propose the last hypothesis.

H3: Although the voting on centre or left- or right-wing parties and the level of trust towards civil servants are not correlated with the individuals' preferences towards the unemployment scheme generosity in CEE, they are relevant in EU-15.

Data and methods

The study has been based on the last wave of the Role of Government survey that was conducted as a part of the International Social Survey Programme[12] in 2016 (ISSP Research Group, 2018). We were able to include 14 countries in our analysis – 7 EU-15 states: Belgium, Denmark, Finland, France, Germany, Spain, Sweden; and 7 CEE countries: Croatia, the Czech Republic, Hungary, Latvia, Lithuania, Slovakia, Slovenia. It allowed us to conduct the estimates for a group of 12 718 respondents.[13]

The answers to the following question have been employed as the dependent variable: *On the whole, do you think it should or should not be the government's responsibility to provide a decent standard of living for the unemployed?* We interpret it as a measure of support towards the unemployment benefits system. Originally, the respondents could choose among four answers. However, the number of individuals that chose the answer *Definitely should not be* was so small that it was decided to combine it with the answer *Probably should not be* and for the sake of simplicity name it *Should not be*. As a result, only three possible categories of the dependent variable were analysed: *Should not be, Probably should be, Definitely should be.*

To model the answers to the chosen question the cumulative logit random intercept model has been estimated (Agresti, 2010, pp. 282–283; Grilli & Rampichini, 2012; Hedeker, 2008):

$$log\frac{\Pr(Y_{ij} \le y_c)}{\Pr(Y_{ij} > y_c)} = \alpha_c - (\boldsymbol{x}'_{ij}\boldsymbol{\beta} + u_j) \qquad c = 1,2, \tag{4.1}$$

where i represents individuals, j denotes countries, and c identifies categories of the explained variable Y_{ij} (the third category is redundant in the model). The vector $\boldsymbol{x}$ in our model consists of explanatory variables that characterise particular respondents (individual level variables). The variable α_c is known as a threshold (or cutpoint) between category c and $c+1$. The greater the expression $\boldsymbol{x}'_{ij}\boldsymbol{\beta}$ is, the higher the probability that a respondent i belongs to a category $c + 1$ or higher. Therefore, each parameter β has the same direction of effect as the regression parameter in an ordinary linear regression. Finally, u_j is a random effect capturing the unobserved heterogeneity of answers to the analysed question at the country level. The random effect is assumed to have a normal $N(0,\sigma_u^2)$ distribution, and its variance σ_u^2 is estimated within the model.

Like in the case of the logistic regression model, the β parameters are not directly interpretable. For this reason, we estimated also the conditional[14] probabilities of choosing specific answers to the analysed question. Firstly, these probabilities were calculated for a baseline respondent. Secondly, these probabilities were estimated for every explanatory variable, assuming that this variable increases by one, ceteris paribus. Thus, interpretation of these estimated probabilities resembles interpretation of parameters in an ordinary linear regression. We have decided that the baseline respondent would be a man, aged from 26 to 45, with primary or lower secondary education, who is an employee but does not belong to a trade union, lives in a two-person household but does not have an unemployed partner, places himself at the middle of the social ladder, attends religious services less than once a week, believes that taxes for those with middle incomes are about right, is neither in favour of nor against supporting declining industries to protect jobs, neither agrees nor disagrees with a statement that most civil servants can be trusted, and votes for centre or liberal parties.

Results

Table 4.1 (its left column) presents the distribution of answers to the analysed question in CEE and EU-15 countries. It may be noticed that at this aggregate level there are only slight differences between CEE and EU-15 countries in respondents' answers concerning the government's responsibility to provide a decent standard of living for the unemployed. In CEE states almost 31% of respondents declared it should not be the government's responsibility, while in EU-15 states it was almost 25%. This means that in both groups of countries the majority of respondents agreed that it is the role of the government to help the unemployed. Additionally, Table 4.1 (right column) presents the distribution of answers to a similar question from the survey concerning the preferences to change the level of government's spending on unemployment benefits. Interestingly, a greater difference can be noticed for this question, because almost 42% of respondents in CEE declared that the government's spending on unemployment benefits should be increased, while in EU-15 states it was less than 30%.

As far as the analysis of impact of individuals' characteristics on the dependent variable is concerned, its results obtained separately for CEE and EU-15 countries

Table 4.1 The percentage of answers (weighted) to the survey questions concerning unemployment benefits

Question: On the whole, do you think it should or should not be the government's responsibility to provide a decent standard of living for the unemployed?			*Question: Please show whether you would like to see more or less government spending on unemployment benefits. Remember that if you say 'much more', it might require a tax increase to pay for it.*		
Possible answers	*% of answers in CEE*	*% of answers in EU-15*	*Possible answers*	*% of answers in CEE*	*% of answers in EU-15*
Should not be	30.9	24.9	*Spend less or much less*	21.8	25.3
Probably should be	41.6	48.4	*Spend the same as now*	36.3	45.2
Definitely should be	27.5	26.6	*Spend more or much more*	41.9	29.5
Cramér's V	0.076		Cramér's V	0.13	

Source: Own elaboration.

Notes: The presented differences between CEE and EU-15 countries are statistically significant at the 0.001 level according to the Pearson chi-squared test. The answers were weighted with the weights provided by the International Social Survey Programme.

are presented in Tables 4.2 and 4.3, respectively. Although the comparison of these estimates must be done with some caution,[15] these results indicate that different individuals' characteristics matter for determining societal preferences concerning the government's responsibility to provide a decent standard of living for the unemployed in CEE and EU-15 countries. For instance, a meaningful difference may be noticed for the question regarding the respondents' self-placement on a social ladder. Assuming that the baseline respondent had self-placed himself at the bottom levels of this ladder instead of the middle, the probability to answer *Definitely should be* to the analysed question would rise from 17.8% to 21.2% in CEE countries and only from 11.4% to 12% in EU-15. The first difference is statistically significant, while the latter is not. Furthermore, the higher support for providing a decent standard of living for the unemployed in CEE is also characteristic of women and respondents with primary or lower secondary education. It contrasts with EU-15 where these factors occurred to be insignificant. Both women and

Table 4.2 Estimation results for the CEE countries

Variable	*Estimated coefficient*	*Standard error*	*Probab. of answering* Should not be *(in %)*	*Probab. of answering* Definitely should be *(in %)*
Baseline respondent	–	–	36.978	17.794
Woman	0.136*	0.053	33.869	19.87
Age group (omitted: 26–45 years)				
15–25 years	−0.176'	0.094	41.166	15.362
46–65 years	−0.173**	0.066	41.082	15.408
above 65 years	−0.307**	0.106	44.366	13.738
Education level (omitted: primary or lower secondary)				
Upper secondary and post-secondary	−0.251***	0.063	42.993	14.413
Tertiary	−0.362***	0.079	45.73	13.098
Labour market status (omitted: employee)				
Self-employed or working for own family's business	−0.122	0.103	39.865	16.077
Unemployed	0.657***	0.108	23.318	29.461
Economically inactive	0.125'	0.074	34.106	19.702
Trade union membership	0.179'	0.098	32.915	20.562
Unemployed partner	0.101	0.138	34.659	19.317
Number of persons in a household (omitted: two)				
One	0.073	0.076	35.29	18.889
Three	−0.052	0.077	38.187	17.052
Four or more	−0.061	0.072	38.422	16.912

Variable	*Estimated coefficient*	*Standard error*	*Probab. of answering* Should not be *(in %)*	*Probab. of answering* Definitely should be *(in %)*
Self-placement on a social ladder (10 pts scale, omitted: level 5)				
Levels 1–4	0.215**	0.07	32.127	21.155
Level 6	−0.01	0.076	37.22	17.642
Levels 7–10	−0.192*	0.074	41.558	15.154
Attending religious services at least once a week	0.164’	0.091	33.247	20.318
Taxes for those with middle incomes (omitted: about right)				
Much too low or too low	0.156	0.123	33.415	20.196
Too high	0.053	0.061	35.747	18.585
Much too high	0.383***	0.089	28.565	24.104
Support for declining industries to protect jobs (omitted: neither in favour of nor against)				
Strongly in favour of	0.948***	0.083	18.522	35.844
In favour of	0.333***	0.074	29.615	23.186
Against or strongly against	−0.259**	0.089	43.188	14.315
Most civil servants can be trusted (omitted: neither agree nor disagree)				
Strongly agree or agree	0.065	0.081	35.484	18.759
Disagree	−0.003	0.066	37.043	17.753
Strongly disagree	−0.047	0.078	38.07	17.122
Party voted for in the last general election: left/right scale (omitted: centre, liberal)				
Far right, right, conservative	0.036	0.094	36.143	18.326
Centre left, left, far left	0.133	0.095	33.926	19.83
Did not vote or other party	0.181*	0.081	32.858	20.604
Threshold *Should not be/Probably should be*:	−0.533	Standard error:		0.253
Threshold *Probably should be/ Definitely should be*:	1.53	Standard error:		0.254
Std. deviation of a random effect:	0.563	ICC:		0.088
Number of countries:	7	Number of observations:		5504

Source: Own elaboration.

Notes: Asterisks denote significance level: *** – 0.001, ** – 0.01, * – 0.05, ’ – 0.1. ICC is an abbreviation for the Interclass Correlation Coefficient. The estimated probabilities are conditional, which means that they are calculated with the assumption that the countries’ random effect is equal to 0. The estimated probabilities of choosing the answer *Probably should be*, as the least volatile, were not presented for the sake of clarity. As in the case of the dependent variable, some of the answers were combined into one category due to the small number of responses.

Table 4.3 Estimation results for the EU-15 countries

Variable	*Estimated coefficient*	*Standard error*	*Prob. of answering* Should not be *(in %)*	*Prob. of answering* Definitely should be *(in %)*
Baseline respondent	–	–	36.402	11.352
Woman	0.078	0.047	34.625	12.157
Age group (omitted: 26–45 years)				
15–25 years	0.135	0.096	33.337	12.783
46–65 years	0.243***	0.059	30.99	14.032
above 65 years	0.099	0.094	34.15	12.383
Education level (omitted: primary or lower secondary)				
Upper secondary and post-secondary	−0.112	0.07	39.026	10.275
Tertiary	0.039	0.07	35.504	11.751
Labour market status (omitted: employee)				
Self-employed or working for own family's business	−0.024	0.087	36.955	11.115
Unemployed	0.926***	0.113	18.482	24.431
Economically inactive	0.352***	0.071	28.691	15.41
Trade union membership	0.072	0.059	34.755	12.096
Unemployed partner	0.463***	0.138	26.492	16.901
Number of persons in a household (omitted: two)				
One	0.124'	0.068	33.588	12.658
Three	−0.071	0.069	38.061	10.657
Four or more	−0.089	0.065	38.49	10.486
Self-placement on a social ladder (10 pts scale, omitted: level 5)				
Levels 1–4	0.062	0.073	34.982	11.99
Level 6	−0.039	0.071	37.303	10.969
Levels 7–10	−0.124'	0.068	39.307	10.167
Attending religious services at least once a week	0.057	0.112	35.087	11.941
Taxes for those with middle incomes (omitted: about right)				
Much too low or too low	0.563***	0.152	24.575	18.365
Too high	−0.159**	0.054	40.151	9.85
Much too high	−0.251**	0.081	42.39	9.059
Support for declining industries to protect jobs (omitted: neither in favour of nor against)				
Strongly in favour of	0.764***	0.078	21.049	21.564
In favour of	0.199**	0.064	31.922	13.519
Against or strongly against	−0.126'	0.07	39.367	10.144

Variable	*Estimated coefficient*	*Standard error*	*Prob. of answering* Should not be *(in %)*	*Prob. of answering* Definitely should be *(in %)*
Most civil servants can be trusted (omitted: neither agree nor disagree)				
Strongly agree or agree	0.16*	0.063	32.779	13.067
Disagree	−0.198**	0.064	41.089	9.51
Strongly disagree	−0.062	0.076	37.846	10.744
Party voted for in the last general election: left/right scale (omitted: centre, liberal)				
Far right, right, conservative	−0.156*	0.075	40.077	9.877
Centre left, left, far left	0.888***	0.076	19.065	23.732
Did not vote or other party	0.554***	0.083	24.751	18.223
Threshold *Should not be/Probably should be*:	−0.558	Standard error:		0.312
Threshold *Probably should be/ Definitely should be*:	2.055	Standard error:		0.313
Std. deviation of a random effect:	0.747	ICC:		0.145
Number of countries:	7	Number of observations:		7214

Source: Own elaboration.

Notes: The same as for Table 4.2.

respondents with primary or lower secondary education are large socio-economic groups that are generally considered disadvantaged in the labour market and have been found to experience economic insecurity in post-socialist countries (Ivlevs, 2014). Finally, the membership in a trade union, also a numerous socio-economic group, occurred to be significant only in the case of CEE (but at the 10% level). However, between CEE and EU-15 countries there are also some similarities that can be noticed for the unemployed and the economically inactive. Being a member of these groups occurred to increase the support for unemployment benefits both in EU-15 and CEE. Such results support H1, which states that in EU-15 and CEE countries the public support for the generous unemployment benefits scheme is higher in socio-economic groups that experience economic difficulties; however, these groups in CEE are significantly larger than in EU-15.

It is also worth noticing that there are meaningful differences for the question whether the level of taxes for those with middle incomes is adequate. In the case of EU-15 the results are consistent with the economic intuition – the respondents who consider the taxes to be too low are substantially greater proponents of the unemployment benefits generosity than individuals who perceive these taxes as about right or too high. However, in the case of CEE countries this regressor occurred to be far from significant with the exception of respondents who declared that these taxes are much too high, because they occurred to be also advocates of generous unemployment benefits. Although such results may suggest that respondents in CEE countries are more prone to fiscal illusion (Winter & Mouritzen, 2001), the studies based on aggregate data do not confirm differences in this respect between CEE and EU-15 countries (Dell'Anno & Dollery, 2014). Therefore, we interpret this result as a sign that in CEE countries there are groups of respondents who expect that in order to improve their level of economic security the government should at the same time decrease taxes and increase benefits. As such, it is another argument supporting H1.

As far as the second hypothesis is concerned, it may be noticed that among the individuals' characteristics that capture economic deprivation three of them occurred to be statistically significant in EU-15: being unemployed, being economically inactive, and having an unemployed partner. Not only one of them – the unemployed partner – occurred to be insignificant in CEE, but also the size of their impact on the individuals' preferences concerning the unemployment benefits was stronger in EU-15 than in CEE. These differences are especially noticeable for the probability of answering *Should not be* to the question whether the state should be responsible for providing a decent standard of living for the unemployed. In both groups of countries this probability is similar for the baseline respondent; for CEE it is equal to almost 37%, while in EU-15 it amounts to 36.4%. However, assuming that the baseline respondent was unemployed, that probability would fall to 23.3% in CEE and to 18.5% in EU-15. In the case of economic inactivity, it would decrease to 34.1% in CEE and 28.7% in EU-15, while for having an unemployed partner it would fall to 34.7% in CEE and to only 26.5% in EU-15. All these results are consistent with H2 and indicate that all individual characteristics associated with economic deprivation that significantly affect the individuals' support for the unemployment benefits system in EU-15 have a greater explanatory power than in CEE.

In order to test the third hypothesis two regressors have been introduced to the model: trust towards civil servants and preferences for political parties. The obtained results indicate that these regressors play a significant role only in EU-15 countries. The EU-15 respondents who trust civil servants, vote for left-wing parties, or abstain from voting declare also stronger support for unemployment benefits than individuals who do not trust civil servants and vote for right-wing parties. At the same time, in the case of CEE states trust occurred to be statistically irrelevant, while in the case of political preferences only the voting abstention had a positive effect on the unemployment benefits support. These results are consistent with H3 stating that these political variables are relevant only in EU-15.

Conclusion

The first aim of this chapter was to compare the unemployment benefits schemes in CEE with their counterparts in EU-15 countries during nearly three decades after the beginning of the economic transition. The analysis shows that CEE countries conduct stricter unemployment benefit policy in terms of unemployment benefit expenditure-to-GDP ratio, net replacement rates, and benefit duration as well as benefit coverage. The baseline result from the empirical literature, which finds support also in many theoretical studies, points to the detrimental impact of generous unemployment benefits scheme on labour utilisation. Therefore, we may conclude, though with caution, that unemployment benefit schemes in CEE countries facilitate the goal of keeping labour utilisation above levels characteristic for EU-15 countries.

The second aim of this chapter was to analyse the differences in the societal preferences between CEE and EU-15 countries concerning the government's responsibility to provide a decent standard of living for the unemployed. The empirical analysis based on the data from the last wave of the ISSP Role of the Government survey for seven CEE and seven EU-15 countries revealed that substantially different sets of respondents' characteristics have an impact on societal preferences concerning the unemployment benefits generosity. In the case of CEE countries such factors as gender, education level, or self-placement on a social ladder play a significant role, whereas in EU-15 we can observe a connection with the level of trust towards civil servants or preferences concerning political parties. The presented theoretical considerations explain these differences as a result of the heterogeneity between CEE and EU-15 countries in terms of accumulated wealth, as well as a consequence of greater maturity of political systems in EU-15 than in CEE.

These considerations allow us to predict that the smaller the economic and political differences between CEE and EU-15 countries would become, the more homogeneous societal expectations concerning the unemployment benefits scheme among these states should be observed. Although changes in societal preferences are not a sufficient condition to initiate economic reforms, we expect that reforms aimed at increasing the unemployment benefits generosity in CEE countries would be more probable than expenditure cuts in this area. As a result, we expect that CEE states may lose a part of their advantage in labour utilisation over EU-15, which is caused by less generous unemployment benefits systems, but at the same time the gap between the societally desired and the actual generosity of the social protection system in CEE states should be decreased.

Acknowledgement

This work was financed by the National Science Centre of Poland [grant number 2015/17/D/HS4/00319], which had no other involvement in any aspect of the study.

Notes

1 For instance, empirical tests verifying the impact of unemployment benefits construction on unemployment rate need to tackle reverse causation, as the extent of support for the unemployed may be adjusted to the current (expected) labour market situation (Glyn, Baker, Howell, & Schmitt, 2003).

2 Other authors, e.g. Vecchi (2017, p. 425), distinguish between universalism (coverage) and generosity (adequacy) to evaluate social welfare schemes.
3 E.g. they do not accept job offers matching their skills and experience or refuse to participate in job training.
4 For example, an open-ended scheme in Poland was transformed into a time-limited one in December 1991. Similarly, in Czechoslovakia in 1992 the one-year duration of unemployment benefit was cut by six months. The same cut, from 12 to 6 months, was introduced in Hungary (Vanhuysee, 2006, p. 74).
5 The remarkable exception was the unconditional eligibility of graduates in Poland and Hungary.
6 Casey (2004) thoroughly discusses and compares the standpoint of the OECD and the European Union on optimal labour market policies.
7 Unfortunately, there are very scarce data on unemployment benefit spending in CEE countries until the year 1994. OECD provides them only for the Czech Republic, Hungary, and Poland. Moreover, they include early-retirement spending for the unemployed. Consequently, the time span of the analysis starts in the year 1995.
8 These observations hold true at least since 2002, when the US Social Security Administration (2019) prepared its first international overview of social security systems, which is available online.
9 In 8 out 10 analysed countries the coefficient of variation (CV) did not exceed 27 percent. Two exemptions were Hungary and Romania with CV amounting to 42 and 47 percent, respectively.
10 Following Osberg and Sharpe (2014) we understand economic insecurity as the anxiety experienced by an individual that is produced by an inability to sufficiently protect against subjectively significant potential economic losses.
11 The theory of valence voting assumes that (Marx, 2015, p. 46): voters' preferences cannot be placed on a single dimension, the saliency of particular dimensions differs across voters and time, and voters choose parties that they perceive as competent to deliver salient policy goals and care much less about policy alternatives. Thus, the valence model is a form of performance voting and predicts that when voters do not perceive the established parties as competent they are willing to vote on new parties.
12 The exemptions were Belgium, where the survey was carried out between 2017 and 2018, and Croatia, where it was conducted in 2017.
13 Sampling weights used in the estimation have been provided along with the individual data by the International Social Survey Programme.
14 'Conditional' means that the random effect is fixed to an arbitrary value (Grilli & Rampichini, 2012), which in our case is the average value of the random effects among countries, i.e. $u_j = 0$.
15 Different results for CEE and EU-15 group may be also caused by the smaller number of observations for CEE (5 504) in comparison to EU-15 (7 214), differences in the way of constructing sampling weights in particular countries, various moments of conducting the survey, or the necessity to translate the questionnaire and adjust it to countries' specificity, among others. Although we add the random effects for particular countries to the model, it does not guarantee that all these potential sources of errors are eliminated.

References

Acemoglu, D., & Shimer, R. (2000). Productivity gains from unemployment insurance. *European Economic Review*, *44*(7), 1195–1224. doi:10.1016/S0014-2921(00)00035-0

Agresti, A. (2010). *Analysis of ordinal categorical data*. Hoboken: John Wiley & Sons.

Allard, G. J. (2005). *Measuring the changing generosity of unemployment benefits: Beyond existing indicators*. (Instituto de Empresa Business School Working Paper No. WP05-18). Madrid: Instituto de Empresa Business School.

Anderson, C. J., & Pontusson, J. (2007). Workers, worries and welfare states: Social protection and job insecurity in 15 OECD countries. *European Journal of Political Research, 46*(2), 211–235. doi:10.1111/j.1475-6765.2007.00692.x

Anesi, V., & de Donder, P. (2013). A coalitional theory of unemployment insurance and employment protection. *Economic Theory, 52*, 941–977. doi:10.1007/s00199-011-0671-1

Atkinson, A. B., & Micklewright, J. (1991). Unemployment compensation and labor market transitions: A critical review. *Journal of Economic Literature, 29*(4), 1679–1727.

Baily, M. N. (1977). On the theory of layoffs and unemployment. *Econometrica, 45*(5), 1043–1063. doi:10.2307/1914058

Blanchard, O., Bean, C., & Münchau, W. (2006). European unemployment: The evolution of facts and ideas. *Economic Policy, 21*(45), 7–59.

Blanchard, O., & Wolfers, J. (2000). The role of shocks and institutions in the rise of European unemployment: The aggregate evidence. *The Economic Journal, 110*(462), 1–33. doi:10.1111/1468-0297.00518

Blekesaune, M. (2007). Economic conditions and public attitudes to welfare policies. *European Sociological Review, 23*(3), 393–403. doi:10.1093/esr/jcm012

Boeri, T., Conde-Ruiz, J. I., & Galasso, V. (2012). The political economy of flexicurity. *Journal of the European Economic Association, 10*(4), 684–715. doi:10.1111/j.1542-4774.2012.01065.x

Boeri, T., & Keese, M. (1992). Labour markets and the transition in Central and Eastern Europe. *OECD Economic Studies, 18*, 133–163.

Boeri, T., & Van Ours, J. (2008). *The economics of imperfect labor markets*. Princeton: Princeton University Press.

Botero, J. C., Djankov, S., La Porta, R., Lopez-de-Silanes, F., & Shleifer, A. (2004). The regulation of labor. *The Quarterly Journal of Economics, 119*(4), 1339–1382.

Caliendo, M., Tatsiramos, K., & Uhlendorff, A. (2013). Benefit duration, unemployment duration and job match quality: A regression-discontinuity approach. *Journal of Applied Econometrics, 28*(4), 604–627. doi:10.1002/jae.2293

Card, D., Chetty, R., & Weber, A. (2007). Cash-on-hand and competing models of intertemporal behavior: New evidence from the labor market. *The Quarterly Journal of Economics, 122*(4), 1511–1560.

Casey, B. H. (2004). The OECD jobs strategy and the European employment strategy: Two views of the labour market and the welfare state. *European Journal of Industrial Relations, 10*(3), 329–352. doi:10.1177/0959680104047024

Centeno, M., & Novo, Á. A. (2009). Reemployment wages and UI liquidity effect: A regression discontinuity approach. *Portuguese Economic Journal, 8*(1), 45–52. doi:10.1007/s10258-009-0038-8

Chetty, R. (2008). Moral hazard versus liquidity and optimal unemployment insurance. *Journal of Political Economy, 116*(2), 173–234. doi:10.1086/588585

Chiu, W. H., & Karni, E. (1998). Endogenous adverse selection and unemployment insurance. *Journal of Political Economy, 106*(4), 806–827.

Commission of the European Communities. (1997). *Modernising and improving social protection in the European Union* (No. COM (97)102). Brussels.

Deegan-Krause, K., & Haughton, T. (2018). Surviving the storm: Factors determining party survival in Central and Eastern Europe. *East European Politics and Societies*, *32*(3), 473–492. doi:10.1177/0888325417728773

Dell'Anno, R., & Dollery, B. E. (2014). Comparative fiscal illusion: A fiscal illusion index for the European Union. *Empirical Economics*, *46*(3), 937–960. doi:10.1007/s00181-013-0701-x

Di Gioacchino, D., Sabani, L., & Tedeschi, S. (2014). Preferences for social protection: Theory and empirics. *Economic Modelling*, *36*, 629–644. doi:10.1016/j.econmod.2013.09.055

Douarin, E., & Mickiewicz, T. (2017). *Economics of institutional change: Central and Eastern Europe Revisited* (3rd ed.). Cham: Palgrave Macmillan.

EBRD. (2011). *Crisis and transition: The people's perspective* (Transition Report 2011). London: The European Bank for Reconstruction and Development.

Emmenegger, P. (2014). *The power to dismiss: Trade unions and the regulation of job security in Western Europe*. Oxford: Oxford University Press.

European Commission. (2006). *Employment in Europe 2006*. Brussels: Directorate-General for Employment, Social Affairs and Equal Opportunities.

Fackler, D., Stegmaier, J., & Weigt, E. (2019). Does extended unemployment benefit duration ameliorate the negative employment effects of job loss? *Labour Economics*, *59*, 123–138. doi:10.1016/j.labeco.2019.03.001

Feldstein, M. (1976). Temporary layoffs in the theory of unemployment. *Journal of Political Economy*, *84*(5), 937–958.

Freeman, R. B. (1994). Transition in Eastern Europe. In O. Blanchard, K. Froot, & J. Sachs (Eds.), *Transition in Eastern Europe* (pp. 1–36). Chicago: University of Chicago Press.

Glyn, A., Baker, D., Howell, D., & Schmitt, J. (2003). *Labor market institutions and unemployment: A critical assessment of the cross-country evidence*. Oxford: Oxford University Press.

Gordon, J. C. (2015). Protecting the unemployed: Varieties of unionism and the evolution of unemployment benefits and active labor market policy in the rich democracies. *Socio-Economic Review*, *13*(1), 79–99.

Grilli, L., & Rampichini, C. (2012). Multilevel models for ordinal data. In R. S. Kenett & S. Salini (Eds.), *Modern analysis of customer surveys: With application using R* (pp. 391–411). Chichester: Jon Wiley & Sons. doi:10.1002/9781119961154.ch19

Grubb, D. (2001). Eligibility criteria for unemployment benefits. In *Labour market policies and the public employment service* (pp. 187–216). Paris: OECD Publishing. doi:10.1787/9789264189836-en

Hagopian, F. (2007). Parties and voters in emerging democracies. In C. Boix & S. C. Stokes (Eds.), *The Oxford handbook of comparative politics* (pp. 582–603). Oxford: Oxford University Press.

Hasselpflug, S. (2005). *Availability criteria in 25 countries* (Danish Ministry of Finance Working Paper No. 12). Copenhagen: Ministry of Finance.

Haughton, T., & Deegan-Krause, K. (2015). Hurricane season: Systems of instability in Central and East European party politics. *East European Politics and Societies*, *29*(1), 61–80. doi:10.1177/0888325414566072

Häusermann, S., Kurer, T., & Schwander, H. (2015). High-skilled outsiders? Labor market vulnerability, education and welfare state preferences. *Socio-Economic Review*, *13*(2), 235–258.

Hedeker, D. (2008). Multilevel models for ordinal and nominal variables. In J. De Leeuw & E. Meijer (Eds.), *Handbook of multilevel analysis* (pp. 237–274). New York: Springer.

Hobolt, S., Tilley, J., & Banducci, S. (2013). Clarity of responsibility: How government cohesion conditions performance voting. *European Journal of Political Research, 52*(2), 164–187. doi:10.1111/j.1475-6765.2012.02072.x

Holmlund, B. (1998). Unemployment insurance in theory and practice. *Scandinavian Journal of Economics, 100*(1), 113–141. doi:10.1111/1467-9442.00093

Holmlund, B. (2014). What do labor market institutions do? *Labour Economics, 30*, 62–69. doi:10.1016/j.labeco.2014.06.007

Howell, D. R., & Rehm, M. (2009). Unemployment compensation and high European unemployment: A reassessment with new benefit indicators. *Oxford Review of Economic Policy, 25*(1), 60–93. doi:10.1093/oxrep/grp010

Immervoll, H., & Knotz, C. (2018). *How demanding are activation requirements for jobseekers?* (IZA Discussion Paper Series No. 11704). Bonn: IZA Institute of Labor Economics.

ISSP Research Group. (2017). *International social survey programme: Work orientations IV - ISSP 2015* (Dataset). doi: 10.4232/1.12848

ISSP Research Group. (2018). *International social survey programme: Role of government V – ISSP 2016* (Dataset). doi:10.4232/1.13052

Ivlevs, A. (2014). Economic insecurity in transition: A primary commodities perspective. *Review of Income and Wealth, 60*(S1), S117–S140. doi:10.1111/roiw.12038

Knotz, C. M. (2018). A rising workfare state? Unemployment benefit conditionality in 21 OECD countries, 1980–2012. *Journal of International and Comparative Social Policy, 34*(2), 91–108. doi:10.1080/21699763.2018.1472136

Lalive, R. (2007). Unemployment benefits, unemployment duration, and post-unemployment jobs: A regression discontinuity approach. *The American Economic Review, 97*(2), 108–112.

Lalive, R., & Zweimüller, J. (2004). Benefit entitlement and unemployment duration: The role of policy endogeneity. *Journal of Public Economics, 88*(12), 2587–2616. doi:10.1016/j.jpubeco.2003.10.002

Langenbucher, K. (2015). *How demanding are eligibility criteria for unemployment benefits, quantitative indicators for OECD and EU countries* (OECD Social, Employment and Migration Working Papers No. 166). Paris: OECD Publishing. doi:10.1787/5jrxtk1zw8f2-en

Layard, R., Nickell, S., & Jackman, R. (2005). *Unemployment: Macroeconomic performance and the labour market* (2nd ed.). Oxford: Oxford University Press.

Le Barbanchon, T. (2016). The effect of the potential duration of unemployment benefits on unemployment exits to work and match quality in France. *Labour Economics, 42*, 16–29. doi:10.1016/j.labeco.2016.06.003

Lehmann, H., & Muravyev, A. (2012). Labour market institutions and labour market performance. What can we learn from transition countries? *Economics of Transition, 20*(2), 235–269. doi:10.1111/j.1468-0351.2012.00435.x

Lippman, S. A., & McCall, J. J. (1976). The economics of job search: A survey. *Economic Inquiry, 14*(2), 155–189. doi:10.1111/j.1465-7295.1976.tb00386.x

Marx, P. (2015). *The political behaviour of temporary workers*. London: Palgrave Macmillan.

Marx, P. (2016). The insider-outsider divide and economic voting: Testing a new theory with German electoral data. *Socio-Economic Review, 14*(1), 97–118. doi:10.1093/ser/mwu022

Mortensen, D. T. (1986). Job search and labor market analysis. In O. C. Ashenfelter & R. Layard (Eds.), *Handbook of labor economics* (pp. 849–919). San Diego and Amsterdam: North Holland. doi:10.1016/S1573-4463(86)02005-9

Mutual Information System on Social Protection. (2019). *Data from: Mutual information system on social protection. Comparative tables* (Dataset). Retrieved from www.missoc.org/missoc-database/comparative-tables/

Nickell, S. (1997). Unemployment and labor market rigidities: Europe versus North America. *The Journal of Economic Perspectives*, *11*(3), 55–74.

Nickell, S., Nunziata, L., & Ochel, W. (2005). Unemployment in the OECD since the 1960s. What do we know? *Economic Journal*, *115*(500), 1–27. doi:10.1111/j.1468-0297.2004.00958.x

OECD. (1992). *OECD employment outlook 1992*. Paris: OECD Publishing.

OECD. (1994). *The OECD jobs study: Facts, analysis, strategies*. Paris: OECD Publishing.

Oesch, D. (2010). What explains high unemployment among low-skilled workers? Evidence from 21 OECD countries. *European Journal of Industrial Relations*, *16*(1), 39–55. doi:10.1177/0959680109355307

Osberg, L., & Sharpe, A. (2014). Measuring economic insecurity in rich and poor nations. *Review of Income and Wealth*, *60*(S1), S53–S76. doi:10.1111/roiw.12114

Pilc, M. (2018). Should the government provide jobs for everyone? Societal expectations and their impact on labour market institutions and outcomes. *Gospodarka Narodowa*, *296*(4), 179–210. doi:10.33119/GN/102229

Rogerson, R., Shimer, R., & Wright, R. (2005). Search-theoretic models of the labor market: A survey. *Journal of Economic Literature*, *43*(4), 959–988. doi:10.1257/002205105775362014

Rohrschneider, R., & Whitefield, S. (2012). *The strain of representation: How parties represent diverse voters in Western and Eastern Europe*. Oxford: Oxford University Press. doi:10.1093/acprof:oso/9780199652785.001.0001

Roosma, F. (2016). *A multidimensional perspective on the social legitimacy of welfare states in Europe*. Ridderkerk: Ridderprint.

Rose, R. (2009). *Understanding post-communist transformation: A bottom-up approach*. New York: Routledge. doi:10.4324/9780203884935

Rueda, D. (2008). *Social democracy inside out: Partisanship and labor market policy in industrialized democracies*. Oxford: Oxford University Press.

Runciman, W. G. (1966). *Relative deprivation and social justice: A study of attitudes to social inequality in twentieth-century England*. Berkeley: University of California Press.

Schmieder, J. F., & von Wachter, T. (2016). The effects of unemployment insurance benefits: New evidence and interpretation. *Annual Review of Economics*, *8*(1), 547–581. doi:10.1146/annurev-economics-080614-115758

Schmieder, J. F., von Wachter, T., & Bender, S. (2012a). The effects of extended unemployment insurance over the business cycle: Evidence from regression discontinuity estimates over 20 years. *The Quarterly Journal of Economics*, *127*(2), 701–752. doi:10.1093/qje/qjs010

Schmieder, J. F., von Wachter, T., & Bender, S. (2012b). The long-term effects of UI extensions on employment. *American Economic Review*, *102*(3), 514–519. doi:10.1257/aer.102.3.514

Singer, M. M. (2013). What goes around comes around: Perceived vulnerable employment and economic voting in developing countries. *European Journal of Political Research*, *52*(2), 143–163. doi:10.1111/j.1475-6765.2012.02066.x

Stovicek, K., & Turrini, A. (2012). *European economy: Benchmarking unemployment benefit systems* (Economic Papers No. 454). Brussels: Directorate-General for Economic and Financial Affairs. doi:10.2765/26084

Tatsiramos, K. (2009). Unemployment insurance in Europe: Unemployment duration and subsequent employment stability. *Journal of the European Economic Association, 7*(6), 1225–1260. doi:10.1162/JEEA.2009.7.6.1225

Tatsiramos, K., & Van Ours, J. C. (2014). Labor market effects of unemployment insurance design. *Journal of Economic Surveys, 28*(2), 284–311. doi:10.1111/joes.12005

Thelen, K. (2014). *Varieties of liberalization and the new politics of social solidarity*. New York: Cambridge University Press.

US Social Security Administration. (2019). *Data from: Social security programs throughout the world* (Dataset). Retrieved from www.ssa.gov/policy/docs/progdesc/ssptw/index.html

Van Ours, J. C., & Vodopivec, M. (2008). Does reducing unemployment insurance generosity reduce job match quality? *Journal of Public Economics, 92*(3–4), 684–695. doi:10.1016/J.JPUBECO.2007.05.006

Vanhuysee, P. (2006). *Divide and pacify: Strategic social policies and political protests in post-communist democracies*. Budapest and New York: Central European University Press.

Vecchi, G. (2017). *Measuring wellbeing: A history of Italian living standards*. Oxford: Oxford University Press.

Venn, D. (2012). *Eligibility criteria for unemployment benefits: Quantitative indicators for OECD and EU countries* (OECD Social, Employment and Migration Working Papers No. 131). Paris: OECD Publishing. doi:10.1787/5k9h43kgkvr4-en

Walker, I., & Smith, H. J. (Eds.). (2002). *Relative deprivation: Specification, development, and integration*. Cambridge, UK: Cambridge University Press.

Winter, S., & Mouritzen, P. E. (2001). Why people want something for nothing: The role of asymmetrical illusions. *European Journal of Political Research, 39*(1), 109–143. doi:10.1023/A:1007185029456

5

PART-TIME EMPLOYMENT IN CENTRAL AND EASTERN EUROPE

A cross-country analysis

Kamila Fialová

Introduction

Part-time (PT) employment is a form of non-standard employment relationships that has been rapidly expanding in Europe over the recent decades (for an overview see Eichhorst & Marx, 2015). The average percentage of PT workers in the European Union was steadily increasing from the late 1990s to 2013 and hovered just below 20% in 2018. However, substantial differences exist between the Central-Eastern European (CEE) and Western European (WE) regions.[1] In 2018, PT employment was rather common in WE, at an average of 22.9% of total employment. In contrast, the average share of PT employment in the CEE region was only 5.9% in 2018.

Though numerous studies have been made on PT work in WE countries, similar studies in the CEE region have been scarce.[2] Eurofound (2011) explains the difference in the prevalence of PT employment between the old (WE) and new (CEE) member states as being due to stronger preferences in CEE for full-time work because of the lower average hourly pay in the region, which makes it difficult for a worker to live on a PT wage. Fialová (2017a, 2017b) examined the trends and determinants of PT employment in CEE countries compared to the WE region and concluded that PT employment in CEE was influenced by different factors. Further, the results of the study indicate that PT employment in CEE countries may be largely viewed as a tool to circumvent labour market rigidity.

The aim of this chapter is to examine the relationship between PT work and labour utilisation in CEE countries compared to the situation in the WE region and to evaluate whether potential expansion of PT employment may facilitate growth in labour utilisation. The chapter describes the main patterns of PT work and the differences between the two regions. The analyses identify the main determinants of PT employment and the key barriers that limit its utilisation in the CEE region for different groups of workers.

Our results indicate that PT employment of prime-aged men is largely driven by business cycle trends, expanded mostly at the expense of full-time positions, and has no significant relationship to labour market inactivity in CEE. Thus, the potential of PT work to significantly increase the labour utilisation of prime-aged men seems rather limited in CEE. In contrast, for both young and older workers, PT employment has a positive relationship to the employment rate without the offsetting effects on full-time positions; it is a viable option to inactivity and may bring about higher labour utilisation. Further, our results suggest that the growth in prime-aged female PT work was mainly at the expense of a shrinking pool of the inactive and was positively related to the total prime-aged female employment rate and labour participation.

This chapter is organised as follows. Firstly, we present the main theoretical considerations and results of empirical literature concerning the impact of PT work on the labour market developments including labour utilisation. Secondly, the following section describes the main determinants of PT employment, as well as the motivation of individuals/firms to accept/offer PT jobs. Thirdly, the next section sketches the development of PT employment in CEE countries. Fourthly, the following section introduces the methodology and data used in the empirical estimation of PT work determinants, and the subsequent section summarises the key findings. The last section concludes.

Part-time employment and labour utilisation

Part-time employment may directly and indirectly influence the general labour force participation rate and the productivity of the labour force and thus affect labour utilisation and the overall economic performance of the country. However, the direction of the overall effect on labour force participation and productivity may be ambiguous, as both positive and negative effects are possible (for an overview see Delsen, 1993; Garnero, Kampelmann, & Rycx, 2014). Consequently, the relationship between PT employment and labour utilisation is not straightforward.

From the macroeconomic perspective, PT employment can bring about many positive consequences. It can represent a feasible alternative to economic inactivity for certain groups of people who are unwilling or unable to work full-time, and thus can boost the overall labour force participation. This concerns mainly younger and older workers, for whom a PT job enables a smoother entrance into or exit from the labour market, prime-aged workers who need to reconcile work and family life, and disabled workers who cannot work full-time (Delsen, 1993). Moreover, PT working arrangements can increase overall labour market flexibility through an adjustment of hours worked and thus help mitigate fluctuating labour costs during the business cycle (Borowczyk-Martins, 2017; Borowczyk-Martins & Lalé, 2019). In this sense, opportunities to work PT are equally important as the opportunities to move from full-time work to PT and back again.[3] However, here also resides the potential drawback of increasing PT employment on the macro level: while the expansion of PT employment may reduce the pool of inactive people, it may also grow at the expense of full-time employment and thus reduce overall labour utilisation.[4]

PT employment also has some drawbacks from the micro perspective. Employers may face higher fixed costs connected with PT employment (recruitment, training etc.). For employees, the negative aspects may include lower wages and fewer fringe benefits, less job security, less access to training and promotion, and less access to unemployment benefits and re-employment assistance (Horemans, Marx, & Nolan, 2016; Kauhanen & Nätti, 2015; OECD, 1999; Wolf, 2002), all of which can lead to a higher risk of poverty. However, as the OECD (2010) shows, at least for certain types of employees, these disadvantages may be compensated for by more family- and study-friendly work arrangements, which can result in greater job satisfaction and productivity of PT employees. This is particularly true for workers who voluntarily choose PT work to allow for other priorities and may be less often the case for other types of workers.

The existing empirical literature on the topic has not come to a consensus regarding the overall effect of PT employment on labour market trends. Favourable effects have been confirmed by some and refuted by others. Positive effects of PT employment on productivity were identified by Garnero et al. (2014) and Künn-Nelen, De Grip, and Fouarge (2013). Been and van Vliet (2017) stress the positive labour market effect of PT work as a 'bridge employment' between full-time employment and retirement. Their results show that PT employment (particularly if it is voluntary) had a significant negative relation to labour market withdrawal among older men in Europe over the period of 1995–2008, without a negative effect on average hours worked. Mourre (2006) shows that the robust development of PT employment was one of the factors that contributed to rising aggregate employment in the euro area in the late 1990s. Similarly, Smith et al. (1998) claim that PT employment accounted for most of the net job creation in Europe in the 1980s and 1990s. In contrast, the results of an analysis conducted by Garibaldi and Mauro (2002) state that the only European country where an increase in PT employment contributed to the growth in total employment was the Netherlands, while in the rest of the European countries, PT jobs tend to replace full-time jobs and have only small net effects on the overall number of hours worked. The results of the analysis carried out by Walwei (1998) indicate that while PT employment can be a viable tool against non-employment, its efficacy in lowering unemployment is limited.

Determinants of part-time employment

The literature indicates that since the late 1980s, trends in PT employment can be attributed to both supply and demand factors (Abhayaratna, Andrews, Nuch, & Podbury, 2008; Allaart & Bellmann, 2007; Euwals & Hogerbrugge, 2006; Tilly, 1991). From the labour demand point of view, PT employment is usually examined under the concept of dual or segmented labour markets and increasing employment precariousness (see Hipp et al., 2015). Under these perspectives, PT work is perceived as a marginalised, secondary form of employment, which represents a source of cheaper labour. Flexibility is usually cited as the main advantage of PT work for employers, as it allows firms to more easily match labour input with business cycle trends. Employers of PT workers can profit from increased productivity, the opportunity to cover unsocial hours and short shifts, and to gain cost advantages resulting from lower hourly wages and premia (Künn-Nelen et al., 2013; Smith et al., 1998; Wolf, 2002).[5] The utilisation of PT work differs across economic sectors; it is widely used in more labour-intensive sectors, such as trade and services (OECD, 2010).

On the supply side, significant differences in motivation to work PT exist between women and men of different ages (OECD, 2010). For women, the two main drivers towards PT employment are motherhood and family-care responsibilities (Fagan & O'Reilly, 1998; see Salladarré & Hlaimi, 2014, for a detailed discussion of female PT employment). Most male part-timers are young labour market entrants and/or students or, on the opposite side of the age spectrum, older and semi-retired workers. For men, PT employment most often occurs at the time of labour market entry or exit, while female PT employment is more evenly distributed across age groups and is a more stable labour market state (Blank, 1994; Delsen, 1998; Rasmussen, Lind, & Visser, 2004). Substantial differences exist between voluntary and involuntary PT employment, both regarding job characteristics and their main drivers (Kauhanen & Nätti, 2015). Green and Livanos (2017) show that younger and older workers, women, workers with less education, and the long-term unemployed are at the greatest risk of being involuntarily limited to PT employment.

The decision to offer or to accept a PT job is a result of many factors (Buddelmeyer et al., 2008; Delsen, 1998; Hipp et al., 2015; Smith et al., 1998). In the short to medium run, PT work is sensitive to business cycle developments. Empirically, PT employment (relative to full-time employment) tends to rise during economic lows and vice versa. The relationship works through several different channels acting both counter- and pro-cyclically (for details see Darby, Hart, & Vecchi, 2001; Delsen, 1998; Lester, 1999; OECD, 1999; Tilly, 1991); generally, the pro-cyclical effects are assumed to be weak. Involuntary PT employment is more sensitive to business cycle trends than voluntary PT employment due to the stronger influence of labour demand factors (Brender & Gallo, 2008; Buddelmeyer et al., 2008; Partridge, 2003). Empirical research on the behaviour of PT employment over the economic cycle has identified countercyclical behaviour of both the total (Blank, 1990; Borowczyk-Martins & Lalé, 2019; Buddelmeyer et al., 2008) and the involuntary PT employment rate (Borowczyk-Martins & Lalé, 2019; Partridge, 2003; Ratti, 1991).

The institutional settings of labour markets tend to have long-term effects on PT employment through several channels, both direct and indirect. The flexibility or rigidity of employment protection legislation (EPL) may have a twofold effect on firm incentives to hire part-timers. Firstly, rigid EPL on full-time jobs may encourage PT work as a means for firms to achieve higher flexibility. Secondly, in contrast, EPL may have an adverse effect by directly limiting PT work. Buddelmeyer et al. (2008) show that PT employment in Europe mostly involves regular, permanent contracts. Therefore, PT employment can be mostly driven by EPL on regular contracts, although regulation on temporary contracts may also exert a certain indirect effect.

Similarly, the tax system settings may have an impact on the supply of PT labour. Joint taxation, upper limits on social contributions, and progressive taxation may discourage a household's secondary earners from taking a full-time position (Delsen, 1998; OECD, 2010). If means-tested and only granted below a certain income threshold, family and child benefits can create an 'unemployment trap' depending on the threshold. At the same time, child benefits may subsidise the PT income of parents who would otherwise opt for full-time work. In contrast, a less-developed subsidised childcare system may be a major disincentive to employment. The overall effect depends on the setting and the generosity of the systems. Further, unemployment benefit systems may create an 'unemployment trap' driven by high net replacement rates and long benefit duration, leading to a negative effect on the probability of transitioning from PT into full-time employment (OECD, 2010).

In the past, due to concerns about the possible undermining of full-time labour standards, trade unions often aimed to restrict the expansion of PT employment in accordance with the insider-outsider theory. This practice has gradually evolved (Smith et al., 1998), and nowadays trade unions often consider the interests of part-timers as well (Rasmussen et al., 2004). Houseman (2001) found a negative relationship between unionisation and PT work in the U.S., although reverse causality ought not to be ruled out – sectors with high shares of part-timers are generally considered harder to unionise (Hernández, 1995). Hevenstone (2010) argues that PT work rises with a decreasing number of strikes and lockouts.

The last set of determinants concerns the structural factors of demographic, social, and economic character that exert long-term effects on the trends in PT employment. Industrial economic structures can account for a significant part of the differences in the prevalence of PT work between countries (Walwei, 1998). The shift towards increasing shares of employment in the service sector is often cited as one of the important factors in the growing prevalence of PT employment since the 1990s (Euwals & Hogerbrugge, 2006; Tilly, 1991).

The schooling rate of the young population and the ageing of the overall population, which is prevalent in European countries, may also be positively related to PT employment. Students often use PT work to finance their education, to gain work experience during their studies, and as a gateway into the labour market, while older workers often use it as a step towards their exit from the labour market.

In contrast, the existence of a robust shadow economy may supply much of the demand for non-standard forms of employment and thus reduce the numbers of PT workers. Packard, Koettl, and Montenegro (2012) show that formal PT jobs at low wages may not be a feasible option for many low-productivity workers due to the interaction of high taxation of labour and entitlements to social assistance benefits; these workers tend to opt for informal employment.

Some determinants are gender specific. For women, the increasing female labour force participation rate is an important determinant in their growing share of PT employment (Buddelmeyer et al., 2008), as is the level of fertility (Delsen, 1998). Nevertheless, the causality between PT employment and these factors is not clear.

The development of part-time employment in the CEE region

PT work is a widespread form of employment in WE: the part-time employment rate (PTR), i.e. the share of part-time workers as a percentage of the total of employed workers, reached an average of 22.9% in 2018 (Figure 5.1 and Table 5.1).[6] CEE countries differed substantially, with an average PTR of only 5.9% in 2018. The highest levels of PT employment in CEE countries were in Estonia and Slovenia, about 10% or more. In contrast, an extremely low PTR of less than 2% was recorded in Bulgaria. Slovakia, Hungary, and Croatia also recorded very low PTRs of around 4% to 5%.

The average share of PT employment as a percentage of total employment in Europe has been increasing since the late 1990s, though the pace decelerated in 2008. In WE, the PTR was steadily rising and stabilised at around 23% after 2013, while PT employment dynamics fluctuated in most CEE countries. The average

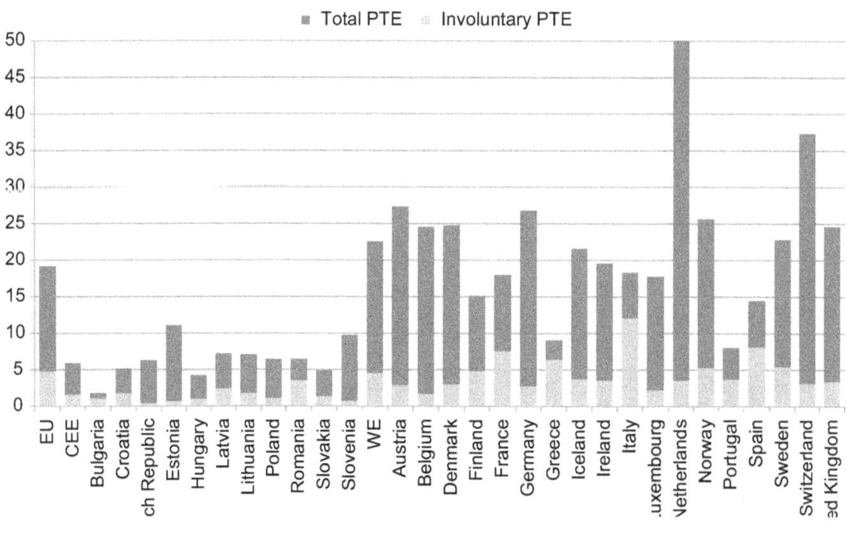

Figure 5.1 Total and involuntary PT employment in Europe (% of total employment), 2018

Source: Eurostat.

Table 5.1 Part-time employment in CEE countries, 2018

	PTR (PT employment as % of total employment)					*Women's share in PT employment (%)*				*Involuntary PT employment (as % of total PT employment)*				
	15–64	*15–24*	*25–49 Males*	*25–49 Females*	*50–64*	*15–64*	*15–24*	*25–49*	*50–64*	*15–64*	*15–24*	*25–49 Males*	*25–49 Females*	*50–64*
Bulgaria	1.8	5.7	1.4	1.5	2.1	51.1	45.9	48.8	56.2	56.9		69.9	51.5	59.9
Croatia	5.2	11.8	2.6	6.3	5.4	60.8	51.4	68.1	52.2	33.8	21.2	46.6	42.0	22.7
Czech Republic	6.3	13.6	1.6	10.4	6.8	77.0	57.0	83.3	73.1	6.5	3.3	8.4	8.4	4.3
Estonia	11.1	27.4	5.2	13.7	10.8	66.3	63.6	68.0	64.9	5.8			6.4	8.2
Hungary	4.2	7.9	1.9	5.0	5.6	67.3	52.5	68.4	71.0	22.9	17.0	38.8	25.1	15.9
Latvia	7.3	15.2	3.8	8.3	8.1	68.0	60.9	67.5	71.2	33.1	17.3	45.3	30.4	34.6
Lithuania	7.1	17.8	3.8	6.8	7.8	63.5	60.0	63.1	65.8	24.4		30.4	25.8	30.5
Poland	6.4	14.5	2.4	8.2	7.8	67.7	59.1	73.8	61.7	15.9	11.6	24.4	18.0	11.6
Romania	6.5	15.0	5.0	5.1	8.4	45.2	43.8	44.0	47.8	54.2	60.6	73.6	50.0	36.8
Slovakia	4.9	8.5	2.6	6.4	5.8	64.0	62.0	66.3	60.5	26.5	21.1	35.1	25.2	24.9
Slovenia	9.7	33.5	3.2	11.3	10.2	67.6	61.1	75.1	60.7	6.5		5.4	12.2	4.1
CEE	5.9	13.8	2.8	7.0	7.0	63.3	55.5	66.9	60.9	26.0	21.7	37.8	26.8	23.0
WE	22.9	35.8	7.8	35.4	23.5	76.3	58.0	79.7	78.7	26.2	25.6	36.8	26.1	24.5

Source: Own elaboration based on Eurostat data.

Notes: Column labels represent age categories.

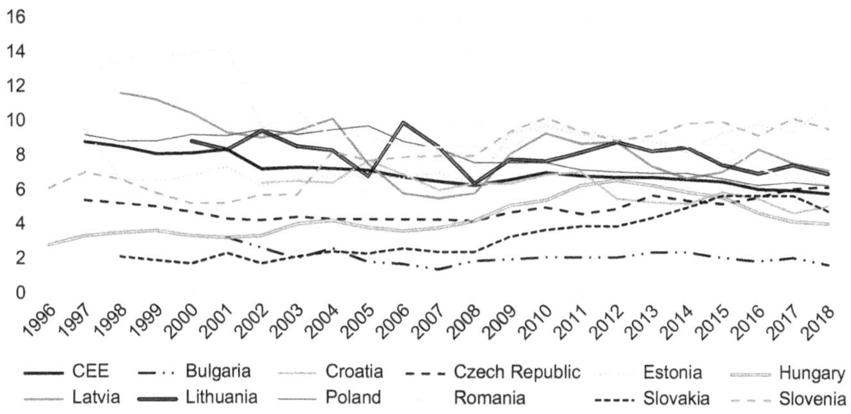

Figure 5.2 Part-time employment in CEE countries (% of total employment), 1996–2018

Source: Own elaboration based on Eurostat data.

share of PT work as a percentage of total employment in CEE generally trended downwards from the late 1990s. The downward trend was particularly evident in Croatia, Poland, and Romania, while an opposite, positive trend was recorded in Slovenia and Slovakia (see Figure 5.2).

The majority of PT employment in Europe is voluntary. In 2018, the share of involuntary PT employment in CEE was comparable to WE, at averages of 26.0% and 26.2%, respectively. In 2018, the highest share of involuntary part-timers among CEE countries, well above 50%, occurred in Bulgaria and Romania. In contrast, very low shares, below 10%, were recorded in Slovenia, the Czech Republic, and Estonia.

Given the different roles that PT employment plays along the life cycle of workers, wide disparities in PTRs exist between different age groups and between the genders. Regarding gender, overall, PT work is more of a female phenomenon (see Table 5.1); most part-timers in both CEE and WE are women. The share of female PT workers as a percentage of the total of PT employed workers in CEE is lower than in WE (63.3% and 76.3%, respectively, in 2018). In both regions, this share is highest in the 25–49 age group, slightly lower among workers aged 50–64, and the lowest in the group of young workers. Within the CEE region, the share of female part-timers is higher in the Czech Republic, Estonia, Hungary, Latvia, Poland, and Slovenia, while lower shares of around 50% have been recorded in Bulgaria and Romania.

When the age structure of PT employment is considered (see Table 5.1), the highest average PTRs are those of young people aged 15–24 in both WE and CEE (35.8% and 13.8%, respectively, in 2018). In WE, a similarly high PTR has also been recorded for prime-aged women, which is not the case in CEE. In both regions, the numbers of part-timers are lowest in the male prime-aged group. The data suggest that while PT work was a less frequent form of employment across all demographic groups in CEE, remarkably large differences were observed for prime-aged women in CEE. They worked PT less frequently than their Western counterparts: in 2018, the average PTR was only 7.0% in CEE, 5 times lower than the 35.4% in WE. Yet women in CEE are involuntary PT workers about as often as in WE: the share of involuntary PT employment in total PT employment was 26.1% in WE and 26.8% in CEE in 2018.

Recent data show that the female prime-age employment rate in CEE was only slightly lower than in WE (at 68.0% and 69.1%, respectively, in 2018).[7] This suggests that women in CEE were more inclined to work full-time rather than in voluntary or involuntary PT employment. This is partly confirmed by Eurostat data on the main reasons for PT employment: Prime-aged women from WE most often named *caring responsibilities* as the main reason for PT work (32.4% of all women working PT in 2017). In CEE, the most frequently cited reason was the *inability to find a full-time job* (30.6%).

Table 5.2 displays cross-country correlations between the share of PT employees and the share of full-time employees, inactive people, and employed people in the total population in respective demographic groups. Observed national employment rates are further adjusted for hours worked, with a factor of 0.6, 0.5, and 0.4 applied to the number of PT employees (full-time equivalents).

In both regions, increasing PT employment was accompanied by falling inactivity and rising employment rates (even in full-time equivalents) for the total labour force, young workers, and older workers. Further, the rise of PT employment was not accompanied by a change in full-time employment of these demographic groups in CEE, as the relationship was insignificant. These results suggest that PT employment was a viable alternative to inactivity for young and older workers in CEE and brought about higher employment rates without the offsetting effects on full-time employment in these groups.

A different picture prevails in the two remaining groups: prime-aged males and females. Among prime-aged men, PT employment expanded at the expense of full-time positions and had no significant relationship to inactivity in either region. Moreover, the correlation between PT employment and the adjusted employment rate was negative and significant for prime-aged men. Thus, the potential of PT jobs to further increase labour force participation and labour utilisation of prime-aged men seems to be limited in CEE countries.

Again, the largest difference between the situation in WE and CEE concerns prime-aged women. PT employment tends to be linked to lower inactivity in both regions. Yet while increasing PT employment is also connected with reductions in female full-time employment in WE, no such relationship seems to exist in CEE, where the correlation is insignificant. Further, we see a positive relationship between PT employment and the observed employment rate in CEE that holds even when employment is measured in terms of full-time equivalents, which is not the case in WE, where it becomes negative. Apparently, the growth of PT employment was related to higher labour force participation and labour utilisation of prime-aged women in CEE countries.

Table 5.2 Relationship between part-time and full-time employment, inactivity and total employment (as a share of the population): coefficients of correlation with part-time employment, 1995–2018

	Full-time employment		*Inactivity*		*Employment rate*		*Adjusted employment rate (0.6)*[a]		*Adjusted employment rate (0.5)*[a]		*Adjusted employment rate (0.4)*[a]	
	CEE	*WE*	*CEE*	*WE*	*CEE*	*WE*	*CEE*	*WE*	*CEE*	*WE*	*CEE*	*WE*
15–64	0.14	−0.24*	−0.40*	−0.69*	0.38*	0.74*	0.33*	0.48*	0.30*	0.38*	0.27*	0.27*
15–24	0.01	−0.01	−0.41*	−0.78*	0.50*	0.75*	0.36*	0.57*	0.30*	0.49*	0.25*	0.41*
25–49 Males	−0.27*	−0.36*	0.10	0.08	−0.17*	0.12*	−0.12*	−0.06	−0.14*	−0.11*	−0.17*	−0.16*
25–49 Females	0.04	−0.72*	−0.36*	−0.36*	0.39*	0.52*	0.28*	−0.05	0.24*	−0.21*	0.21*	−0.36*
50–64	0.10	0.17*	−0.25*	−0.66*	0.29*	0.69*	0.23*	0.54*	0.21*	0.49*	0.19*	0.44*

Source: Own elaboration based on Eurostat data.

Notes: * Statistically significant at the 0.05 level. [a] Observed national employment rates adjusted for hours worked with a factor 0.6, 0.5 and 0.4 applied to the number of PT employees. Number of observations: WE 431, CEE 231. Row labels represent age categories.

These simple correlation coefficients cannot explain the direction of causality and underlying factors which affect both activity and working-time decisions. Still, they suggest that these variables developed within policy and institutional frameworks in which increased opportunities to work PT enabled the expansion of labour utilisation for certain groups, particularly women and young and older workers in CEE. The results also indicate that the supply of PT jobs may ultimately lead to a different trade-off, i.e. between full-time and PT employment, which is particularly evident for prime-aged men in CEE countries. Consequently, the expansion of PT employment at the expense of full-time employment may lead to a drop of labour utilisation of prime-aged men in the region unless the potential decline in labour force participation is offset by an increase in labour productivity.

Empirical estimation of part-time work determinants: methodology and data

This analysis of PT employment determinants is divided into two parts. Firstly, we examine a simple model estimating the effect of economic development, and secondly, we estimate a more comprehensive model specification including additional variables. The methodology mainly builds on the approach established by Buddelmeyer et al. (2008), which is applied to CEE countries. To exploit both intra- and inter-regional variation, we pool data from the countries under examination. The sample covers 29 European countries from 1998 to 2018.[8] Separate analyses were run for CEE and WE countries, and the significance of the differences was tested using standard Chow tests.

The business cycle: short- and medium-term effects

The part-time employment rate (PTR) is trending in most of the countries examined, and the presence of unit roots was confirmed using Phillips-Perron and Augmented Dickey-Fuller tests. To address the issue of non-stationarity, we use the annual change in the PTR as the dependent variable (ΔPTR). To analyse the effect of business cycles on the PTR, the following model specification is used:

$$\Delta PTR_{it} = \alpha_i + \beta BC_{it} + \varepsilon_{it} \tag{5.1}$$

where α_i are country dummies and *BC* denotes the measure of the cyclical position of the economy. Coefficients are obtained using fixed-effects estimation. This model breaks down the development of the PTR into a cyclical component and a linear country-specific trend, which corresponds to the country-specific intercept in the equation. To proxy the country's position in the business cycle, we use (i) estimates of the output gap and (ii) real GDP growth.[9] Taking into account the model-based nature of the output gap estimates, real GDP growth is used for a robustness check. In this specification, lagged independent variables are also included.[10]

The role of labour market institutions and structural factors: long-term effects

To examine the effects of other factors, the basic model (5.1) is complemented with a more comprehensive model including institutional and structural variables. The specification is close to those utilised by Riboud, Sánchez-Páramo, & Silva-Jáuregui (2001), Cazes & Nešporová (2003), and Nickell, Nunziata, & Ochel (2005). The regression equation takes the following form:

$$PTR_{it} = \alpha + \beta BC_{it} + \sum_{k=1}^{K} a_k X_{kit} + \sum_{j=1}^{J} b_j X_{jit} + \varepsilon_{it}, \tag{5.2}$$

Where α is the intercept, *BC* denotes the measure of the cyclical position of the economy, X_k are labour market institutional variables, and X_j are variables describing structural factors.

Most of the variables utilised are trending rather than stationary. To test for the panel unit roots, a Fisher-Maddala-Wu test was employed. The results of this test reject the null hypothesis of non-stationarity of the residuals, i.e. no cointegration, for the estimated model specifications (5.2). Further, we tested for groupwise heteroskedasticity using a modified Wald statistic and for first-order autocorrelation in the residuals, using the Lagrange Multiplier, Likelihood Ratio, and Wald tests. Based on the results, some autocorrelation and groupwise heteroskedasticity was detected in the dataset. Therefore, the equation is estimated by feasible generalised least squares (see also Nickell et al., 2005).

Some of the variables may suffer from endogeneity, especially variables relating to the business cycle and labour force participation (see also Buddelmeyer et al., 2008). For the former, employment trends directly affect economic growth through household disposable income and consumption. Therefore, to check the robustness of the estimates, the output gap was instrumented by the growth rate of fixed capital investments. Further, labour force participation was instrumented by its two-year-lagged values.

Our results are partly limited by the fact that factors affecting PT employment are highly interrelated and interact in complex ways with each other and with their environment, including the cultural values and informal institutions of society (see discussion in Hipp et al., 2015). The impact may vary for different groups of workers, and the demographic composition of the workforce also plays a role. As a result, it is problematic for empirical research to reveal macro-to-micro links and directions of causality. From this perspective, the following analysis describes the basic correlations between PT work and specific factors; the power of the model to explain the causality more deeply is limited.

Data

Most data were obtained from Eurostat. Some of the variables were not available in the Eurostat database and were supplemented by indicators drawn from the OECD database. Unfortunately, the OECD data is not available for all the CEE countries. Therefore, the OECD variables were omitted or replaced by indicators from other sources in several specifications.

PTR data comes from the Eurostat Labour Force Survey and is self-reported by individuals. Involuntary PT employment is a self-reported state by respondents for whom a PT job is an involuntary substitute for a full-time position. Real annual GDP growth data comes from the Eurostat database; the output gap is the model estimate of the European Commission (DG-ECFIN-AMECO database).

The institutional factors cover the following variables. We adopt OECD employment protection legislation indices on the strictness of employment protection (for details see OECD, 2004); version 1 of the EPL index is employed for both regular and temporary employment contracts. We utilise the indicator of Labour Freedom from the Heritage Foundation in several specifications (its inverse value is used to maintain the logic of strictness of employment protection). Consequences of the tax system are addressed using the OECD total tax wedge on labour income, which shows the percentage of gross labour income (100% of average national wage) that goes towards personal income and social security taxes. This variable was replaced with the Eurostat implicit tax rate on labour in several specifications. The power of trade unions is approximated by trade union density, i.e., the share of trade union members of the total number of paid employees in an economy (OECD database). To investigate the consequences of a country's family policy, we use the share of governmental expenditures on children and families from total government outlays, provided by Eurostat. To examine the effects of unemployment benefits, we use the share of the average unemployment benefit of a childless single person who formerly received an average wage on the average national wage (OECD database).

Among the structural factors, the average gross wage in US dollars (PPPs, expressed in logarithm) reflects the wage level in the economy (OECD database). Other variables are from Eurostat: the share of temporary employees of the total number of employees, employment in services as a share of total employment in the economy, total fertility rate, the ratio of students in the population aged 15–24, total female labour force participation, and the index of ageing (the ratio of people aged 65+ on the population younger than 15). The last variable is the model estimate of the size of the shadow economy from research by Medina and Schneider (2018) based on a MIMIC model approach.

Determinants of part-time employment in CEE: results

The aggregated results of model 5.1 estimations are presented in Table 5.3. In both CEE and WE, the output gap exerts a significant negative impact on increases in both the total and involuntary PTR: when the economy operates below its potential, the PTR tends to grow, meaning that PT employment grows more than full-time employment.[11] This is consistent with the labour demand effect on the PTR and reflects firms' desires for flexibility and changes in the composition of employment across sectors. Furthermore, the significant negative effect of the

Table 5.3 Business cycle effects on the part-time employment rate and the involuntary part-time employment rate: total working population aged 15–64

Dependent variable	*Total PTR*						*Involuntary PTR*	
	(i)		*(ii)*		*(iii)*		*(iv)*	
	CEE	*WE*	*CEE*	*WE*	*CEE*	*WE*	*CEE*	*WE*
Output gap	0.013	−0.199*			−0.058*	−0.363**	0.022	−0.060
Output gap (−1)	−0.094**	−0.050					−0.056**	−0.043*
Output gap (−2)	−0.056*	−0.241**					−0.047**	−0.284**
GDP growth			0.032	−0.090				
GDP growth (−1)			−0.031	−0.115**				
GDP growth (−2)			−0.084*	−0.223**				
Instrumented variables	No	No	No	No	Yes	Yes	No	No
No observations/ groups/max periods	214/ 11/21 (a)	315/ 15/21 (b)	218/ 11/21 (a)	378/ 18/21 (c)	218/ 11/21 (a)	315/ 15/21 (b)	214/ 11/21 (a)	309/ 15/21 (b)

Source: Own elaboration based on Eurostat and European Commission data.

Notes: * Statistically significant at the 0.05 level; ** at the 0.01 level. Dependent variable: year-to-year difference in the total PT employment rate/involuntary PT employment rate. Coefficients obtained by fixed-effects estimation. Where indicated, the two-stage least squares fixed-effects estimator with instrumental variables is utilised; the instrument used is the growth rate of fixed capital investment. The panel is unbalanced. Countries included: CEE: Bulgaria, Croatia, the Czech Republic, Estonia, Hungary, Latvia, Lithuania, Poland, Romania, Slovakia, Slovenia; WE: Austria, Belgium, Denmark, Finland, France, Germany, Greece, Ireland, Italy, Luxembourg, the Netherlands, Portugal, Spain, Sweden, the United Kingdom for equations (b), equation (c) adds Iceland, Norway, and Switzerland. Time period: 1998–2018.

business cycle on involuntary PTR is consistent with the involuntary PT effect. In CEE, the main channel of influence is the lagged output gap, meaning that the effect mostly occurs with a delay, as the concurrent output gap coefficient does not prove significant. However, the magnitude of the business cycle effect on the PTR is rather limited: a negative output gap of 1% in periods *t-1* and *t-2* tends to be associated with an increase in the PTR in *t* of approximately 0.15 percentage points.

The results point to the differences between CEE and WE in terms of the effects of business cycles on PT employment rates. In WE, the channels of business cycle influence on the PTR are both the concurrent and the lagged output gap, indicating that the effect occurs within the same year and in the following years.[12] The effect of business cycles on the PTR is also slightly stronger in WE compared to the particular outcome for CEE, regardless of whether approximated by the output gap, GDP growth, or instrumented. The significance of the reported differences in the effect of business cycles on PTR in CEE and WE was tested using a standard Chow test. The results reject the hypothesis of the stability of coefficients between the two groups of countries at a 5% significance level for both total PTR and the involuntary PTR.[13] This suggests that business cycles affect trends in PT employment to different degrees in WE and CEE.

Table 5.4 displays the effects of the business cycle on the PTR separately in four demographic sub-groups in the CEE region. For older workers, the effect of the output gap on the total PTR is not significant. In contrast, the results show a significant negative lagged effect of the output gap on the PTR of young workers. Similarly, a significant negative lagged effect was found for prime-aged men. The business cycle effect on the PTR was negative for prime-aged females as well, but this was not confirmed by robustness checks. Generally, the results indicate that PT work is used by employers as a flexibility device to cope with changing economic conditions during the business cycle, mainly regarding the employment of young workers and prime-aged males.

In order to explain the progression of the PT employment rate in the long run, the analysis is expanded to factors of institutional and structural natures: the main findings are presented in Table 5.5. Firstly, the negative effect of business cycles identified in previous analyses was confirmed. The results reveal further differences in factors that affect the PTR in CEE and WE, as indicated by the results of Chow tests.

Our results suggest that, in CEE, institutional factors generally do not show significant and robust effects on PTR developments. Employment protection legislation has an ambiguous influence on the PTR. The estimated coefficients indicate that EPL on regular contracts tends to diminish the PTR, which is consistent with the finding that most PT contracts are permanent (Buddelmeyer et al., 2008), and rigorous EPL thus limits the use of PT contracts by firms. However, the outcome is not robust in different specifications. EPL on temporary contracts is not significant in our estimations. The inverse value of the labour freedom indicator has a significant positive effect that contradicts the result for EPL on regular contracts.

Table 5.4 Business cycle effects on the part-time employment rate in CEE: demographic sub-groups

Sub-group	*15–24*			*25–49 Females*			*25–49 Males*			*50–64*		
	(i)	*(ii)*	*(iii)*	*(iv)*	*(v)*	*(vi)*	*(vii)*	*(viii)*	*(ix)*	*(x)*	*(xi)*	*(xii)*
Output gap	−0.112		−0.228**	0.025		−0.052	0.015		−0.047**	0.035		−0.036
Output gap (−1)	−0.137			−0.096*			−0.087**			−0.098*		
Output gap (−2)	−0.191*			−0.084*			−0.038*			−0.031		
GDP growth		−0.075			0.037			0.054*			0.065	
GDP growth (−1)		−0.068			−0.032			−0.024			−0.023	
GDP growth (−2)		−0.315*			−0.096*			−0.044*			−0.050	
Instrumented variables	No	No	Yes	No	No	Yes	No	No	Yes	No	No	Yes
No observations	210	214	214	214	218	218	214	218	218	214	218	218

Source: Own elaboration based on Eurostat and European Commission data.

Notes: * Statistically significant at the 0.05 level; ** at the 0.01 level. Dependent variable: year-to-year difference in part-time employment rate. Coefficients obtained by fixed effects estimations. Where indicated, the two-stage least squares fixed-effects estimator with instrumental variables is utilised; the instrument used is the growth rate of fixed capital investment. The panel is unbalanced. Countries included: see CEE group in Table 5.3. Time period: 1998–2018.

Table 5.5 Part-time employment determinants: results of empirical estimations

	(i)		*(ii)*		*(iii)*		*(iv)*		*(v)*		*(vi)*		*(vii)*	
	CEE	*WE*	*CEE*	*WE*	*CEE*	*WE*	*CEE*	*WE*	*CEE*	*WE*	*CEE*	*WE*	*CEE*	*WE*
Output gap	−0.103**	−0.109*	−0.156**	−0.069*	−0.067**	−0.099*	−0.054*	−0.107*	−0.091**	−0.060	−0.083**	−0.134*	−0.126**	−0.019
EPL regular			−0.691*	−0.884									−0.138	3.081**
EPL temporary			0.542	−2.308**									0.213	−2.523**
Labour freedom	319.006**	−322.778**									192.582**	−231.304**		
Tax wedge on labour			−0.180**	0.053									−0.061	0.083
Implicit tax on labour	−0.028	0.342**									−0.015	0.101		
Trade union density			−0.001	−0.052**									−0.001	−0.062**
Government expenditures on family and children	−0.296	0.564**	0.464**	0.529**							−0.336*	−0.174	0.308*	−0.705**
Unemployment benefit share on average wage			0.014	−0.014									0.031**	−0.023
Employment in services					−18.569**	28.337**	−12.155**	20.289**	−13.805*	−1.786	−12.069**	34.747**	−25.693**	38.478**
Temporary jobs					0.050*	−0.119*	0.109**	−0.115*	0.121**	0.269**	0.006	−0.147	−0.018	−0.082
Shadow economy					0.171**	−0.276**	0.183**	−0.277**	0.129	0.239*	0.138**	−0.463**	0.233**	−0.087
Total fertility					1.300	2.774*	1.820	2.039	1.975	4.465**	0.517	1.549	−1.584	1.631
Female participation					0.197**	0.172**	0.204**	0.183**	0.308**	0.341**	0.053	0.127	0.150**	0.161*
Schooling rate					0.117**	0.038	0.092**	0.053	0.082**	0.124**	0.201**	0.087	0.258**	0.116*
Index of ageing					−0.010	0.033	0.031**	0.037*	−0.017	0.057**	0.012	0.073*	0.060**	−0.045*
Log average gross wage PPP							−2.253**	6.915**					−4.885**	18.849**
Constant	3.017	9.969**	12.470**	24.475**	−7.277*	−16.449**	7.015	−85.365**	−14.713*	−29.366**	−9.168*	−18.906*	36.645**	−221.110**
No observations	88	120	59	173	156	225	117	225	150	225	88	117	56	163
groups/max. periods	11/8 (a)	15/8 (b)	7/13 (c)	15/13 (d)	11/16 (e)	15/16 (f)	8/16 (g)	15/16 (h)	11/16 (i)	15/16 (j)	11/8 (a)	15/8 (b)	7/13 (c)	15/13 (d)
Instrumental vars.	No	No	No	No	No	No	No	No	Yes	Yes	No	No	No	No

Source: Own elaboration based on Eurostat, European Commission, OECD, and Heritage Foundation data.

Notes: * Statistically significant at the 0.05 level; ** at the 0.01 level. Dependent variable: part-time employment rate. Coefficients obtained by FGLS allowing for heteroskedasticity and common-across-group first order serial correlation. Where indicated, a two-stage least squares fixed-effects estimator with instrumental variables is utilised; the instruments used are the growth rate of fixed capital investment to instrument output gap; labour force participation is instrumented by its two-year-lagged values. The panel is unbalanced. Time period: (a) and (b) 2005–2012; (c) and (d) 2001–2013; (e)–(j) 1998–2013. Countries covered: (b), (d), (f), (h) and (j) Austria, Belgium, Denmark, Finland, France, Germany, Greece, Ireland, Italy, Luxembourg, the Netherlands, Portugal, Spain, Sweden, and the United Kingdom; (c) the Czech Republic, Estonia, Hungary, Latvia, Poland, Slovakia, and Slovenia, (g) adds Lithuania and (a), (e) and (i) add Bulgaria, Croatia, and Romania.

Nevertheless, these two indicators seem to cover different aspects of labour protection in CEE – the correlation between these two variables is insignificant.

Taxation of labour exerts an adverse effect on the PTR in CEE, although it is not robust and significant across all different model specifications. Negative effects may reflect a high marginal taxation, which discourages second earners from working PT. Trade union density is not significant in explaining trends in the PTR. Generally, trade unions are much weaker in CEE than in WE, where trade union density is almost 3 times as high (average 12.6% vs. 38.6% in 2013). The weaker trade unions may fail to have an influence on PT employment in the CEE region. The positive estimated coefficient for government expenditures on family and children probably reflects a favourable effect of state family policies on reconciliation of work and family life and the motivation of mothers to return to the labour market via PT jobs. However, the effect is not robust in different specifications. Finally, the ratio of unemployment benefits on the average wage does not show a clear effect.

In contrast to institutional variables, several structural variables prove significant as PTR determinants in CEE. Specifically, employment in services exerts a significant negative impact on PT employment, which contradicts results of previous literature and our outcomes for the WE region. We may hypothesise that PT employment developments have followed different patterns in the CEE region. While the expansion of PT jobs in WE has been closely related to the growth of employment in services, no such trend occurred in CEE countries. Here, PT employment has not expanded the way that it was recorded in WE, and also, employment in services has not been its major determinant. Instead, the share of temporary jobs and the shadow economy both seem to have a positive relationship to the PTR in our results. The positive association between PT employment and temporary jobs suggests that these two flexibility schemes together help firms ameliorate labour market rigidity. Further, the positive effect of the shadow economy may reflect the simultaneous engagement of workers in both the formal and informal economies, as the widespread shadow economy in CEE usually does not involve total informality but rather underreporting of wages or hours worked (see European Commission, 2004; Williams, 2009).

Among the two gender-specific variables, the total fertility rate exerts some positive effect; it is not robust though. In contrast, female labour force participation has a significant positive relationship to PTR developments, which confirms our previous results in correlation analysis.[14] Similarly, our results indicate a significant positive effect of the schooling rate on PTR, which suggests that students in CEE do combine their studies and employment under PT contracts. Further, the positive effect of the index of ageing is not robust across different specifications. Finally, the average gross wage has a negative impact on PTR in the CEE region. A low wage level in CEE countries may not enable workers to live solely on a PT wage. Therefore, workers often use PT jobs as a second, supplementary source of household income or in case of the inability to find a full-time job. When wages increase, not only does the PTR tend to fall, meaning that PT employment grows less than full-time employment, but also supplied labour grows. This is consistent with the domination of the substitution effect of the change in wage and is in contrast with the situation in WE, where the income effect seems to dominate.

Compared to CEE, the PTR is affected by different factors in the WE region. EPL has a significant negative effect on the PTR for temporary contracts and when measured by the inverse value of the labour freedom indicator. Taxation of labour shows a weak positive effect on the PTR; however, it is not robust for different specifications. In contrast to CEE, higher trade union density seems to diminish the PTR in WE, which is in line with the traditional insider-outsider theory. Finally, EPL on regular contracts, unemployment benefits, and government expenditures on families and children do not show a clear effect. Among the structural factors, three determinants with unambiguous and robust effects on the PTR were identified in WE: employment in services, female labour force participation, and average gross wage all tend to boost the PTR. The average gross wage positively influences the PTR, probably because higher average wage levels in WE make it possible for a worker to live on a PT wage. The estimation results do not show an unambiguous, significant, and robust effect of temporary employment, shadow economy, schooling rates, index of ageing, or the total fertility rates in WE.

Conclusion

This chapter has considered part-time (PT) employment in Central and Eastern European (CEE) countries as compared to Western Europe (WE). Although the CEE countries are heterogeneous in their levels of PT employment, generally, PT work is less widespread than it is in WE, and its prevalence is also influenced by other factors.

In CEE, PT work is used as a flexibility device for coping with changing economic conditions: the business cycle has a significant negative effect on the PT employment rate (PTR). When the economy operates below its potential, PT employment tends to grow more than full-time employment. The main channel of influence is the lagged output gap, meaning that the effect mostly occurs with a delay. However, the magnitude of the business cycle effect on the PTR is rather limited and weaker compared to the particular outcome for WE. A further difference between CEE and WE regions concerns the relationship between PT employment and employment in services: while the expansion of PT jobs in WE was closely related to the growth of employment in services, no such trend occurred in CEE countries.

PT employment is positively related to the share of temporary jobs in CEE, which indicates that these two more-flexible tools help firms overcome labour market rigidity. Similarly, the positive effect of the shadow economy on the PTR probably reflects the simultaneous engagement of many workers in both the formal and the informal economy, as the widespread shadow economy in CEE often does not entail complete informality but rather underreporting of wages or hours worked. These findings all suggest that PT employment in CEE is widely used as a tool to circumvent labour market rigidity together with other forms of non-standard employment relationships and informal employment.

PT work engaged in by younger workers is influenced to a large extent by the employers' need for flexibility during the business cycle, while PT employment of experienced, older workers is less sensitive to economic trends. For both young and older workers, potential growth in PT employment may have certain positive consequences: regarding older workers, a wider utilisation of PT work may help reduce the financial burden of an ageing population. For the young, PT jobs offer a gateway to the labour market, helping young workers gain experience and serving as stepping stones towards employment. Our results indicate a positive effect of the schooling rate on the PTR, which suggests that students in CEE do combine their studies and employment under PT contracts. For both young and older workers, PT employment has a positive relationship to the employment rate; without the offsetting effects on full-time employment, it is a viable option to inactivity and may bring about higher labour utilisation. Greater utilisation of PT work in these groups may be stimulated by changes to employment protection legislation and tax systems to encourage firms to offer more PT contracts.

To a large extent, PT employment of prime-aged men is driven by business cycle trends and is involuntary to a large degree. Our results show that among prime-aged men, PT employment mostly expanded at the expense of full-time positions and had no significant relationship to inactivity. In this respect, we may not expect that potential growth in PT work by prime-aged men would facilitate better labour utilisation unless the potential decline in labour force participation is offset by an increase in labour productivity. Moreover, the relatively low wages in CEE pose an obstacle to more widespread PT employment of prime-aged men.

The largest differences in patterns of PT employment between CEE and WE concern prime-aged women. Female involvement in PT work is not sensitive to business cycle trends in CEE, which suggests that their PT work is usually a more stable labour market state driven by structural and institutional determinants with long-term effects. Women in CEE use PT jobs to balance work and family life radically less often than their Western counterparts. This can be probably attributed to longer state-paid maternity leaves guaranteed in the CEE region, which discourage mothers from returning early to the labour market on a PT basis (although generally the state expenditure in this area is substantially lower in CEE than in WE). Moreover, once mothers do return to the labour force, they tend to choose full-time work, probably as a result of low aggregate wage levels, although the limited willingness of firms to offer PT contracts may also be an important factor. In this sense, PT employment is not unambiguously related to national fertility levels. Yet female labour force participation has a significant positive relationship to PTR developments.

Our results do not indicate an existence of a trade-off between female PT and full-time employment in CEE and suggest that, so far, the growth in PT jobs was mainly at the expense of a shrinking pool of the inactive and was positively related to the total prime-aged female employment rate and labour participation. A potential growth of prime-aged female PT employment in CEE in the future may have a lasting positive effect on female labour participation only in the case that the growth remains at the expense of inactivity and does not turn to offset full-time employment. Yet the prime-aged female employment rate is only slightly lower in CEE than in WE, and the employment rate in full-time equivalents is even higher in CEE. This casts doubts on the magnitude of potential future expansion in female labour participation driven by PT employment growth in CEE. Nevertheless, institutional changes enabling the rise of PT work by motivating both firms to offer PT positions and women to accept them may have several positive consequences. The most important is the positive effect on productivity related to shorter career breaks connected with motherhood and greater job satisfaction due to more flexible work conditions offered by many PT jobs. To minimise the potential adverse effects on labour force participation and overall labour utilisation, opportunities to work PT are equally as important as opportunities to move from PT back to full-time work.

Acknowledgement

This work was supported by the Czech Science Foundation under the grant 'Social stratification in the Czech Republic and Central Europe: 1968–2018' [18–09220S].

Notes

1 The CEE group includes the following countries: Bulgaria, Croatia, the Czech Republic, Estonia, Hungary, Latvia, Lithuania, Poland, Romania, Slovakia, and Slovenia. WE countries include Austria, Belgium, Denmark, Finland, France, Germany, Greece, Ireland, Italy, Luxembourg, the Netherlands, Portugal, Spain, Sweden, and the United Kingdom; we also add non-EU Iceland, Norway, and Switzerland, which we classify as WE for the purposes of this chapter to gain more data.

2 PT work has received large attention in WE (see e.g. Booth & van Ours, 2013; Buddelmeyer, Mourre, & Ward, 2004, 2008; Garibaldi & Mauro, 2002; Gash, 2008; Mourre, 2006; Smith, Fagan, & Rubery, 1998; OECD, 2010). For a detailed overview of literature on the topic, see Hipp, Bernhardt, and Allmendinger (2015).

3 In many countries with widespread PT employment, flows out of PT into full-time employment are relatively rare, and people tend to stay in their PT jobs even after their original reasons for taking PT work cease to exist (OECD, 2010).

4 The OECD (2008) shows that, in the Netherlands, which has the most widespread incidence of PT employment in Europe, high levels of utilisation of PT contracts by women after childbirth pulled down the average working time to a very low level and reduced overall labour utilisation. The resulting negative effects include lower overall productivity growth and lower rates of return to education, which is especially damaging for female life-cycle career prospects and life-time earnings.

5 Analyses that compare the willingness of companies to offer PT work in CEE and WE are still lacking, although this may also be a factor contributing to the large differences in PT employment between these two regions.

6 Unless stated otherwise, the aggregate data concern workers aged 15–64.

7 Among CEE countries, the lowest employment rates of below 60% were recorded in Croatia and Romania. In contrast, high employment rates around 70% were the case in the Baltic countries, Slovenia, and the Czech Republic.
8 As some of the variables employed in the following estimations were not available for all countries and years, several model specifications rely on limited samples. The exact details of country samples are given below the estimation results tables.
9 The causality between PT employment and the output gap might be questionable, as employment directly affects economic growth through household disposable income and consumption. In order to test the robustness of the results to this possible endogeneity, a Granger predictive causality test was performed. The test rejected the null hypothesis of no Granger causality for all specifications in the CEE region except for prime-aged females. Moreover, we instrument the output gap by the growth rate of fixed capital investment to further support the idea that the direction of the causality in the applied regression models is correct. No significant alteration of the results occurred.
10 The number of lags to be covered was tested using a Wald test, the results of which indicate that two periods' lags are sufficient.
11 The robustness of this result was confirmed by both the estimation based on the use of instrumental variables to account for possible endogeneity of the output gap variable and the estimation based on the real GDP growth variable instead of the output gap. In both cases, the effect of the business cycle is weaker.
12 The results for WE support the findings of Buddelmeyer et al. (2008), who used a similar method and report a significant negative effect for EU-15 countries in 1984–2001.
13 The value of the test statistics $F(3,25)$ was 3.71 for total PTR in model specification (i) and 3.65 for involuntary PTR in specification (iv) as presented in Table 5.3.
14 The causality between PT employment and the female participation rate might be questioned, as a greater supply of PT positions may enable labour market participation for women with small children, etc., who might otherwise remain out of the labour market. Our results are broadly confirmed when instrumental variables techniques are used to correct for possible issues of reverse causality (column v. of Table 5.5). To test the robustness of the results to possible reverse causality, a Granger causality test was performed. The results rejected the null hypothesis of no Granger causality for WE but could not reject the hypothesis for CEE.

References

Abhayaratna, J., Andrews, L., Nuch, H., & Podbury, T. (2008). *Part-time employment: The Australian experience* (Productivity Commission Staff Working Paper). Melbourne: Australian Government Productivity Commission.

Allaart, P., & Bellmann, L. (2007). Reasons for part-time work: An empirical analysis for Germany and the Netherlands. *International Journal of Manpower*, *28*(7), 557–570.

Been, J., & van Vliet, O. (2017). Early retirement across Europe: Does non-standard employment increase participation of older workers? *KYKLOS*, *70*(2), 163–188.

Blank, R. M. (1990). Are part-time jobs bad jobs? In G. Burtless (Ed.), *A future of lousy jobs? The changing structure of U.S. wages* (pp. 123–155). Washington, DC: Brookings Institute.

Blank, R. M. (1994). *The dynamics of part-time work* (Working Paper No. 4911). Cambridge: National Bureau of Economic Research.

Booth, A. L., & van Ours, J. C. (2013). Part-time jobs: What women want? *Journal of Population Economics*, *26*(1), 263–283.

Borowczyk-Martins, D. (2017). Why does part-time employment increase in recessions? *IZA World of Labor*, 397. doi:10.15185/izawol.397

Borowczyk-Martins, D., & Lalé, E. (2019). Employment adjustment and part-time work: Lessons from the United States and the United Kingdom. *American Economic Journal: Macroeconomics*, *11*(1), 389–435.

Brender, A., & Gallo, L. (2008). *The response of voluntary and involuntary female part-time workers to changes in labor-market conditions* (Bank of Israel Research Department Discussion Paper No. 2008.08).

Buddelmeyer, H., Mourre, G., & Ward, M. (2004). *Recent developments in part-time work in EU-15 countries: Trends and policy* (Discussion Paper No. 1415). Bonn: IZA.

Buddelmeyer, H., Mourre, G., & Ward, M. (2008). *Why do Europeans work part-time? A cross-country panel analysis* (Working Paper No. 872). Frankfurt-am-Main: European Central Bank.

Cazes, S., & Nešporová, A. (2003). *Labour markets in transition: Balancing flexibility and security in Central and Eastern Europe*. Geneva, Switzerland: ILO.

Darby, J., Hart, R. A., & Vecchi, M. (2001). Labour force participation and business cycle fluctuations: A comparative analysis of Europe, Japan and the United States. *Japan and the World Economy*, *13*(2), 113–133.

Delsen, L. (1993). Part-time employment and the utilisation of labour resources. *Labour*, *7*(3), 73–91.

Delsen, L. (1998). When do men work part-time? In J. O'Reilly & C. Fagan (Eds.), *Part-time prospects: An international comparison of part-time work in Europe, North America and the Pacific Rim* (pp. 57–76). London: Routledge.

Eichhorst, W., & Marx, P. (Eds.). (2015). *Non-standard employment in post-industrial labour markets: An occupational perspective*. Cheltenham: Edward Elgar Publishing.

Eurofound. (2011). *Part-time work in Europe – European company survey 2009*. Dublin: European Foundation for the Improvement of Living and Working Conditions.

European Commission. (2004). *Undeclared work in an enlarged union. An analysis of undeclared work: An in-depth study of specific items*. Brussels: European Commission.

Euwals, R., & Hogerbrugge, M. (2006). Explaining the growth of part-time employment: Factors of supply and demand. *Labour*, *20*(3), 533–557.

Fagan, C., & O'Reilly, J. (1998). Conceptualising part-time work: The value of an integrated comparative perspective. In J. O'Reilly & C. Fagan (Eds.), *Part-time prospects: An international comparison of part-time work in Europe, North America and the Pacific Rim* (pp. 1–31). London: Routledge.

Fialová, K. (2017a). Part-time employment and business cycle in Central and Eastern Europe. *Národohospodářský obzor/Review of Economic Perspectives*, *17*(2), 179–203.

Fialová, K. (2017b). Why don't Eastern Europeans work part-time? *Ekonomický časopis*, *65*(2), 125–142.

Garibaldi, P., & Mauro, P. (2002). Anatomy of employment growth. *Economic Policy*, *17*(34), 67–113.

Garnero, A., Kampelmann, S., & Rycx, F. (2014). Part-time work, wages, and productivity: Evidence from Belgian matched panel data. *ILR Review*, *67*(3), 926–954.

Gash, V. (2008). Preference or constraint? Part-time workers' transitions in Denmark, France and the United Kingdom. *Work, Employment & Society*, *22*, 655–674.

Green, A. E., & Livanos, I. (2017). Involuntary non-standard employment in Europe. *European Urban and Regional Studies*, *24*(2), 175–192.

Hernández, A. (1995). The impact of part-time employment on union density. *Journal of Labor Research, 16*(4), 485–491.
Hevenstone, D. (2010). National context and atypical employment. *International Sociology, 25*(3), 315–347.
Hipp, L., Bernhardt, J., & Allmendinger, J. (2015). Institutions and the prevalence of nonstandard employment. *Socio-Economic Review, 13*(2), 351–377.
Horemans, J., Marx, I., & Nolan, B. (2016). Hanging in, but only just: Part-time employment and in-work poverty throughout the crisis. *IZA Journal of European Labor Studies, 5*(5). doi:10.1186/s40174-016-0053-6
Houseman, S. N. (2001). Why employers use flexible staffing arrangements: Evidence from an establishment survey. *ILR Review, 55*(1), 149–169.
Kauhanen, M., & Nätti, J. (2015). Involuntary temporary and part-time work, job quality and well-being at work. *Social Indicators Research, 120*(3), 783–799. doi:10.1007/s11205-014-0617-7
Künn-Nelen, A., De Grip, A., & Fouarge, D. (2013). Is part-time employment beneficial for firm productivity? *ILR Review, 66*(5), 1172–1191.
Lester, A. (1999). Labour demand and the economic cycle. *Reserve Bank of Australia Bulletin,* February, 35–38.
Medina, L., & Schneider, F. (2018). *Shadow economies around the world: What did we learn over the last 20 years?* (Working Paper No. WP/18/17). Washington, DC: IMF.
Mourre, G. (2006). Did the pattern of aggregate employment growth change in the euro area in the late 1990s? *Applied Economics, 38*(15), 1783–1807.
Nickell, S., Nunziata, L., & Ochel, W. (2005). Unemployment in the OECD since the 1960s. What do we know? *Economic Journal, 115*(500), 1–27.
OECD. (1999). Focus on part-time work. In *Employment outlook* (pp. 14–46). Paris: OECD.
OECD. (2004). *Employment outlook.* Paris: OECD.
OECD. (2008). Increasing working hours: Helping reconcile work and family. In *OECD economic surveys: Netherlands* (pp. 99–118). Paris: OECD.
OECD. (2010). How good is part-time work? In *Employment outlook* (pp. 211–266). Paris: OECD.
Packard, T. G., Koettl, J., & Montenegro, C. (2012). *In from the shadow: Integrating Europe's informal labor.* Washington, DC: The World Bank.
Partridge, M. D. (2003). Part-time workers and economic expansion: Comparing the 1980s and 1990s with US state data. *Papers in Regional Science, 82*(1), 51–73.
Rasmussen, E., Lind, J., & Visser, J. (2004). Divergence in part-time work in New Zealand, the Netherlands and Denmark. *British Journal of Industrial Relations, 42*, 637–658.
Ratti, R. A. (1991). Involuntary part-time employment: Cyclical behavior and trends over 1968–1987. *Economics Letters, 35*, 461–464. doi:10.1016/0165-1765(91)90020-L
Riboud, M., Sánchez-Páramo, C., & Silva-Jáuregui, C. (2001). *Does Eurosclerosis matter? Institutional reform and labor market performance in Central and Eastern European countries in the 1990s.* Washington, DC: World Bank.
Salladarré, F., & Hlaimi, S. (2014). Women and part-time work in Europe. *International Labour Review,153*(2), 293–310.
Smith, M., Fagan, C., & Rubery, J. (1998). Where and why is part-time work growing in Europe? In J. O'Reilly & C. Fagan (Eds.), *Part-time prospects: An international comparison of part-time work in Europe, North America and the Pacific Rim* (pp. 35–56). London: Routledge.

Tilly, C. (1991). Reasons for the continuing growth of the part-time employment. *Monthly Labor Review, 114*(3), 10–18.

Walwei, U. (1998). Are part-time jobs better than no jobs? In J. O'Reilly & C. Fagan (Eds.), *Part-time prospects: An international comparison of part-time work in Europe, North America and the Pacific Rim* (pp. 96–115). London: Routledge.

Williams, C. C. (2009). The commonality of envelope wages in Eastern European economies. *Eastern European Economics, 47*(2), 37–52.

Wolf, E. (2002). Lower wage rates for fewer hours? A simultaneous wage-hours model for Germany. *Labour Economics, 9*(5), 643–663.

Part II

LABOUR MARKET REFORMS AND UTILISATION

Learning from countries' experiences

6

STRUCTURES, INSTITUTIONS, AND AGENCY

The drivers of the expansion of precarious employment in Poland

Adam Mrozowicki

Introduction

Flexible workforce and low wages – along with the weak enforcement mechanisms of labour law – were sometimes considered important sources of comparative advantages of Central and Eastern European (CEE) economies (Maciejewska, Mrozowicki, & Piasna, 2016; Muszyński, 2019). However, they also proved to generate high social costs in terms of increased social exclusion risk and lower wages of precarious workers, worse representation by trade unions, the threat of exclusion from decent pensions in the future, and limited access to banking services (such as credits), to mention just a few (Czarzasty, 2016; Kiersztyn, 2018; Teisseyre, 2012). Some of the Eastern European countries experienced a sharp increase of temporary employment in the 2000s. Examples include Croatia, Hungary, Poland, Slovakia, and Slovenia (Eurostat, 2019a). In Poland, the share of temporary employed rose from 5.6% of employees aged 15–64 in 2000 to 28.3% in 2014 and only slightly declined to 24.3% in 2018. In other countries, precarity meant rather very low wages than the experience of temporary employment. Examples are Bulgaria, Romania, Lithuania, Latvia, with the share of temporary employees as low as 1.1% (Romania), 1.6% (Lithuania), 2.7% (Latvia), 4.0% (Bulgaria) (Eurostat 2019b). Yet all of them score very low in terms of median gross hourly earnings (adjusted to purchasing power standards) in comparison to other European Union countries (Eurostat, 2019c).

In this context, it is astonishing that the expansion of precarity did not generate sharp social conflicts in CEE countries. As documented by Vandaele (2018), average days not worked due to strikes were lower in the most of Eastern European countries in 2000–2017 as compared to Western European ones. Other forms of social protests, including media and social campaigns, occurred in some of CEE countries, such as Poland, Croatia, or Romania, following austerity measures implemented in the post-crisis period after 2009 (Bernaciak & Kahancová,

2017). However, their coverage, tools, and intensity were much lower than in the case of the south of Europe and even Nordic countries, despite the tradition of mass workers' protests in some CEE societies, such as Poland, in the socialist past.

The chapter examines the situation in Poland, in which precarisation of work – at least with respect to the expansion of temporary contracts – has been most advanced in Central and Eastern Europe. It analyses three drivers of precarisation: (a) socio-economic structures typical of the Polish variety of capitalism, (b) the three pillars of socio-economic institutions underlying precarity, including legal regulations, normative expectations, and cultural-cognitive schemes (Scott, 2008, p. 51), and (c) agential responses of workers aimed at surviving, managing, or possibly resisting precarisation (Hardy, 2015). Particular attention is paid to two latter factors – institutions and workers' agency – which are held responsible for the perpetuation of precarity.

We understand precarity as a relational category in line with suggestions of scholars such as Dörre (2019) and Lorey (2015). The best summary of such a perspective is given by Dörre, who suggests that employment can be called precarious 'if it does not allow for subsistence above a certain cultural and socially defined level' (Dörre, 2019, p. 19). At the subjective level, precarious employment is considered risky and insecure from the perspective of a worker (Kalleberg, 2009). Precarity is related to the problems of labour utilisation, as understood in this volume, in at least two ways. Firstly, it often reflects skills mismatch on the labour market as precarious workers tend to work below their formal qualifications, being trapped in perpetuating, insecure contracts, doing cheap, dead-end internships (as in the United Kingdom or the US), and being involved in transitory labour market programmes (as in the case of Germany) (Standing 2011, pp. 72–73). Secondly, it means work intensification due to the need for continuous 'work for labour' – 'work that does not have exchange value but which is necessary or advisable' (Standing, 2011, p. 120). Such work is not reported in statistics, but it is widespread and common in flexible labour markets. It involves, among others, searching for jobs, commuting, and doing work-related business, such as networking, in formal 'leisure' time.

Two questions are addressed in the chapter which are connected to the general theme of the volume. Firstly, what is the relationship between the expansion of precarious employment in Poland and socio-economic and institutional factors related to the course of capitalist transformations in the country? Secondly, from an institutional perspective focused on shared understanding and logics of action (Scott, 2008, p. 51), the solidification of flexible labour regime calls for the analysis of the social consciousness of those affected by it. Thus, it can be asked do individuals reproduce such a regime in their ways of thinking or rather tend to question them?

The chapter suggests that precarious employment in Poland emerged as a result of the low-cost model of business competition adopted in the country after 1989, policy measures to counteract high unemployment in early 2000s by flexibilising

Labour Code regulations, in line with European employment strategies, and the weakness of industrial relations actors and institutions in regulating and monitoring employment conditions, as well as global economic trends, such as the economic slowdown in late 2000s (Maciejewska et al., 2016). The chapter also argues that the institutional and socio-economic factors partially converged with subjective interpretations of reality among young precarious workers which tended to 'normalise' precarity through their life strategies and social consciousness. Yet the convergence is incomplete, which opens some space for critique of precarisation.

The chapter is structured as follows. Dealing with the first question, its first part examines the forms and drivers of the work-related precarity in Poland, paying attention to socio-economic factors, cultural/ideological and political factors, and labour relations contexts of precarisation. In the second part of the chapter, the typical patterns of managing precarious employment encountered among young (18–35 years old) people in Poland in the course of the PREWORK research project carried out in 2016–2020 are presented. In the conclusion, the main findings are summarised and limitations of the study are elaborated.

The Polish flexible capitalism: the rise and perpetuation of precarious employment

As discussed earlier (Mrozowicki, Karolak, & Krasowska, 2017, pp. 230–235), Poland underwent at least three waves of precarisation driven – among others – by the macro-social reforms, employer strategies, and collective labour weakness: (1) the first wave in the 1990s mostly connected with the consequences of system change including the restructuring and privatisation of state-owned industry which resulted in massive job losses; (2) the second wave in the late 1990s until the global economic crisis in 2008 characterised by attempts to attract foreign direct investments (FDIs), fight unemployment and adjust the Polish economy and law to the requirements related to the EU accession; (3) the third wave connected to the economic slowdown in Poland in 2008–2010 and the consequences of anti-crisis legislation adopted in 2009.

Looking at Figure 6.1, several remarks can be made on the characteristics of the Polish variety of precarity. Firstly, the share of those with temporary employment contracts has grown systematically since the late 1990s, whereas the share of part-timers stagnated at a low level. The Polish variety of labour market flexibilisation, likewise in other CEE countries (Eurostat, 2019a), is characterised by low shares of part-time jobs as compared to the EU-28 average (19.1% in 2018 in the EU-28 as compared to 6.4% in Poland). It seems to be connected with low wages in these countries, which makes it very difficult to live without a full-time job, as well as with the prevalence of civil law contracts that offer more advantages to employers than part-time contracts (Maciejewska et al., 2016, p. 248). It also needs to be noted that part-time employment can be an important way of increasing labour utilisation for some groups (e.g. parents, adult learners, workers with disabilities), which does not need to be connected with precarity. This observation

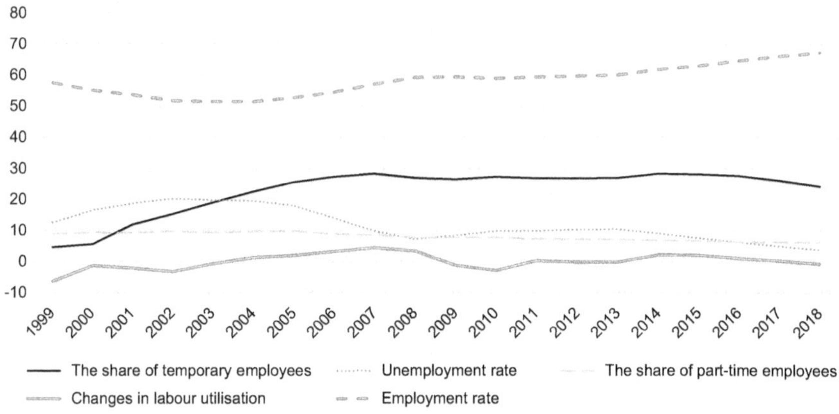

Figure 6.1 Basic characteristics of the Polish labour market

Notes: Labour utilisation is measured as hours worked per capita. The figure presents changes in labour utilisation per year (in %). Unemployment, part-time, and temporary employment statistics are presented for age category 15–64.

Source: Own elaboration based on (Eurostat, 2019a) and (OECD, 2020).

is supported by a decrease of involuntary part-time employment (in age category 15–64) in Poland from 32.3% in 2014 to 15.9% in 2018 (the EU-28 average is 24.8%; Eurostat, 2019a).

Secondly, the employment rate in Poland, following a decline in the period of very high unemployment in the early 2000s, kept on growing. While in 2004 the employment rate was 64.6% for 15- to 64-year-olds in EU-15 and 51.4% in Poland, in 2018 the difference was much lower: 68.7% in EU-15 and 67.4% in Poland. As argued elsewhere, growing employment rates were mostly achieved by replacing permanent jobs with temporary jobs, in particular in the time of high unemployment in 2001–2004 (Maciejewska et al., 2016, p. 247). Falling unemployment rates and growing employment rates can also be related to mass emigration abroad after the European Union enlargement. While in 2002, the number of Poles residing abroad was 786 thousand, it grew to 2.270 thousand in 2007 and in fact still continued to grow despite a short period of decline as result of the global economic crisis in 2009–2010. In 2018, there were 2.445 thousand Poles abroad (GUS, 2019a); the fact which might have also influenced the levels of labour utilisation, understood in quantitative terms as hours worked per capita, which grew in 2002–2007 until the moment of economic slowdown in 2009.

Thirdly, Poland observed a sharp rise in the share of temporary employees in 1999–2007, followed by some decline in the period of economic slowdown in 2007–2009, growth until 2014, and a subsequent slow decline. In the youngest category, temporary employment affects slightly more female workers than male: 66.9% of employed women aged 15–24 are temporarily employed as compared to 59.1% of men. Lower-status employees are more often temporarily employed than other groups: almost 39.2% of lower-status employees worked with contracts of limited duration in 2018 as compared to 8.4% of managers. Low education coexists with lower employment rates in most of the EU countries; in Poland it was 43.1% in 2018 as compared to 88.7% for those with tertiary education (Eurostat, 2019a). Education level also correlates with unemployment rates, with greater rates among those with primary and vocational education (as compared to university graduates; Eurostat, 2020). Taking into account these observations and the high level of temporary employment among lower-status groups, it could be cautiously suggested that temporary employment serves as a tool of labour market activation of lower-skilled workers.

Fourthly, it has to be remembered that the category of temporary employees in the Eurostat statistics covers a variety of work situations of those with fixed-term contracts. In Poland, it includes both workers with temporary employment contracts covered by the Labour Code and those with contracts regulated by the civil law, which concerns contracts of mandate (*umowa zlecenie*) and contracts for a specific task *(umowa o dzieło)*. At the present moment, the most precarious forms of contracts are specific task contracts (see Table 6.1).

According to the most recent data, in 2018 there were 1.3 million people who worked solely based on civil law contracts in Poland (8% of the employed aged 15–64); a slight growth as compared to 2017 when the number was 1.25 million. Simultaneously, 1.5 million workers in Poland (9.3% of the employed) earned less than minimum wage in the same year (GUS, 2019b). Taking into account that temporary employment meant approximately 30% lower wages than permanent

Table 6.1 The forms of paid work in Poland and their occurrence

Contract type	*Minimum wage*	*Working time regulated by Labour Code*	*Protection against dismissals*	*Social security & health care contribution*	*Trade union membership rights*
Permanent employment contract	Monthly	Yes	Yes	Yes	Yes
Temporary employment contract	Monthly	Yes	Yes	Yes	Yes
Part-time employment contract	Pro rata	Pro rata	Yes	Pro rata	Yes
Contract of mandate	Hourly[a]	No	No	Yes	Yes[d]
Contract for specific task	No	No	No	No	Yes[d]
Self-employment[b]	Hourly[abc] /No	No	No	Yes	Yes[d]

Sources: Own elaboration based on Karolak (2020) and Mrozowicki and Maciejewska (2016).

Notes: a) since 2016; b) solo self-employed except for agriculture; c) in case of dependent self-employed; d) starting from 2019.

employment, it can be suggested that the very high number of civil law and temporary contracts in Poland fosters the development of precarity (Kiersztyn, 2012, p. 107).

The drivers of precarity in Poland: structures, institutions, and social agency[1]

It has been mentioned that the emergence and perpetuation of precarisation can be explained by three groups of factors: (a) socio-structural factors, which refer to the specific variety of capitalism that emerged in Poland after the end of state socialism; (b) institutional factors, which concern, among others, legal regulations of labour market, but also the emergent patterns of expectations among workers regarding issues such as working conditions, career patterns, or job quality; and (c) agential factors which refer to individual and collective responses to precarious working conditions (Hardy, 2015; for an extended discussion see: Mrozowicki, 2019).

Socio-structural factors are conditioned by the semi-peripheral position of Poland in global capitalism, of which one of the important characteristics has been the scarcity of domestic capital. The goal of attracting foreign direct investments (FDIs) by keeping labour costs low, labour market deregulation, employment flexibilisation, lowering corporate income tax and creating investor-friendly Special Economic Zones became an important aspect of economic policies in the 1990s and 2000s (Maciejewska et al., 2016). More recently, the concepts such as a 'dependent market economy' (Nölke & Vliegenthart, 2009, p. 672) were used to describe the type of economies whose comparative advantages are 'based on institutional complementarities between skilled, but cheap labour, the transfer of technological innovations within transnational enterprises, and the provision of capital via foreign direct investment (FDI)'. Rapacki and Czerniak (2019, p. 200) coined the term 'patchwork capitalism' to depict the model of market economy, which combines three layers: '(1) proto-capitalist legacy, (2) socialist legacy, and (3) imprints of diverse models of contemporary Western-type capitalism, with a predominant role of the last layer'.

From this perspective, some aspects of precarity, for instance a strong emphasis on the omnipotence of domestic firm owners in labour relations, might reflect the 'manor' organisational culture (Hryniewicz, 2004) and derive from the 'proto-capitalist' nature of the economic system. Other aspects are direct consequences of the policies of liberalisation, privatisation, and deregulation pursued in Poland and other CEE countries after the end of state socialism, thus deriving from the imitation of neoliberal models of Anglo-Saxon capitalism in the early 1990s. Thus, the final result in terms of the Polish variety of precarity is the mixture of both long-term and medium-/short-term factors. In the labour market, industrial relations, and social security dimensions, the Polish capitalism type is characterised by low labour costs, limited coverage and decentralisation of collective bargaining, and limited social protection of citizens, all of which support the emergence of precarity (Rapacki & Czerniak, 2019, p. 187). On the one hand, low-skilled workers are more exposed to the risk of precarity, as demonstrated by higher unemployment rates among those with primary and vocational education. On the other hand, we observe precarisation also among university graduates, observed also in other developed countries. In Poland, it is additionally fostered by the mismatch between employers' demands for technically skilled workers and the characteristics of the education system. Successive governments promoted general secondary education and tertiary education (often in the fields not requiring significant public investments, such as social science and humanities) and marginalised vocational schools (Jasiecki, 2013, pp. 345–359).

Regarding institutional factors, important drivers of precarisation included successive Labour Law reforms aimed at employment flexibilisation. They included, among other things, (1) the legislation on temporary work agencies (2003) resulting in quick growth in the numbers of temporary agency workers, often employed with civil law contracts, (2) the temporary introduction in 2003–2004 and, later on, as part of anti-crisis legislation in 2009–2011, of the possibility of concluding an unlimited number of temporary contracts, and (3) the extension of the reference periods for calculating working time from 4 to 12 months (first as part of anti-crisis law in 2009 and then permanently in the Labour Code in 2013). Additionally, until 2016, it was possible to extend a temporary employment contract for an unlimited number of years. Temporary employment contracts were connected with shorter termination periods than permanent contracts. In this way, an incentive to overuse this extension of temporary employment had been created for employers to abuse. The emphasis on employment flexibility also reflected Poland's preparation to EU accession and adjusting the country's regulation to the European Employment Strategy.

An additional explanation of the expansion of temporary and civil law contracts in Poland in the 2000s is proposed by Muszyński (2019). He argues that intentional policies aimed at employment flexibilisation mattered less than employers' strategies aimed at bypassing Labour Law and quickly growing the minimum wage, stiff regulations, and high costs of open-ended employment contracts by turning to civil law contracts. Limited trade union influence and density both at the national level and in the private sector, as well as restricted prerogatives of the State Labour Inspectorate to monitor the compliance of contracts with Labour Law, supported further employment destandardisation in Poland. It can be suggested that the explanations focused on changes in formal institutions (Labour Law) and employers' and workers' adaptive strategies are not mutually exclusive but rather reinforce and supplement each other.

As argued by Muszyński (2019), we can also observe a gradual conversion of the employment contracts regulated by the Labour Code and civil law contracts, in which the latter acquire some properties of the former. However, this is a new situation which results from attempts to re-regulate Polish labour markets started by the late government of the Civic Platform (PO) and the Polish People's Party (PSL) in 2014–2015 and continued after the victory of the Law and Justice (PiS) party in parliamentary elections in 2015. Until 2016, there were clear advantages for the employers to offer workers temporary employment contracts with shortened termination periods. The reforms included, among others, changes to the Labour Code which equalised notice periods for temporary and permanent contracts; established obligatory social security contributions on contracts of mandate; introduced minimum hourly wage for contracts of mandate and the solo self-employed; as well as modified the Trade Union Act to enable the unionisation of civil law workers and the self-employed.

The recent reforms were at least partially driven by workers' collective agency, namely trade union pressure. It combined political coalitions (NSZZ Solidarność and PiS), mass media campaigns against 'junk contracts' (as civil law contracts were labelled), international pressure at the EU level and in ILO, inter alia regarding the discrimination of workers with temporary employment contracts (Mrozowicki & Maciejewska, 2017). However, these recent forms of mobilisation against the precarity co-exist with more general collective passivity and withdrawal of workers. Trade union density in the country stabilised at one of the lowest levels in the EU, 12.9%, in 2019, with great disparity observed between the private sector (4%) and public sector (29%) levels of union membership (Badora, 2019). As argued elsewhere (Mrozowicki & Maciejewska, 2017), the main achievement of trade unions was changing the frames of the discourse on civil law contracts and creating political pressure to re-regulate some dimensions of the labour market. However, this did not translate into lessening the asymmetry between employers and workers in Poland, which laid the basis for precarisation.

At the moment of writing this chapter, marked by historically lowest unemployment rates in Poland after 1989 (3.3% in December 2019), the labour market bargaining power of workers has increased. Yet no sharp decline in temporary contracts and civil law contracts is observed. This might point to a deeper institutional embeddedness of precarity which goes beyond legal regulations and present economic conditions. As argued by Scott, institutions also concern 'normative rules that introduce a prescriptive, evaluative, and obligatory dimension into social life' (Scott, 2008, p. 54) as well as 'internalised symbolic representations of the world' (Scott, 2008, p. 57). These normative and cognitive dimensions of institutional reality refer to the emergence of social norms that made precarity a legitimate part of socio-economic reality in Poland, as well as internalisation of such norms as a part of the taken-for-granted reality of society members. On the employers' side, the aforementioned disrespect to economic and labour law can be mentioned. For instance, in 2010, 46.7% of owners of small and medium enterprises in Poland confirmed that bypassing or even breaking economic legislation can be sometimes justified (Męcina, 2013, p. 286). On the employees' side, the factors legitimising precarity include the rise of individualistic attitudes and strong belief in meritocratic rules and entrepreneurship among workers in general and younger ones in particular. The ideology of meritocracy makes people believe that their failures are the matter of insufficient efforts rather than structural constraints (Littler, 2018). The ideology of entrepreneurship, in turn, is not limited to the desire to start individual businesses but also concern for the need to 'manage one's life' like a firm, controlling, regulating, and governing the individual *self* (Lorey, 2015, original emphasis).

While ideologies of meritocracy and entrepreneurship are central to late capitalism, they proved to be particularly successful in the post-socialist world, echoing the 'myth of the market' as a remedy for an overregulated socialist economy and the promise of social advancement by individual efforts (Kolarska-Bobińska, 1998). As the result of a strong belief in the advantages of Western and, more precisely, the US type of capitalism, the attitudes such as the expectation of state support or social assistance, were often reduced to the criticised 'legacy' of socialism, or the traits of *homo sovieticus*, and opposed to self-reliance, resourcefulness, and self-responsibility of modern individuals. On the one hand, as a consequence of long-term socialisation to entrepreneurship and self-reliance, excessive labour market flexibility might not have been necessarily seen as a problem, in particular by younger workers. On the other hand, trade union mobilisation against the 'junk contracts' in the late 2000s and 2010s as well as general 'disenchantment' of neoliberalism, visible in the subsequent (2015 and 2019) victories of the conservative and anti-liberal Law and Justice (PiS) in parliamentary elections, indicate some changes in the social consciousness of Poles, involving more open critique of precarity. In the next part of the chapter, a closer look is taken at the recent research on young precarious workers in Poland to examine the 'agential' responses of individual workers to precarisation.

The meanings of precarious employment among young people

It was suggested earlier that young people belong to a group particularly affected by labour market precarity. In order to examine the impact of precarious employment on socio-economic consciousness, life strategies, and civic involvement of young people, a Polish-German research project NCN-DFG PREWORK in 2016–2020 was carried out.[2] It consisted of both qualitative and quantitative modules. In the former one, 63 qualitative biographical narrative interviews were conducted with workers aged 18–35 who experienced various forms of precarious employment in Poland. They were employed in non-standard forms of employment (different from full-time, open-ended contracts), low-paid jobs, being temporarily unemployed following a sequence of temporary jobs or doing unpaid or low-paid traineeships. Each interview included a complete life story, questions of clarifications of life events, and a range of additional questions on the issues such as the meanings of education, work, family life, class identifications, civic activism, and future plans. Additionally, the project team, led by Juliusz Gardawski and Jan Czarzasty (Czarzasty, 2020; Gardawski, 2020), carried out a survey (CATI) of a representative sample of young people aged 18–30 in Poland (*N* = 1000). A similar approach was followed in a mirror project carried out in Germany within a team led by Vera Trappmann.[3]

For the purpose of this chapter the most important question of the project concerns the effects of the precarisation on the socio-economic consciousness and life strategies of young precarious workers. The PREWORK CATI survey in Poland suggests that almost half (48.8%) of young working Poles confirmed to have worked in precarious conditions, defined in the survey question as short-term, low-paid jobs, in the past. Table 6.2 summarises the answers of the interviewees regarding their current employment situation and their desired type of contracts, i.e. the ones which they would choose if they were able to do so.

Table 6.2 makes it clear that a permanent employment contract is not necessarily the most desired form of employment: experienced by 35.8% of interviewees as their current form of employment, it was desired by 39.9% of young working Poles studied (and 43.5% of young Poles interviewed in general). However, 27.3% of young working Poles wished to be solo self-employed and 26.9% wished to be employers; 47.8% of those with permanent contracts would prefer to become self-employed or employers. Permanent employment was chosen statistically more often by women (50.4%) than men (32.8%), who opted more frequently for self-employed and employer status. By contrast, a tiny minority wished to be employed with any kind of temporary employment; only 6 interviewees (out of 224 in total working with civil law contracts and temporary employment contracts) wanted to keep such contracts.

While a strong desire to be an employer is nothing new in Poland and it was noted in earlier research, for instance among blue-collar workers in the 1990s (Gardawski, 2000), it is striking that over one-fourth of our interviewees declared their wish to be solo self-employed, a situation often connected with a rather high level of precarity and *de facto* dependency on large contractors. The preference for starting an individual business over permanent employment

Table 6.2 The current and desired type of work situation among young Poles (in %)

Work situation	*Working Poles (N = 574)*		*Young Poles (N = 1000)*
	Current	*Desired*	*Desired*
Solo self-employed	15.9	27.3	26.6
Employer	4.2	26.9	22.5
Permanent employment contract	35.8	39.9	43.5
Temporary employment contract (incl. probation period)	29.4	0.9	1.5
Contract for specific task	1.9	0.2	0.5
Contract of mandate	9.7	0.9	0.7
Informal employment	0.5	0.2	0.7
Other answers/No answers	2.6	3.7	3.9

Source: Own elaboration based on The PREWORK CATI survey.

Notes: $N = 1000$ Poles, aged 18–30.

fits well into the ideologies of meritocracy and entrepreneurship, as well as the notion of the 'rationality of individualised agency and personal responsibility'. According to Kubala (2019, p. 294), who coined this term based on the discourse analysis of focus group interviews with working Poles, it includes, among others, the equalisation of freedom and entrepreneurship and the definition of social justice as the result of 'individual agency and systemic deregulation of social life'.

Further elaboration of the result is possible by looking closer at the meanings of precarious employment and biographical responses to it reflected in qualitative interviews with young people. In the subsequent sections, a simplified version of the typology of work-related life strategies is presented consisting of two types only (cf. for a full version Mrozowicki et al., 2020; Mrozowicki & Trappmann, 2020).

Longing for security and social status: orientation to stable work

The first type of work-related life strategies present in two-thirds of the qualitative sample (41 cases) was found in the life stories of those who expressed a desire to be employed in stable, permanent jobs. Precarious 'labourers' working in blue-collar occupations tended to see their work mostly in terms of decent income, good social relations with colleagues, and predictable working time schedules ('Monday till Friday, eight hours per day'). In the case of those aspiring to or performing white-collar jobs ('professionals'), work was seen more typically as a matter of social status, sometimes connected with a dream of social advancement, predictable working life, and career patterns. Finally, there were also the narratives of those who aspired to a stable job, but subjectively saw no chance of achieving it (feeling 'blocked').

An example of the labourers' narrative was, among others, Marianna, 25 years old, unemployed, who recalled how lucky she was when she had found a replacement contract in the post office following the completion of an evening secondary school. As in the case of other informants in this type, she identified dignified work with 'dignified salary' and regular working time which would make it possible to fulfil family duties:

MARIANNA: I passed secondary school with very good grades, As and Bs (. . .) I wanted to work in a kind of office capacity, mostly due to the working hours. (. . .) So, I said I would give myself two weeks to find work that I wanted. If I failed, I would take anything, just so the hours suit me (. . .) I walked, I walked, I was already depressed (. . .) And finally it was raining. (. . .) I entered the post office soaked through, my make-up blurred, water in my shoes. (. . .) I said that I was looking for work. And she [the woman working in the post office] says I am taking you (. . .) This was for me . . . you know what it was for me? Like I got really, really lucky. I was so happy, I said: I will be a lady from the post office. Post lady. Elegant clothes. I have to be

> nice at the counter, clean, smelling nice, eloquent, computer, office work. I liked it. It was good (. . .)

Przemek, another interviewer with very low education (completed primary school only), who formerly worked in construction and at the moment of interviewing had taken a free driving licence course sponsored by the Voluntary Labour Corps, saw 'dignified' work as a matter of individual achievement: completing a forklift course would be a step towards this individual achievement, as it would mean that 'he could make it and didn't give up'. Other labourers tended to compensate low wages and instability by pointing at good social relations at work or beyond it.

Labour market precarity becomes more acute if social relations and family support fail, local opportunities on the labour market are limited (as in the case of small cities affected by structural unemployment), and objective educational resources are very low. Once individuals do not see meaningful ways to leave the zone of precarity and at the same time remain critical of it, the 'blocked' type emerges. In such 'blocked' cases, precarity was not subjectively normalised. Instead, social suffering was manifested into the feeling of incapacity to cope with biographical predicaments (e.g. difficult family situations, broken relationship, illness) overlapping with labour market and economic problems. An example was Helena, a 19-year-old shop attendant coming from a large family in a small town, whose early adulthood was marked by the experience of violence and alcohol abuse at home. Narrating about her work situation, she also openly talked about the lack of choices and 'exploitation':

HELENA: I have, this contract, junk contract, this does not count for your seniority.

INTERVIEWER: Contract of mandate?

HELENA: Yes. This completely, as I said, at least my employer, this is another employer, that I met, who does not care completely that when I have my work obligation, I take it. I come to work and do it. This is exploitation. Since I came to work, I have to do what they want. Not what my responsibility is; that is, I do more duties than are mine. These are the facts. But what can a young person do, who wants to work and does not want to be blocked? Most people simply surrender, agree to the exploitation, because they do not have another choice.

Regardless of how much stable employment was desired, most of our informants were either temporarily unemployed or employed in temporary or civil law contracts. Being objectively precarious, the most of them, unlike Helena, tended to justify it both by objectifying the characteristics of labour markets and employers' expectations, as well as the 'transitory' nature of their situation. Adaptation to instability was connected with orientation to meritocracy rules. The belief that as time passes and experience could be gained, achieving desired stabilisation and finding trustworthy work was clear in the interview with 26-year-old Marta. She was an intern in the law office, paid very little from the employment office funds, and hoped to get a better paid and permanent position in the future:

> MARTA: This is for me surely an interim situation which has to be there, and this is all. Honestly, among my friends almost nobody has a contract of employment. In any case, it is difficult to expect that somebody right after studies will trust you like that. Of course, you can give a temporary, etc. a trial period agreement. (. . .) Most friends work in corporations, this is for them also a transit period. Because either they are waiting for some agreement or possibly take into account the fact that they will change their job. This is not beneficial, let us not fool ourselves. Not without a reason these are called junk contracts.

Marta, even though she believed in the transitory nature of her unstable and low-paid work, remained critical of her situation and referred to the category of 'junk contracts', which became popular in the last decade in Poland as a result of trade union campaigns against the civil law contracts. We could find a similar critique of precarity in the interview with Julian, 25-year-old librarian in a medium-sized town in central Poland, earning just above the minimum wage:

> JULIAN: I am this state precarian. The state maintains me, I believe it takes care of me. Maybe I feel that the state should, but on the other hand, I have no feeling of stability. Not yet. The stability appears when you have your own space. You have your own work with some income, and not such that allows you just to eat, and everybody in the family and so on, but lets you get dressed, go from time to time to the cinema, what you like. To save a few zloty, to be able to invest. The lowest national wage is definitely not enough.

The incongruence of social status factors (education and income) was particularly strong in the case of those with higher education degrees who found themselves in the situation of labour market precarity and subjectively aspired to better quality jobs. The critique of precarious working conditions also increased as informants got older and if employment insecurity was combined with the lack of social and family support, family problems, or malfunctioning health beyond the sphere of work, the feeling of isolation and the unmet needs in the domain of consumption (which also includes cultural needs). However, even in such cases it rarely led to any kind of involvement in protest actions or trade union activities. Exceptions included the cases of those who joined trade unions which existed in their firms, mostly for pragmatic reasons such as access to social benefits, and three cases of highly educated precarious 'professionals', who supported new left-wing parties (the 'Together' party), explaining it by their critique of the expansion of civil law contracts.

Longing for creativity, entrepreneurial success, and freedom

In the second type of life strategies (22 cases in our sample), an unstable employment situation tended to be redefined as the consequence of individual choices rather than external conditions to which one needs to adapt. On the one hand, there were the stories of precarious 'creatives' who focused on individual self-fulfilment, autonomy, and passion, as well as their need to escape from the limitations of bureaucratic work organisations (often identified with corporations), such as inflexible working hours and strong dependency on employers. On the other hand, there was the subtype of 'bricoleurs' who, in accordance to the meaning of the 'bricolage' concept (Lévi-Strauss, 1968), made use and recombined all possible resources (social networks, skills, competences) to pursue their individual goal of economic advancement, mostly by attempts to establish and maintain an individual small business. Finally, a small fraction in the Polish sample, represented the subtype of 'withdrawn' from the world of regular employment in favour of alternative lifestyles beyond work, such as squats or experimental spaces of social entrepreneurship (e.g. a self-managed small brewery).

The creatives' subtype was mostly present in the biographical interviews with NGOs and cultural sector workers. Their critique of a 'standard' work situation as the means of restraining and controlling individual needs and aspirations resembled the ideology of 'new spirit of capitalism' (Boltanski & Chiapello, 2005; Bove, Murgia, & Armano, 2017). Precarity was defined as a cost for self-fulfilment, and work-related biographical decisions were presented in terms of a specific trade-off between creativity and stability. A good example can be found in the story of 27-year-old Dagmara, an activist of a small, radical trade union, Workers' Initiative, who, at the moment of interviewing, worked informally by giving private lessons and selling vegan products:

> DAGMARA: When I finished my studies, I had to maintain myself, I simply found the first possible job which was in catering. So, the first one with 10-hour shifts and they paid PLN 10 per hour, contract of mandate. So, contract of mandate, I had (. . .) no awareness at the time that a contract of mandate in this kind of work is not legal (. . .) [Now] I think that a certain stabilisation is necessary, meaning, (. . .) it's not about getting a job and spending my life there until retirement. But I want to be able to try, if something does not work out, e.g. I want to quit my work, because I will have terrible conditions, I would not want to be afraid of it (. . .) [But] I would never see myself as a workaholic, who dedicates her whole life to work.

Dagmara pointed, on the one hand, to her growing awareness of the legal need to have a permanent contract, and on the other hand, to her reluctance to sacrifice other goals in her life for employment stability. In other cases, too, the clear advantages of having employment contracts in terms of access to sick leave and minimum pay were mentioned. However, the creatives – and even more the 'withdrawn' – refused to see stable work as the central aspect of their lives and highly valued the opportunity to change their jobs if the jobs appeared boring or unsatisfactory. Moreover, as in the case of Alicja, a self-employed worker in an NGO, they saw insecurity as the biographical price for performing interesting and engaging work:

> ALICJA: I keep working in places which I co-create myself, so for me it is, I am not able to criticise that because it is a part of me, like I am giving a part of me. (. . .) I do not have any security, sometimes I am not insured, and I can write four applications during a week for which nobody pays me, but I know that this is my step towards maintaining myself somehow.

Another way of managing precarity was found in the narratives of precarious 'bricoleurs'. They referred to the discourses of self-reliance, resourcefulness, and entrepreneurship in justifying their indifference or reluctance towards having a full-time employment contract. In the words of Paweł, a 21-year-old electrician seeking an idea for a business, in order to make good money, one simply needs to 'put down one's laziness' and 'motivate him- or herself'. Disbelief in the advantages of having a standard employment contract was connected with cost-benefit calculation (higher earning in the case of self-employment or civil law contract), distrust in the employment protection by the Labour Code in the context of excessive (and exclusive) power of employers to hire and fire, as well as the scepticism with respect to decent pensions in the future, and the quality of public services (such as public health care). Marian, another electrician, decided to change his qualifications and financed (from a short loan) an IT course in order to become a programmer. At the moment of interview, he was working as a coder in an IT corporation with a civil law contract and expressed his indifference about the advantages of stable employment.

> MARIAN: I read a lot of articles in which they write that programmers earn so much, that their work is so great. (. . .) These work conditions, that they have foosball, that they have . . . a playroom, Fridays off, that they have some trips and many other conveniences for employees. And for me this was simply impossible (. . .) I simply decided to check it, decided to check it, there was a course (. . .) [After the course], I wanted [to go to] Warsaw. Because I knew this is the future here, in terms of this sector (. . .) [I got] the contract of mandate (. . .) Looking at what our government is doing, I do not believe in the pension [system]; even if I get one, it will be at the starvation level. So, I prefer to save up. (. . .) So, I do not look at it. I have health insurance, those things.

Similar reluctance to contribute to the pension system and public services also emerged from the CATI PREWORK survey (Gardawski, 2020): 55.3% of young working Poles (as compared to 11.9% of young working Germans) supported the claim that the 'universal mandatory pension system must be abolished, and citizens must be able to decide for themselves whether they want to save for their pensions'. Simultaneously, 46.4% of Poles (and 21.6% of Germans) confirmed that 'taxes should be drastically reduced, and citizens should be allowed to finance education, health care, etc. themselves'. At the same time, 72.1% of the Polish interviewees expressed the belief that 'free health care should be provided for all citizens', and 88.2% claimed that 'employees who wish to be employed on a permanent basis (contract for an indefinite time) should have a guaranteed indefinite contract'. Thus, the results indicate a contradictory nature of the socio-economic consciousness of Poles rather than the normative acceptance of precarity.

It needs also to be mentioned that despite the 'normalisation' of an unstable work situation in the narratives of those oriented to creativity, autonomy, and freedom, they also included the important potentials of social critique of precarity. The critique emerged as the result of the personal exhaustion with the work from one project to another and failed entrepreneurial projects. It was also caused by work intensification related to both self-employment and project-based work in NGOs and creative-sector cultural institutions. While in the case of 'bricoleurs' the main target of criticism was the state (seen in terms of limiting individual entrepreneurship'), in the narratives of 'creatives' (and some 'withdrawn') some attempts to counteract radical individualisation and social injustice of short-term contracts by the involvement in collective actions were observed. It was only among trade union members of the Workers' Initiative (such as the aforementioned Dagmara) and the supporters of the 'Together' party in our sample that we observed a direct identification of the 'precariat'. Thus, political socialisation appeared to be crucial in developing a discourse of critique of precarity.

Conclusion

The discussion on precarisation intensified following the global economic crisis by the end of the first decade of the 21st century (Dörre, 2019). The debate is connected with labour utilisation, as the precarity often co-exists with the underemployment of high-skilled workers, as well as work intensification of all categories of precarious employees who seek to maximise their income by multiplying short-term jobs (Standing, 2011). This chapter aimed at providing answers to the questions of the socio-economic, institutional, and 'agential' drivers of precarity in Poland. Looking closer at the latter factors, the chapter also explored the relationship between labour market precarity and workers' ways of managing it.

Paying attention to the interplay of three kinds of factors, the chapter contributes to the existing studies on the development of precarity, which tend to analyse them separately and focus either on institutional (Muszyński, 2019) or subjective aspects (Bove et al., 2017; Poławski, 2012). The analysis in the first part led us to conclude that the rise of precarity in Poland has been the result of the intersecting and interacting factors such as the semi-peripheral position of the country, institutional reforms aimed at flexibilising employment, and the adaptive strategies of employers striving to minimise labour costs in the context of the weakness of trade unions and the state in counteracting such practices. The empirical study presented in the second part suggested that institutional and socio-structural changes were partially 'normalised' in the socio-economic consciousness and life strategies of young Poles. From an institutional perspective, they became a part of shared and taken-for-granted assumptions about the nature of the labour market reality. However, the research also suggested that 'normalisation' was incomplete. A large part of young working Poles still consider stable, open-ended contracts to be a norm and recognise very high biographical costs of excessive labour market flexibility in terms of a disrupted work–life balance, career development, and the lack of stable and decent income.

The analysis presented in the chapter has some limitations. It focused on a single country with low unemployment and a high occurrence of temporary jobs. It would be very interesting to explore the situation in societies such as some Baltic countries (Latvia and Lithuania) or in Romania or Bulgaria, in which precarity does not overlap with employment destandardisation but with rather very low wages. Additionally, a better understanding of some of the traits of socio-economic consciousness of young Poles, which include a simultaneous critique of precarity and very strong preference for self-employment would also require comparative analysis. Arguably, strong reliance on individual resourcefulness combined with the disbelief in the role of the state in protecting its own citizens against economic misfortunes has deep roots in the Polish organisational and economic culture of the 19th and 20th centuries (Gardawski, 2020). In this context, it would be interesting to know what the institutional sources of the 'normalisation' of precarity in other CEE countries are.

Acknowledgement

This chapter was prepared within the project PREWORK ("Young precarious workers in Poland and Germany: a comparative sociological study on working and living conditions, social consciousness and civic engagement") funded by the National Science Centre in Poland and the German Research Foundation (DFG). The NCN project number is UMO-2014/15/G/HS4/04476; the DFG project number is TR1378/1–1.

Notes

1 This section is a shortened and modified version of the theoretical framework presented in the book *Oswajanie niepewności* (*Managing Uncertainty*) which I co-edited with Jan Czarzasty (Mrozowicki et al., 2020) and several earlier papers (Maciejewska et al., 2016; Mrozowicki, 2019).

2 The project PREWORK ("Young precarious workers in Poland and Germany: a comparative sociological study on working and living conditions, social consciousness and civic engagement") was funded by the National Science Centre in Poland (UMO-2014/15/G/HS4/04476) and the German Research Foundation (DFG) (TR1378/1–1). It was carried out by the Warsaw School of Economics (Juliusz Gardawski, Jan Czarzasty,

Magdalena Andrejczuk), University of Wrocław (Adam Mrozowicki, Agata Krasowska, Mateusz Karolak, Aleksandra Drabina-Różewicz, Jacek Burski), and Freie Universität Berlin together with Leeds University Business School (Vera Trappmann, Alexandra Seehaus, Jule-Marie Lorenzen, Denis Neumann). More information on the project can be found on the website www.prework.uni.wroc.pl and in publications (Mrozowicki & Czarzasty, 2020; Czarzasty, Trappmann, Mrozowicki, & Andrejczuk, 2018).

3 In this chapter, we will focus on the Polish part of the project only. Some of the results – including the types of coping with precarity in Poland and Germany – were jointly elaborated and presented in earlier papers (Czarzasty et al., 2018; Mrozowicki, Trappmann, Seehaus, Karolak, & Krasowska, 2020; Mrozowicki & Trappmann, 2020).

References

Badora, B. (2019). *Związki zawodowe w Polsce. Komunikat 138/2019*. Warszawa. Retrieved from www.cbos.pl/SPISKOM.POL/2019/K_138_19.PDF

Bernaciak, M., & Kahancová, M. (2017). Introduction: Innovation against all odds? In M. Bernaciak & M. Kahancová (Eds.), *Innovative union practices in Central and Eastern Europe* (pp. 7–20). Brussels: ETUI.

Boltanski, L., & Chiapello, E. (2005). *The new spirit of capitalism*. London: Verso.

Bove, A., Murgia, A., & Armano, E. (2017). Mapping precariousness: Subjectivities and resistance. An introduction. In E. Armano, A. Bove, & A. Murgia (Eds.), *Mapping precariousness, labour insecurity and uncertain livelihoods: Subjectivities and resistance* (pp. 1–12). Abingdon: Routledge.

Czarzasty, J. (2016). Who speaks for whom? Interest representation for non-standard employees. *Warsaw Forum of Economic Sociology*, *7*(1), 105–120.

Czarzasty, J. (2020). Od stoczniowców do prekariuszy. Trzydzieści lat badań nad gospodarką dobrze urządzoną w SGPiS/SGH. In A. Mrozowicki & J. Czarzasty (Eds.), *Oswajanie niepewności. Studia społeczno-ekonomiczne nad młodymi pracownikami sprekaryzowanymi* (pp. 73–99). Warszawa: Wydawnictwo Naukowe 'Scholar'.

Czarzasty, J., Trappmann, V., Mrozowicki, A., & Andrejczuk, M. (2018). Prekaryjność po polsku i niemiecku: świadomość ekonomiczna i strategie ludzi młodych. In J. Czarzasty & C. Kliszko (Eds.), *Świat (bez) pracy. Od fordyzmu do czwartej rewolucji przemysłowej* (pp. 395–418). Warszawa: Oficyna wydawnicza SGH.

Dörre, K. (2019). Precariousness the Eurozone: Causes, effects and developments. In S. Schmalz & B. Sommer (Eds.), *Confronting crisis and precariousness: Organised labour and social unrest in the European Union* (pp. 15–32). London and New York: Rowman & Littlefield Publishers.

Eurostat. (2019a). *Eurostat employment statistics*. Brussels. Retrieved from https://ec.europa.eu/eurostat/statistics-explained/index.php/Employment_statistics

Eurostat. (2019b). *Temporary employment*. Retrieved from https://ec.europa.eu/eurostat/web/products-eurostat-news/-/DDN-20190524-1

Eurostat. (2019c). *Wage and labor costs*. Retrieved from https://ec.europa.eu/eurostat/statistics-explained/index.php/Wages_and_labour_costs#Gross_wages.2Fearnings

Eurostat. (2020). *Unemployment rates by sex, age and educational attainment*. Retrieved from https://appsso.eurostat.ec.europa.eu/nui/show.do?dataset=lfsq_urgaed&lang=en

Gardawski, J. (2000). Robotnicy przemysłowi w pierwszej dekadzie transformacji: ciągłość i zmiana. In H. Domański, A. Ostrowska, & A. Rychard (Eds.), *Jak żyją Polacy?* (pp. 313–334). Warszawa: Wydawnictwo IFiS PAN.

Gardawski, J. (2020). Wizje gospodarki dobrze urządzonej młodzieży polskiej i młodzieży niemieckiej. In A. Mrozowicki & J. Czarzasty (Eds.), *Oswajanie niepewności. Studia społeczno-ekonomiczne nad młodymi pracownikami sprekaryzowanymi* (pp. 277–313). Warszawa: Wydawnictwo Naukowe 'Scholar'.

GUS. (2019a). *Informacja o rozmiarach i kierunkach czasowej emigracji z Polski w latach 2004–2018*. Warsaw. Retrieved from https://stat.gov.pl/obszary-tematyczne/ludnosc/migracje-zagraniczne-ludnosci/informacja-o-rozmiarach-i-kierunkach-czasowej-emigracji-z-polski-w-latach-2004–2018,2,12.html

GUS. (2019b). *Wybrane zagadnienia rynku pracy. Dane dla 2018 roku*. Warszawa. Retrieved from https://stat.gov.pl/obszary-tematyczne/rynek-pracy/pracujacy-zatrudnieni-wynagrodzenia-koszty-pracy/wybrane-zagadnienia-rynku-pracy-dane-dla-2018-roku,9,7.html

Hardy, J. (2015). The institutional, structural and agential embeddedness of precarity: An engagement with guy standing. *Warsaw Forum of Economic Sociology*, *6*(11), 7–25.

Hryniewicz, J. T. (2004). *Polityczny i kulturowy kontekst rozwoju gospodarczego*. Warszawa: Wydawnictwo Naukowe 'Scholar'.

Jasiecki, K. (2013). *Kapitalizm po polsku. Między modernizacją a peryfriami Unii Europejskiej*. Warszawa: Wydawnictwo IFIS PAN.

Kalleberg, A. L. (2009). Precarious work, insecure workers: Employment relations in transition. *American Sociological Review*, *74*(1), 1–22.

Karolak, M. (2020). Społeczno-ekonomiczne konteksty prekaryzacji pracy młodych w Polsce. In A. Mrozowicki & J. Czarzasty (Eds.), *Oswajanie niepewności. Studia społeczno-ekonomiczne nad młodymi pracownikami sprekaryzowanymi* (pp. 49–72). Warszawa: Wydanictwo Naukowe 'Scholar'.

Kiersztyn, A. (2012). Analiza ekonomicznych konsekwencji zatrudnienia na czas określony dla jednostek i gospodarstw domowych. In M. Bednarski & K. Frieske (Eds.), *Zatrudnienie na czas określony w polskiej gospodarce. Społeczne i ekonomiczne konsekwencje zjawiska* (pp. 93–121). Warszawa: Instytut Pracy i Spraw Socjalnych.

Kiersztyn, A. (2018). Non-standard employment and subjective insecurity: How can we capture job precarity using survey data? In A. L. Kalleberg & S. Vallas (Eds.), *Precarious work* (pp. 91–122). Bingley: Emerald Publishing.

Kolarska-Bobińska, L. (1998). *Egalitaryzm i interesy grupowe w procesie zmian ustrojowych* [Egalitarism and group interests in the process of system change] (W. Adamski, Ed.) Warszawa: Wydawnictwo IFIS PAN.

Kubala, K. (2019). *Racjonalność w dyskursach o pracy w Polsce (po)transformacyjnej*. Łódź: Wydawnictwo Uniwersytetu Łódzkiego.

Lévi-Strauss, C. (1968). *The savage mind*. London: Weidenfeld and Nicolson.

Littler, J. (2018). *Against meritocracy: Culture, power and the myths of mobility*. London and New York: Routledge.

Lorey, I. (2015). *State of insecurity: Government of the precarious*. London: Verso.

Maciejewska, M., Mrozowicki, A., & Piasna, A. (2016). The silent and crawling crisis: International competition, labour market reforms and precarious jobs in Poland. In M. Myant, S. Theodoropoulou, & A. Piasna (Eds.), *Unemployment, internal devaluation and labour market deregulation in Europe* (pp. 229–254). Brussels: ETUI.

Męcina, J. (2013). Postawy przedsiębiorców wobec prawa i ocena warunków prowadzenia działalności gospodarczej. In J. Gardawski (Ed.), *Rzemieślnicy i biznesmeni. Właściciele małych i średnich przedsiębiorstw prywatnych* (pp. 241–287). Warszawa: Wydawnictwo Naukowe 'Scholar'.

Mrozowicki, A. (2019). Precarity and counter-movements in the European semi-peripheries: The case of Poland. In S. Schmalz & B. Sommer (Eds.), *Confronting crisis and precariousness organised labour and social unrest in the European Union* (pp. 169–188). London and New York: Rowman & Littlefield Publishers.

Mrozowicki, A., & Czarzasty, J. (Eds.). (2020). *Oswajanie niepewności. Studia społeczno-ekonomiczne nad młodymi pracownikami sprekaryzowanymi*. Warszawa: Wydawnictwo Naukowe Scholar.

Mrozowicki, A., Karolak, M., Czarzasty, J., Gardawski, J., Drabina-Różewicz, A., Krasowska, A., & Andrejczuk, M. (2020). Prekaryzacja pracy a świadomość społeczna i strategie życiowe ludzi młodych: ramy teoretyczne. In A. Mrozowicki & J. Czarzasty (Eds.), *Oswajanie niepewności. Studia społeczno-ekonomiczne nad młodymi pracownikami sprekaryzowanymi* (pp. 17–48). Warszawa: Wydanictwo Naukowe 'Scholar'.

Mrozowicki, A., Karolak, M., & Krasowska, A. (2017). Between commitment and indifference: Trade unions, young workers and the expansion of precarious employment in Poland. In V. Deilteil & V. Kirov (Eds.), *Labour and social transformation in Central and Eastern Europe: Europeanization and beyond* (pp. 228–246). London and New York: Routledge.

Mrozowicki, A., & Maciejewska, M. (2016). *The rise of the dual labour market: Fighting precarious employment in the new member states through industrial relations (PRECARIR) Country report: Poland.* Bratislava. Retrieved from www.celsi.sk/en/publications/research-reports/detail/13/the-rise-of-the-dual-labour-market-fighting-precarious-employment-in-the-new-member-states-through-industrial-relations-precarir-country-report-poland/

Mrozowicki, A., & Maciejewska, M. (2017). Bricolage unionism. Unions' innovative responses to the problems of precarious work in Poland. In M. Bernaciak & M. Kahancová (Eds.), *Innovative union practices in Central and Eastern Europe* (pp. 139–159). Brussels: ETUI.

Mrozowicki, A., & Trappmann, V. (2020). Precarity as a biographical problem? young workers living with precarity in Germany and Poland. *Work, Employment and Society, (forthcoming)*.

Mrozowicki, A., Trappmann, V., Seehaus, A., Karolak, M., & Krasowska, A. (2020). Typologia strategii życiowych pracowników sprekaryzowanych. In A. Mrozowicki & J. Czarzasty (Eds.), *Oswajanie niepewności. Studia społeczno-ekonomiczne nad młodymi pracownikami sprekaryzowanymi* (pp. 349–368). Warszawa: Wydawnictwo Naukowe 'Scholar'.

Muszyński, K. (2019). *Polityka regulacji zatrudnienia w Polsce. Kryzys ekonomiczny a destandaryzacja stosunków pracy*. Warszawa: Wydawnictwo Naukowe 'Scholar'.

Nölke, A., & Vliegenthart, A. (2009). Enlarging the varieties of capitalism: The emergence of dependent market economies in East Central Europe. *World Politics*, *61*(4), 670–702.

OECD. (2020). *Labour productivity and utilisation.* doi:10.1787/02c02f63-en

Poławski, P. (2012). Prekariat: stabilizacja w gorszym segmencie rynku pracy. In M. Bednarski & K. Frieske (Eds.), *Zatrudnienie na czas określony w polskiej gospodarce. Społeczne i ekonomiczne konsekwencje zjawiska* (pp. 122–147). Warszawa: Instytut Pracy i Spraw Socjalnych.

Rapacki, R., & Czerniak, A. (2019). The empirical results of subspace clustering – A summary. In R. Rapacki (Ed.), *Diversity of patchwork capitalism in Central and Eastern Europe* (pp. 185–209). London and New York: Routledge.

Scott, R. W. (2008). *Institutions and organisations: Ideas and interests*. Los Angeles, London, New Delhi, Singapore, and Washington, DC: Sage.
Standing, G. (2011). *Precariat: A new dangerous class*. London: Bloomsbury Academic.
Teisseyre, P. (2012). Wpływ zatrudnienia na czas określony na szanse partycypacji na rynku nieruchomości. In M. Bednarski & K. W. Frieske (Eds.), *Zatrudnienie na czas określony w polskiej gospodarce. Społeczne i ekonomiczne konsekwencje zjawiska* (pp. 192–204). Warszawa: Instytut Pracy i Spraw Socjalnych.
Vandaele, K. (2018). *Strikes – Map of Europe*. Brussels. Retrieved from www.etui.org/Services/Strikes-Map-of-Europe.

7

SKILLS UTILISATION AND GENDER

Estonian case study

Maryna Tverdostup

Introduction

Having a highly skilled labour force is a necessary but not a sufficient condition for an economy to grow. To achieve steady growth and to facilitate worker welfare, individual skills should be productively used at a workplace. The extent of successful job utilisation largely relates to the correspondence between the employers' demand for specific skills and qualifications and the employees' supply of these skills. Even when having comparable productive human capital, as a constellation of skills, abilities, and knowledge, individuals may apply those on the job to a different extent due to different skill demands of occupied positions, different motivation, and intrinsic factors and employer discrimination. The latter results in a disproportional allocation of workers into skill-intense jobs and/or tasks, based on workers' innate characteristics. Gender aspect is particularly relevant in this context, given the vast evidence on the gender gaps in human capital, gendered occupation segregation (Blau & Kahn, 2017), and discrimination (Altonji & Blank, 1999). Therefore, gender disproportionalities in skills utilisation constitute a focal point of this chapter.

In the 'task framework' pioneered by Autor, Levy, and Murnane (2003), the demand side of the labour market is largely shaped by skill requirements of the job. Following this framework, all occupations can be classified according to the specific tasks that are then linked to the skills and abilities of the workers required to perform these tasks (Autor & Handel, 2013). As a result, the specific skill demands determine a job profile, and employers have unambiguously higher demand for workers with these specific abilities. Several studies have considered implications of this framework for the gender disparity in labour utilisation. Among others, Black and Spitz-Oener (2010) and Green (2012) underline drastic differences between males and females in a job task specialisation, relying on the actual task composition of jobs. The latter appears particularly relevant in the context of technological change (Lindley, 2010).

This chapter employs the direct measures of skill use at work (henceforth SUW) intensities to identify gender differences in labour utilisation. Using the survey data from the Program of International Assessment of Adult Competencies (PIAAC) for Estonia, the chapter analyses gender gaps in four information-processing SUW domains (reading, writing, numeracy, and information and communication technologies (henceforth ICT), and in three generic SUW domains (task discretion, influence, and planning). These seven domains identify major skill demands, associated with different tasks. Since the SUW measures rely on the self-reported frequencies of performing specific job tasks, they allow us to study the magnitude of gender disparities.

The major focus of the analysis is understanding which factors drive the gender gap in SUW. Identifying why the differences emerge is crucial for two major reasons. Firstly, gender differences in task specialisation may be due to actual men–women disparities in human capital and other observable characteristics, which implies that SUW gaps do not yield labour underutilisation. However, SUW disparities may be due to factors other than mere human capital differences. Skilled men and women may segregate into different jobs due to gendered entry barriers, job preferences, employer stereotypes, and discrimination. Moreover, even when occupying a formally identical position, men and women may be exogenously entitled by the employer, or may self-select, into different tasks. The latter signals skills underutilisation. Secondly, policy actions should be tailored according to the underlying nature of gender gaps in job tasks. If the reason of the gaps lies in the mere human capital differences, policy interventions should tackle closing the human capital gaps through skills accumulation and improvement via education and training. If the gap emerges due to the gendered job segregation, given a comparable human capital profile, policy actions should facilitate reducing job segregation by promoting equal employment opportunities, acknowledging gender-specific job preferences, and fighting employers' statistical and taste discrimination.

The chapter disentangles three major sets of factors behind the gender SUW gaps: demographic, human capital, and job related. The analysis focuses on Estonia, as a country with the highest gender wage gap in Europe (18.7% in 2018). Despite numerous gender equality actions, the persistent wage disparity signals potential disparity in SUW, which negatively reflects on female earnings. Gender wage and employment disparities remain a topical issue for most post-communist CEE countries. Metcalfe and Afanassieva (2005) discuss that neo-traditionalism and a traditional gender identity has a huge influence on females' employment prospects, career progression, and, eventually, wage.

Employing a multivariate OLS regression approach and Gelbach (2016) decomposition technique, this chapter answers the following research questions: (1) Does the gender gap in SUW remain significant if the demographic, human capital, and employment characteristics of individuals are controlled for? (2) What are the main factors driving the gender gap in SUW? (3) Given demographic, human capital, and employment characteristics fixed, does a more intense SUW yield comparable returns for men and women?

While the first two questions tackle the existing gender disparity in SUW, the third question suggests whether fostering females' SUW has a potential to increase their earnings and narrow the gender wage gap. The results of the chapter document significant gender gaps in writing, reading, numeracy, and influence SUW. Even when controlling for a full set of demographic, human capital, and employment characteristics, women are using these skills systematically less intensively than men. Gelbach decomposition analysis reveals that the main observed reason behind females' lower SUW intensity is employment segregation. Men and women (self-) select into different industries and occupations, even when having a comparable human capital and demographic profile. Further analysis of gender-specific returns to SUW show that women are likely to get higher wage returns to more intensive SUW, suggesting that fostering females' skill application at work has the potential to narrow down the gender wage disparity.

The rest of the chapter is structured as follows. The second section provides a brief literature overview of the gender gap in SUW and the factors behind it, as well as a number of stylised facts about gender disparities in the Estonian labour market. The third section provides an overview of data and empirical method, followed by the presentation of results in the subsequent section. The last section summarises the findings and concludes.

Skills utilisation and gender

Gender disparity in skill use (SUW) and the factors behind it: literature overview

Several recent papers discuss disproportionalities of male and female job task composition as additional factors behind the gender wage gap – a persistent labour market inequality (for a comprehensive overview of gender wage gap dynamics see Blau & Kahn, 2017). Black and Spitz-Oener (2010) is one of the few papers focusing on gender gaps in tasks in Germany and the United States over the recent decades. The study applies the task-based approach introduced by Autor et al. (2003) to directly compare the composition of male and female job tasks. The paper documents that a change in the composition of work over the last decades has been larger for women than for men, hence being one of the factors behind the gender wage gap decline. Olivetti and Petrongolo (2016), as well as Rendall (2017), arrive at a similar conclusion.

However, despite some advancements in female labour market returns and changing composition of female work, the gender wage gap and employment segregation persist (Blau & Kahn, 2017). Occupational and industry segregation underlines gender differences in job tasks and suggests that men and women apply different skills to different extents. The relevant question is: why do gender gaps in SUW persist?

Here, the existing literature offers a variety of explanations. The most canonical refer to gender disparities in human capital. While the gender gap in education level narrowed down and even reversed in the last decades (Becker, Hubbard, &

Murphy, 2010; Goldin, Katz, & Kuziemko, 2006), education specialisation remains strongly gendered (Blau, Ferber, & Winkler, 2014; Ceci & Williams, 2011; Gemici & Wiswall, 2014). Boys are taking systematically more mathematical and technical subjects, while girls attend more philological and social science disciplines and are substantially less likely to enrol in STEM (science, technology, engineering, mathematics) majors. As a result, men and women accumulate different skills and are simply trained for different types of job tasks, where males' tasks are likely more skill intense. Men are much more prone to have better mathematical and technical skills (Ellison & Swanson, 2010; Wang & Degol, 2017), while females are performing better in verbal tests and have stronger reading comprehension, perceptual speed, and associative memory (Goldin et al., 2006).

Non-cognitive competencies and certain psychological attributes may differ drastically across males and females (Becker et al., 2010). Females are found to be more risk averse and have a lower propensity to negotiate or compete; however, they may have an advantage in interpersonal skills (Blau & Kahn, 2017). Furthermore, a number of experimental studies proved females' lower leadership skills and competitiveness (Gneezy, Niederle, & Rustichini, 2003). Mueller and Plug (2006) reported a significant gender gap in extroversion, conscientiousness, neuroticism, agreeableness, and openness to experience. The results suggest that men are considerably more antagonistic (non-agreeable) and open to experience, as well as substantially less neurotic, extravert, and conscientious. The study by Fortin (2008) documents gender differences in self-esteem, external locus of control, importance of money/work, and importance of people/family. The paper reports women's having lower self-esteem, higher external locus of control, and placing a major priority on people/family rather than money/work. These dimensions are tightly linked to gender gaps in job preferences (Gemici & Wiswall, 2014), enforcing gender segregation into occupations.

Gender disparity in work experience is viewed as another dimension of the gender human capital gap. Work experience closely relates to skills and qualifications acquired through labour market participation. Moreover, work experience by itself transmits information about certain job- or industry-specific skills, as well as task-specific human capital (Gibbons & Waldman, 2004).

Substantial gender disparities in various human capital domains unambiguously reflect on males' and females' job task composition and the extent of various SUW. These differences are unbiased, since the underlying skills and abilities differ across men and women. However, the SUW gap may emerge due to factors other than human capital profile. The major factor is gender occupational and industry segregation, with males dominating in managerial and highly professional positions (Blau & Kahn, 2017). Discrimination is another well-recognised barrier, particularly in male-dominated jobs and industries (Goldin, 2014; Reuben, Sapienza, & Zingales, 2014). Stereotypes and gender identity norms are another driver of gendered career choices and self-selection into specific jobs (Correll, 2001). Job preferences may also drive gendered self-selection into employment. Among others, Wiswall and Zafar (2018) discuss that women tend to value job stability and work flexibility, while men have stronger preferences for jobs with earning growth prospects. Unlike the human capital differences, these factors may be uncorrelated with skills and abilities. As a result, female skills may be used to only a partial extent.

Gender gaps in the Estonian labour market: stylised facts

Despite a number of positive developments, including education and job access improvements, increasing labour market commitment of women, rising social awareness, and growing gender equality in society, a number of gender imbalances persist in the European labour market (Blau & Kahn, 2017). Estonia is a special case in this context. Despite experiencing rapid economic growth, adopting the state-of-the-art technological advances, and promoting gender equality and inclusion, Estonia reveals the highest gender pay disparity in Europe. The unadjusted gender wage gap was equal to 18.7% in 2018, as compared to the European average of 16% in 2017 (Eurostat gender wage gap in EU statistics), while the employment rate of women in Estonia ranks among the highest in Europe (71.4%, compared to the EU average of 63.4%; Eurostat gender statistics).

Figure 7.1 depicts the dynamics of the gender gap in wage and female employment rates in Estonia, as compared to EU-15 and CEE countries. Two stark

Figure 7.1 Labour market dynamics

Source: Own elaboration based on Eurostat and Estonia statistics.

observations arise. Firstly, the gender gap in Estonia remains significantly higher compared to EU-15 and CEE averages, despite a generally declining trend. This pattern had already been documented in 2002 and remained consistent up until 2017, albeit a gradual convergence to the EU-15 average. Secondly, the female employment rate in Estonia is considerably higher, compared to both the EU-15 and CEE average. This signals women's stronger labour market commitment, coupled with particularly good childcare services and flexible employment contracts, thus allowing women to return to work soon after childbirth and to work a preferred number of hours.

Multiple studies tackle the gender pay disparity in Estonia, reporting persistent disparity unexplained by the broad range of individual and employment controls (Anspal, 2015; Meriküll & Mõtsmees, 2017; Rõõm & Kallaste, 2004; Tverdostup & Paas, 2017; among others). A dramatic gender wage gap in Estonia appears even more surprising in light of numerous gender equality initiatives (Anspal, Kraut, & Rõõm, 2010).

The policy actions aim at different aspects of the society and the labour market. Firstly, policy programmes aim at reducing gender inequality on a societal level, including: (i) increasing societal awareness of principles of equal opportunities and equal pay, and their provision in law; (ii) improving legal awareness among managers in the private sector; (iii) gender mainstreaming. Secondly, policy actions facilitate reconciliation of work and family life to reduce the gender wage gap, including: (i) sharing parental leave; (ii) flexible parental leave; (iii) part-time work upon return from parental leave; and (iv) flexible and need-based childcare. Thirdly, various policy actions target organisational practices aiming to reduce the gender imbalance: (i) collecting and analysing the data accounting for a gender aspect; (ii) increasing employees' awareness regarding the gender wage gap; (iii) overcoming gender-specific job design, associated with females' lower wages; (iv) promoting equal job access and transparency of hiring procedures (Anspal et al., 2010). Fourthly, policy actions facilitate gender wage convergence through reduced occupation and education segregation. The governmental Action Plan for the reduction of the gender pay gap was approved in 2012, and gender wage gap dynamics has been under precise policy attention ever since. Nonetheless, the recent statistics suggest the gender wage gap is yet far from closing (see Figure 7.1).

Data and methods

Data

The empirical analysis relies on the Programme of International Assessment of Adult Competencies (PIAAC) database for Estonia, collected as a part of the Survey of Adult Skills (OECD, 2013a). The PIAAC survey was conducted in 2011/2012 and collected information on 5307 currently employed respondents in Estonia. The database has many advantages. Firstly, it provides unique information on cognitive skills of adults in three domains: literacy, numeracy, and problem solving in a technology-rich environment. Secondly, it includes self-reported measures of SUW. The latter are based on a set of specific questions covering a wide range of job activities. Thirdly, the PIAAC survey includes detailed demographic and employment characteristics of the respondents.

Table 7.1 provides a list of all the variables used in the analysis. The chapter focuses on gender disparities in seven SUW domains, namely: writing, reading, numeracy, ICT, task discretion, planning, and influence. The first four measures refer to the information-processing abilities, while the latter three refer to generic abilities, which reflects the respondents' autonomy over key aspects of their work (OECD, 2013b, p. 43). While the SUW measures primarily assess the task composition of jobs, they also capture motivational components to a certain extent. Satisfied and motivated employees are likely to have a higher SUW, compared to demotivated workers performing identical job tasks. Thus, it appears important to measure both detailed job segregation and intrinsic factors related to the current job.

The analysis relies on the ready-made PIAAC SUW indices, derived by applying the Item Response Theory. Each of the SUW domains relies on a set of background questions asking how frequently a respondent performs certain activity at work. These individual items are then integrated into a one-dimensional continuous index, with a higher value corresponding to more intensive SUW (for more details see OECD, 2013b, pp. 43–44).

The analysis of gender gaps in SUW will incorporate three groups of factors – demographic, human capital, and employment controls. Demographic characteristics include gender, age, immigrant status, test language, cohabitation status, and the presence of progeny. Human capital profile includes a number of detailed characteristics. Formal education degree and total years of work experience are the most frequently used human capital measures (see Becker et al., 2010; Blau & Kahn, 2006; Gayle & Golan, 2012; Goldin et al., 2006; Hanushek, Schwerdt, Wiederhold, & Woessmann, 2015; Niederle & Vesterlund, 2010; among others), because they are easy to measure, unlike cognitive and non-cognitive abilities. The PIAAC survey is the only data source that provides consistent test-based measures of cognitive skills of the adult population for all European countries. This chapter exploits this advantage and controls for the gender difference in actual cognitive abilities (in literacy, numeracy, and problem solving in a technology-rich environment), as these may differ dramatically across men and women with an identical education level and work experience (Christl & Köppl-Turyna, 2017; Nollenberger, Rodriguez-Planas, & Sevilla, 2016; Tach & Farkas, 2006).

Employment profile includes an extensive list of controls related to the occupied position. Unfortunately, occupation and industry are both defined in broad categories (one-digit ISCO classification for occupation and one-letter ISCED Rev.4 industry). Therefore, controlling for these leaves a lot of within-category variation when it comes to a specific job. Thus, additional controlling for the wage rate provides a more precise job identifier within occupation than an industry

Table 7.1 Definitions and empirical measures of the main variables

	Variable	*Definition*
Demographic	*Gender*	0 – Male, 1 – Female
	Age	The youngest respondent is aged 15, the oldest 65 years.
	Immigrant status	0 – Respondent was born in a country of survey, 1 – Respondent is a first-generation immigrant.
	Estonian test language	0 – Test language Russian, 1 – Test language Estonian
	Cohabiting	Living with a spouse or a partner: 0 – No, 1 – Yes
	Children	Have children: 0 – No, 1 – Yes
Human capital	*Formal education degree*	Education groups are defined according to International Standard Classification of Education (ISCED) 2011 as follows: 1 – low – early childhood education, primary and lower secondary education; 2 – medium – upper secondary and postsecondary non-tertiary education; 3 – high – short-cycle tertiary education, bachelor or equivalent level, master or equivalent level, doctoral or equivalent level
	Total work experience	Total years of employment
	Literacy skill	Test-based cognitive skill measure, ranging from 0 to 500 points. Reported as a set of 10 plausible values and defined as 'understanding, evaluating, using, and engaging with written text to participate in society, to achieve one's goals, and to develop one's knowledge and potential' (OECD, 2013a, p. Foreword-3).
	Numeracy skill	Test-based cognitive skill measure, ranging from 0 to 500 points. Reported as a set of 10 plausible values and defined as 'the ability to access, use, interpret, and communicate mathematical information and ideas, in order to engage in and manage the mathematical demands of a range of situations in adult life' (OECD, 2013a, p. Foreword-3).
	Problem solving in technology-rich environment	Test-based cognitive skill measure, ranging from 0 to 500 points. Reported as a set of 10 plausible values and defined as 'the abilities to solve problems for personal, work and civic purposes by setting up appropriate goals and plans, and accessing and making use of information through computers and computer networks' (OECD, 2013a, p. Foreword-4).
Employment	*Occupation*	9 categories, based on the International Standard Classification of Occupations as of year 2008 (ISCO-08), 1-digit level: 1. Managers 2. Professional 3. Technicians and associate professionals 4. Clerical support workers 5. Service and sales workers 6. Skilled agricultural, forestry, and fishery workers 7. Craft and related trades workers 8. Plant and machine operators and assemblers 9. Elementary occupations

(*Continued*)

Table 7.1 Continued

	Variable	*Definition*
Employment	*Industry*	19 categories, based on The International Standard Industrial Classification of All Economic Activities (ISCED Rev.4)
	Wage	Hourly wage, PPP adjusted
	Work hours	Number of work hours per week
	Contract type	Types of contract: 1 – An indefinite contract, 2 – A fixed-term contract, 3 – A temporary employment agency contract, 4 – An apprenticeship or other training scheme, 5 – No contract, 6 – Other
	Work satisfaction	The variable identifies whether the respondent is satisfied with his/her current job. Categorical variable: 1 – Extremely satisfied, 2 – Satisfied, 3 – Neither satisfied nor dissatisfied, 4 – Dissatisfied, 5 – Extremely dissatisfied
	Work challenge	The variable asks if the respondent feels challenged enough at his/her current job. Binary variable: 0 – Challenged enough, 1 – Not challenged enough
	Learning at work	The index of learning at work, which includes three component activities: learning by doing, learning from co-workers, keeping up to date. The variable is a ready-made, PIAAC-derived measure.
	Readiness to learn at work	Index of readiness to learn at work, which includes components of on-going job training and participation in learning activities. The variable is a ready-made, PIAAC-derived measure.
Skills use at work (SUW)	*Information-processing SUW (all indices range from 0 to 5, with 0 corresponding to minimal skill use and 5 to maximal skill use):*	
	(i) Writing	Index measure, defined as 'Reading documents (directions, instructions, letters, memos, e-mails, articles, books, manuals, bills, invoices, diagrams, maps)' (OECD, 2013b, p. 43).
	(ii) Reading	Index measure, defined as 'Writing documents (letters, memos, e-mails, articles, reports, forms)' (OECD, 2013b, p. 43).
	(iii) Numeracy	Index measure, defined as 'Calculating prices, costs or budgets; use of fractions, decimals or percentages; use of calculators; preparing graphs or tables; algebra or formulas; use of advanced math or statistics (calculus, trigonometry, regressions)' (OECD, 2013b, p. 43).
	(iv) ICT	Index measure, defined as 'Using e-mail, Internet, spreadsheets, word processors, programming languages; conducting transactions online; participating in online discussions (conferences, chats)' (OECD, 2013b, p. 43).
	Generic SUW (all indices range from 0 to 5, with 0 corresponding to minimal skill use and 5 to maximal skill use):	
	(v) Task discretion	Index measure, defined as 'Choosing or changing sequence of job tasks, the speed of work, working hours; choosing how to do the job' (OECD, 2013b, p. 43).
	(vi) Influence	Index measure, defined as 'Instructing, teaching or training people; making speeches or presentations; selling products or services; advising people; planning others' activities; persuading or influencing others; negotiating' (OECD, 2013b, p. 43).
	(vii) Planning	Index measure, defined as 'Planning own activities; planning activities of others; organizing own time' (OECD, 2013b, p. 43).

Source: Own elaboration.

group. Moreover, including the number of work hours and contract directly measures employment type, which eventually reflects on the extent of SUW. Along with the classical job-related measures, the analysis includes job-attitude variables, which capture readiness to learn at work, on-going learning, job satisfaction, and job challenge sufficiency. These factors are crucial determinants of job motivation and fulfilment, which are important determinants of SUW intensity. More satisfied and motivated employees are more likely to invest a higher effort in their job, compared to otherwise similar but unsatisfied and demotivated workers.

Despite the analysis reliance on the extensive set of controls, a few limitations should be acknowledged. Firstly, because of a cross-sectional structure of the data, only SUW and employment outcomes of currently employed respondents are considered in the analysis. Secondly, the SUW measures are self-reported, which leaves space for arbitrary responses. However, the individual deviations in SUW as a dependent variable do not bias the estimates of major effects.[1] Thirdly, non-cognitive abilities, job preferences, as well as employer discrimination, cannot be assessed with the data in hand. These factors will remain uncontrolled in the analysis and should be recognised when interpreting the results.

Empirical strategy

Following the research questions, the chapter conducts a threefold empirical analysis. Firstly, the gender gaps in seven SUW domains (presented at the bottom of Table 7.1) are analysed using a multivariate OLS regression approach. The following two models are estimated, with the first one corresponding to a baseline model and the second one to a full specification:

$$In\,SUW_{ji} = \alpha + \beta \cdot Female_i + \varepsilon_j, \tag{7.1}$$
$$In\,SUW_{ji} = \alpha + \beta \cdot Female_i + \boldsymbol{D}_i' \cdot \gamma + \boldsymbol{HC}_i' \cdot \theta + \boldsymbol{EC}_i' \cdot \mu + \varepsilon_i, \tag{7.2}$$

where SUW_{ji} corresponds to the SUW index, in particular domain $j \in \{1, \ldots, 7\}$ of respondent i, resulting in seven models, each estimating SUW gap in one of the seven domains; $Female_i$ is a female indicator, and coefficient β stands for the unexplained gender gap in SUW; $\boldsymbol{D}$ is a vector of demographic covariates, and $\boldsymbol{\gamma}$ is a vector of respective coefficients; $\boldsymbol{HC}$ is a vector of human capital controls, and $\boldsymbol{\theta}$ stands for a vector of respective coefficients; $\boldsymbol{EC}$ represents a vector of employment controls and $\boldsymbol{\mu}$ a vector of respective coefficients; ε_I is an error term. The estimation procedure accounts for the population weight.

The regression of a form (7.1) is estimated first, providing evidence of unadjusted or raw gaps in SUW. Then adjusted, or unexplained gaps are assessed by estimating the model of specification (7.2). It allows us to isolate the variation in the SUW intensity which originates from (i) different demographic profiles of men and women in the sample; (ii) different educational attainments, work experience, cognitive abilities; (iii) different job profiles, including occupation, industry, wage, hours worked, and contract type; and (iv) different motivation and job satisfaction. Once controlling for all these factors, the unexplained gender gaps signal potential unobserved heterogeneity in intrinsic factors and possible discrimination, related to the types of tasks and extent of responsibilities men and women are entitled too, given all aforementioned characteristics fixed. Equation (7.1) is estimated across all ISCO occupation groups.

However, the OLS estimation is not a sound tool for eliciting the contributions of individual regressors. Order of adding covariates into the model affects the individual coefficient estimates in OLS regression, causing path-dependent inferences. Gelbach (2016) developed a decomposition methodology allowing us to overcome a bias resulting from the sequence of adding controls. The estimation procedure relies on how the omitted variables bias the formula and derives individual effects conditional on all covariates (full specification), unlike the classical decomposition methodologies like Oaxaca-Blinder (Cardoso, Guimarães, & Portugal, 2016; Grove, Hussey, & Jetter, 2011; see also Gelbach, 2016 for more details).

Gelbach estimation procedure allows us to isolate an unbiased effect of individual variables on the outcome of interest through a two-stage procedure. On the first stage, an auxiliary model is estimated, which includes a baseline variable (set of variables), in our case, a female dummy. On the second stage, a full specification regression is estimated. The overall contribution of controls is decomposed into the conditional contributions of individual variables, allowing us to get their order-invariance absolute contribution to explaining a disparity in the outcome variable (in our context, the gender gap in SUW).

Therefore, multivariate OLS regression is a valid tool to answer the first research question, namely, examine raw and unexplained gender gaps in SUW. Gelbach decomposition tackles the second question and estimates path-independent contributions of individual factors in order to explain gender disparities in SUW.

To address the third research question and explore the gender-specific wage returns to different SUW domains, the following regression is estimated separately for males and females:

$$\text{In } W_i = \alpha + \beta \cdot \text{In } SUW_{ij} + \boldsymbol{D}_i' \cdot \gamma + \boldsymbol{HC}_i' \cdot \theta + \boldsymbol{EC}_i' \cdot \mu + \varepsilon_i, \tag{7.3}$$

where W_i stands for an hourly wage of respondent i and coefficient β captures gender-specific wage returns to more intense SUW. The remaining parameters are defined as in equation (7.2). Given the high correlation between different SUW domains, seven separate regressions are estimated for women and seven for men, each controlling for one SUW. As with the multivariate OLS estimation, population weights are included in the analysis.

One technical feature of the PIAAC data is measurement of literacy, numeracy, and problem-solving abilities, which are included in the analysis as controls for human capital. As mentioned in Table 7.1, each cognitive skill is reported as a set of 10 plausible values and is accompanied by a set of 80 replication weights to correctly estimate standard errors.[2] Descriptive analysis accounts for a full set of plausible values and applies the jackknife replication method to measure average skills of men and women (OECD, 2013a). However, regression and Gelbach decomposition estimations incorporate only first plausible value due to computational difficulties.[3] A similar approach was used by Anspal (2015), Hanushek et al. (2015), and Smith and Fernandez (2017), because it occurs that the estimation results based on the first value are not significantly different from the results based on the full set of plausible values.

Empirical analysis

Descriptive profile

Table 7.2 presents the average characteristics of the Estonia PIAAC sample by gender. The demographic profile is somewhat different across men and women, with women being on average older (41 vs. 39 years), more likely to have children (77.3% vs. 70.3%), and less likely to cohabit (74.4% vs. 81.6%). The human capital profile differs a lot across men and women. Men possess on average higher numeracy and problem-solving skills (respectively 7 and 4 points higher); however, they hold less formal education than women (only 22.4% of men have higher education, as compared to 31.4% of women). Notably, total work experience is comparable across the genders.

The employment profile also reveals a number of differences by gender. Women are more likely to occupy higher positions (skilled and semi-skilled white-collar occupations), while men substantially outnumber women in semi-skilled blue-collar positions. Nonetheless, females work considerably fewer hours per week (38 vs. 41) and earn substantially lower hourly wages (8.3 EUR vs. 11.81 EUR). Interestingly, above 80% of respondents reported insufficient challenge at work, signalling potential over-qualification. However, considerably fewer females reported insufficient challenge (80.1% among females vs. 85.4% among males).

Moving to the SUW intensity, Table 7.2 reveals a number of important patterns. Firstly, the only skill domain having, on average, an insignificant gender gap is the influence SUW. Writing and reading at work reveal a female-favouring gender gap, while numeracy, ICT, task discretion, and planning SUW are applied by men considerably more often. However, the average gaps in SUW do not account for underlying differences of male and female demographic, human capital, and employment profiles. Therefore, the descriptive evidence on SUW gaps tells little about the true disparities.

Gender gaps in skill use: regression and decomposition analysis

Regression analysis

Table 7.3 presents the regression estimates of the gender gaps in seven SUW domains. Model I incorporates only a female control, following equation (7.1); thus, it represents an unadjusted gender gap. Model II includes a full set of demographic, human capital, and employment-related controls, following equation (7.2). Thus, model II represents unexplained gender SUW disparities.[4]

Table 7.2 Summary statistics by gender

Variable	*Total sample*	*Female*	*Male*	*Gender difference*
Demographics				
Age, years	40 (.168)	41 (.230)	39 (.245)	***
Immigrant, %	11.8 (.004)	12.5 (.006)	11.1 (.006)	
Cohabiting, %	77.9 (.006)	74.4 (.008)	81.6 (.008)	***
Have child(ren), %	73.9 (.006)	77.3 (.007)	70.3 (.009)	***
Human capital				
Literacy, points	279 (.779)	280 (.868)	279 (1.281)	
Numeracy, points	278 (.662)	275 (.891)	282 (1.036)	***
Problem solving, points,	277 (1.192)	275 (1.473)	279 (1.540)	**
Low education, %	49.8 (.006)	40.8 (.009)	59.1 (.010)	***
Medium education, %	23.5 (.005)	27.8 (.008)	18.5 (.008)	***
High education, %	27.0 (.006)	31.4 (.008)	22.4 (.008)	***
Total work experience, years	19 (.169)	19 (.233)	19 (.245)	
SUW (indices)				
(1) Information processing skills				
Writing skills	1.731 (.013)	1.749 (.017)	1.699 (.020)	**
Reading skills	2.040 (.014)	2.059 (.019)	2.021 (.021)	**
Numeracy skills	2.012 (.015)	1.952 (.019)	2.073 (.023)	***
ICT skills	2.157 (.019)	2.113 (.024)	2.211 (.031)	**
(2) Other generic skills				
Task discretion skills	1.996 (.013)	1.909 (.016)	2.088 (.020)	***
Influencing skills	2.014 (.015)	2.016 (.021)	1.995 (.022)	
Planning skills	2.230 (.014)	2.187 (.018)	2.276 (.021)	***
Employment				
Skilled occupation[1], %	46.1 (.006)	51.2 (.009)	40.7 (.010)	***
Semi-skilled white-collar[2], %	18.3 (.005)	27.9 (.008)	8.1 (.005)	***
Semi-skilled blue-collar[3], %	27.7 (.006)	11.4 (.006)	45.1 (.010)	***
Elementary occupation[4], %	7.7 (.003)	9.3 (.005)	6.1 (.004)	***
Work hours	40 (.155)	38 (.204)	41 (.232)	***
Average hourly wage, EUR	9.87 (.146)	8.30 (.185)	11.81 (.225)	***
Satisfied with work, %	79.5 (.005)	80.1 (.007)	78.8 (.008)	
Not challenged enough, %	82.8 (.005)	80.2 (.007)	85.4 (.007)	***
Learning at work, index	1.991 (.014)	1.992 (.018)	1.989 (.021)	
Ready to learn at work, %	1.890 (.012)	1.864 (.016)	1.917 (.018)	**
N	5 307	2 880	2 427	

Source: Own elaboration based on the PIAAC data for Estonia.

Notes: All mean and standard error estimates account for the population weight. Cognitive skills are measured using all 10 plausible values and 80 replication weights. Mean difference is estimated using Somers' D significance test. Asterisks denote significance level: * $p< 0.10$, ** $p < 0.05$, *** $p < 0.01$

1 The category includes ISCO codes 1, 2 and 3 (see Table 7.1)
2 The category includes ISCO codes 4 and 5 (see Table 7.1)
3 The category includes ISCO codes 6, 7 and 8 (see Table 7.1)
4 The category includes ISCO code 9 (see Table 7.1)

There are several things to note. The most distinct evidence is a substantial variation in the female coefficient across specifications. In model I, females have a higher use of reading SUW (4.7%, $p < 0.05$), while males report a more intense numeracy (5.4%, $p < 0.05$), task discretion (5.7%, $p < 0.01$), and planning (3.5%, $p < 0.05$) SUW. Further inclusion of all controls in model II changes the coefficients dramatically. Inclusion of the complete set of controls reverses gender gaps in writing, reading, and influence from female- to male-favouring. However, inclusion of all controls turns task discretion and planning SUW gaps from male-favouring to insignificant. This implies that given demographic, human capital, and employment characteristics fixed, women use writing (6.5%, $p < 0.05$), reading (7.3%, $p < 0.01$), and influence (8.0%, $p < 0.01$) abilities less intensively than men, while the gender gap in task discretion and planning abilities use appears insignificant. Numeracy SUW gap (5.5%, $p < 0.1$) and insignificant ICT SUW gap remain robust to inclusion of controls.[5]

The unexplained SUW gap in writing, reading, numeracy, and influence, even when controlling for a full set of variables, signals that there are factors beyond the controlled ones which drive the gender disparity in SUW. These will be discussed later in this section.

Decomposition analysis

The empirical results provided in Table 7.3 answered the first research question, documenting that gender SUW gaps persist in several domains. To address the

Table 7.3 Gender gaps in SUW – total sample

Model	*Writing*	*Reading*	*Numeracy*	*ICT*	*Task discretion*	*Influence*	*Planning*
I	0.0161	0.0472**	–0.0541**	–0.0214	–0.057***	0.005	–0.0347**
	(0.0328)	(0.0227)	(0.028)	(0.0268)	(0.0208)	(0.0294)	(0.0188)
N	*2145*	*2419*	*2201*	*1821*	*2525*	*2394*	*2463*
II	–0.0654**	–0.0732***	–0.0553*	–0.0164	–0.0019	–0.0801***	–0.0111
	(0.0314)	(0.0205)	(0.0325)	(0.0247)	(0.0236)	(0.0308)	(0.0218)
N	*2 145*	*2 419*	*2 201*	*1 821*	*2 525*	*2 394*	*2 463*

Source: Own elaboration based on the PIAAC data for Estonia.

Notes: Ordinary least square regression. Dependent variable is log of SUW index. Only female coefficients are reported – β parameters in equations (7.1) and (7.2). Model specifications are as follows: I controls for female dummy; II adds age, age squared, immigration status, language of the test, cohabiting status, children, education level, years of work experience, literacy, numeracy, problem-solving skills, occupation, industry, hourly wage, work hours per week, type of the contract, learning at work, readiness to learn at work, job satisfaction, and sufficient job challenge. Both models incorporate population weight. Standard errors in parentheses. Complete model estimates are available upon request. Asterisks denote significance level: * $p < 0.10$, ** $p < 0.05$, *** $p < 0.01$

second question and to elicit unbiased contributions of different demographic, human capital, and employment factors on the gender gap in SUW, Gelbach decomposition analysis was performed. Table 7.5 presents Gelbach decomposition results. The base estimation model controls for the female dummy only, following equation (7.1), while the full specification corresponds to equation (7.2). Individual covariates from equation (7.2) are grouped into nine categories, with some categories incorporating only one variable (education, work experience, occupation, industry, wage) and some categories merging several related variables (demographic characteristics, cognitive skills, work hours and contract type, intrinsic factors). Table 7.4 reports the contribution of each category to the gender gap in specific SUW domain, where negative contributions imply a reduction and positive contributions increase of the raw gaps, reported in model I of Table 7.3.

Controlling for all factors, the covariates unrelated to employment reveal a very weak or no explanatory power. The total work experience and cognitive skills have no significant association with the gender gap in any SUW domain. Formal education reveals only weak significant association with ICT SUW (narrowing the gap by 0.0053 points, $p < 0.1$), and demographic characteristics only associate with the gender gap in reading (widening the gap by 0.0096 points, $p < 0.1$) and ICT (narrowing the gap by 0.0123 points, $p < 0.05$). This result gives an interesting insight into the nature of the gender gaps in SUW. Insignificant associations suggest that, given fixed employment characteristics, more total experience, a higher education level, or a better cognitive skills profile does not yield more intense SUW. The only domain in which both demographic profile and education somewhat narrow the gender gap is an ICT SUW. This can relate to (i) on average, the younger age of males in our sample (see Table 7.2); (ii) specific field of education, since, based on the earlier evidence, males are likely to hold degrees in STEM disciplines more often.

Employment-related factors have the highest explanatory power, suggesting that gender segregation into employment is a major factor explaining gender disparity in SUW. Gelbach decomposition outlines two important findings. Firstly, occupation variables significantly associate with all SUW domains and contribute to widening the gender gaps. The absolute contributions vary from 0.1099 points ($p < 0.01$) for the influence SUW to 0.0221 points ($p < 0.1$) for the task discretion SUW. Secondly, an hourly wage, number of work hours, type of employment contract, and industry also significantly associate with the gender gap in all SUW domains; however, they contribute to narrowing the gender disparity (except the industry variable in the case of writing and reading SUW).

These two stark observations can be explained by the fact that one-digit ISCO level is used to define occupation. The occupation categories are defined very broadly, and they leave a lot of heterogeneity within each ISCO group. As a result, a man and a woman may fall in the same ISCO one-digit group but carry out very different obligations. The results suggest that jobs occupied by males are likely to be more skill intense compared to jobs occupied by women, albeit both male' and female positions belong to the same ISCO category. Controlling for an industry,

Table 7.4 Gelbach decomposition of gender gaps in SUW

Groups of factors	*Writing*	*Reading*	*Numeracy*	*ICT*	*Task discretion*	*Influence*	*Planning*
1. Demographic factors	0.0013	0.0096*	–0.0038	–0.0123**	–0.0086	–0.0094	–0.0046
	(0.008)	(0.006)	(0.007)	(0.006)	(0.006)	(0.007)	(0.006)
2. Education	0.0008	–0.0022	0.0003	–0.0053*	–0.0019	0.0053	0.0005
	(0.004)	(0.003)	(0.004)	(0.003)	(0.003)	(0.004)	(0.003)
3. Work experience	–0.0010	–0.0010	0.0015	0.0014	–0.0012	0.0026	0.0026
	(0.003)	(0.002)	(0.004)	(0.005)	(0.003)	(0.003)	(0.002)
4. Cognitive skills	0.0131	–0.0084	–0.0147	–0.0017	0.0016	0.0036	–0.0025
	(0.010)	(0.006)	(0.015)	(0.011)	(0.006)	(0.008)	(0.005)
5. Occupation	0.0937***	0.0951***	0.1008***	0.0797***	0.0221*	0.1099***	0.0289***
	(0.019)	(0.013)	(0.017)	(0.014)	(0.012)	(0.017)	(0.011)
6. Industry	0.0283*	0.0337***	–0.0683***	–0.0309***	–0.0147	0.0444***	0.0139
	(0.015)	(0.010)	(0.016)	(0.010)	(0.011)	(0.015)	(0.010)
7. Wage	–0.0296**	–0.0374***	–0.0111	–0.0336***	–0.0313***	–0.0576***	–0.0327***
	(0.013)	(0.008)	(0.011)	(0.010)	(0.009)	(0.012)	(0.008)
8. Work hours, contract type	–0.0274***	–0.0066*	–0.0143***	–0.0072*	0.0018	–0.0209***	–0.0195***
	(0.006)	(0.004)	(0.005)	(0.004)	(0.004)	(0.006)	(0.004)
9. Intrinsic factors	–0.0017	–0.0012	–0.0023	–0.0102*	–0.0144***	–0.0134*	–0.0048
	(0.006)	(0.005)	(0.005)	(0.006)	(0.005)	(0.008)	(0.004)
Total contribution	0.0703**	0.1169***	–0.0033	–0.0189	–0.0601***	0.0640**	–0.0282*
	(0.028)	(0.021)	(0.024)	(0.023)	(0.018)	(0.026)	(0.016)
N	2 145	2 419	2 201	1 821	2 525	2 394	2 463

Source: Own elaboration based on the PIAAC data for Estonia.

Notes: Gelbach decomposition results. Dependent variable is log of the SUW index. The variables are grouped as follows: (1) age, age squared, immigration status, language of the test, cohabiting status, and children; (2) own highest education level; (3) total years of work experience; (4) literacy, numeracy and problem solving test scores; (5) ISCO 1 digit occupation dummies; (6) ISIC Rev. 4 level 1 industry dummies; (7) hourly wage PPP adjusted; (8) work hours per week, type of the employment contract; (9) on-the-job learning and readiness to learn, job satisfaction, and sufficient challenge. Standard errors in parentheses. Asterisks denote significance level: * $p < 0.10$, ** $p < 0.05$, *** $p < 0.01$.

an hourly wage, number of hours worked per week, and a type of employment contract narrows down the job definition and captures more characteristics of the actual position. While two jobs can fall in the same ISCO category, they may have a different wage level; employees may have a different number of working hours and a different type of employment contract, which tells a lot about the actual job tasks. Therefore, these additional employment characteristics help pin down a more detailed job profile, reducing occupation heterogeneity within each ISCO category.

Naturally, working longer hours and holding a permanent, full-time contract are associated with more intense SUW, as an employee spends more time at the workplace. Moreover, a higher wage can, firstly, be associated with a more complex and skill-demanding position, and, secondly, by itself serve as a motivation to use skills more intensively at work. These speculations point towards a more intensive SUW by employees with full-time, permanent contracts, earning higher wages. Given the descriptive evidence in Table 7.2, males are more likely to be such employees. Therefore, controlling for these additional employment characteristics narrow the SUW disparities considerably.

Gender-specific returns to skill use

The results so far have revealed that gender employment segregation is the major driver of the gender gaps in SUW. However, does a gender-equal use of skills actually yield gender equal-labour market returns? The results from the Table 7.5 reveal gender-specific wage returns to different SUW domains, following equation (7.3) from Section 7.2.

The estimates in Table 7.5 control for a full set of demographic, human capital, and employment controls. The results signal that there exists a positive association between higher SUW and wage rate, given all other fixed characteristics.

Table 7.5 Gender-specific returns to SUW

Sample:	*Writing*	*Reading*	*Numeracy*	*ICT*	*Task discretion*	*Influence*	*Planning*
(a) Women	0.03	0.10***	0.01	0.11***	0.03	0.10***	0.08***
	(0.02)	(0.03)	(0.02)	(0.03)	(0.02)	(0.02)	(0.03)
N	*1 284*	*1 419*	*1 282*	*1 143*	*1 493*	*1 408*	*1 452*
(b) Men	0.05*	0.12***	0.04	0.04	0.11***	0.04	0.02
	(0.03)	(0.04)	(0.03)	(0.05)	(0.04)	(0.03)	(0.04)
N	*859*	*998*	*917*	*676*	*1 030*	*984*	*1 009*

Source: Own elaboration based on the PIAAC data for Estonia.

Notes: Ordinary least square regression. Dependent variable is log hourly wage. Only SUW coefficients are reported. The estimates follow equation (7.3). Regressions presented in (a) are estimated only for females, while regressions from panel (2) only for males. All models incorporate population weight. Complete model estimates are available upon request. Standard errors in parentheses. $* \ p < 0.10$, $** \ p < 0.05$, $*** \ p < 0.01$.

Moreover, women, on average, have a higher benefit from a more intense SUW relative to men.

Specifically, 1% higher ICT SUW among women is associated with 0.11% ($p < 0.01$) higher hourly wage; 1% increase in reading and influence SUW are both associated with 0.1% ($p < 0.01$) hourly wage raise; planning SUW yield 0.08% ($p < 0.01$) hourly wage premium in response to a 1% SUW rise. For men, only reading and task discretion SUW are strongly associated with a wage increase (a 1% increase in respective SUW corresponds to a 0.12% and 0.11% wage rise ($p < 0.01$), while writing SUW exhibits a statistically and economically weak association (0.05%, $p < 0.1$). This gives suggestive evidence that increasing SUW has a potential to raise females' wages and contribute to narrowing the gender wage gap in Estonia.

Conclusion

The chapter analyses the gender gap in skills utilisation, measured by on-the-job skill use (SUW). The analysis focuses on Estonia and addresses three major research questions.

Firstly, the chapter explores raw and unexplained gender gaps in use of four information-processing SUW and three generic SUW. The analysis suggests that, even when controlling for a full set of demographic, human capital, and employment characteristics, women are using writing, reading, numeracy, and influence SUW systematically less than otherwise comparable men do. An additional heterogeneity analysis across ISCO groups (not presented in the chapter; available upon request) reveals no gender gaps in SUW among managers, clerical support workers, and craft and related trades workers. In other occupations, the information-processing gender SUW gaps are more prevalent for skilled and semi-skilled white-collar occupations, while generic SUW gaps are for semi-skilled blue-collar and elementary occupations.

Secondly, the chapter explores the major drivers of the observed gender gaps in cognitive SUW. The results of a Gelbach decomposition reveal that demographic and human capital characteristics have limited power in explaining gender gaps in on-the-job SUW, once the detailed employment characteristics are controlled for. Even when having the same education, skills, and experience profile as men, women tend to use their abilities less. The major reason for females' lower SUW intensity lies in employment segregation. Therefore, increasing females' net skills or training or facilitating their labour market commitment per se has little potential to close gender gaps in SUW.

Occupation and industry segregation, selection into employment contracts, work time, and wage differences appear as major factors explaining gender gaps in all SUW domains. This suggests that employment segregation not only reflects on the gender wage disparity (Blau & Kahn, 2017) but also results in labour underutilisation and underuse of skills. Employment segregation appeared to be particularly relevant in the context of CEE counties (Fodor & Glass, 2018). The extent of labour market segregation and selection into private and public sectors are particularly important in shaping females' labour market opportunities as compared to males'. Persistent employment segregation in CEE countries is largely a result of path dependence and persistence of gendered norms, which largely affect hiring processes and job opportunities of females (Metcalfe & Afanassieva, 2005).

Thirdly, the analysis reveals a wage premium for more intense SUW to be somewhat higher among women than among men. Namely, the results suggest, however not unequivocally, that women get premium to more SUW domains than men. It may indicate that fostering females' higher SUW will not only increase labour utilisation but has a potential to decrease the gender pay gap. The latter appears particularly relevant for Estonia as a country with Europe's highest gender pay gap.

All things considered, the results indicate that females' skills are underused in the Estonian labour market. Given individual and societal losses associated with skill underutilisation, policy actions should foster a gender SUW gaps convergence. However, the latter should be shaped according to the underlying reason of the disparity. The research suggests that the gaps, in the case of Estonia, are likely to be driven by employment segregation, and therefore policy interventions should aim at reducing the gender misbalance in industries and occupations. However, this requires the identification of the underlying reason for employment segregation.

Whether employment selection arises from the internal, individual-level factors or external forces imposed by employers or society is an open question, and it cannot be addressed with the data in hand.

The first group of factors – internalised factors – incorporates preferences, non-cognitive skills, and motivation. These are unobserved in the data and may systematically differ across men and women. As discussed, women are more likely to have a stronger preference for family and the household as opposed to work. This may eventually result in a higher effort level in family and household activities, compared to on-the-job ones. If female-specific job preferences are characteristic for the industries and/or occupations with a low SUW intensity, it results in females' out-selecting into employment requiring a lower SUW.

Similar to preference, non-cognitive skills, discussed briefly also, may drive down females' SUW. In particular, females' stronger focus on external versus internal locus of control may largely explain the gender gap in the influence SUW. The same applies to self-confidence and competitive behaviour. These characteristics largely determine females' socioemotional skills and are likely to strongly correlate with generic SUW. Females may experience lower intrinsic and/or monetary incentives to apply a skill extensively, with intrinsic incentives largely linked to individual preferences and work satisfaction, and monetary incentives linked to job characteristics such as wage, various compensation schemes, job appeal, career progression, etc. Albeit the estimation procedure controls for various employment characteristics, males' and females' motivation response is not observed. To put it simply, men's and women's motivation levels may change differently in response to identical compensation schemes or career progression perspectives.

While internalised factors are predominantly affecting individuals' choices of SUW effort, the second group of factors – external factors – is mostly shaping the task environment in a way that it is either more or less skill demanding and challenging. Among the external unobserved factors, the most common one is the pure statistical and taste discrimination. Employers may simply allocate different tasks and responsibilities to men and women with similar demographics, human capital profiles, and positions. This may be due to the employers' belief that men have a somewhat higher competence in performing specific tasks, compared to females (statistical discrimination). Alternatively, an employer may prefer to give males certain tasks and obligations due to concerns other than the male's higher skills, i.e. taste discrimination. One cannot elicit discrimination with the data in hand. However, given the vast evidence that gender discrimination exists (among others, Altonji & Blank, 1999), it is very likely that discrimination affects females' SUW intensity.

Given the varying drivers of employment segregation, reducing the gender gaps in labour utilisation requires complex policy interventions. In Estonia, most of the existing gender equality actions tackle gender misbalance in hiring procedures and career progression in various occupations and/or industries. These policy initiatives are crucial for facilitating gender balance at the job application level. At this stage, policy interventions should (i) promote more equal employment opportunities for men and women in highly skill-intense and challenging occupations and (ii) introduce diverse affirmative action policies aiming to encourage female job applications in male-dominated jobs, without restricting males' employment opportunities.

However, these initiatives may not be enough to offset the gender gaps in labour utilisation. Given the discussion, females may (i) out-select from skill-intense occupations due to job preferences and tastes; (ii) exhibit different motivation levels; (iii) possess different non-cognitive abilities, which reflect on their generic SUW; (iv) face employers' taste and statistical discrimination, resulting in the allocation to tasks different than men. Because of factor (i), women may not even reach the stage of job entry; as a result, the conventional gender balance policies will not help prevent skills underutilisation. Factors (ii) through (iv) may widen SUW gaps for men and women employed under identical job titles. As a result, policies beyond mere job access are needed.

To correctly shape the policy mechanism, further investigation into the psychological factors, such as job preferences and motivation, is needed. These will help us better understand females' self-selection into employment and potentially foster more skill-intense job choices through aligning them with women's job preferences and tastes. Furthermore, policy attention should focus on job composition as a conjunction of tasks performed by employees. Analysing job segregation on the occupation and industry level hides potential task disparity between men and women. Thus, narrowing down gender segregation into occupations and industries does not necessarily eliminate the labour utilisation gap if the disparity in tasks and responsibilities between men and women is assigned to persist.

Acknowledgements

This project was funded by the European Union's Rights, Equality and Citizenship Programme (2014–2020) No. 820778 (InWeGe – Income, Wage and Gender) by the European Union. The content of this project represents the views of the authors only and is their sole responsibility. The European Commission does not accept any responsibility for use that may be made of the information it contains. The author is thankful to Tiiu Paas, Jaanika Meriküll, and Tairi Rõõm for their feedback and valuable suggestions in early versions of this research.

Notes

1 A random measurement error in independent variable biases an estimate against zero, even though an average value of an independent variable may stay unaffected, whereas a random measurement error in dependent variable will not bias regression estimates. For more details see https://web.stanford.edu/class/polisci100a/regress5.pdf.

2 The replication procedure repeatedly selects the sub-samples and estimates the descriptive statistics of interest from these sub-samples. Standard errors are calculated using the variability of the statistics derived from these sub-samples. For more details see OECD (2013a).

3 Regression and decomposition analysis accounts for all three skill domains simultaneously. Incorporating 10 plausible values for each skill with 80 replication weights and one population weight results in $810 \times 810 \times 810$ replications.

4 To check for potential multicollinearity, VIF were computed. The estimates rule out multicollinearity concerns. Results are available upon request.
5 A heterogeneity analysis of SUW gaps across ISCO groups was done as an additional robustness check, given that SUW intensity is largely dependent on the type of job one performs (see Table 7.1 for occupation groups definition). The most notable finding is a substantial variation of unexplained gaps across occupation groups. In two high occupation categories (ISCO 1, corresponding to managers, and ISCO 3, corresponding to technicians and associate professionals), as well as in one medium-level occupation (ISCO 7, representing craft and related trades workers), no significant gender gaps are found. In the remaining occupations, reading, numeracy, and influence SUW gaps, whenever significant, are male-favouring. The results are available upon request.

References

Altonji, J. G., & Blank, R. M. (1999). Race and gender in the labor market. *Handbook of Labor Economics*, *3*, 3143–3259. doi:10.1016/S1573-4463(99)30039-0

Anspal, S. (2015). Non-parametric decomposition and the choice of reference group: A study of the gender wage gap in 15 OECD countries. *International Journal of Manpower*, *36*(8), 1266–1280. doi:10.1108/IJM-03-2015-0047

Anspal, S., Kraut, L., & Rõõm, T. (2010). *Sooline palgalõhe Eestis: empiiriline analüüs. Uuringuraport* [Gender pay gap in Estonia: An empirical analysis. Study report]. Eesti Rakendusuuringute Keskus CentAR, Poliitikauuringute Keskus PRAXIS, Sotsiaalministeerium.

Autor, D. H., & Handel, M. J. (2013). Putting tasks to the test: Human capital, job tasks, and wages. *Journal of Labor Economics*, *31*(S1), S59–S96. doi:10.1086/669332

Autor, D. H., Levy, F., & Murnane, R. J. (2003). The skill content of recent technological change: An empirical exploration. *The Quarterly Journal of Economics*, *118*(4), 1279–1333. doi:10.1162/003355303322552801

Becker, G. S., Hubbard, W. H., & Murphy, K. M. (2010). Explaining the worldwide boom in higher education of women. *Journal of Human Capital*, *4*, 203–241. doi:10.1086/657914

Black, S. E., & Spitz-Oener, A. (2010). Explaining women's success: Technological change and the skill content of women's work. *The Review of Economics and Statistics*, *92*(1), 187–194. doi:10.1162/rest.2009.11761

Blau, F. D., Ferber, M. A., & Winkler, A. E. (2014). *The economics of women, men, and work* (7th ed.). Upper Saddle River, NJ: Pearson.

Blau, F. D., & Kahn, L. M. (2006). The US gender pay gap in the 1990s: Slowing convergence. *ILR Review*, *60*(1), 45–66. doi:10.1177/001979390606000103

Blau, F. D., & Kahn, L. M. (2017). The gender wage gap: Extent, trends, and explanations. *Journal of Economic Literature*, *55*(3), 789–865. doi:10.1257/jel.20160995

Cardoso, A. R., Guimarães, P., & Portugal, P. (2016). What drives the gender wage gap? A look at the role of firm and job-title heterogeneity. *Oxford Economic Papers*, *68*(2), 506–524. doi:10.1093/oep/gpv069

Ceci, S. J., & Williams, W. M. (2011). Understanding current causes of women's underrepresentation in science. *Proceedings of the National Academy of Sciences*. doi:10.1073/pnas.1014871108

Christl, M., & Köppl-Turyna, M. (2017). *Gender wage gap and the role of skills: Evidence form PIAAC dataset* (GLO Discussion Paper No. 63). Maastricht: Global Labour Organization (GLO).

Correll, S. J. (2001). Gender and the career choice process: The role of biased self-assessments. *American Journal of Sociology*, *106*(6), 1691–1730. doi:10.1086/321299

Ellison, G., & Swanson, A. (2010). The gender gap in secondary school mathematics at high achievement levels: Evidence from the American mathematics competitions. *Journal of Economic Perspectives*, *24*(2), 109–128. doi:10.1257/jep.24.2.109

Eurostat employment statistics. Retrieved from https://appsso.eurostat.ec.europa.eu/nui/show.do?dataset=lfsi_emp_a&lang=en

Eurostat gender statistics. Retrieved from https://ec.europa.eu/eurostat/statistics-explained/index.php/Gender_statistics

Eurostat gender wage gap in EU statistics. Retrieved from https://ec.europa.eu/eurostat/statistics-explained/index.php/Gender_pay_gap_statistics

Fodor, É., & Glass, C. (2018). Labor market context, economic development, and family policy arrangements: Explaining the gender gap in employment in Central and Eastern Europe. *Social Forces*, *96*(3), 1275–1302. doi:10.1093/sf/sox080

Fortin, N. M. (2008). The gender wage gap among young adults in the United States the importance of money versus people. *Journal of Human Resources*, *43*(4), 884–918. doi:10.3368/jhr.43.4.884

Gayle, G. L., & Golan, L. (2012). Estimating a dynamic adverse-selection model: Labour-force experience and the changing gender earnings gap 1968–1997. *The Review of Economic Studies*, *79*(1), 227–267. doi:10.1093/restud/rdr019

Gelbach, J. B. (2016). When do covariates matter? And which ones, and how much? *Journal of Labor Economics*, *34*(2), 509–543. doi:10.1086/683668

Gemici, A., & Wiswall, M. (2014). Evolution of gender differences in post-secondary human capital investments: College majors. *International Economic Review*, *55*(1), 23–56. doi:10.1111/iere.12040

Gibbons, R., & Waldman, M. (2004). Task-specific human capital. *American Economic Review*, *94*(2), 203–207. doi:10.1257/0002828041301579

Gneezy, U., Niederle, M., & Rustichini, A. (2003). Performance in competitive environments: Gender differences. *The Quarterly Journal of Economics*, *118*(3), 1049–1074. doi:10.1162/00335530360698496

Goldin, C. (2014). A grand gender convergence: Its last chapter. *American Economic Review*, *104*(4), 1091–1119. doi:10.1257/aer.104.4.1091

Goldin, C., Katz, L. F., & Kuziemko, I. (2006). The homecoming of American college women: The reversal of the college gender gap. *Journal of Economic Perspectives*, *20*, 133–156. doi:10.1257/jep.20.4.133

Green, F. (2012). Employee involvement, technology and evolution in job skills: A task-based analysis. *ILR Review*, *65*(1), 36–67. doi:10.1177/001979391206500103

Grove, W. A., Hussey, A., & Jetter, M. (2011). The gender pay gap beyond human capital heterogeneity in noncognitive skills and in labor market tastes. *Journal of Human Resources*, *46*(4), 827–874. doi:10.2139/ssrn.2240312

Hanushek, E. A., Schwerdt, G., Wiederhold, S., & Woessmann, L. (2015). Returns to skills around the world: Evidence from PIAAC. *European Economic Review*, *73*, 103–130. doi:10.1016/j.euroecorev.2014.10.006

Lindley, J. (2010). *The gender dimension of technical change and job polarisation* (Discussion Papers in Economics No. 0510). Guildford: University of Surrey.

Meriküll, J., & Mõtsmees, P. (2017). Do you get what you ask? The gender gap in desired and realised wages. *International Journal of Manpower*, *38*(6), 893–908. doi:10.1108/IJM-11-2015-0197

Metcalfe, B. D., & Afanassieva, M. (2005). Gender, work, and equal opportunities in Central and Eastern Europe. *Women in Management Review*, *20*(6), 397–411. doi:10.1108/09649420510616791

Mueller, G., & Plug, E. (2006). Estimating the effect of personality on male and female earnings. *ILR Review*, *60*(1), 3–22. doi:10.1177/001979390606000101

Niederle, M., & Vesterlund, L. (2010). Explaining the gender gap in math test scores: The role of competition. *Journal of Economic Perspectives*, *24*(2), 129–144. doi:10.1257/jep.24.2.129

Nollenberger, N., Rodriguez-Planas, N., & Sevilla, A. (2016). The math gender gap: The role of culture. *American Economic Review*, *106*(5), 257–261. doi:10.1257/aer.p20161121

OECD. (2013a). *Technical report on the survey of adult skills (PIAAC)*. OECD Publishing. Retrieved from www.oecd.org/skills/piaac/_Technical%20Report_17OCT13.pdf

OECD. (2013b). *The survey of adult skills: Reader's companion*. OECD Publishing. doi:10.1787/9789264204027-en

Olivetti, C., & Petrongolo, B. (2016). The evolution of gender gaps in industrialized countries. *Annual Review of Economics*, *8*, 405–434. doi:10.1146/annurev-economics-080614-115329

Rendall, M. (2017). *Brain versus brawn: The realization of women's comparative advantage* (Working Paper No. 491). University of Zurich, Institute for Empirical Research in Economics.

Reuben, E., Sapienza, P., & Zingales, L. (2014). How stereotypes impair women's careers in science. *Proceedings of the National Academy of Sciences*. doi:10.1073/pnas.1314788111

Rõõm, T., & Kallaste, E. (2004). Females-males in Estonian labour market: Evaluation of wage differences. *Publication of PRAXIS Center for Policy Studies*, (8).

Smith, W. C., & Fernandez, F. (2017). Education, skills, and wage gaps in Canada and the United States. *International Migration*, *55*(3), 57–73. doi:10.1111/imig.12328

Statistics Estonia gender wage gap in Estonia statistics. Retrieved from www.stat.ee/news-release-2019-122

Tach, L. M., & Farkas, G. (2006). Learning-related behaviors, cognitive skills, and ability grouping when schooling begins. *Social Science Research*, *35*, 1048–1079. doi:10.1016/j.ssresearch.2005.08.001

Tverdostup, M., & Paas, T. (2017). Gender-specific human capital: Identification and quantifying its wage effects. *International Journal of Manpower*, *38*(6), 854–874. doi:10.1108/IJM-05-2016-0111

Wang, M. T., & Degol, J. L. (2017). Gender gap in science, technology, engineering, and mathematics (STEM): Current knowledge, implications for practice, policy, and future directions. *Educational Psychology Review*, *29*(1), 119–140. doi:10.1007/s10648-015-9355-x

Wiswall, M., & Zafar, B. (2018). Preference for the workplace, investment in human capital, and gender. *The Quarterly Journal of Economics*, *133*(1), 457–507. doi:10.1093/qje/qjx035

8

UTILISATION OF RETURNING MIGRANTS' SKILLS AND LABOUR

The case of Lithuania

Egidijus Barcevičius, Luka Klimavičiūtė, and Lukas Pukelis

Introduction[1]

During the last two decades Lithuania has experienced a significant outflow of its labour force, primarily to EU countries as well as to Norway and the United States of America. This has been driven by several factors, such as much higher income levels in the destination countries, lack of economic opportunities, weak social protection in the home country, and migrant network effects. EU membership since 2004 has had a facilitating effect in that joining the EU has dramatically decreased barriers to mobility and employment for Lithuanian citizens. High labour mobility was also experienced by many other Central and Eastern European (CEE) countries (such as Bulgaria, Estonia, Latvia, Poland, Romania) that entered the EU in 2004 and 2007. While emigration has advantages and disadvantages, on balance, it tends to have a negative influence on the economic performance of the sending countries, because migrants are usually younger, more active in the labour market, and, often, better educated than the general population.

During the last few years emigration from Lithuania has slowed down, and a significant number of emigrants have returned. Much of the literature views return migration to CEE positively, assuming it may improve the demographic structure and economic performance of these countries. Empirical evidence concerning the number of returnees, as well as the outcomes of return, is inconclusive (see for example Hazans, 2019; Hazans & Philips, 2011; Kaczmarczyk, Anacka, & Fihel, 2016; Lulle, Krisjane, & Bauls, 2019; Smoliner, Förschner, Hochgerner, & Nová, 2013). It shows that a significant share of migration from CEE is temporary, short term, circular; yet many workers return permanently after spending multiple years abroad. Various authors show that returnees may or may not earn an income premium for their experience abroad, are more likely to be self-employed, and may also face difficulties in finding employment, at least during the first year after coming back. The outcomes of return depend on the level of education, qualification, type, and duration of work abroad, the region of return, timing and duration of return, and other factors.

Return migration may increase labour productivity and labour utilisation (both quantitative and qualitative aspects as defined in this book), provided returnees can draw on their skills and work experience to find good-quality employment. Labour market institutions, such as active labour market policies and support by the public employment service (PES), may play a facilitating role. The core aim of this chapter is thus to analyse the status of return migrants in the Lithuanian labour market and the likely implications of return migration to labour productivity and utilisation. We will also consider, to the extent allowed by the data, the role that different institutions play in facilitating labour market integration of the returnees. The findings are pertinent to other countries of the CEE, such as Estonia, Latvia, and Poland, that show a trend towards increasing return migration.

We start this chapter by presenting contextual data concerning return migration and labour productivity and utilisation in Lithuania and carrying out a brief literature overview. Next, we introduce the data sources and explain the methodological choices. Afterwards, we carry out an empirical analysis in two steps. Firstly, we use Lithuanian LFS (Labour Force Survey) data for 2013–2018 to analyse the recent returnees. While this data presents important evidence concerning labour market status of the returnees, it only covers the recent returnees. This data can be used for the analysis of the role of institutions only to a limited extent because of the relatively small sample size. In order to understand the experiences of a wider sample of returnees, researchers usually draw on surveys (convenience samples, with or without quotas and answer weighting) or interviews. In this chapter we proceed to experiment with another approach and use emerging big data–type tools and machine-based automatic text processing to analyse articles on return migration in the main news portals for 2004–2018. We assess both the sentiment of the articles and the most prominent narratives. While such a method has not been used often for the analysis of return migration, we assume that it provides a promising angle to understand the labour market status of the returnees and the role of institutions. We agree that texts from news portals may be biased, may construct reality, and reflect both authentic migrant experiences as well as the perception of these experiences in the society. This is advantageous for the purposes of our research, as both the individual story of the returnees and the reception by the society are two sides of the same coin; this may explain the 'return of innovation' versus 'bitter' return (see e.g. Cassarino, 2004; Cerase, 1974; Coniglio & Brzozowski, 2016).

The research presented in this chapter shows some evidence of positive selection of the Lithuanian returnees: according to the LFS data, the recent returnees are younger than the general labour force; fewer among them have low education; more of them have medium-level education. The recent returnees are significantly less likely to work and much more likely to be self-employed. We used the news portals to consider the further career paths of returnees. The narratives vary, but if we try to single out the most prominent topics (based on the LDA algorithm and other techniques), it seems to suggest that returnees' work and skills are being accepted in the labour market. Our findings point towards a likely positive effect of return migration on labour productivity, although the effect on labour utilisation is less clear and may be negative during the initial stages of return (especially if labour utilisation is understood in quantitative terms of the number of hours worked). Further, our data does not show that labour market institutions play a significant role in positive selection or quick integration of the returnees. Rather this is associated with broader factors, such as the economic environment in the country and actions of the central government institutions.

Setting the context: return migration, labour productivity, and labour utilisation in Lithuania

Around 650-thousand Lithuanian citizens emigrated in 2004–2018 (Figure 8.1), mostly to the United Kingdom, Germany, Ireland, Spain, Norway, and the United States of America. The net migration during this period was around 428 thousand; it was the key factor contributing to the decrease in population in the country from 3.4 million people in 2004 to 2.8 million in 2018. The net migration rate of Lithuania per 1000 inhabitants reached -25.2 in 2010 and throughout 2004–2018 was consistently one of the highest among the CEE countries that entered the EU in 2004 and 2007. Figure 8.1 also shows a number of emigration peaks that are related to the membership in the EU in 2004, the economic crisis in 2009–2011, as

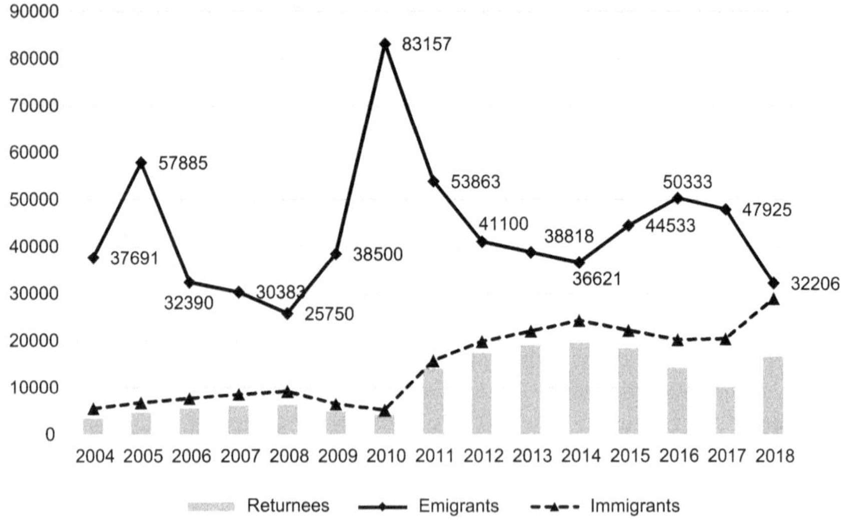

Figure 8.1 Emigration, immigration, and return migration (number of people), Lithuania 2004–2018

Source: Statistics Lithuania.

well as Brexit when Lithuanian emigrants made an effort to formally secure their legal status given the uncertainties of the United Kingdom's exit terms.

Recent years have shown an increase of immigration to Lithuania, and therefore the migration balance has improved markedly. In 2018 the net migration rate per 1000 inhabitants was -1.2. Further, 2019 was the first year in two decades when this rate turned slightly positive. What makes immigration to Lithuania (and some other CEE countries) unique compared to West European countries is that most immigrants are returnees. Throughout 2004–2018 the majority of immigration to Lithuania (74 per cent) consisted of returning Lithuanian citizens (see Figure 8.1).

The high level of emigration has negative macroeconomic consequences on sending countries by decreasing the potential level of GDP due to shrinking labour force and related effects such as brain drain (Bodvarsson & den Berg, 2009; OECD, 2013; Skibinska, 2019). For example, in 2011 Holland et al. estimated that due to emigration Lithuania's long-term GDP will be around 6 per cent lower, while the effect on GDP per capita will be -1.24 per cent[2] (Holland et al., 2011). According to a more recent IMF study, during 1999–2014 the high levels of emigration decreased the annual growth rates by around 0.6 to 0.9 percentage points in a number of CEE countries, including Lithuania (Atoyan et al., 2016).

Many authors agree that emigration has partly contributed to lowering unemployment and increasing employment in high-emigration countries of CEE due to absorbing the 'slack labour' (Hazans, 2016; Hazans & Philips, 2011; Kaczmarczyk & Okolski, 2008). The actual extent of such contribution is difficult to calculate given the context of rapid economic growth, injection of EU structural funds, and fluctuating demand for labour after 2004. Notably, based on analysis of several CEE countries, including Lithuania, Škuflić and Vučković (2019) argue that emigration may actually increase unemployment in sending countries as it amplifies the mismatch between labour supply and demand.[3]

The effects of emigration on labour productivity and utilisation are multifaceted. At first glance, it can be expected that labour productivity in the outflow countries would decrease if mobile workers were better educated and/or more skilled than stayers. Quantitatively, the labour utilisation (understood as the number of hours worked per capita) may be expected to increase given a smaller labour force, growing economies, high demand for labour, and increasing wages. The likely effects on the qualitative aspect of labour utilisation (understood as the extent to which skills of the employed are used in the economy) are mixed. On the one hand, emigration may lead to skills mismatches, but on the other, it may force employers to hire and train less-educated and thus previously underemployed workers. Indeed, many authors agree that migration has negative effects on productivity in CEE (Holland et al., 2011; Atoyan et al., 2016). There is evidence of brain drain, as, for example, emigrants tend to be more educated or skilled than stayers; this, however, may fluctuate across countries and over time (Hazans, 2016; Hazans & Philips, 2011).[4] Many authors argue that brain drain is taking place due to the mere fact that many highly educated or skilled persons have emigrated;[5] moreover, a significant number of mobile persons gain education and skills abroad and stay in the foreign countries, which is a loss from the sending country's perspective, not least in terms of (potential) labour productivity and utilisation.

Figure 8.2 and Figure 8.3 show that in 2004–2018 the labour productivity and labour utilisation (the quantitative aspect in terms of hours worked per capita) of Lithuania and some other CEE countries grew faster than on average in the EU-28, which also points towards faster economic growth and convergence towards the other EU countries. In the absence of a counter-factual scenario, the actual effects of labour mobility on labour productivity and utilisation are difficult to discern from other factors. It is quite certain that labour productivity in the sending countries would have been even higher if the rate of emigration had been lower. This, however, assumes that most of the more-productive and skilled workers that emigrated would have had employment in their home countries, which was not always the case (hence the term 'labour overflow'; see Kaczmarczyk & Okolski, 2008). While extensive emigration may have put pressure on the labour market, resulting in higher utilisation of labour (both quantitative and qualitative aspects), this may have been moderated by migration-related, unfavourable trends in the demographic structure of the sending countries.[6]

Much of the literature on migration from CEE sees return migration as a factor that may help alleviate the negative effects of labour outflow. Return migration

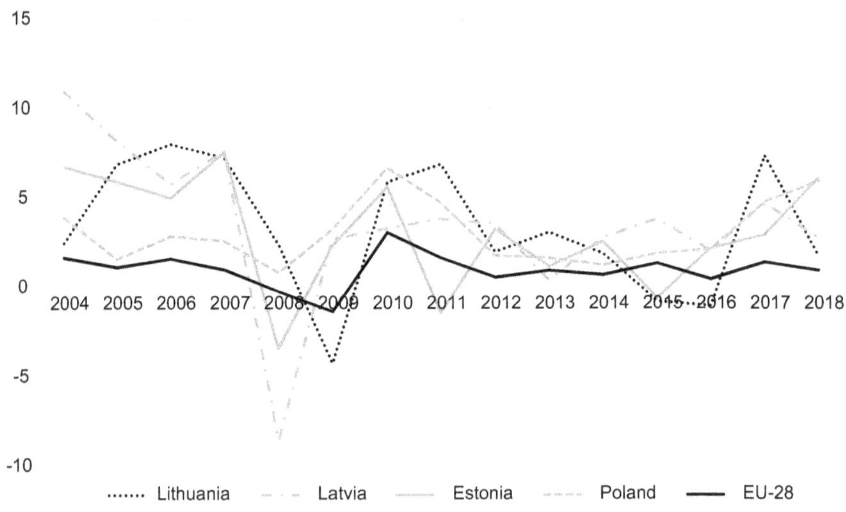

Figure 8.2 Labour productivity in selected CEE countries, annual growth rate (%) 2004–2018

Source: OECD (2019).

Notes: Labour productivity measured as GDP per hour worked.

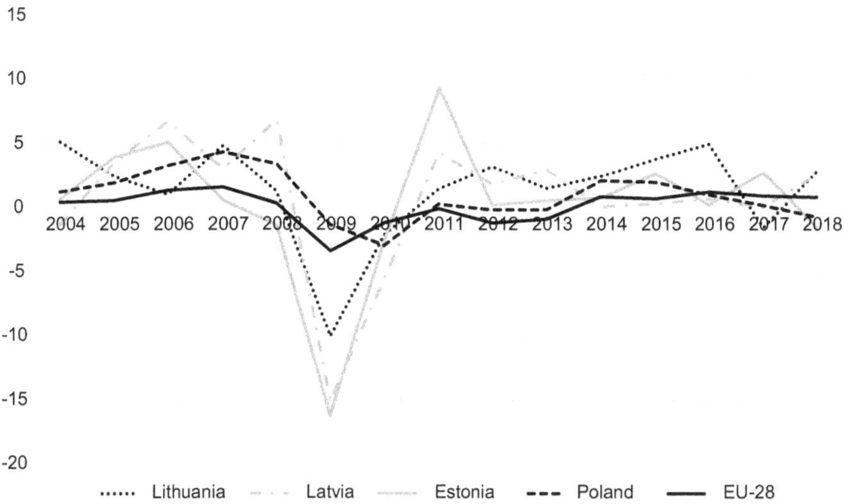

Figure 8.3 Hours worked per capita in selected CEE countries, annual growth rate (%) 2004–2018

Source: OECD (2019).

could be expected to have positive influence on labour productivity and utilisation, especially if three conditions are fulfilled. Firstly, there is positive selection of the returnees in terms of education or skills. Secondly, returnees should find employment in jobs where they can productively use their skills and qualification. Thirdly, in order to have a macroeconomic effect, the number of returnees must be substantial.

Empirical data from Lithuania and other CEE countries shows a complicated picture. Several studies argue that returnees tend to be more skilled or educated than stayers, especially given that returnees tend to increase their human capital abroad (Coniglio & Brzozowski, 2016; Hazans & Philips, 2011; Martin & Radu, 2012; Smoliner et al., 2013). Nevertheless, the positive selection of returnees is not always the case (Anacka & Wójcicka, 2019; Hazans, 2016; Kaczmarczyk et al., 2016).

What concerns the labour market status of the returnees is that various studies find that returnees may or may not receive income premia compared to stayers. They are more likely to be employed or self-employed or work in high-value-added sectors or sectors experiencing labour shortages than stayers. Other authors argue that returnees are more likely to be unemployed, at least during the initial phase of return. This has been explained either as a positive sign (returnees are more entrepreneurial; they have savings and may afford to be selective when choosing jobs) or a negative development (returnees may lack country-specific skills or networks, they are being treated with caution by employers and the society; Hazans, 2018; Karolak, 2016; Martin & Radu, 2012; Smoliner et al., 2013). The returnees to CEE are indeed a very heterogeneous group in terms of their education, skills, working experience abroad, and motivation to return. Empirical research shows that those with higher education and those who worked in jobs commensurate with the level of their qualification find it relatively easy to integrate (see e.g. Barcevičius (2016) for Lithuania; Hazans (2019) for Latvia, Klein-Hitpaß (2016) for Poland). Conversely, return is more likely to turn 'bitter' for those with lower skills, including those who worked abroad below the level of their qualification (Anacka & Wójcicka, 2019; Kaczmarczyk et al., 2016; Žvalionytė, 2015). This may lead to a repeated emigration; conversely, the situation of returnees who initially find it difficult to adapt may improve over time (Coniglio & Brzozowski, 2016; Grabowska, 2016; Žvalionytė, 2012).

Finally, the estimates on the propensity of the mobile workers to return range from 18 to 60 per cent for Estonia, Latvia, and Lithuania; the actual number depends on individual migrant characteristics, the economic situation in the home countries, and wider economic circumstances (Hazans, 2016; Krisjane, Apsite-Berina, & Berzins, 2016; Žvalionytė, 2015). Overall, despite considerable repeated or circular migration, the actual stock of population with migration experience has been on the increase. In the medium to long term this may have economy-wide effects in terms of labour productivity and utilisation, especially in countries like Lithuania, which is a small country with a large migrant population.

Labour market institutions have a role facilitating return and supporting returnees to find quality employment in their home countries. This volume considers a wide range of such institutions, including the public employment service (PES), labour market regulation, training and education, trade unions and collective bargaining, and others. Further, specific institutions and programmes have been created in CEE to encourage return and integration of returnees into the labour market (see, for example, Boros & Hegedus, 2016; Budginaitė, 2012a; Coniglio & Brzozowski, 2016).[7] The labour market institutions of Lithuania as well as other CEE countries have undergone significant changes during the last two decades due to the transition to a market economy, EU membership, economic crises, new or emerging social risks, and changing priorities within the society. Despite visible progress, the key current challenges are limited funding for the labour market policy and limited trust in the society, including contested discussion concerning the effectiveness of these institutions. In comparison to the EU average, participation in the active labour market policies in Lithuania is low (around 13 per cent in 2016), and trade union membership is very limited (around 8 per cent in 2016); however, close to 80 per cent of unemployed people used PES for job searching[8] (European Commission, 2018). To the extent allowed by data, in the empirical analysis we will discuss whether the labour market institutions make a difference when it comes to supporting labour market integration of the returnees.

Data and methodology

We carry out empirical analysis based on two distinct methods and data sets, which, however, complement each other by offering different angles to answering the key questions of this chapter.

Statistical analysis of the LFS data set

We use the 2013–2018 Lithuanian LFS data to explore returnees' socio-demographic characteristics and employment patterns in comparison to those of non-migrants. As done in other research (e.g. Martin & Radu, 2012), we define return migrants as those born in Lithuania who resided abroad one year prior to the survey. Our sample includes 162 returnees over the age of 15 as well as 77,614 non-migrants.[9] The dataset includes important socio-demographic information, including age, gender, marital status, education, employment status, and self-employment. This information helps us compare returnees with other residents in Lithuania and assess to what extent their employment patterns differ.

Using LFS has notable limitations. The LFS lacks a question on whether the respondent has *ever* resided abroad, so we are limited to running our analysis only on *recent returnees* rather than those with any migration experience. Recent returnees might still be in the process of looking for work given that they returned within the last year, and so the analysis might underestimate the employment rates of all returnees. Furthermore, the sample of returnees is small, limiting our ability to run more complex models and angles to analyse the data.

We nevertheless proceed with the analysis of the LFS in order to check whether the characteristics of returnees have changed since earlier research. We also explore the limitations of using the LFS with the aim to understand the potential of other tools, such as text mining, to address some of those shortcomings.

In order to assess how non-migrants and returnees differ in the labour market, we run a logistic regression with a variable set to 1 if the respondent is working and 0 otherwise. Note that zero in this case represents both the inactive and the unemployed. The main explanatory variable in the second regression is the returnee variable, allowing us to assess whether returnees are more or less likely to be working compared to non-migrants. We also control for socio-demographic variables mentioned earlier.

We run four more logistic regressions to explore how working patterns differ among returnees and non-migrants. In these, we explore whether having a higher degree affects returnees' employment. We then look at the differences of using a public employment office among the two groups and the likelihood of being a student as well as self-employment patterns.

Finally, to compare not only returnees' and migrants' likelihood of working, but also how they do once they find jobs, we compare their salaries using an ordinary least-squares regression (OLS). The dependent variable is the net salary, which indicates monthly wage measured after taxes and coded in 15 categories, from 0 to 900+ euros. In addition to the socio-demographics outlined, we also control for occupation, which is coded in nine categories based on ILO categorisation (ILO, 2012), where 1 indicates managers and 9 stands for elementary occupations.

Text mining of media articles on return migration

The key limitation of the LFS-based data is that it captures only the recent returnees, who lived in a foreign country a year ago. In order to reach a more diverse group of returnees, researchers in CEE countries have used surveys (relying mostly on quota-based convenience samples) and/or interviews. In this chapter we apply yet another method, which assumes that texts about the returnees in the major news portals are a good proxy for, firstly, understanding the status of the returnees in the labour market and society and, secondly, exploring to what extent the state or municipal institutions are associated with success or otherwise of the returnees. The texts of interest include factual reports, interviews with returnees or their family members, comments by journalists, statements by public institutions, reflections by employers, etc.

We have collected news media articles from the most popular Lithuanian web portals (delfi.lt, 15min.lt, vz.lt, lrt.lt, alfa.lt, lrytas.lt, balsas.lt.). Data collection was carried out in two steps: first, we scraped all the articles from the portals that either had a tag related to emigrants or showed up when we posted queries with the keyword 'emigrant' to the portal search engine. The result of this first step was a corpus of web portal texts related to emigrants. In the second step, we narrowed our search to focus on returnees only. We did so by keeping only the articles that contained the roots forms for the verb 'return' (in Lithuanian: 'grįž*') and a noun 'emigrant' (in Lithuanian 'emigrant*'). The first step of the data collection yielded more than 3000 articles, and 1017 articles were left after the filtering in the second step.

Afterwards, the selected texts were pre-processed for analysis. All the pre-processing procedures had the same core steps: lemmatising, lowercasing, removing numbers, punctuation, pronouns, and stop-words.

We then proceeded to perform quantitative and qualitative analysis of the collected texts. More specifically, we applied three methods: sentiment-coloured word-clouds, topic-modelling, and word-embeddings using the word2vec algorithm. Word clouds are a technique to visualise word frequencies in the text/corpus. A word-cloud algorithm produces a picture with the most common words in a text/corpus, where the font size of each word represents its frequency in text, with more common words being larger. For this method we performed additional pre-processing, keeping only those parts of speech which carry a sentiment value: verbs, adjectives, and adverbs. We then compiled dictionaries of positive and negative words that occur in our corpus and used them to colour the word-cloud figures.

Topic modelling is a technique that allows us to summarise a corpus of documents and extract the most commonly occurring topics (collections of words). For this method, we also did additional pre-processing steps by including bi-grams (commonly occurring two-word phrases) in the analysis. For the analysis, we implemented a classical LDA (Blei, Ng, & Jordan, 2003) topic modelling algorithm.

Finally, word2vec is a word clustering algorithm, which embeds words in a low-dimensional space. It does so by analysing text using a sliding window approach and trying to predict each word in a window using other words as input features. As a result, words that are used in a corpus in a similar way (interchangeably) are clustered closely together. The algorithm is most often used to detect the most similar and most different words in a text/corpus (Goldberg & Levy, 2014). All the data collection and analysis were done using Python programming language.

Recent returnees: labour market performance based on LFS data

Table 8.1 summarises the descriptive statistics of our LFS sample. In the first column, we present descriptive statistics for the entire sample. The second column – non-migrants – describes those Lithuanian nationals who either have lived in Lithuania their entire lives or have returned from abroad more than a year ago. The third column illustrates the main socio-demographic characteristics of recent returnees. In the fourth column, we show the differences between non-migrants and recent returnees, including whether these differences are statistically significant.

Table 8.1 Descriptive statistics of the sample, LFS data for the period 2013–2018

	All sample 1	*Non-migrants* 2	*Recent returnees* 3	*Differential (t-test)* 2–3
Age (median)	50–54 years-old	50–54 years-old	30–34 years-old	2.703***(0.273)
Male	0.446	0.446	0.525	–0.0787**(0.039)
Single	0.231	0.231	0.506	–0.276***(0.033)
Married	0.580	0.580	0.346	0.235***(0.039)
Divorced, legally separated, or widowed	0.189	0.189	0.148	–0.316***(0.051)
Low education	0.178	0.178	0.080	0.098***(0.030)
Medium education	0.547	0.546	0.679	–0.133***(0.039)
High education	0.276	0.276	0.241	0.035 (0.035)
Employed (Y/N)	0.562	0.562	0.475	0.087** (0.039)
Observations	77,776	77,614	162	

Source: Own elaboration based on LFS data 2013–2018.

Notes: Standard errors in parentheses; *** denotes significance at 0.01; ** denotes significance at 0.05. To ensure anonymity, Lithuanian Statistics provided the age variable grouped in 5-year intervals, hence the differential indicates the difference between two age groups. Classification of education levels follows the approach of EU LFS: High refers to tertiary education, Medium – to upper secondary and post-secondary non-tertiary education, and Low to the rest (CIRCABC, 2019).

It is immediately apparent that recent returnees differ from non-migrants. Recent returnees are younger, and more of them are male and single compared to the rest of the Lithuanian population. Fewer returnees have low education, and more of them have acquired medium education. These observations go in line with similar research performed previously (Hazans & Philips, 2011; Martin & Radu, 2012). Unlike in previous research, however, in our dataset we do not see significant differences between the shares of degree holders among the general population and the returnees.

Given that recent returnees are different from non-migrants at least in some regards, we control for their socio-demographic characteristics when assessing their position on the labour market. The first column in Table 8.2 summarises the results of the regression, which estimates whether returning from abroad affects one's likelihood of working. We find that the recent returnees are 86 per cent less likely to be working than the general population.

In order to check whether the impact is different for more- and less-educated returnees, we then limit the sample to returnees only and estimate the effect of having a higher degree on whether a person is working using a logistic regression (see column 2 in Table 8.2). The results are significant, meaning that work outcomes among returnees are differentiated by education. To be more precise, returnees who are degree holders have double the odds of working compared to returnees who do not hold a degree.

If recent returnees are more likely to be not working compared to the general labour force, are they more likely to reach out to public employment office to find work? To answer this question, we run another logistic regression (see column 3 in Table 8.2) with a dependent variable set to 1 if a respondent contacted the public employment office within four weeks prior to taking the survey and 0 otherwise.[10] We find that returnees are 66 per cent less likely to contact a public employment office to find work compared to non-returnees. Regarding other institutional involvement, returnees also appear less likely to participate in regular education, even when we control for age and other socio-demographic characteristics (see column 4 in Table 8.2).

Given findings in the literature that returnees are also more prone to be self-employed (Karolak, 2016; Martin & Radu, 2012), we also assess whether returnees are more likely to be self-employed than non-migrants (see column 3 in Table 8.2). In line with other research, we find that returnees have more than twice the odds of being self-employed. Based on econometric analysis, some scholars (Démurger & Xu, 2011; McCormick & Wahba, 2001) argue that savings and skills acquired abroad foster entrepreneurship upon return. Nevertheless, drawing on interviews with Polish returnees, Karolak (2016) points out that many businesses started by returnees soon fail, the primary motivation for starting a business is the hesitancy to work 'for a Polish boss', and that few self-employed returnees employ others. This calls into question whether self-employment among Lithuanian returnees is a sign of entrepreneurship or difficulty integrating into the Lithuanian labour market.

Table 8.2 Work-related regression results

		(1) DV: Employed (Y/N)	*(2) DV: Employed (Y/N)*	*(3) DV: Public employment office (Y/N)*	*(4) DV: Student (Y/N)*	*(5) DV: Self-employed (Y/N)*
Returnee		0.141***		0.342***	0.482***	2.630***
		(0.051)		(0.130)	(0.137)	(0.723)
Employment status a year ago (ref. employed)	Unemployed	0.021***				
		(0.001)				
	Inactive	0.005***				
		(0.000)				
Age (ref.: 15–29-year-olds)	30–44-year-olds	0.577***		1.866***	0.035***	2.054***
		(0.042)		(0.227)	(0.002)	(0.155)
	45–59-year-olds	0.438***		2.367***	0.008***	2.254***
		(0.032)		(0.309)	(0.001)	(0.173)
	60+ year-olds	0.103***		1.806***	0.000***	2.523***
		(0.008)		(0.351)	(0.000)	(0.214)
Females (ref. Males)		0.855***		1.522***	1.489***	0.623***
		(0.027)		(0.123)	(0.057)	(0.020)
Marital Status (ref. Single)	Married	1.277***		1.117	0.200***	1.102
		(0.077)		(0.125)	(0.014)	(0.065)
	Divorced, legally separated, or widowed	1.044		1.018	0.202***	1.089
		(0.072)		(0.137)	(0.032)	(0.076)
Education (ref. Low)	Medium	3.531***		1.195		0.782***
		(0.168)		(0.154)		(0.058)
	High	6.412***		0.576***		0.499***
		(0.354)		(0.081)		(0.038)
Higher degree (Y/N)			2.113**			
			(0.797)			
Employed (Y/N)				0.123***	0.079***	
				(0.012)	(0.003)	
Constant		10.648***	0.757	2.433***	4.588***	0.111***
		(0.627)	(0.138)	(0.324)	(0.144)	(0.010)
Observations		77,776	162	4,845	77,776	43,084
Pseudo R^2		0.694	0.018	0.140	0.706	0.026

Source: Own elaboration.

Notes: *** denotes significance at 0.01; ** denotes significance at 0.05. Results are reported in odds ratios. DV stands for a dependent variable. Y/N informs that the variable could take only two values: 1 – for Yes, 0 – for No. Reference categories are specified next to each variable. Robust standard errors are noted in parentheses.

So far, we have learned that returnees – especially those with less education – are less likely to be working than non-migrants but more likely to be self-employed. However, we know little about the reasons behind these patterns. These findings could imply that recent returnees are at a disadvantage in the Lithuanian labour market compared to non-migrants, or on the contrary, returnees might simply still be looking for jobs given that they returned within the previous year.

To assess returnees' labour market position more in depth, we limit the sample to the working population only and estimate the impact that being a returnee has on one's wage. If we find that returnees earn less for the same jobs than non-migrants, we could argue that recent returnees are at a disadvantage. As shown in Table 8.3, we indeed find a somewhat negative effect, although significant only at 10 per cent. The model has some limitations. Although we control for occupation, occupation is coded in nine broad categories (from managers to elementary occupations), but returnees and non-migrants might occupy different positions within these broad categories. It is likely that at the initial stages of return, mobile

Table 8.3 OLS regression results regrading wages

		(1) *Dependent Variable: Net salary*
Returnee		–1.130* (0.635)
Occupation		–0.280*** (0.012)
Age (ref.: 15–29-year-olds)	30–44-year-olds	1.065*** (0.096)
	45–59-year-olds	1.226*** (0.097)
	60+ year-olds	0.781*** (0.115)
Females (ref. Males)		–1.764*** (0.050)
Marital Status (ref. Single)	Married	–0.015 (0.084)
	Divorced, legally separated, or widowed	–0.110 (0.100)
Education (ref. Low)	Medium	1.059*** (0.116)
	High	2.857*** (0.129)
Constant		7.584*** (0.152)
Observations		35,811
R^2		0.120

Source: Own elaboration.

Notes: *** denotes significance at 0.01; ** denotes significance at 0.05; * denotes significance at 0.1. Occupation is coded in nine categories based on ILO categorisation (ILO, 2012), where 1 indicates managers and 9 stands for elementary occupations. Reference categories are specified next to each variable. Robust standard errors are noted in parentheses.

workers may occupy relatively lower positions within these categories than non-migrants. Nevertheless, we know little about the further career progress of the returnees. Other research shows that over the years the effect of former migration dissipates or may turn into advantage (Barcevičius, 2016; Grabowska, 2016).

Given that circular migration has been observed in Lithuania in the past (Barcevičius & Žvalionytė, 2012), we attempt to address it in our research by looking at respondents who say that their current place of work is abroad. We indeed find stark differences between recent returnees and non-migrants regarding their place of work: in our sample, 0.3 per cent of non-migrants work abroad compared to 39 per cent of recent returnees.[11] These statistics could help explain some of the employment patterns explored in this chapter. Nevertheless, we are careful not to overstate the impact of circular migration. Returnees who work abroad might work both in high-skilled and low-skilled occupations; they can work on a temporary or full-time basis (for example, remotely), so circular migration could have both an upward and downward pressure on their wages as well as an effect on employment rates.

Overall, our limited sample size does not allow us to explore what implications a foreign workplace has on returnees' employment patterns. We believe it is an important area of research to explore by introducing complementary methods and data samples, as it could provide insights into the effects of emigration and return migration on important questions, including the effects of migration on labour productivity and utilisation in the country.

Experiences of return as mediated through the most popular news websites

Media analysis has been applied in migration research, including, for example, the refugee crisis (e.g. Berry, Garcia-Blanco, & Moore, 2015) and return migration to Lithuania (e.g. Budginaitė, 2012b). This analysis has been carried out by coding the texts manually, using a pre-set coding structure, which requires a lot of resources and may even miss important topics. In this section we experiment with emerging big data–type tools and machine-based automatic text processing. Such tools allow for a more inductive approach; they can be applied quickly and on a large data-set. Admittedly, the data set used in our analysis (1017 articles dealing with return migration) is relatively limited. They key reason is that the sheer number of articles on return migration has not been very large, and some texts have already been archived, hidden, or deleted and are not available for scraping. Nevertheless, the data set is sufficient to explore the method as well as draw some inferences on questions of interest to this chapter.

Our data shows that the overall number of texts dealing with return migration has been on the increase (Figure 8.4). While specific numbers should be treated with caution, as older articles are more difficult to scrape, the trend itself is plausible. It is in line with the overall tendency of increasing return migration as well as higher interest in the topic from journalists and the society.

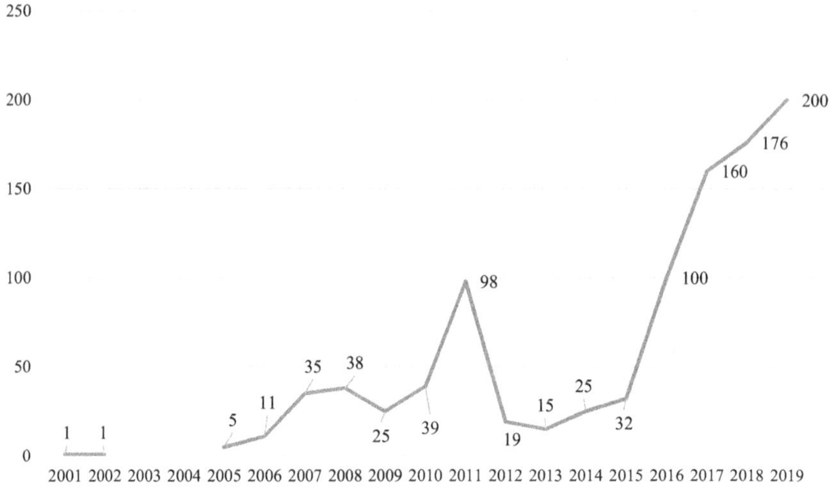

Figure 8.4 Number of articles on return migration scraped from the main news portals

Notes: We could not assign a concrete date for 37 articles that most likely come from the period 2012–2015.

Source: Own elaboration.

Next, we have checked the overall sentiment of the media regarding the returnees. Word cloud analysis shows that overall return migration received rather positive coverage. The dominating words are ‘good’, ‘new’, ‘important’, ‘possible’. The negative words, such as ‘difficult’, ‘not be able to’, ‘mistake’, ‘suspected’ are visible but less frequent. Analysis by portal and by time showed a certain variation. For example, the main business portal vz.lt had somewhat neutral coverage, featuring words such as ‘service’, ‘client’, ‘tax’, ‘construction’. The more positive stories featured words like ‘new’, ‘possible’, ‘important’, while the more negative reports included ‘prohibited’, ‘does not contribute’. There was some fluctuation in our dataset over the years. In 2017–2019 the key words were ‘new’, ‘now’, ‘good’, ‘true’, ‘possible’, ‘need’, ‘want’, ‘return’, ‘worked’. The words with clearly negative connotations were ‘difficult’, ‘bitter’, ‘mistake’, ‘suspected’, ‘not be able to’. We ran the word2vec algorithm specifically with the bi-gram ‘acquired abroad’. It shows that words that can be used interchangeably with this bigram include ‘specific’, ‘ability’, ‘professional’, ‘patience’, ‘deficiency’, ‘diploma’, ‘international experience’.

We carried out topic modelling, based on the LDA algorithm, to see how different words in our textual data cluster into topics. We firstly asked to generate one most prominent topic based on 20 words. The algorithm returned a collection of words as presented in Table 8.4. While the meaning of the topic is subject to interpretation, the words seem to cluster into a narrative, saying that presently

Table 8.4 LDA topic modelling algorithm, 1 topic, 20 words

0.021*"is" + 0.007*"time" + 0.006*"person" + 0.006*"many" + 0.006*"in Lithuania" + 0.005*"emigrant" + 0.005*"have" + 0.005*"work" + 0.004*"country" + 0.004*"Lithuania" + 0.004*"may" + 0.003*"say" + 0.003*"good" + 0.003*"here" + 0.003*"hello"

Source: Own elaboration

many persons who used to be emigrants have work in Lithuania and are satisfied with their return.

In order to carry out a more detailed analysis, we have varied the number of topics (up to 50) and changed the number of words per topic from 10 to 30. Based on this analysis, we singled out the following narratives that are most prominent in our dataset:

i Being in Lithuania, work, new life;
ii Bringing family and children back to Lithuania;
iii A returnee creating or having a business in Lithuania;
iv Health procedures and medical operations (emigrants returning for health checks or medical procedures);
v Owning property (a house, a flat) in Lithuania;
vi Emigrant suspected of a crime; car crash; investigation being carried out;
vii 'Four million' – a project by the national broadcasting company (LRT) about Lithuanian migrants

We also checked how various state and labour market institutions (including the key policy instruments used by these institutions) feature in the texts on return migration. The assumption is that if an institution is mentioned frequently and is presented in a positive context, then its role is visible and acknowledged as such in society. If this is not the case, it does not necessarily mean that an institution is not important; nevertheless, this is a useful proxy showing that an institution is not perceived as making much difference on the decisions and labour market status of the return migrants. In order to understand the context in which an institution is presented, we ran a word cloud analysis as well as the word2vec algorithm, which shows the words in our data set that are most similar to the selected institution.

As demonstrated in Table 8.5, central government institutions were mentioned most frequently in our dataset (Parliament, President, Government). It means that return migration, as well as the success or unsuccess of return, are associated frequently with the overall economic and social environment in the country. The words that feature most in our dataset alongside these institutions are: 'new', 'important', 'good', 'big', 'service', 'need', 'tax', 'suggest'. These words are related to the modus operandi of the institutions (suggesting, making, or justifying decisions, responding to needs). Analysis based on the word2vec algorithm shows that, among other things, Parliament is discussed frequently in the context of the

Table 8.5 The number of articles mentioning specific institution, programme, or concept

	In Lithuanian [a]	*No of articles*
Central or municipal level institutions		
Parliament	Parlamentas, Seimas	567
President	Prezidentas	519
Government	Vyriausybė	380
Municipality	Savivaldybė	172
Labour market institutions and organisations		
Ministry of Social Affairs and Labour	Socialinės apsaugos ir darbo ministerija, SADM	28
Public employment service	Darbo birža, Užimtumo tarnyba	198
State Social Insurance Fund Board	Sodra	31
Trade union	Profesinė sąjunga, profsąjunga	129
Labour council	Darbo taryba	97
Labour market and related instruments		
Social model	Socialinis modelis	7
Labour code	Darbo kodeksas	25
Collective agreement	Kolektyvinis susitarimas, kolektyvinė sutartis	4
Unemployment benefit	Nedarbo pašalpa, nedarbo išmoka, bedarbio pašalpa	41
Minimum salary	Minimalus atlyginimas	53
Pension	Pensija	333
Social insurance	Socialinis draudimas	48
Programmes aimed specifically at returnees		
"I choose Lithuania"	„Renkuosi Lietuvą"	45
"Create for Lithuania"	Kurk Lietuvai	10
Important concepts		
Training	Mokymai	100
Education	Švietimas, išsilavinimas	184
Knowledge, skills	Žinios, įgūdžiai	268
Productivity	Produktyvumas	20
Entrepreneurship	Verslumas	46
Business	Verslas	733
Work	Darbas	935
Unemployment	Nedarbas	138
Acquired abroad	Užsienyje įgytas	37
Low qualification, unqualified	Žema kvalifikacija, nekvalifikuotas	71

Source: Own elaboration.

Notes: [a] Given that the endings of words in Lithuanian change depending on the case, gender, and tense, we run the search using the root parts of these words.

demographic situation in the country. Government is visible in the discussion on the economic aspects of migration and strategies to encourage return.

Further, we considered institutions and organisations that oversee implementing or mediating labour market policy. They include the Ministry of Social Affairs and Labour, State Social Insurance Board, the Public Employment Service, trade unions, and labour councils. Table 8.5 shows that some of these institutions featured frequently in the texts on return migration, especially the PES. The word clouds concerning the PES and the Social Insurance Fund Board are very illustrative, with the following words dominating: 'need', 'pay', 'contribution payment', 'debt', 'now'. The trade unions and labour councils also featured quite frequently in the dataset. It is an unexpected finding given the low trade union membership in the country; further, the majority of labour councils have been established only since 2017, when they became mandatory for companies with 20+ employees.[12] The word clouds regarding these organisations are quite telling in that the dominating words are 'wish', 'need', 'not be able to', or 'be impossible'. They seem to point to a tension between the potentially helpful role of these organisations as well as the underlying difficulties.

Finally, we checked various policy instruments, such as pensions, social insurance, minimum salary, unemployment benefit, training, and others. In this paragraph we present only the more interesting or more conclusive evidence. Thus, pensions were mentioned frequently in articles on return migration. The word cloud and word2vec analysis showed that pensions are considered small and compared frequently to the minimum salary or social benefits. The word cloud on articles featuring the unemployment benefit has linked it to the words 'need', 'want', 'work', while the word2vec algorithm revealed that 'very small' is used almost interchangeably with 'unemployment benefit'. The programme 'I Choose Lithuania', which was created to facilitate return, has also been noticed. It is associated with the words such as 'want', 'need', 'returning', 'now', 'possible', 'important', 'difficult' and is seen through the narrative of offering the returnees help to overcome difficulties.

We also checked to what extent and in which capacity important concepts such as 'entrepreneurship', 'business', 'work', and 'unemployment' appear in our data set. The word 'work' is featured in almost all articles, showing that finding, having, and doing work is considered very important when discussing returnees. The word2vec algorithm shows that work is often used interchangeably with 'well paid', 'will create it ourselves', as well as words such as 'need', 'search', 'overtime'. The word 'business' goes often together with the words 'returned emigrants'. Words such as 'low qualification', 'unqualified' are used often in the texts. However, interestingly, the closely associated words in the word2vec analysis were 'need', 'lack employees', 'difficult find'.

Further, analysis shows that the concepts of knowledge, skills, and productivity appear often in the articles and are associated frequently with 'new', 'important', 'create', 'offer', 'need'; yet also 'do not contribute' was quite visible in the texts. The word2vec analysis shows that 'knowledge' can be used quite interchangeably with 'work offer', while 'skills' is used closely with phrases like 'professional', 'quality', 'gained abroad', 'well paid'. When it comes to productivity, it is often used together with words such as 'new', 'need', 'important'; 'high', 'increasing'. A number of texts, however, point towards 'smaller' or 'decreasing' productivity as well as 'loss making', although this may reference the texts on increasing salaries, the middle-income trap, and the need to increase productivity to stay competitive.

Conclusion

In this concluding section we combine the evidence from LFS and text mining to draw conclusions about the status of returnees in the Lithuanian labour market, the role of institutions, and the potential influence of return migration on labour productivity and utilisation in Lithuania. Statistical analysis and text mining are rarely used together, partly because such a combination crosses the boundaries of distinct academic fields. Nevertheless, we believe that the two methods can complement each other and, at least partly, compensate for each other's limitations. The LFS dataset provides pertinent answers. However, it can be only used to analyse the recent returnees. Text mining allows us to consider return migration overall and explore the role of institutions that are in charge of facilitating labour market integration.

The key downside of text mining is that the algorithm-generated outputs leave a lot of leeway to subjective interpretation. Nevertheless, the method does have a quantitative side (e.g. it can show what words are used more or less often, in what contexts) and thus provide useful information, which may be difficult to notice by using more structured approaches. Certainly, it is important to ask whether the news portals provide an accurate reflection of reality or should be treated as a selective view of journalists and reporters, mediated by the editorial policy of a specific news outlet. This, however, does not present a major issue to our analysis. On the one hand, while individual narratives in the media may not be representative, we assume that an entirety of these narratives reflect well whether the returnees are successful and are perceived as such or the opposite is true. On the other hand, media narratives may also entail an element of a self-fulfilling prophecy. In other words, even if media narratives were different from the statistically objective reality (which is difficult to capture given that no truly representative data set on returnees exists), the more positive narratives could bolster self-confidence of the returnees and their acceptance in the society and thus initiate some kind of a virtuous cycle. Meanwhile, a vicious cycle would be more likely if we observed a trend towards more negative media coverage.

The first empirical question is, then, whether we see evidence of positive selection of returnees. The LFS data shows that the recent returnees are younger; fewer among them have low education as compared to the general labour force; more of them have medium-level education. We do not find that returnees are more likely to hold higher education degrees. If we look at this from the perspective of labour productivity, we could argue that return migration is likely to have a positive influence. Importantly, human capital manifests itself not only in the formal level of education but also in professional skills and work experience that mobile workers gain abroad, as well as foreign language, communication, and interpersonal abilities. Our data set allows us to explore whether the society and employers recognise the time abroad as useful or, on the contrary, they see returnees as those who worked in low qualification jobs and/or choosing to return because they could not fit in abroad. This is pertinent to the analysis of both labour productivity and utilisation. The analysis of the dataset revealed a variety of narratives, positive and negative. However, the most visible stories tend to highlight skills, abilities, diplomas, and experiences that were acquired abroad. The texts also refer to unqualified work quite frequently, but not necessarily in connection to the migrant experiences abroad or in the home country; e.g. many of these texts seem to point to the lack of workers in the home country. In summary, the texts suggest that migration experience is being acknowledged, which points to a positive influence of return migration on labour productivity as well as on labour utilisation (especially the qualitative aspect).

Next, we consider whether the returnees find employment in jobs where they can use productively their skills and qualification. This is also pertinent to the question of labour utilisation. The analysis of the LFS data showed that, compared to the general labour force, the recent returnees are significantly less likely to work and much more likely to be self-employed. The labour market status depends on the level of education, as returnees who have higher education degrees are much more likely to work than those with lower levels of education. We also find an indication, albeit not very strong statistically, that salaries of working recent returnees are somewhat lower than those in the general population. This is plausible, as it might be related to the fact that recent returnees are only starting in their careers in Lithuania. Nevertheless, there is no data in the LFS which would allow us to explore the further career paths of the returnees. Other research shows that over the years the effect of migration disappears or even turns into an advantage. This is supported by the media texts on return migration. If we try to identify the single most prominent topic, based on the LDA algorithm, it seems to suggest that returnees have work and are satisfied with their status. If we expand the number of topics, the narratives of creating or having business, owning property, and growing family are more visible than narratives pointing towards difficulties of return. Further, in our dataset the words 'work' and 'business' are often associated with returnees, albeit work may also be associated with job search and (working) overtime. All in all, although the LFS data indicates that recent returnees are less likely to be employed, the textual data set does not show that the return migrants are perceived as failing to find work. On the contrary, the stories of successful return are relatively more visible. From the perspective of labour productivity and utilisation we can again point towards a likely positive effect of return migration on labour productivity. The effect on labour utilisation is more complex. It may be negative on the quantitative aspect of labour utilisation, especially during the initial stages of return.

Thirdly, we consider the role of institutions and some of the labour market policies. LFS-based data shows that recent returnees are significantly less likely to use PES; they are also less likely to participate in regular education. Analysis of the texts from news portals provides some explanation for this, as the labour market institutions (Public Employment Service, Social Insurance Board) are associated with paying taxes and contributions, while the level of protection is not considered high. Importantly, central government institutions appear frequently in the texts on return migration. While specific narratives about these institutions are not easy to discern, this shows that in the media discourse the situation of the returnees is linked to the overall economic and social environment in the country. Several initiatives to encourage return (such as 'I Choose Lithuania') were created recently; they do not appear frequently in the media, but when they do, they are usually part of the more positive narrative. When looking at this from the perspective of labour productivity and utilisation, we do not find, then, that labour market institutions play a significant role in positive selection or quick integration of the returnees in the labour market. Rather, this is associated with broader factors, such as the labour market dynamics and quality of government in the country.

Notes

1 We would like to thank Lukas Trišauskas (Data Scientist, PPMI) for his valuable contribution to data collection, in particular for scraping the web to collect texts analysed in this chapter. We are also grateful to Irma Budginaitė, as some of the media articles for 2005–2011 come from Budginaitė (2012b).
2 The model used for Lithuania did not take account of remittances. However, according to the authors: '[remittances] cannot fully address the loss of labour input on capacity output in the longer-term' (Holland, Fic, Rincon-Aznar, Stokes, & Paluchowski, 2011, p. 5).
3 In other words, the skilled mobile workers are difficult to replace, which leads to structural unemployment.
4 For example, according to Hazans (2016), 'post-accession Baltic emigrants were less educated than the pre-accession ones'.
5 I.e. without consideration whether the mobile workers are more or less educated than stayers.
6 Quantitatively, labour utilisation is measured as hours worked per capita. If stayers are older and thus less active in the labour market, this moderates the relative increase (if any) in labour utilisation even in the context of high demand for labour.
7 A characteristic example includes the portal 'I choose Lithuania' (in Lithuanian: 'Renkuosi Lietuvą', www.renkuosilietuva.lt), which provides information to (prospective) returnees, offers consultations, and features personal stories of successful return.
8 In 2018 this was the highest percentage among EU-28. It is probably influenced by the fact that registration is necessary to access benefits.
9 Due to the structure of the LFS, the same respondents are interviewed four times over the course of one and a half years. To exclude repeat data from the same respondents, we only consider responses given the fourth time LFS participants were interviewed (in other words, we use the fourth wave of the LFS only).
10 Both people currently employed and those out of work were asked whether they contacted public employment services if they indicated that they were looking for work.
11 Note: the statistic is for illustrative purposes only and does not imply that 39 per cent of all returnees in Lithuania work abroad. We cannot make that statement because we are using a pooled dataset without applying weights.
12 This obligation was introduced in the latest reform of the Labour Code in 2017.

References

Anacka, M., & Wójcicka, A. (2019). *Impacts of return migration in Poland* (Working Paper Horizon 2020 Grant Agreement No. 727072). REMINDER project.

Atoyan, R., Christiansen, L., Dizioli, A., Ebeke, C., Ilahi, N., Ilyina, A., . . . Zakharova, D. (2016). *Emigration and its economic impact on Eastern Europe* [Staff Discussion Notes]. IMF.

Barcevičius, E., & Žvalionytė, D. (2012). *Užburtas ratas? Lietuvos gyventojų grįžtamoji ir pakartotinė migracija*. Vaga.

Barcevičius, E. (2016). How successful are highly qualified return migrants in the Lithuanian labour market? *International Migration, 54*(3), 35–47. doi:10.1111/imig.12224

Berry, M., Garcia-Blanco, I., & Moore, K. (2015, December). *Press coverage of the refugee and migrant crisis in the EU: A content analysis of five European countries* (pp. 1–276). Report Prepared for the United Nations High Commission for Refugees, United Nations.

Blei, D. M., Ng, A. Y., & Jordan, M. I. (2003, March). Latent Dirichlet allocation. *The Journal of Machine Learning Research, 3*, 993–1022. doi:10.5555/944919.944937

Bodvarsson, Ö. B., & den Berg, H. V. (2009). *The economics of immigration: Theory and policy*. Springer.

Boros, L., & Hegedus, G. (2016). European national policies aimed at stimulating return migration. In R. Nadler, Z. Kovacs, B. Glorius, & T. Lang (Eds.), *Return migration and regional development in Europe: Mobility against the stream* (pp. 333–357). Palgrave Macmillan. doi:10.1057/978-1-137-57509-8

Budginaitė, I. (2012a). Politiniai grįžtamosios migracijos veiksniai: politikos priemonės ir jų sėkmė. In E. Barcevičius & D. Žvalionytė (Eds.), *Užburtas ratas? Lietuvos gyventojų grįžtamoji ir pakartotinė migracija* (pp. 167–213). Vaga.

Budginaitė, I. (2012b). Visuomeniniai grįžtamosios migracijos veiksniai: Grįžusių migrantų įvaizdis viešojoje erdvėje ir visuomenės požiūris. In E. Barcevičius & D. Žvalionytė (Eds.), *Užburtas ratas? Lietuvos gyventojų grįžtamoji ir pakartotinė migracija* (pp. 214–270). Vaga.

Cassarino, J.-P. (2004). Theorising return migration: The conceptual approach to return migrants revisited. *International Journal of Multicultural Societies, 6*(2), 253–279.

Cerase, F. P. (1974). Expectations and reality: A case study of return migration from the United States to Southern Italy. *International Migration Review, 8*(2), 245–262.

Coniglio, N. D., & Brzozowski, J. (2016). Migration and development at home: Bitter or sweet return? Evidence from Poland. *European Urban and Regional Studies, 25*(1), 85–105. doi:10.1177/0969776416681625

CIRCABC. (2019). *Educational attainment, early leaving from education and training, transition from school to work (complementary methodological information)*. Retrieved from https://circabc.europa.eu/sd/a/3b3f4939-5e18-478d-b954-42e112f8ed05/SECTION1_EA.htm

Démurger, S., & Xu, H. (2011). Return migrants: The rise of new entrepreneurs in rural China. *World Development, 39*(10), 1847–1861. doi:10.1016/j.worlddev.2011.04.027

European Commission. (2018). *Draft joint employment report from the commission and the council accompanying the communication from the commission on the Annual Growth Survey 2019* (COM(2018) 761 final).

Goldberg, Y., & Levy, O. (2014). Word2vec explained: Deriving Mikolov et al.'s negative-sampling word-embedding method. *ArXiv*, arXiv:1402.3722. Retrieved from http://arxiv.org/abs/1402.3722

Grabowska, I. (2016). *Movers and stayers: Social mobility, migration and skills*. Peter Lang. doi:10.3726/978-3-653-05817-8

Hazans, M. (2016). Migration experience of the Baltic Countries in the context of economic crisis. In M. Kahanec & K. F. Zimmermann (Eds.), *Labour migration, EU enlargement, and the great recession* (pp. 297–344). Springer. doi:10.1007/978-3-662-45320-9_13

Hazans, M. (2018). *An in-depth analysis of the emigration of skilled labour: Latvia* (pp. 1–51). Labour Market Policy Thematic Review 2018. European Centre of Expertise in the Field of Labour Law, Employment and Labour Market Policy (ECE).

Hazans, M. (2019). *What kind of foreign experience boosts returnees' earnings? Evidence from Latvia*. Inaugural Baltic Economic Conference, Vilnius.

Hazans, M., & Philips, K. (2011). *The post-enlargement migration experience in the Baltic labour markets* (IZA Discussion Papers).

Holland, D., Fic, T., Rincon-Aznar, A., Stokes, L., & Paluchowski, P. (2011). *Labour mobility within the EU: The impact of enlargement and the functioning of the transitional arrangements. Final report*. Study carried out on behalf of the Employment, Social Affairs and Inclusion Directorate General of the European Commission (contract VC/2010/1159).

ILO. (2012). *International standard classification of occupations: Structure, group definitions and correspondence tables*. International Labour Office.

Kaczmarczyk, P., Anacka, M., & Fihel, A. (2016). Migration as an asset? Polish returnees at the time of the crisis. In M. Kahanec & K. F. Zimmermann (Eds.), *Labuor migration, EU enlargement, and the great recession* (pp. 219–245). Springer. doi:10.1007/978-3-662-45320-9

Kaczmarczyk, P., & Okolski, M. (2008). *Economic impacts of migration on Poland and the Baltic states* (Fafo-Paper No. 2008:01, pp. 1–67).

Karolak, M. (2016). From potential to actual social remittances? Exploring how Polish return migrants cope with difficult employment conditions. *Central and Eastern European Migration Review*, *5*(2), 21–39. doi:10.17467/ceemr.2016.02

Klein-Hitpaß, K. (2016). Return migrants as knowledge brokers and institutional innovators: New theoretical conceptualisations and the example of Poland. In R. Nadler, Z. Kovacs, B. Glorius, & T. Lang (Eds.), *Return migration and regional development in Europe: Mobility against the stream* (pp. 55–81). Palgrave Macmillan. doi:10.1057/978-1-137-57509-8

Krisjane, Z., Apsite-Berina, E., & Berzins, M. (2016). Circularity within the EU: The return intentions of Latvian migrants. In R. Nadler, Z. Kovacs, B. Glorius, & T. Lang (Eds.), *Return migration and regional development in Europe: Mobility against the stream* (pp. 215–240). Palgrave Macmillan. doi:10.1057/978-1-137-57509-8

Lulle, A., Krisjane, Z., & Bauls, A. (2019). Diverse return mobilities and evolving identities among returnees in Latvia. In R. G. Anghel, M. Fauser, & P. Boccagni (Eds.), *Transnational return and social change: Hierarchies, identities and ideas* (pp. 103–123). Anthem Press. Retrieved from https://repository.lboro.ac.uk/articles/Diverse_return_mobilities_and_evolving_identities_among_returnees_in_Latvia/9486533

Martin, R., & Radu, D. (2012). Return migration: The experience of Eastern Europe. *International Migration*, *50*(6), 109–128.

McCormick, B., & Wahba, J. (2001). Overseas work experience, savings and entrepreneurship amongst return migrants to LDCs. *Scottish Journal of Political Economy*, *48*(2), 164–178.

OECD. (2013). *Coping with emigration in Baltic and East European countries*. OECD Publishing. doi:10.1787/9789264204928-en

OECD. (2019). *Labour productivity and utilisation (indicator)*. doi:10.1787/02c02f63-en

Skibinska, M. (2019). *The aggregate and redistributive effects of migration for the sending country* (Preliminary draft).

Škuflić, L., & Vučković, V. (2019). The effect of emigration on unemployment rates: The case of EU emigrant countries. *Economic Research-Ekonomska Istraživanja*, *31*(1), 1826–1836. doi:10.1080/1331677X.2018.1516154

Smoliner, S., Förschner, M., Hochgerner, J., & Nová, J. (2013). Comparative report on re-migration trends in Central and Eastern Europe. In T. Lang (Ed.), *Return migration in Central Europe: Current trends and an analysis of policies supporting returning migrants* (pp. 11–57). Leibniz-Institut für Länderkunde e.V. (IfL).

Žvalionytė, D. (2012). Grįžtamosios ir pakartotinės migracijos tendencijos. In E. Barcevičius & D. Žvalionytė (Eds.), *Užburtas ratas? Lietuvos gyventojų grįžtamoji ir pakartotinė migracija* (pp. 75–100). Vaga.

Žvalionytė, D. (2015). Migracijos patirtis – privalumas ar trūkumas Lietuvos darbo rinkoje? *Politologija*, *78*(2), 58–93.

9

THE ECONOMIC EFFECTS OF THE MINIMUM WAGE IN SLOVENIA

Suzana Laporšek and Matija Vodopivec

Introduction

One of the greatest challenges that CEE countries have faced since the beginning of their transition to market economies in the 1990s has been to strike an appropriate balance between achieving economic growth and maintaining a tolerable degree of income equality. Under the previous regimes, centrally planned wage grids resulted in egalitarian wage distributions and low income inequality, which, combined with policies of full employment, resulted in low productivity (Orazem & Vodopivec, 1995). Even in Slovenia, which, as a constituent republic of Yugoslavia, functioned under a system of workers' self-management with some degree of market prices, large government transfers redistributed funds from high-performing firms to underperforming ones, limiting the scope for firm-specific wage premia and its concomitant inequality (Kraft & Vodopivec, 1992). Following a period of rapidly increasing wage inequality immediately after the onset of transition, Slovenia introduced a statutory minimum wage in 1995. Following this introduction, by far the biggest change in minimum-wage policy came in 2010, when the government introduced a considerable increase in the minimum wage.

The economic effects of the minimum wages are some of the most debated topics both in theoretical and empirical literature. The literature on the effects of the minimum wage on employment is especially voluminous, but the findings are not unanimous. This is the case also for the CEE countries, as shown in the next section. Nevertheless, Neumark (2018) indicates that most of the empirical evidence suggests that minimum wages have a negative effect on employment, especially of low-skilled workers. With regard to the minimum wage effects on wage distributions, several studies report minimum wage increases creating spikes in the wage distribution (see Neumark & Wascher, 2010, for an overview), whereas evidence on the effects on wages higher up in the wage distribution (i.e., spill-over effects) is inconclusive. Studies on the CEE countries, however, mostly report positive effects of the minimum wage increases on wages of workers at or above the minimum wage (Eriksson & Pytlikova, 2004, for the Czech Republic and Slovakia; Ferraro, Meriküll, & Staehr, 2018, for Estonia, Harasztosi & Lindner, 2019, for Hungary). One of the least researched topics in the minimum wage literature is the effects of the minimum wage increases on firm performance. Available studies mostly deal with the effects on firm exit and profitability, mostly reporting negative effects. For the CEE countries, only two studies investigate the effects of minimum wages on firm profitability, confirming the negative effects (Harasztosi & Lindner, 2019, for Hungary, and Babiak, Chorna, & Pertold-Gebicka, 2019, for Poland).

In this chapter, we examine the effects of Slovenia's dramatic 22.9% minimum wage increase in March 2010 on a variety of economic outcomes in Slovenia including employment, wages, and firm performance. An in-depth study of the 2010 minimum wage increase is relevant not only because of the magnitude of the increase but also because it provides a case study of the effects of such an increase immediately following a deep recession. The minimum wage change increased the minimum-to-average wage ratio from 41.2% to 47.6% (Eurostat, 2019), which put Slovenia in the forefront among the EU countries and affected a growing share of the workforce – between 2005 and 2009, about 5% of workers earned minimum wage, whereas in 2011 this share increased to 8.8% (own calculations, Statistical Office of the Republic of Slovenia, 2017).

What are the main findings of this chapter? As found in other countries, the minimum wage in Slovenia has a significant impact on the wage distribution, both via direct effects (i.e., by creating spikes at the minimum wage) as through spill-over effects, i.e., by creating upward pressure on wages higher up in the wage distribution that result in wage increases. This effect was particularly pronounced in Slovenia after its 2010 minimum wage increase, given the increase's magnitude in terms of its level relative to the average wage as well as the share of workers it directly affected. While the minimum wage increase mainly affected less educated workers, it also resulted in a surprisingly large increase in the share of minimum-wage workers with at least general secondary education: their share among all minimum-wage workers grew from 25.3% in 2008 to 41.8% in 2015. A parallel development was an increase in the share of high-skilled occupations in the structure of minimum wage recipients. Our worker-level analysis of the effects of the minimum wage increase on the employment probability of workers finds that workers who were below the minimum wage were disproportionally, adversely affected: the increase in their relative price of labour made them less likely to remain in employment. Finally, our firm-level analysis shows that after accounting for the increased probability of exit amongst firms most affected by the minimum wage increase, surviving firms responded to the minimum wage increase with increased investment, decreased sales, and a decline in profitability.

As the above discussion suggests, there are a variety of channels through which minimum wages can influence a country's labour utilisation. Taking the broader definition of labour utilisation which encompasses the total contribution of human labour to GDP, minimum wages can have an important effect not only through their direct effect on employment and the number of hours worked but also through their indirect effects. To the extent that they make certain categories of jobs economically unviable, they provide an impetus for retraining, upskilling, and investment into higher-value-added jobs.

The structure of this chapter is as follows. We first provide a literature review on the economic effects of the minimum wage. Next, we provide a more detailed description of the context of the minimum wage increase in March 2010 in Slovenia, followed by an international comparison of the Slovenian minimum wage to the CEE and EU-15 countries. We continue with a presentation of micro data. In the empirical part of the chapter, we first present characteristics of the minimum-wage workers in Slovenia by their demographic characteristics and sector of employment. We then examine the effects of the minimum wage increase in 2010 on the wage distribution, the employment probability of individual workers and firm performance. Finally, we summarise the main empirical results and provide policy implications of the minimum wage changes on labour utilisation.

Literature review on the minimum wage effects

In this section we provide a literature review on the effects of minimum wages on employment, wage distribution, and firm performance, issues we later empirically analyse for Slovenia.

Minimum wage effects on employment

The effect of minimum wage on employment has been one of the most debated topics in economics. Still, economic theory does not provide a common answer on the minimum wage effects on labour market outcomes. On the one hand, a simple supply-and-demand model predicts that setting the minimum wage above the equilibrium wage increases a firm's marginal costs with a negative effect on employment. On the other hand, monopsony models and their extensions show that a minimum wage can increase employment (for an overview of models see Boeri & van Ours, 2013). As there is no consensus in a theory, empirical evidence is crucial for understanding the minimum wage effects.

The empirical literature on the minimum-wage employment effects is long-standing and voluminous. Early empirical studies, which were mostly based on time-series analysis and studying the effects of the changes in the national minimum wage on aggregate employment, mostly report negative employment effects. According to Brown, Gilroy, and Kohen (1982), the consensus of early studies was that a 10% increase in the minimum wage reduces teenage employment by 1% to 3%. This consensus was challenged by the new minimum wage research in the beginning of the 1990s, which were applying quasi-experimental approach and reported no or of positive effects of minimum wage increase on employment (Card, 1992a, 1992b; Card & Krueger, 1994; Katz & Krueger, 1992). These findings triggered continuous research on minimum wages which had two poles – research identified with the new minimum wage and its critics (for an overview see Neumark & Wascher, 2010; Schmitt, 2013).

Recent studies on the effects of minimum wages on labour market results mostly apply quasi-experimental methods, and several of them use individual level data, which is the approach we apply also in our analysis. Most studies show that high minimum wages negatively affect worker and job flows, reduce employment and inhibit its recovery (see, for example, Neumark, Salas, & Wascher, 2014, and Dube, Lester, & Reich, 2016, for the United States; Abowd, Kramarz, Margolis, & Philippon, 2000, and Portugal & Cardoso, 2006, for France and Portugal, respectively; Galán & Puente, 2015, for Spain; Bossler & Gerner, 2019, and Caliendo, Fedorets, Preiss, Schröder, & Wittbrodt, 2019, for Germany). Studies also show that these effects are stronger for vulnerable groups and that they disproportionally affect sectors with high shares of minimum wage recipients. But there are also many empirical studies that report positive and/or statistically insignificant effects of minimum wages on employment and labour market transitions (for example, Allegretto, Godoey, Nadler, & Reich, 2018, for the United States; Stewart, 2003, 2004; Dickens & Draca, 2005; Dickens, Riley, & Wilkinson, 2009, 2012; and Bryan, Salvatori, & Taylor, 2013, for the United Kingdom; and König & Möller, 2009, for Germany).

There are only a few studies on the minimum wage effects on labour market outcomes in the CEE countries. For Croatia, Blažević Burić (2013) reported small yet positive effects of the minimum wage increase in the 2000–2010 period. Moreover, Nestić, Babić, and Blažević Burić (2018) showed that minimum wage increases in the 2009–2015 period in Croatia, at most, affected tradable low-wage sectors, yet these sectors had a smaller employment decline compared to the manufacturing industry as a whole and non-tradable low-wage sectors. Kertesi and Köllő (2003) analysed the effects of a large minimum wage increase over the 2000–2002 period in Hungary and found significant negative effects on employment in small firms and on job-finding probabilities of low-wage workers, with the effects being stronger in low-wage segments of the market and depressed regions. Disemployment effects were reported also by a recent study for Hungary by Harasztosi and Lindner (2019). Similar findings were reported also by Fialová and Mysíková (2009) for the Czech Republic, by Baranowska-Rataj and Magda (2015) and Majchrowska, Broniatowska, and Żółkiewski (2016) for young workers in Poland, and by Hinnosaar and Rõõm (2003) for Estonia. In contrast, Ferraro, Hänilane, and Staehr (2018) reported no or small effects of the minimum wage increase on employment retention for the directly affected workers in Estonia. No significant effects of minimum wage increase on employment were reported also by Pantea (2017) for Romania and Šuminas (2015) for Lithuania.

Minimum wage effects on wage distribution

A fairly extensive body of empirical research shows that minimum wage increases affect wage distributions by increasing the concentration of workers paid at the minimum (for an overview of studies see Neumark & Wascher, 2010) as well as through spill-over effects, i.e., by creating upward pressure on wages higher up in the wage distribution that result in wage increases.

Regarding spill-over effects, theoretical literature provides several explanations (see Stewart, 2012a, 2012b, for in-depth overviews). Minimum wage hikes may (i) decrease the demand for low-paid workers and, depending on their substitutability, increase demand for more skilled (and higher paid) workers with positive effects on their wages (Gregory, 2014); (ii) trigger increases of wages above the minimum wage in order to preserve wage differentials necessary to stimulate worker effort (Grossman, 1983); and (iii) increase the reservation wages of job seekers, forcing employers to raise their wage offers in order to attract new workers (Manning, 2003).

Empirical literature provides various findings of the effects of the minimum wage increases on wages higher up in the distribution. Several studies for the United States reported significant spill-over effects, being especially high for workers with wages close to the new minimum wage (Card & Krueger, 1995; DiNardo, Fortin, & Lemieux, 1996; Lee, 1999; Manning, 2003; Neumark, Schweitzer, & Wascher, 2004). On the other hand, studies for the United Kingdom found small or no minimum wage spill-over effects (Stewart, 2012a, 2012b; Dickens & Manning, 2004). Some studies even reported negative spill-over effects. For example, Centeno, Duarte, and Novo (2011) showed that minimum wage increases during 2006–2010 in Portugal created negative spill-over effects on other individuals' wages, suggesting that firms adjust the other wage gains downwards to accommodate exogenous increases in the minimum wage.

Regarding the CEE countries, most empirical studies report positive wage effects of the minimum wage increases for workers at or above the minimum wage. For example, Ferraro, Meriküll, et al. (2018) found substantial spill-over effects up to the 20th percentile of the wage distribution in Estonia. Harasztosi and Lindner (2019) showed in the case of Hungary, that due to minimum wage increase, the average wage at the highly exposed firms increased by 54% more than at firms with no exposure to the minimum wage. Eriksson and Pytlikova (2004) find on high wage effects for the Czech Republic and Slovakia.

Minimum wage effects on firm performance

The effect of minimum wage on firm performance has received relatively little attention in the literature. Draca, Machin, and Van Reenen (2011) showed that the minimum wage introduction in the United Kingdom resulted in a significant reduction of firms' profitability, yet they found no evidence that these profitability reductions further resulted in increases in firm exits. Rohlin (2011) reported negative effects of minimum wage increases on firm entry in the United States but of small effects on firm exit. In contrast, Luca and Luca (2017) and Aaronson, French, Sorkin, and To (2018) found considerable effects of minimum wage increases on restaurant exits in the United States.

To our knowledge, there are only two studies that analyse the effects of minimum wage increases on firm performance in CEE countries. Harasztosi and Lindner (2019) showed that considerable minimum wage increases in 2001 in Hungary had reduced profits, by which the effects were stronger in the short run. Also, Babiak et al. (2019) reported a decline in firms' profits due to the 2008 minimum wage increase in Poland.

A closer look at the 2010 minimum wage change in Slovenia

The adoption of the 2010 Minimum Wage Act (Official Gazette of the Republic of Slovenia, No. 13/10) brought one of the most substantial changes in Slovenia's minimum wage after its introduction in 1995. First, the law considerably increased the minimum wage level – from 597 EUR to 734 EUR gross, or by 22.9% – supposedly to bring it in line with minimum consumption basket per person (IMAD, 2013). Following the minimum wage change, the minimum-to-average wage ratio increased by 6.4 percentage points, from 41.2 to 47.6% (or to 43.2% for firms with a gradual adjustment schedule). This ratio further increased in the following years, reaching its peak at 51.5% in 2013, and it settled at 50.1% in 2018 (Figure 9.1; Eurostat, 2019). Second, the law altered the adjustment mechanism of the minimum wage to macroeconomic parameters. The new law introduced automatic, full indexation to consumer price index growth and allowed

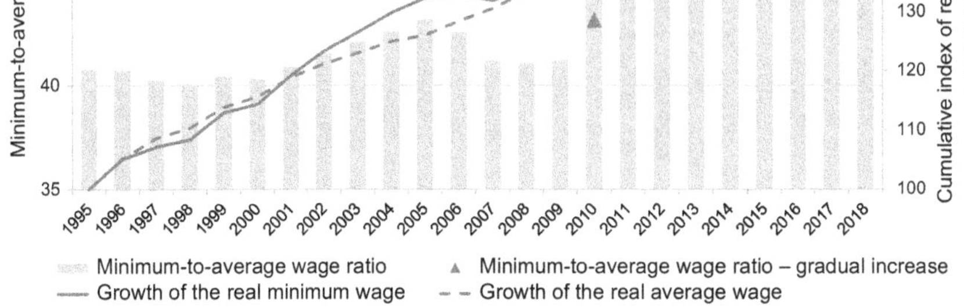

Figure 9.1 The ratio between the minimum and average gross wages and cumulative indices of real minimum and real average gross wage growth, 1995–2018

Source: Own elaboration based on data from the SI-STAT (Statistical Office of the Republic of Slovenia, 2019) and overview of the minimum wage legislation.

for additional increases to reflect wage, employment, or GDP growth. Because of the unprecedented rate of increase, the 2010 law stipulated that employers could apply for a gradual transition – consisting of three discrete jumps – to the new mandated minimum wage, to be completed by December 31, 2011.[1]

Moreover, the 2010 Minimum Wage Act contributed to a strong divergence of growth between the minimum wage and the average wage. Compared to 2008, the real minimum wage amount increased alone by 20% in 2010 and by 38.9% until 2018. The increase in real average wage was substantially lower – only by 13.8% in the 2008–2018 period (Statistical Office of the Republic of Slovenia, 2019). As shown in Figure 9.1, before the 2010 minimum wage change both real minimum wage and average wage recorded similar growth trends. In 2010 the gap between the real minimum and real average wage growth remarkably increased and, mostly due to the subsequent reduction of the real average wage, in 2013 the gap between the cumulative index of the real minimum and real average gross wage growth reached its maximum. Among the reasons for this strong divergence of growth trends is the minimum wage increase, on one hand, and a small but steady decrease of real average wages during 2011–2013 caused by the decline of general economic activity as well as austerity measures applied to the public sector, on the other.

Slovenia's adoption of the new minimum wage coincided with an unusually large contraction of the GDP. As shown in Figure 9.2, in 2009 the economic activity decreased by 7.8% in real terms, followed by small declines in 2012 and 2013. In this period the minimum wage increased by 20% in real terms.

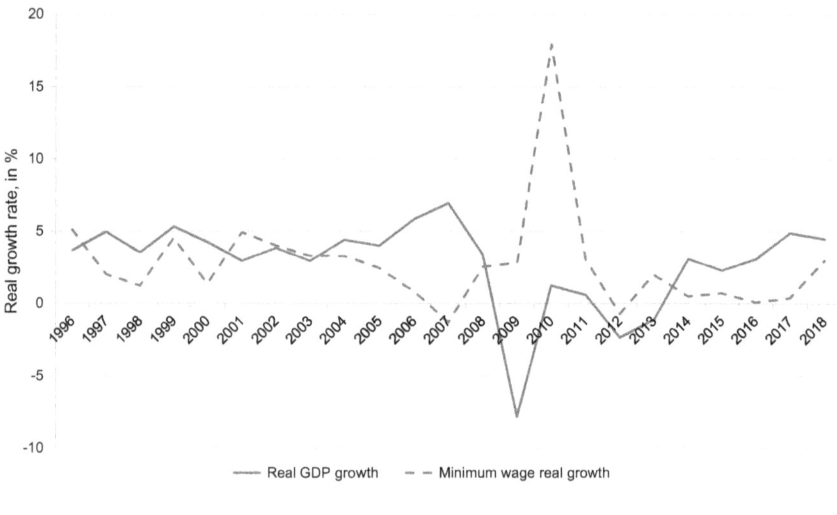

Figure 9.2 The minimum wage real growth and real GDP growth in Slovenia, 1996–2018, in %

Sources: Own elaboration based on (Statistical Office of the Republic of Slovenia, 2019; Eurostat, 2019).

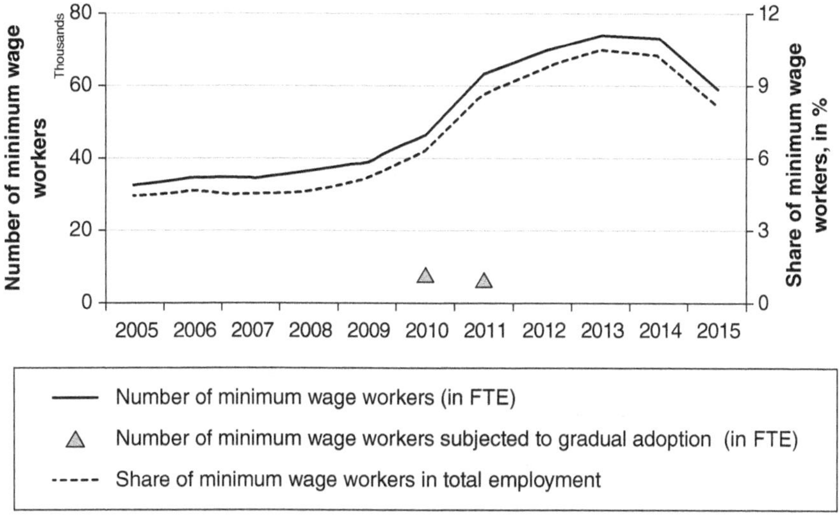

Figure 9.3 Number and share of FTEs receiving a wage set at the minimum wage, yearly averages, 2005–2015

Source: Own elaboration based on combined unemployment, employment, and earnings registry data, Statistical Office of the Republic of Slovenia.

Notes: Year is defined as March to February. Data present average number and shares of FTEs receiving a wage set at the minimum wage. Shares of minimum-wage workers receiving a wage set at the minimum wage are calculated as % of total FTEs. Minimum-wage workers were identified using the combined unemployment, employment, and earnings registry data. According to our definition, a minimum-wage worker is a worker whose hourly wage is equal to the statutory minimum wage in that year +/ – 2.5 %.

It comes as no surprise that in the wake of the 2010 Minimum Wage Act, the number of minimum wage-workers increased. As shown in Figure 9.3, less than 40-thousand full-time equivalent workers (FTEs), so less than 6% of total employment, received a wage set at the minimum wage in 2009 and prior. In 2010 this number increased to 47-thousand (i.e., to 6.4%) and in 2011 further to 63-thousand (i.e., to 8.8%). Out of these, 6.5-thousand FTEs were subjected to the gradual increase of the minimum wage. A trend of a steady increase of FTEs receiving the minimum wage continued to 2013, reaching 74-thousand (i.e., 10.5%), followed by a decline to 59-thousand (8.2% of total employment).

Slovenia's minimum wage in the CEE and EU-15 perspective

With the 2010 minimum wage change, the Slovenian minimum wage significantly increased compared to the minimum wages in other CEE countries, which is still the case today. According to the last available data for 2019, Slovenia records the highest nominal hourly minimum wage, set at 5.1 euros per hour in January 2019. This is high above the minimum wage levels in other CEE countries, where the minimum wage ranged between 1.7 and 3.4 euros per hour (see Figure 9.4). This is, on average, about one-third of the average minimum wage in the old EU member states (WSI, 2019; Schulten & Luebker, 2019). Measuring the minimum wage in purchasing power standard (PPS), the divergence between CEE countries reduces, with Slovenia still recording the highest hourly minimum wage (5.8 euros), closely followed by Poland (5.3 euros), Lithuania (5.1 euros) and Romania (5.1 euros) (WSI, 2019). Overall, recent trends show an increase of minimum wages in all CEE countries, with the exception of Latvia (see Figure 9.4).

The minimum wage gap between the CEE countries and the EU-15 countries with a statutory minimum wage is smaller in terms of the minimum-to-average wage ratio. In all the CEE countries, with the exception of the Czech Republic, the minimum wage has reached more than 40% of average wage, which is comparable to the EU-15 average (Figure 9.5). The minimum-to-average ratio is the highest in Slovenia (50.1% in 2018). Estonia, Slovakia and the Czech Republic, on the other hand, record the lowest minimum-to-average wage ratio among the CEE countries, being also below the EU-15 average (Eurostat, 2019). In all the CEE countries the minimum-to-average ratio increased during the last decade, with

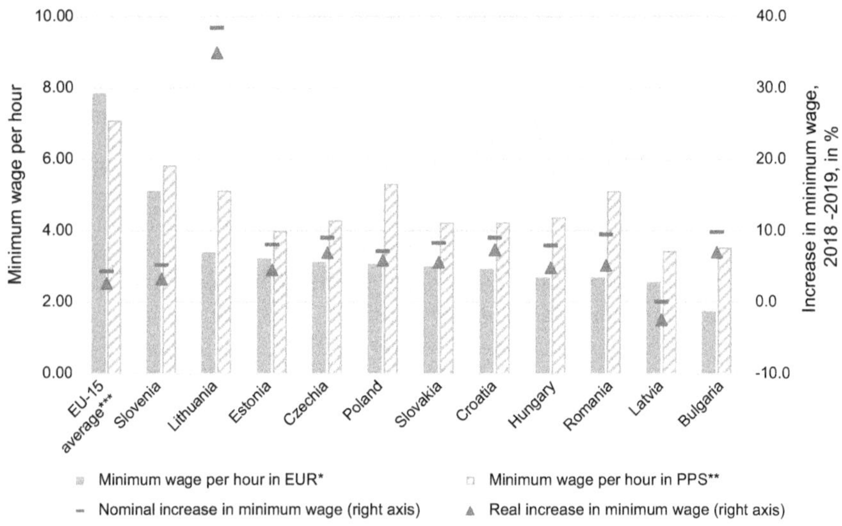

Figure 9.4 Hourly minimum wage in euros and PPS and nominal and real developments in minimum wage between 2018 and 2019 in %

Source: WSI, 2019.

Notes: Nominal and real developments of minimum wage refer to a growth rate of the minimum wage of 1 January 2019 compared to 1 January 2018.

*Conversion in euros by reference to the annual average rate 2018.

**Conversion in PPS on a euro basis by reference to the private consumption PPS 2017 provided by the World Bank.

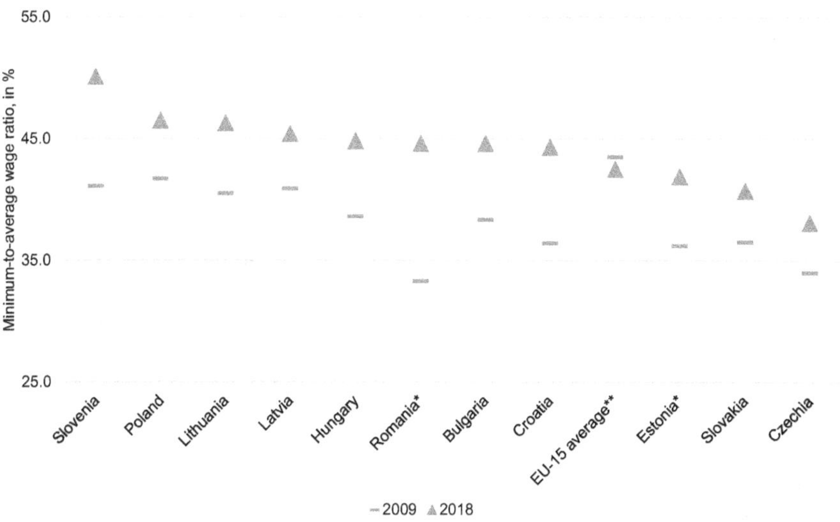

Figure 9.5 The minimum wage as the percentage of average wages of workers employed full time in the EU Member States, 2007–2015

Sources: Eurostat, 2019.

Notes: Countries are ranked by decreasing value of the minimum-to-average ratio in 2018.

*For Estonia and Romania, we present data for 2017 instead for 2018.

**The EU-15 average refers to average of old EU Member States with a statutory minimum wage (i.e., Belgium, France, Germany, Greece, Ireland, Luxembourg, Malta, the Netherlands, Portugal, Spain, and the United Kingdom).

the increase being the highest in Romania (due to several substantial increases starting in 2014) and Slovenia (mostly on the account of the 2010 minimum wage increase). In contrast, in the EU-15 countries this ratio has slightly decreased.

Data used for analysis of the minimum wage effects

While the already-presented analysis focused on aggregate statistics, the remaining analysis in this chapter focuses on the effects of the 2010 minimum wage increase using individual-level, matched employer–employee data. The database was compiled by linking several administrative databases covering the entire Slovenian workforce and the universe of firms. For each worker, the data contains information on employment, unemployment, and wages for the 2005–2015 period. For each firm, accounting data is linked with annual reports to provide a detailed picture of each firm's operations. The resulting database combines the following administrative data sources:

i *Work history data*. It contains starting and ending dates of an employment spell, the type of appointment, occupation, employer identification code and personal characteristics (gender, age, and education). The data are collected as a part of social insurance and are maintained by the Statistical Office of the Republic of Slovenia (2017).

ii *Data on registered unemployment.* It contains starting and ending dates of an unemployment spell, destinations of exit from unemployment, as well as information on the receipt of unemployment insurance benefits. Personal and family characteristics pertaining to each spell are also included. The data are provided by the Employment Service of Slovenia (2017).

iii *Worker earnings data.* It contains information on earnings associated with each employment spell of an individual (amount of earnings, number of hours worked, starting and ending date of earnings period). This database is provided by the Pension and Disability Insurance Institute of Slovenia (2017).

iv *Accounting data on enterprises.* Data consist of the yearly profit and loss statements, as well as balance sheets, for all incorporated businesses in Slovenia between 1991 and 2015, from the Agency of the Republic of Slovenia for Public Legal Records and Related Services (AJPES, 2017a). This database is used to calculate firm-level estimates of productivity.

v *Slovenian Business Registry data set.* It includes information on the four-digit industry, the year the firm started operating and the firm's type and ownership structure (private and state ownership, ownership by domestic and foreign owners and whether a firm is a publicly traded stock company or a limited liability company), obtained from AJPES (2017b).

Who are minimum-wage workers in Slovenia?

As shown in Figure 9.3, the number of minimum wage recipients substantially increased with the 2010 minimum wage increase. An in-depth analysis of their demographic characteristics and characteristics of their employment gives the following interesting findings.

Minimum-wage workers in Slovenia are predominately men – in the 2005–2015 period their share among all minimum wage earners increased from 47% in 2005 to 54% in 2015 – and of 30 to 49 years of age. Nevertheless, if we compare shares of minimum-wage workers within age categories, we can observe that young workers are most affected by the minimum wage. Namely, before the minimum wage change in 2008, 12.1% of all young FTEs under the age of 25 were minimum wage earners; in 2011 their share increased to 21.3%, with further increases in later years. A similar increase of minimum-wage workers share can be observed in the 25–29 age group – after the 2010 minimum wage increase their share has increased 4.5 percentage points to 12.4%.

Minimum-wage workers are mostly low skilled. Almost two-thirds of minimum-wage workers have primary or vocational secondary education. Interestingly, after 2010 we can observe a change in the educational structure of minimum-wage workers – there was a remarkable increase in the minimum-wage workers with a general secondary education (their share among all minimum-wage workers increased from 19% in 2008 to 30.7% in 2015) and tertiary education (from 6.3% in 2008 to 11.1% in 2015), implying that the increase of the minimum wage also affected highly educated workers. This might be attributed to the fact that the minimum wage increase in 2010 was substantial, and firms did not raise the wages of some high-skilled workers whose wages were at the new minimum wage. Nevertheless, the share of minimum wage recipients among all workers with tertiary education is quite small but not entirely negligible – standing at 2.9% in 2015.

Most of the minimum-wage workers work in very low or low-skilled occupations – in 2015, their share in the structure of all minimum-wage workers stood at 80%. With regard to the share of minimum-wage workers among all workers in the certain occupation group, we can, expectedly, observe an especially high increase in very low and low-skilled occupation groups. Interestingly, however, is that we can also observe a slight increase in shares in medium and high occupations after 2010. This goes in line with the finding on the education structure of new minimum wage recipients.

About 20% of all minimum-wage workers in Slovenia are employed in construction, followed by manufacturing (18.6% in 2015) and retail (16.9% in 2015). Nevertheless, if we observe shares of minimum-wage workers within individual industry affiliation, the minimum wage is more prevalent in administrative and support services and in other service activities (21.2% and 22% of workers employed in these industry affiliations received minimum wage in 2015, respectively), construction (21.5% in 2015) and accommodation and food service activities (17.8% in 2015). The latter was at most exposed to the 2010 minimum wage change – the share of minimum-wage workers increased namely by 9.4 percentage points between 2009 and 2011.

As pointed out already, Slovenia's adoption of the new minimum wage coincided with a large contraction of GDP. A closer look by the industry affiliations shows that during the recession period the value added decreased at most in manufacturing (by 16% in 2009 compared to the previous year, followed by a recovery in 2010–2011 and a further slight drop in value added in 2012 and 2013), construction (by 13.4% in 2009 compared to previous year, by which a further decrease can be observed by 2013) and accommodation and food service activities (by 10.9% in 2009 compared to previous year, followed by a recovery in 2010 and 2011 and a 5% drop in 2012). In Figure 9.6 we observe the relation between the change in value added and trends in the number and share of minimum-wage workers by industry affiliations that were most affected by the recession. As already noted above, in 2010 the number and share of minimum-wage workers increased in all observed industry affiliations. Although the increase of minimum-wage workers in 2010 followed a reduction in value added in 2009, it is interesting that the number and shares of minimum-wage workers increased also in later years when growth in value added resumed (with an exception of construction, where value added fell for the entire period 2009–2013), followed by a decline in 2014 and 2015.

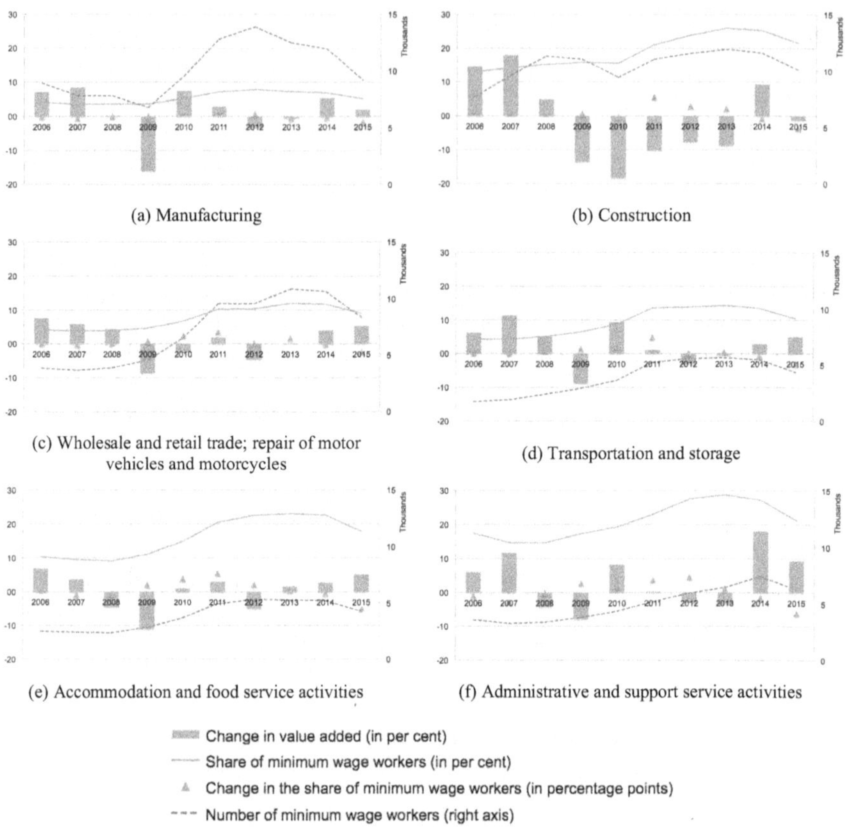

Figure 9.6 Change of value added compared to previous year (in %) and number and share of FTEs receiving a wage set at the minimum wage by selected industry affiliations, 2006–2015

Source: Own elaboration based on combined unemployment, employment, and earnings registry data, Statistical Office of the Republic of Slovenia and data obtained from SI-STAT (Statistical office of the Republic of Slovenia, 2019).

Worker-level analysis of the minimum wage shocks: effects on wages

The increase of the minimum wage in March 2010 resulted in a remarkable increase in the concentration of low wage workers at the minimum wage. As shown in Figure 9.7, the legislative change caused an increased concentration at the bottom of the wage distribution and, due to a sharp increase of the number of minimum wage earners, created a spike at the minimum. The concentration of workers at or very near the minimum wage persisted also during 2011–2013, with, interestingly, the spike increasing from one year to another. The concentration

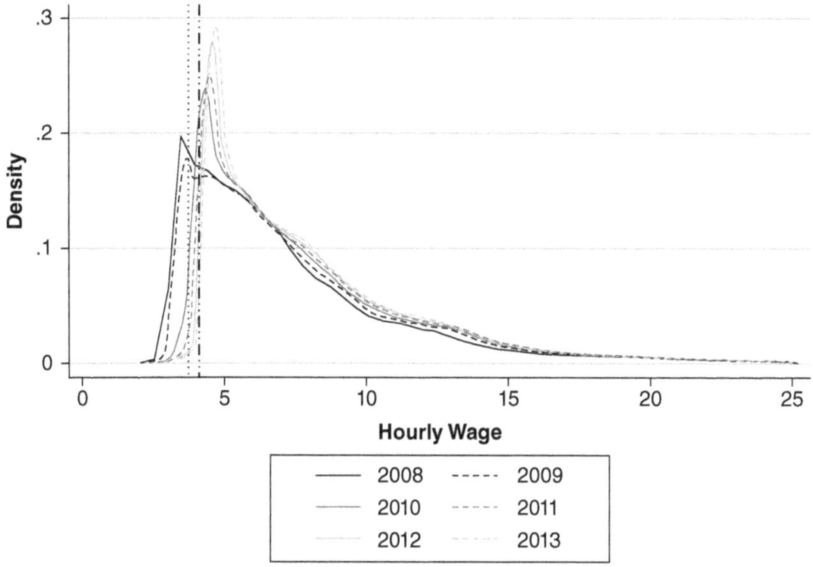

Figure 9.7 Wage distribution – non-agricultural workers in dependent employment, 2008–2013

Source: Own elaboration based on combined unemployment, employment, and earnings registry data, Statistical Office of the Republic of Slovenia.

Note: Hourly wage refers to the average annual hourly gross nominal wage at a given employer expressed in euros.

of minimum-wage workers at the minimum wage is particularly pronounced in market services, where the share of minimum-wage earners was high also before the legislative change.

In a recent paper with another co-author (Laporšek, Vodopivec, & Vodopivec, 2019), we further examined the spill-over effects in a difference-in-differences framework. We compared changes in wages during the control and treatment periods as experienced by workers in the wage group immediately above the level of the new minimum wage and workers in wage groups higher up in the wage distribution. The estimates showed positive and statistically significant spill-over effects of the minimum wage increase, with these effects being more pronounced for treatment groups with wage levels closer to the new minimum wage. In general, we observed spill-over effects at wage levels that are up to 150% of the new minimum wage – in other words, the wages of workers up to 50% higher than the new minimum wage received pay increases that can be directly attributable to the minimum wage increase. The spill-over effects were higher among young and older workers, especially for wage levels near the new minimum wage.

Worker-level analysis of the minimum wage shocks: effects on employment

Given that the previous section documented that the 2010 minimum wage increase had a considerable effect on the wage distribution in Slovenia, in another recent study (Laporšek, Orazem, Vodopivec, & Vodopivec, 2019) we examined the extent to which the increase affected the probability of staying in employment.[2] The results of this study are summarised in Table 9.1, which presents probit estimates of the probability of remaining in employment among individuals in Slovenia who had held a job a year before the minimum wage was increased. The estimation reflects the probability of being employed – possibly at a new

Table 9.1 Employment probability among individuals employed in March 2009, using static firm-level minimum wage shock values from 2009

Dependent variable is probability of employment: $E_{i\tau+1k}$	*before increase*	*after increase*				
	2009	*2010*	*2011*	*2012*	*2013*	*2014*
Firm minimum wage shock – values from March 2009, α_S	0.398*** (0.0189)	0.443*** (0.0229)	0.139*** (0.0179)	0.037** (0.0182)	–0.03 (0.0187)	–0.108*** (0.0185)
Ratio of minimum wage to predicted MRP – values from March 2009, α_M	–0.132*** (0.0021)	–0.219*** (0.0037)	–0.147*** (0.0039)	–0.11*** (0.0041)	–0.082*** (0.004)	–0.069*** (0.004)
Predicted marginal revenue product, α_W	–0.003*** (0.0002)	–0.002*** (0.0004)	0.009*** (0.0004)	0.017*** (0.0004)	0.024*** (0.0004)	0.025*** (0.0004)
Output shock, α_q	0.027*** (0.0033)	0.147*** (0.0051)	0.128*** (0.0097)	0.193*** (0.0111)	0.098*** (0.0104)	0.557*** (0.0102)
Effect of the MRP on employment probability, $\frac{\partial E_{i\tau+1k}}{\partial \widehat{\omega}_{i\tau}}$	0.010	0.019	0.023	0.027	0.031	0.031
Observations	4,633,521	4,633,355	4,632,751	4,632,593	4,632,905	4,632,891
Pseudo R-squared	0.121	0.096	0.083	0.081	0.084	0.094

Source: Laporšek et al. (2019).

Notes: Reported above are marginal effects from the following equation:

$$E_{i\tau+1k} = \begin{cases} 1, & -\varepsilon_{i\tau+1K} > (\alpha_0 + \alpha_W \widehat{\omega}_{i\tau} + \alpha_M \dfrac{MW_{\tau+1}}{\widehat{\omega}_{i\tau}} + \alpha_S MW^K_{-i,\tau+1} + \alpha_q dq^K_{-K,\tau+1}) \\ 0, & otherwise. \end{cases}$$

Regressions are estimated on individual-level monthly data. Years are defined to begin in March of each year to coincide with the March 2010 minimum wage increase. Monthly dummies were included in all specifications. Standard errors clustered by individuals are in parentheses. Statistical significance: *** $p < 0.01$, ** $p < 0.05$, * $p < 0.1$

employer – conditional on having been employed in March 2009, i.e., before the minimum wage change. We explain in more detail the definition of variables, included in the model, and interpret their effect.

We use the worker's predicted marginal revenue product (MRP) in March 2009 as the primary regressor of interest. Calculated based on a range of individual-level covariates from a regression where log(wages) is the dependent variable, the MRP is our preferred measure instead of an individual's actual wage in March 2009 because it is less prone to underreporting for tax purposes and idiosyncratic factors that do not reflect an individual's options outside their current firm. Furthermore, our regressions assume that the firm minimum wage shocks remain static at their levels in March 2010. Taking the period from March 2009 to February 2010 as the baseline, we estimate the probability of employment with 12 consecutive monthly observations beginning in March of the year 2010 and ending in February of the following year. Therefore, the column labelled 2010 shows the coefficients for the first 12 months after the increase of the minimum wage (March 2010–February 2011). Because the sample is conditioned on March 2009 employment, the coefficients reflect the changing probability of employment since March 2009.

The firm-level minimum wage shock variable (α_s) measures the change in the cost of employing all the other workers in the firm due to the minimum-wage policy; therefore it is the cross-wage effect on a given worker's employment. The positive coefficients mean that firms facing larger minimum wage shocks are substituting away from other, now more expensive workers and towards this less expensive worker. The positive effect in 2009 suggests some substitution began in the year before implementation, potentially reflecting anticipation effects. In contrast, the effect dissipates and eventually turns negative where only the initial shock is allowed to affect probability of employment. This result is suggesting that in the longer term, workers may be hurt by working in firms with other workers receiving wage increases due to the minimum wage.

The ratio of the minimum wage to the worker's MRP (α_M) always lowers the probability of employment. There is a small effect even in the year before the minimum wage increase was implemented, but the effect becomes larger in the first year of the implementation. The effect dissipates but remains statistically significant five years after the initial increase.

The worker's predicted MRP in March 2009 appears in two places: in the ratio of minimum wage to MRP and then as a separate independent variable. The total effect of the marginal revenue product on conditional employment probability is $\frac{\partial E_{i\tau+1k}}{\partial \widehat{\omega_{i\tau}}} = f(\cdot)\left(\alpha_W - \alpha_M \frac{MW_{\tau+1}}{(\widehat{\omega_{i\tau}})^2}\right)$, where $f(\cdot)$ is the normal density function evaluated at sample values. Because the estimated minimum wage effect (α_M) is always negative, the estimated effect of marginal revenue product on employment was positive for the full sample range of values of $\hat{\omega}_{i\tau}$ as shown in the last row of the table. The impact is largest for the least skilled, meaning that a small increase in skills will have the largest impact on employment prospects for individuals at the bottom of the skill distribution. Although the estimated effect is non-linear, roughly speaking, the effect of the increase in the minimum wage is that an individual at the middle of the skills distribution had a probability of being employed that was 1.9% higher than someone at the bottom of the skills distribution in 2010. By 2014, the probability had increased to 3.1%.

Firm-level responses to the minimum wage shocks

The previous sections have documented the effects of the minimum wage increase on the labour market outcomes of individual workers – but what are the effects from the perspective of the firm? In addition to reducing employment, the standard neoclassical model predicts that in a competitive market, the response of firms to an increase in the minimum wage will be to substitute labour with capital inputs. The increased minimum wage is also predicted to decrease a firm's profitability, possibly to the point of making it no longer feasible to remain in operation. Although there is a sizable literature concerning how the minimum wage affects individuals' employment and wages (see discussion earlier in the chapter), relatively few papers examine the effect of a minimum wage increase on a firm's input, output, investment, and exit decisions.

This section examines the effects of Slovenia's 2010 minimum wage increase on a variety of firm-level outcomes, based on the research performed by Vodopivec, Orazem, Vodopivec, and Laporšek (2019). The analysis rests on a detailed longitudinal database on the universe of firm employment, investment, compensation, output, and returns to examine how firms respond to multiple labour market policies at once. Such an empirical approach is well grounded in theory: as shown by Pries and Rogerson (2005), the effects of a given labour market policy will depend on its interactions with other labour market policies, and their model shows that minimum wages and dismissal costs both significantly affect worker turnover. In this chapter, worker-level information for each firm allows us to estimate the heterogeneous effects of common minimum wage and severance policies on the wage bills of each firm. Hence, our identification of the effects comes from the differential effects of common policies on otherwise similar firms.

Minimum-wage shock effects on employment

Let the new 2010 minimum wage to be implemented be designated as MW_{10}. For each firm with $N_{ij,09}$ employees, $N^{S}_{ij,09}$ will be subminimum workers for whom the expected wage $W^{e}_{ijl,09} = S'_{ijl,09}\beta^{S}_{09} < MW_{10}$. The remaining $N_{ij,09} - N^{S}_{ij,09}$ workers will have $W^{e}_{ijl,09} \geq MW_{10}$. Only the first group will have their expected wages rise as a direct result of the imposed minimum wage. Therefore, we measure the proportional change in the firm *i* wage bill attributable to the increase in the minimum wage as:

$$MW_{ij,10} = \left(\left(\sum_{l=1}^{N^{S}_{ij,09}} MW_{10}\right) - W^{e}_{ijl,09} \right) / \sum_{l=1}^{N^{S}_{ij,09}} W^{e}_{ijl,09} \qquad (9.1)$$

This measure says that, holding constant the mix of skills employed in the firm in 2009, the future implemented minimum wage law would raise the firm's wage bill by the proportion $MW_{ij,10}$.

As shown in Table 9.2, compared to employment levels in 2009 before the minimum wage increase, firms experiencing larger minimum wage shocks had

Table 9.2 Regressions of employment based on firm-level data using static minimum wage shock – firms with more than 10 workers, using shock calculated based on predicted wages, 2010–2015

Dependent variable: Growth in individual-level employment	*2010*	*2011*	*2012*	*2013*	*2014*	*2015*
Minimum wage shock – current year relative to 2009	–0.011***	–0.013***	–0.017***	–0.019***	–0.016***	–0.019***
	(0.003)	(0.003)	(0.003)	(0.003)	(0.003)	(0.004)
ln (Potential severance pay)	0.01	0.003	–0.006	–0.013	–0.01	–0.026***
	(0.011)	(0.009)	(0.008)	(0.008)	(0.009)	(0.009)
Output shock (current year relative to 2009)	0.164	0.312***	0.307***	0.247***	0.339***	0.319***
	(0.105)	(0.057)	(0.042)	(0.037)	(0.046)	(0.046)
Net Herfindahl-Hirschman Index	0.046	0.279	0.351**	0.332**	0.207	0.234
	(0.204)	(0.178)	(0.158)	(0.165)	(0.182)	(0.183)
Firm-level share of foreign sales	0.024	0.079***	0.151***	0.195***	0.238***	0.257***
	(0.035)	(0.03)	(0.026)	(0.027)	(0.03)	(0.03)
Firm's market share	0.023	0.036	–0.107	0.169	–0.109	0.015
	(0.262)	(0.223)	(0.192)	(0.197)	(0.219)	(0.212)
Firm's age	–0.006**	–0.011***	–0.015***	–0.016***	–0.018***	–0.013***
	(0.003)	(0.003)	(0.003)	(0.003)	(0.003)	(0.003)
Firm's age^2*100	0.011*	0.018***	0.025***	0.025***	0.027***	0.021***
	(0.006)	(0.005)	(0.005)	(0.005)	(0.006)	(0.005)
Constant	–0.00200	0.0439	0.0976***	0.116***	0.166***	0.144***
	(0.0385)	(0.0371)	(0.0361)	(0.0417)	(0.0503)	(0.0512)
Inverse Mills ratio	–0.802***	–0.677***	–0.582***	–0.507***	–0.556***	–0.398***
	(0.153)	(0.0855)	(0.0645)	(0.0641)	(0.0720)	(0.0683)
Observations	7,023	7,023	7,023	7,023	7,023	7,023
Number of censored observations	325	727	1107	1482	1771	2035
Minimum wage aggregate effect	–0.191	–0.145	–0.157	–0.148	–0.117	–0.155
Severance pay aggregate effect	0.0966	0.0174	–0.0350	–0.0594	–0.0457	–0.131

Source: Own elaboration based on combined unemployment, employment, and earnings registry data, Statistical Office of the Republic of Slovenia and data obtained from SI-STAT (Statistical Office of the Republic of Slovenia, 2019; Vodopivec et al., 2019).

Notes: Coefficients refer to estimates corrected for selection using Heckman's two-step procedure where the selection regression also includes two measures of the Lerner index for market power. Values for the minimum wage shock are fixed and are equal to the firm-level values in 2010 assuming the workforce composition is unchanged from March 2009. Growth variables use the mean of both periods in the denominator to provide a symmetric measure of growth. Regressions also include dummy variables for incorporation type. Standard errors in parentheses. Statistical significance: *** $p < 0.01$, ** $p < 0.05$, * $p < 0.1$.

lower employment growth that persisted over time. Consistent with the Lazear (1990) prediction, firms facing greater severance costs cut back on employment growth. The effect gets larger over time as it becomes more difficult for firms to avoid severance costs over the longer horizon. The other market factors behave as expected. Sectoral output and exposure to export market demand raises employment. Selection matters negatively, meaning that firms that were more likely to survive expanded employment at a slower rate (Vodopivec et al., 2019).

Minimum-wage shock effects on other firm response variables

As shown in Table 9.3, firms experiencing larger minimum wage shocks face different effects on their wage bills: wage bill growth decreases for larger firms but rises for smaller firms. Apparently, larger firms are able to restructure their operations so that they substitute away from the rising cost of low-skilled workers, but smaller firms have to absorb the costs. Firms experiencing larger minimum wage shocks substitute away from labour and towards capital. Capital investment rises immediately for small firms. Larger firms initially decrease their capital investments, perhaps to alleviate the cost of the minimum wage shock, but they also increase their capital investments after a 4-year lag. Firms experiencing larger minimum wage shocks lower the growth of their operating costs in the near term by cutting back on input growth. In equilibrium, assuming firms are operating at an efficient scale and with diminishing marginal product, neoclassical theory suggests that as marginal costs rise with the minimum wage increase, firms will cut back on output – a prediction borne out in the data. It would be implausible that mandated higher wages would raise firm profits if firms were already maximising profits, and that is what we find: both large and small firms experiencing larger minimum wage shocks had lower rates of return, and the lower returns became larger in magnitude over time (Vodopivec et al., 2019).

Conclusion

Statutory minimum wages are an important feature of labour market policy in the CEE countries. As the most direct policy lever for influencing wage growth at the bottom of the wage distribution, CEE governments have employed them to ensure that the benefits of economic growth are shared by the most vulnerable groups. However, as we have shown in this chapter, the recent experience of Slovenia's large 2010 increase can also serve as evidence of the potential for minimum-wage policy to result in unintended effects on a variety of economic outcomes – all of which have important implications for labour utilisation.

The results in this chapter show that the 2010 minimum wages had a variety of effects observable at both the individual and firm level. At the individual level, we document that the large increase was in fact binding in practice, as it

Table 9.3 Summary of key regression coefficients and marginal effects using static minimum wage shock – firms with more than 10 workers, using shock calculated based on predicted wages, 2010–2015

Growth rates of:	*2010*	*2011*	*2012*	*2013*	*2014*	*2015*
Employment based on individual-level data	–0.0114***	–0.0132***	–0.0165***	–0.0186***	–0.0156***	–0.0185***
	(0.003)	(0.0027)	(0.0026)	(0.0029)	(0.0034)	(0.0036)
	[–0.19***]	[–0.15***]	[–0.16***]	[–0.15***]	[–0.12***]	[–0.16***]
Wage bill	–0.0076**	–0.0083***	–0.008***	–0.0056*	–0.0052	–0.0055
	(0.0036)	(0.0031)	(0.003)	(0.0032)	(0.0037)	(0.0039)
	[–0.23**]	[–0.17***]	[–0.12***]	[–0.07*]	[–0.08]	[–0.13]
Investment	–0.0087***	–0.0032	0.0022	0.0112**	0.018***	0.0253***
	(0.0029)	(0.0031)	(0.0038)	(0.0045)	(0.0052)	(0.0055)
	[–0.21***]	[–0.06]	[0.03]	[0.12**]	[0.2***]	[0.32***]
Operating costs	–0.015***	–0.0179***	–0.0166***	–0.0159***	–0.0212***	–0.0203***
	(0.0015)	(0.0021)	(0.0028)	(0.0033)	(0.0038)	(0.0041)
	[–0.47***]	[–0.58***]	[–0.3***]	[–0.25***]	[–0.45***]	[–0.66***]
Sales	–0.0095***	–0.0082***	–0.0053*	–0.0044	–0.0029	–0.0012
	(0.003)	(0.0031)	(0.0029)	(0.0032)	(0.0038)	(0.004)
	[–0.44***]	[–0.35***]	[–0.12*]	[–0.08]	[–0.06]	[–0.04]
Operating rate of return	–0.0037***	–0.0193***	–0.0137***	–0.0071***	–0.0125***	–0.0139***
	(0.0013)	(0.006)	(0.0022)	(0.0012)	(0.0019)	(0.0024)
	[–0.56***]	[–3.42***]	[–1.07***]	[–0.53***]	[–2.51***]	[–5.9***]

Source: Own elaboration based on combined unemployment, employment, and earnings registry data, Statistical Office of the Republic of Slovenia and data obtained from SI-STAT (Statistical Office of the Republic of Slovenia, 2019; Vodopivec et al., 2019).

Notes: Estimates are corrected for selection using Heckman's two-step procedure where the selection regression also includes two measures of the Lerner index for market power. Marginal effects are reported in square brackets. Values for the minimum wage shock are fixed and are equal to the firm-level values in 2010 assuming the workforce composition is unchanged from March 2009. Growth variables use the mean of both periods in the denominator to provide a symmetric measure of growth. Regressions also include dummy variables for incorporation type. Standard errors in parentheses. Statistical significance: *** $p < 0.01$, ** $p < 0.05$, * $p < 0.1$.

resulted in considerable growth in the number of individuals receiving the minimum wage, particularly amongst the young, male, and low-skilled occupations. In addition to directly affecting workers whose wages were previously below the newly raised threshold, the minimum wage increase resulted in considerable spill-over effects; we find robust evidence of increases in the wages of workers up to 150% of the new minimum wage. We find that the large increase resulted not only in changes in the wage distribution but also in the probability of remaining in employment; we find evidence of direct effects on low-wage workers in particular, as well as evidence of indirect effects of working in a firm with lower average wages in general. At the firm level, we corroborate the negative effects of the minimum wage increase on employment growth but also document a variety of interesting firm-level responses. Affected firms responded to the increase in the relative price of labour by disproportionally exiting the market, with remaining firms substituting labour inputs with capital. Furthermore, we find a decrease in profitability amongst affected firms, which is consistent with theoretical predictions.

Taken together, the results support the contention that minimum wages have a negative, direct effect on labour utilisation. The results from our analysis of Slovenia's 2010 minimum wage increase show that the minimum wage had a negative effect on employment, particularly among low-skilled workers. The effects on total hours worked were similar. At the same time, the minimum wage resulted in an increase in investment by firms which survived the minimum wage shock, as firms substituted labour for capital. All these factors serve to decrease labour utilisation. At the same time, however, the minimum wage increase may conceivably have positive, indirect effects in the long term. To the extent that it makes certain categories of jobs economically unviable, a high minimum wage provides an impetus for retraining, upskilling, and investment into higher-value-added jobs. Alas, the latter aspect was outside the scope of our present analysis.

We should emphasise several factors concerning the results discussed in this chapter which may limit the extent to which the results could be generalised to other CEE countries. First, the magnitude of the increase was quite large, amounting to 22.9%. The magnitude of this increase strongly exceeded that of previous minimum wage adjustments following the introduction of a minimum wage in 1995 and brought Slovenia to the forefront among the EU countries by the ratio of the minimum to the average gross wage. Second, it coincided with a large contraction of the GDP due to economic crisis and, in contrast to many other countries, was uniformly applied without exemptions for younger workers or labour market entrants. All these factors served to arguably magnify its effects.

Acknowledgement

This publication has received financial support from the European Union Programme for Employment and Social Innovation 'EaSI' (2014–2020).

Notes

1 The conditions for adopting a gradual transition were very lenient. A gradual increase of the minimum wage could be adopted by firms for which immediate transition would lead to large losses that would jeopardise the existence of these firms or to layoffs of a large number of workers for business reasons. According to the Labour Inspectorate (2010) a gradual transition to the stipulated minimum wage was adopted by 1,611 companies.

2 A detailed description of the methodological approach is available in Laporšek et al. (2019).

References

Aaronson, D., French, E., Sorkin, I., & To, T. (2018). Industry dynamics and the minimum wage: A putty-clay approach. *International Economic Review*, *59*, 51–84. doi:10.1111/iere.12262

Abowd, J. M., Kramarz, F., Margolis, D. N., & Philippon, T. (2000). *The tail of two countries: Minimum wages and employment in France and the United States* (IZA Discussion Papers No. 203). Bonn: Institute for the Study of Labor.

AJPES. (2017a). *Accounting data on enterprises*. Ljubljana: AJPES.

AJPES. (2017b). *Slovenian business registry data set*. Ljubljana: AJPES.

Allegretto, S., Godoey, A., Nadler, C., & Reich, M. (2018). *The new wave of local minimum wage policies: Evidence from six cities* (CWED Policy Brief). Berkeley: Center on Wage and Employment Dynamics.

Babiak, M., Chorna, O., & Pertold-Gebicka, B. (2019). *Minimum wage increase and firm profitability: Evidence from Poland* (Working Papers No. IES 2019/14). Prague: Charles University Prague, Faculty of Social Sciences, Institute of Economic Studies.

Baranowska-Rataj, A., & Magda, I. (2015). *The impact of the minimum wage on job separations and working hours among young people in Poland* (Institute of Statistics Working Papers No. 45). Warsaw: Warsaw School of Economics.

Blažević Burić, S. (2013). Is employment decreasing due to minimum wage increase? *Economic Research-Ekonomska istraživanja*, *26*, 69–100.

Boeri, T., & van Ours, J. C. (2013). *The economics of imperfect labor markets*. Princeton: Princeton University Press.

Bossler, M., & Gerner, H.-D. (2019). Employment effects of the new German minimum wage: Evidence from establishment-level microdata. *ILR Review*. doi:10.1177/0019793919889635

Brown, C., Gilroy, C., & Kohen, A. (1982). *The effect of the minimum wage on employment and unemployment: A survey* (NBER Working Paper No. 846). Cambridge: National Bureau of Economic Research.

Bryan, M., Salvatori, A., & Taylor, M. (2013). *The impact of the national minimum wage on employment retention, hours and job entry: A report to the Low Pay Commission*. Essex: Institute for Social and Economic Research (ISER) University of Essex.

Caliendo, M., Fedorets, A., Preiss, M., Schröder, C., & Wittbrodt, L. (2019). The short-run employment effects of the German minimum wage reform. *Labour Economics*, *53*, 46–62. doi:10.1016/j.labeco.2018.07.002

Card, D. (1992a). Using regional variation in wages to measure the effects of the federal minimum wage. *Industrial and Labor Relations Review*, *46*(1), 22–37. doi:10.2307/2524736

Card, D. (1992b). Do minimum wages reduce employment? A case study of California, 1987–1989. *Industrial and Labor Relations Review*, *46*(1), 38–54. doi:10.1177/001979399204600104

Card, D., & Krueger, A. B. (1994). Minimum wages and employment: A case study of the fast food industry in New Jersey and Pennsylvania. *American Economic Review*, *84*(4), 772–793.

Card, D., & Krueger, A. B. (1995). *Myth and measurement: The new economics of the minimum wage*. Princeton: Princeton University Press.

Centeno, M., Duarte, C., & Novo, A. A. (2011). *The impact of the minimum wage on low-wage earners*. Lisbon: Bank of Portugal.

Dickens, R., & Draca, M. (2005). *The employment effects of the October 2003 increase in the national minimum wage* (CEP Discussion Paper No. 693). London: Centre for Economic Performance.

Dickens, R., & Manning, A. (2004). Spikes and spill-overs: The impact of the national minimum wage on the wage distribution in a low-wage sector. *The Economic Journal*, *114*(494), C95–C101.

Dickens, R., Riley, R., & Wilkinson, D. (2009). *The employment and hours of work effects of the changing national minimum wage* (Technical Report). London: Low Pay Commission.

Dickens, R., Riley, R., & Wilkinson, D. (2012). *Re-examining the impact of the national minimum wage on earnings, employment and hours: The importance of recession and firm size* (Technical Report). London: Low Pay Commission.

DiNardo, J., Fortin, N. M., & Lemieux, T. (1996). Labor market institutions and the distribution of wages, 1973–1992: A semiparametric approach. *Econometrica*, *64*(5), 1001–1044. doi:10.2307/2171954

Draca, M., Machin, S., & van Reenen, J. (2011). Minimum wages and firm profitability. *American Economic Journal: Applied Economics*, *3*(1), 129–151. doi:10.1257/app.3.1.129

Dube, A., Lester, T. W., & Reich, M. (2016). Minimum wage shocks, employment flows, and labor market frictions. *Journal of Labour Economics*, *34*(3). doi:10.1086/685449

Employment Service of Slovenia. (2017). *Data on registered unemployment*. Ljubljana: Employment Service of Slovenia.

Eriksson, T., & Pytlikova, M. (2004). Firm-level consequences of large minimum-wage increases in the Czech and Slovak Republics. *Labour*, *18*, 75–103.

Eurostat. (2019). *Statistical database*. Retrieved from http://stats.oecd.org/Index.aspx

Ferraro, S., Hänilane, B., & Staehr, K. (2018). Minimum wages and employment retention: A microeconometric study for Estonia. *Baltic Journal of Economics*, *18*(1), 51–67. doi: 10.1080/1406099X.2018.1485422

Ferraro, S., Meriküll, J., & Staehr, K. (2018). Minimum wages and the wage distribution in Estonia. *Applied Economics*, *50*(49), 5253–5268. doi:10.1080/00036846.2018.1486017

Fialová, K., & Mysíková, M. (2009). The minimum wage: Labor market consequences in the Czech Republic. *Czech Journal of Economics and Finance*, *59*(3), 255–274.

Galán, S., & Puente, S. (2015). Minimum wages: Do they really hurt young people? *The B.E. Journal of Economic Analysis & Policy*, *15*(1). doi:10.1515/bejeap-2013-0171.

Gregory, T. (2014). *When the minimum wage bites back: Quantile treatment effects of a sectoral minimum wage in Germany* (Centre for European Economic Research Discussion Paper No. 14-133). Manheim: Centre for European Economic Research.

Grossman, J. B. (1983). The impact of the minimum wage on other wages. *The Journal of Human Resources*, *18*(3), 359–378.

Harasztosi, P., & Lindner, A. (2019). Who pays for the minimum wage? *American Economic Review, 109*(8), 2693–2727. doi:10.1257/aer.20171445

Hinnosaar, M., & Rõõm, T. (2003). *The impact of minimum wage on the labour market in Estonia: An empirical analysis* (Working Papers of Eesti Pank No. 2003/8). Tallinn: Eesti Pank.

IMAD. (2013). *Minimalna plača v Sloveniji v obdobju krize* [Minimum Wage in Slovenia in Time of Crisis]. Retrieved from www.umar.gov.si/

Katz, L. F., & Krueger, A. B. (1992). The effect of the minimum wage on the fast food industry. *Industrial and Labor Relations Review, 46*(1), 6–21. doi:10.2307/2524735

Kertesi, G., & Köllő, J. (2003). *The employment effects of nearly doubling the minimum wage – The case of Hungary* (Budapest Working Papers No. 2003/6). Budapest: Institute of Economics, Hungarian Academy of Sciences

König, M., & Möller, J. (2009). Impacts of minimum wages: A microdata analysis for the German construction sector. *International Journal of Manpower, 30*(7), 716–741.

Kraft, E., & Vodopivec, M. (1992). How soft is the budget constraint for Yugoslav firms? *Journal of Comparative Economics, 16*(3), 432–455. doi:10.1016/0147-5967(92)90166-5

Labour Inspectorate. (2010). *Minimum wage*. Retrieved from www.gov.si/drzavni-organi/organi-v-sestavi/inspektorat-za-delo/

Laporšek, S., Orazem, P. F., Vodopivec, M., & Vodopivec, M. (2019). *Long-term responses to large minimum wage shocks: Sub-minimum and super-minimum workers in Slovenia* (IZA Discussion Paper Series No. 12123). Bonn: Institute of Labor Economics.

Laporšek, S., Vodopivec, M., & Vodopivec, M. (2019). Spillover effects of a minimum wage increase – Evidence from Slovenia. *Post-Communist Economies, 31*(5), 603–622. doi:10.1080/14631377.2019.1578582

Lazear, E. P. (1990). Job security provisions and employment. *The Quarterly Journal of Economics, 105*(3), 699–726. doi:10.2307/2937895

Lee, D. S. (1999). Wage inequality in the United States during the 1980s: Rising dispersion or falling minimum wage? *The Quarterly Journal of Economics, 114*(3), 977–1023. doi:10.1162/003355399556197

Luca, D. L., & Luca, M. (2017). *Survival of the fittest: The impact of the minimum wage on firm exit* (Harvard Business School Working Paper No. 17-088). Boston: Harvard Business School.

Majchrowska, A., Broniatowska, P., & Żółkiewski, Z. (2016). Minimum wage in Poland and youth employment in regional labor markets. *Emerging Markets Finance and Trade, 52*(9), 2178–2194. doi:10.1080/1540496X.2015.1068611

Manning, A. (2003). *Monopsony in motion: Imperfect competition in labor markets*. Princeton: Princeton University Press.

Minimum Wage Act. Official Gazette of the Republic of Slovenia, No. 13/10.

Nestić, D., Babić, Z., & Blažević Burić, S. (2018). Minimum wage in Croatia: Sectoral and regional perspectives. *Economic Research/Ekonomska istraživanja, 31*(1), 1981–2002.

Neumark, D. (2018). Employment effects of minimum wages. *IZA World of Labor, 6*. doi:10.15185/izawol.6.v2

Neumark, D., Salas, J. M. I., & Wascher, W. (2014). Revisiting the minimum wage-employment debate: Throwing out the baby with the bathwater? *Industrial and Labor Relations Review, 67*(2.5), 608–648. doi:10.1177/00197939140670S307

Neumark, D., Schweitzer, M., & Wascher, W. L. (2004). Minimum wage effects throughout the wage distribution. *Journal of Human Resources, 39*(2), 425–450. doi:10.2307/3559021

Neumark, D., & Wascher, W. L. (2010). *Minimum wages*. Cambridge: The MIT Press.

Orazem, P. F., & Vodopivec, M. (1995). Winners and losers in transition: Returns to education, experience, and gender in Slovenia. *The World Bank Economic Review*, *9*(2), 201–230.

Pantea, S. (2017). *Did minimum wage increases reduce employment? Panel data evidence from Romania* (MPRA Paper No. 79863). Munich: University Library of Munich.

Pension and Disability Insurance Institute of Slovenia. (2017). *Worker earnings data*. Ljubljana: Pension and Disability Insurance Institute of Slovenia.

Portugal, P., & Cardoso, A. R. (2006). Disentangling the minimum wage puzzle: An analysis of worker accessions and separations. *Journal of the European Economic Association*, *4*(5), 988–1013.

Pries, M., & Rogerson, R. (2005). Hiring policies, labor market institutions, and labor market flows. *Journal of Political Economy*, *113*(4), 811–839. doi:10.1086/430333

Rohlin, S. M. (2011). State minimum wages and business location: Evidence from a refined border approach. *Journal of Urban Economics*, *69*(1), 103–117. doi:10.1016/j.jue.2010.08.001

Schmitt, J. (2013). *Why does the minimum wage have no discernible effect on employment?* (Center for Economic and Policy Research Working Paper). Washington, DC: Center for Economic and Policy Research.

Schulten, T., & Luebker, M. (2019). *WSI minimum wage report 2019*. Düsseldorf: Hans-Böckler-Stiftung.

Statistical Office of the Republic of Slovenia. (2017). *Work history data*. Ljubljana: Statistical Office of the Republic of Slovenia.

Statistical Office of the Republic of Slovenia. (2019). *SI-STAT database*. Retrieved from www.stat.si/statweb

Stewart, M. B. (2003). *Modelling the employment effects of the minimum wage*. Warwick: University of Warwick.

Stewart, M. B. (2004). The employment effects of the national minimum wage. *The Economic Journal*, *114*(494), C110–C116. doi:10.1111/j.0013-0133.2003.00200.x

Stewart, M. B. (2012a). Quantile estimates of counterfactual distribution shifts and the effect of minimum wage increases on the wage distribution. *Journal of the Royal Statistical Society: Series A (Statistics in Society)*, *175*(1), 263–287. doi:10.1111/j.1467-985X.2011.01007.x

Stewart, M. B. (2012b). Wage inequality, minimum wage effects, and spillovers. *Oxford Economic Papers*, *64*(4), 616–634.

Šuminas, M. (2015). Effects of minimum wage increases on employment in Lithuania. *Ekonomika*, *94*(2), 96–112.

Vodopivec, M., Orazem, P. F., Vodopivec, M., & Laporšek, S. (2019). *How do firms respond to minimum wage shocks and firing costs? The case of Slovenia*. Paper presented at the 31st Annual Conference of the European Association of Labour Economists (EALE), Uppsala, Sweden.

WSI. (2019). *WSI minimum wage database*. Retrieved from www.boeckler.de/wsi-tarifarchiv_44064.htm

10

THE ROLE OF OLD-AGE PENSION SYSTEMS AS LABOUR MARKET INSTITUTIONS

The Czech Republic and Poland compared

Paweł Łuczak and Michał Polakowski

Introduction

During the last three decades CEE countries not only underwent a deep economic restructuring, but they also experienced multiple social transformations of various kinds. A rapid demographic change, including an ongoing 'ageing of society', is one of them (Chawla, Betcherman, & Banerji, 2007). In general, CEE countries experienced a shift towards longer-living, lower-fertility and higher-educated societies (Lutz et al., 2019). However, it should be noted that the post-communism transformation brought about 'an intergenerational rift', according to which new market possibilities for older cohorts were much more limited than the possibilities of younger and middle-aged people living in CEE (Botev, 2012).

Against this backdrop, particular labour market institutions that facilitate an early withdrawal from the labour market or prolong careers can be considered as a crucial determinant of labour utilisation of older workers in this region. In this chapter we focus on one particular labour market institution, namely the pension system.[1] Indeed, analysing a statutory retirement age as a labour market institution has become a common endeavour in labour economics, especially the strand accentuating the inherent imperfection of labour markets (Boeri & Van Ours, 2013). The comprehensive review of studies, based on experiences of Western countries, showed that, after a statutory retirement age is raised, people delay their retirement often to an exceptionally large extent (Blundell, French, & Tetlow, 2016). Therefore, we formulate the general hypothesis that a similar effect might be observed in the CEE region: an increase of a statutory retirement age brings about an immediate increase in labour market participation of older workers in the region.

In order to examine this hypothesis, we narrow down the number of cases to two countries: the Czech Republic and Poland. We selected those countries due to substantial heterogeneity of institutional arrangements concerning pension systems, as they represent two divergent policy paths concerning pension reforms that were taken in CEE during the transition period (Müller, 2002). At the same time, those two countries are comparable in demographics and socio-economic development. Even though the Czech Republic and Poland adopted qualitatively different pension systems, they share a legacy of low retirement ages. This is why both countries have been increasing them lately, albeit at a different pace, because the timing of the reforms varied between countries. What is more, the increase in the retirement age was reversed by the Polish parliament in 2016, which makes the comparison of these countries even more meaningful.

The general aim of this chapter is to assess whether old-age pension systems in both countries facilitate keeping labour utilisation of older people at a high level. In other words, we want to explore to what extent pensions systems promote early or late retirement of older workers. In line with the book's profile, this chapter focuses on current differences in the labour market institutional framework. Therefore, the time scope of this study covers the period from the end of the 1990s, due to the fact that the aforementioned reconfigurations of the pension system took place at that time.

The chapter shows that in both countries there were many piecemeal reforms that aimed at curbing the extent of early retirement and prolonging the careers of older people. However, in the short term such reforms were moderately successful, as they were accompanied by a 'retirement run' of those who were eligible and could lose their early retirement right. The comparison of our cases also shows some surprising results, given the hypothesis. For example, despite similar, low minimum retirement ages for women, we documented different gains in the employment rates for this group in both countries. We put an interpretation on such results by arguing that the role of pension system reforms, and in particular legislation concerning a retirement age, should not be considered as a panacea with regard to increasing labour utilisation of older workers in CEE. Thus, we conclude that successful policies that aim at increasing the contribution of older workers' human capital to GDP in the region should also focus on other formal institutions that in practice play a role of functional equivalents to the pension system such as disability pensions or unemployment benefits. Those policies should also concentrate on the issue of improving labour market conditions of those older people who express the greatest willingness to withdraw from labour markets as early as possible.

The chapter is structured as follows. The following section identifies how different elements of a pension system need to be constructed to keep labour utilisation of older workers at a high level. Then we provide a brief description of the older people's situation in the labour market in CEE and, in the next section, we look at labour utilisation of older workers in the analysed countries. Next, we discuss in detail the pension reforms with reference to the retirement age changes in the Czech Republic and Poland. The last section concludes and provides recommendations that also go beyond our two cases.

Public pension system as a determinant of a labour utilisation of older workers

In the past, early retirement policies were common in many countries, as governments used these measures to decrease unemployment through a reduction of labour supply (Boeri & Van Ours, 2013). From a political economic perspective, employers and trade unions often cooperated with each other regarding the usage of early retirement schemes in order to externalise costs of labour market restructuration on the public purse (Ebbinghaus, 2006). During the last 10–15 years we have witnessed a change in this respect with the increases of the statutory retirement age and limiting early retirement routes. Currently, as pension reforms are regarded as a key measure for promoting longer careers among older people (OECD, 2019a), experts tend to argue that an increase in the retirement age is an inevitable adjustment of pension systems (Góra, 2019).

Among the various drivers of individuals' retirement decisions, the role of financial incentives stemming from institutional pension design that make retirement more or less attractive clearly stands out (De Preter, Van Looy, & Mortelmans, 2013). Some researchers even argue that a situation of older workers contradicts standard labour market theory, because an impact of labour market institutions, such as pensions, on their decision is so strong that older workers are not actually free to choose the number of their working hours (Börsch-Supan, Bucher-Koenen, Kutlu-Koc, & Goll, 2018). Consequently, one could expect that an increase of a basic parameter of any pension system, that is a statutory retirement age, brings about an immediate change of labour market utilisation of older workers. Indeed, the cross-country study shows that an increase in a minimal age for claiming pension benefit by one year is associated with an increase in the participation rate of older workers by approximately 0.8 percentage points (Geppert, Guillemette, Morgavi, & Turner, 2019).

Nevertheless, some studies cast doubts on such simple causality, as they indicate a successful reform concerning increasing the retirement age in a given country is conditioned on an adequate labour demand for older workers (Etgeton, 2018). In other words, when a demand for labour of older people decreases, the value attached to a pathway that leads outside a labour market may increase. It should be also noted here that older workers in their transition to retirement may use institutional pathways outside the pension system such as unemployment benefits or disability benefits (Ardito, 2017). Indeed, a recent study (Geppert et al., 2019) suggests that one underlying cause of increasing labour participation among older workers lies in reducing the possibilities of using these alternative retirement paths entailing unemployment and disability schemes.

Moreover, pension systems consist of different dimensions. Thus, when we look at the implications for labour utilisation, a retirement age should be analysed with reference to a high complexity of different elements of the pension system, such as an 'earning test' for those who retire and want to continue work and benefit generosity and actuarial adjustments concerning the level of a future pension benefit stemming from delaying retirement (Blundell et al., 2016). In this vein, the recent comparative study aimed at understanding the impact of pension rules and laws on the behaviour of older people with regard to work and retirement (Börsch-Supan et al., 2019) proposed a useful framework for assessing whether a pension system is attractive for early or late retirement (Table 10.1). This framework helps us to identify how pension systems need to be constructed in order to keep the labour utilisation at the high level.

We add to the framework presented in Table 10.1 the issue of a benefit formula, because adjustments concerning the level of a future pension benefit stemming

Table 10.1 The scale of attractiveness of early retirement and late retirement

	not attractive	*ambiguous*	*attractive*	*very attractive*
Attractiveness of early retirement:				
Statutory eligibility age	⩾ 65, changing quickly	⩾ 65, changing slowly or not at all	< 65, changing quickly	< 65, changing slowly or not at all
Benefit deduction for earlier retirement	No early retirement possible	High deductions, making early retirement unattractive	Low deductions, making early retirement attractive	Flat benefits independent of retirement age
Part-time pensions before normal retirement	No part-time employment	Depends on pension fund/ kind of work	Depends on age	Possible for all employees
Special groups	No early retirement possible	No early retirement in public pension system	Early retirement for physically demanding jobs or long history (narrow eligibility)	Early retirement for long contribution history (broad eligibility) or flat benefits
Attractiveness of late retirement:				
Mandatory retirement	For all segments of the labour market	For some large segments of the labour market	For some small segments of the labour market	Mandatory retirement is illegal
Subsidies/costs for employers	No subsidies but high costs	No subsidies but low costs	Low subsidies	High subsidies
Earnings limits	Strict earnings test			No earnings test
Benefit increases for later retirement	No increase at all	Less than actuarial	Actuarial	More than actuarial

Source: Adapted from Börsch-Supan et al. (2019, p. 8).

from delaying retirement depend on general rules of how pension benefits are calculated (D'Addio, Keese, & Whitehouse, 2010). In defined contribution and nonfinancial defined contribution systems, the rules seem to be quite straightforward, because when older workers continue employment, they become eligible to higher benefits, as there is an additional contribution to a pension fund. In defined benefit systems, pension benefits are typically determined with years of earnings. Hence, an additional year of employment might, apart from the obvious possibility to add additional years to an entitlement, enhance a composition of contribution record taken into account in a formula by including a year with high earnings at the expense of dropping out a year with lower earnings (OECD, 2011a, p. 53). The latter would be especially important for those workers who experienced a considerable growth in earnings in the last phases of their careers. In general, there was a tendency to believe that pension formulas based on the defined contribution principle provide older workers with greater incentives to prolong their careers than in the defined benefit systems (Lacomba & Lagos, 2009). However, a recent study (Qi, Helgertz, & Bengtsson, 2018), which evaluated the shift to the nonfinancial defined contribution system, found that this effect is a function of educational and occupational composition of the workforce of senior people: if a majority of older workers have low educational attainment and skills, the overall outcome concerning labour utilisation might be very small and even negative.

To sum up, while the role of pension systems regarding labour utilisation of older workers is fundamental, its importance has to be also assessed in combination with other factors, such as the general labour market situation of older workers in a given country.

The context: specificity of labour markets situation of older workers in CEE

Health and education remain core elements of human capital formation. When we look at the older workforce in the CEE region, we should bear in mind that those elements of human capital were to a great extent shaped by specific economic and societal factors related to a state-socialism economy. Hence, it is important to look at the determinants of labour utilisation of this group through a historically oriented lens. Only then can we understand the existing differences between CEE countries and wealthier Western Europe in such issues as mortality or life expectancy.

The post-communist transformation brought about a substantial improvement to the health of the population in the CEE, which manifested itself, for instance, by a dramatic decline of deaths caused by ischaemic heart disease (Ginter & Simko, 2012). Among all transition countries, Poland and the Czech Republic might be regarded as champions of such improvements (Golinowska, 2009, p. 229), even though the life expectancy, especially for males in those two countries, is still lower than in the EU-15. Measures of healthy life years (i.e. the number of remaining years that a person of specific age is expected to live without any severe or moderate health problems) for Polish and Czech women are, as is documented by Eurostat, good, and they are very close to the EU average (Eurostat database), which theoretically can facilitate prolonging careers in the labour market of older women. The same indicators for Polish and Czech men are well below EU's average. From the perspective of labour utilisation, it is important to look at general health indicators of different segments of the labour market. In this vein, we could take the example of the huge gaps in life expectancy between men with the highest and the lowest educational levels: those gaps[2] point to highly diversified labour market chances for older people, especially men, in the Czech Republic and Poland.

Prevailing educational attainment among the current older workforce in CEE is to a very large degree the result of educational systems that were in place during state socialism. Data presented in a comprehensive study (Kogan, Gebel, & Noelke, 2008) documented an exceptionally small share, also given the EU-15 average, of older people in the Czech Republic who had only lower-secondary education or less.[3] A similar pattern was also detected by the authors in the share of older workers with upper-secondary or post-secondary no-tertiary education (ISCED 3–4): the percentage for the Czech population was two times higher than the EU-15 average. In general, public authorities throughout the period of state socialism in CEE were greatly aimed at producing lower-grade specialities i.e., a worker who can be employed in industrial sectors as well as in state bureaucracy (Michael, Kogan, & Gebel, 2012). The role of tertiary education remained limited, and it was additionally discouraged by low differences in wages between tertiary-educated people and skilled manual workers or technicians (Kogan et al., 2008).

From a labour demand side, the post-communist transformation brought about very dramatic reconfigurations of the work environment, including the privatisation or liquidation of many state companies. At the same time, countries from the CEE region experienced a rapid tertiarisation that could be regarded as a 'structural correction of over-industrialised economies' as well as – especially in Visegrad countries – inflow of FDI investments that contributed to the re-industrialisation of the economies (Lux, 2018). We could argue that many new investments that counterbalanced a negative external shock to the labour market were much more favourable to younger workers, as the cost of (re)training these workers was lower than for older workers. Furthermore, from a territorial perspective, those new investments were unevenly distributed, i.e. some regions of countries were underinvested; the urban–rural divide was also a serious problem in this respect (Domański, 2003).

To sum up, the specificity of the labour market situation of older workers in CEE stems from a combination of improvements of general quality of life in the last years and hardships and challenges that the elderly faced before and during the transformation.

Labour market utilisation of older workers in the Czech Republic and Poland

Data

The empirical analysis is based on a broad range of data. Apart from the data derived from comparable databases established by OECD and Eurostat, we also looked at the data collected by national entities such as the Ministry of Labour and Social Policy in the Czech Republic and the Social Insurance Institution (ZUS) in Poland. We employed these data to detect and compare trends over the study period. A cautionary note should be made here: the pension system tends to be 'slow-moving objects', and legal amendments do not always translate into fast policy changes, not to mention changes that could be observed at the individual level.

In order to complement the analysis and to delve into the situation of older workers, we also used the wave of the Survey of Health, Ageing and Retirement in Europe (SHARE) from 2017. This dataset provides detailed information on many aspects of life of the elderly for a probabilistic sample of older people in many European countries, including the Czech Republic and Poland. We used the SHARE data for a merely descriptive purpose by employing a simple binary variable logistic regression model.

Macro-level data

As outlined in the book's introduction, the employment rate is a basic indicator measuring quantitative aspects of labour utilisation. Figure 10.1 presents this indicator for both countries, as well as for the EU-15 average, with a differentiation of gender. The data clearly show that, throughout the period under study, the Czech Republic and Poland differed not only in the levels of employment rates, but also in the dynamics of their changes. Interestingly, when examining the employment rate for older women, situations in the Czech Republic and Poland were remarkably similar (and close to EU-15) at the beginning of the period of the study and began to diverge during the first decade of the twenty-first century. In the same time, the employment rate for older men in Poland considerably declined, which only widened the gap between Polish and Czech (and the EU-15) measures. Throughout the period of the study, employment rates for Czech men and women were generally steadily increasing, with only one episode of decline for the former group which took place during the economic slowdown in 2009. Overall, unlike in the Polish case, the employment rate for the Czech men has been above the EU-15 average, whereas this measure for the Czech women has been gradually catching up to the EU average.

As shown in Table 10.2, dynamics of growth of the employment rate in CEE varied with regard to educational levels of older people. The Polish case clearly stands out, because the employment rate of low-educated older workers between

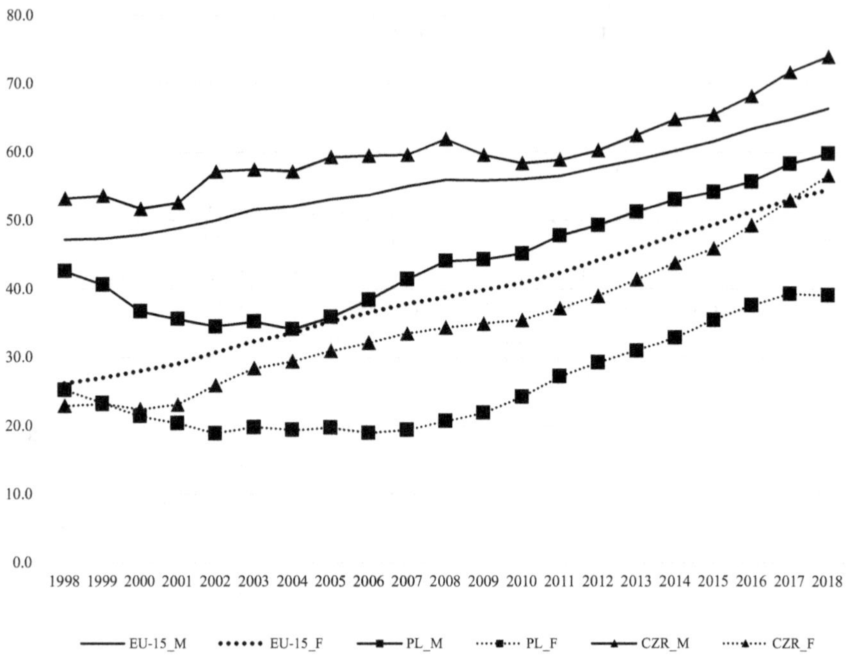

Figure 10.1 Employment rate of older men and women (55–64) between 1998 and 2018, percentage points

Source: Eurostat [lfsi_emp_a].

Notes: M denotes men, F denotes women.

Table 10.2 Change in employment rates of older workers by educational level between 2000 and 2017, percentage points

	Below upper secondary education	*Upper secondary or post-secondary non-tertiary education*	*Tertiary education*
Czech Republic	**13.9**	**22.6**	**15.9**
Poland	**2.9**	**19.7**	**18.1**
Estonia	15.2	20.6	20.9
Hungary	21.2	23.2	17.1
Latvia	15.1	23.0	19.9
Lithuania	10.8	15.7	23.2
Slovak Republic	19.9	26.5	16.2
Slovenia	6.9	22.4	19.6

Source: OECD (2019b, p. 24).

2000 and 2017 increased only marginally, and this group is significantly lagging behind workers with higher educational attainment. It suggests that, by employing the book's definition of labour utilisation, the contribution of human capital to GDP in Poland by those with the lowest education level is minor. On the contrary, in the Czech Republic the growth of employment rates among older people with different educational levels was much more even.

Job opportunities for older workers could be measured at a macro level by at least two indicators: retention rates and full-time earnings ratio between workers aged 55 and 64 and 25 and 54 (OECD, 2019a). Concerning the former measure, which is regarded as a key determinant of prolonging careers and increasing employment of older people (Hardy, Kiełczewska, Lewandowski, & Magda, 2018), both countries made significant progress between 2008 and 2018, as they experienced almost the same level of age growth of retention rate.[4] Therefore, one of the causes of the increase to the employment rates for senior workers is that they are more likely to stay in their jobs (Lewandowski, 2017). When it comes to the earnings ratio between different groups of workers (OECD, 2019a), the Czech Republic had a very even relation in the last decade,[5] whereas Poland experienced a considerable change over this period. The latter suggests that wage increases that have taken place recently in the Polish economy mostly affected the situation of younger workers, leaving older workers behind.

Micro-level data

Having in mind that we frame a pension system as a formal labour market institution that either facilitates an early withdrawal from the labour market or prolongs employment, we now provide a brief overview of the individual-level characteristics of older workers concerning their preferences for retiring as soon as possible. The analysis of a likelihood that the older workers are looking for an early retirement option enriches a cross-country comparison of institutional-level factors, i.e. by directing the attention of potential voters, which is important from a political process perspective, as it leads to increasing or decreasing the retirement age (Conde-Ruiz & Galasso, 2004). Such analysis also helps determine an optimal shape of the pension system in a given country that suits needs of older workers, i.e. by asking whether women really prefer to retire early or they face 'involuntary' early retirement (Dorn & Sousa-Poza, 2010).

Concerning the comparative perspective, Table 10.3 presents distributions of older workers (currently at employment or self-employed) with reference to their preference for an early retirement options in selected CEE and Western countries. There is a substantial difference in distributions between the Czech Republic and Poland, as in the former case we see a much lower share of older workers who are looking for an early retirement. Those two countries exemplify the general diversity within the CEE region. It should be noted that strong preferences for earlier retirement are quite widespread in Europe, and the CEE region is not unique in this regard.

Table 10.3 Preferences for early retirement of older workers in selected European countries, percentage points

	Yes	*No*	*N*
Central and Eastern Europe			
Czech Republic	**45.9**	**53.1**	**567**
Poland	**58.3**	**40.4**	**1169**
Bulgaria	41.3	58.0	547
Romania	55.4	44.6	327
Slovakia	33.0	67.0	966
Slovenia	72.1	26.4	455
Continental Europe			
Belgium	38.3	60.8	1117
France	65.4	34.2	638
Germany	50.8	48.8	1087
Nordic countries			
Denmark	37.6	60.6	1267
Sweden	31.5	67.0	672
Southern Europe			
Greece	56.9	42.8	559
Italy	68.9	30.8	929
Spain	70.7	28.3	823

Source: Own elaboration based on SHARE data (7th Wave, 2017).

Notes: Older workers (those aged 50 years and more) were asked the following question: 'Thinking about your present job, would you like to retire as early as you can from this job?'

Binomial logistic regressions, run separately for both countries, were performed to ascertain the effects of selected variables on the likelihood that the older workers are looking for an early retirement option. The simple model consists of independent variables that hypothetically determine labour utilisation of older workers, especially regarding postponing a withdrawal from the labour market. Therefore, we include in the model variables of a gender, due to the gender gaps in the analysed cases, together with the variable concerning living with a partner, because previous analyses of retirement behaviours have shown that individual retirement decisions are in fact results of negotiations within couples (Atalay, Barrett, & Siminski, 2019; Lalive & Parrotta, 2017). Health status is an obvious driver of labour utilisation of older workers, so in the model we included two variables related to this aspect: subjective assessment of health and objective measure of body mass index (BMI). Finally, our simple model also includes the variable CASP-12, which measures the quality of life in older age. CASP-12 is composed of four subscales: control, autonomy, self-realisation, and pleasure. The higher the score on the scale, the better quality of life. Unfortunately, due to data constraints we were not able to include other potentially important variables concerning education or occupation. Table 10.4 presents the results of the analysis.

When interpreting the results, we should keep in mind many disadvantages of logistic regression such as problems with omitted variables and the fact that

Table 10.4 Logistic regression predicting likelihood of looking for early retirement based on subjective health, CASP index, gender, BMI, and living with a partner

	Coefficients	*Odds ratio*	*95% confidence intervals for odds ratio*	
			Lower	*Upper*
Poland				
Constant	2.156*** (0.604)	8.638		
Subjective health (dummy): 1 – worse than very good, 0 – excellent or very good	0.499** (0.157)	1.648	1.212	2.240
CASP index	–.075*** (0.012)	0.928	0.907	0.949
Gender (dummy): 1 – female, 0 – male	0.088 (0.127)	1.092	0.852	1.399
BMI	0.030** (0.013)	1.030	1.003	1.058
Living with a partner (dummy): 1 – no, 0 – yes	–0.630*** (0.177)	0.533	0.376	0.754
Czech Republic				
Constant	2.669** (0.902)	14.421		
Subjective health (dummy):1 – worse than very good, 0 – excellent or very good	0.764*** (0.206)	2.147	1.434	3.214
CASP-12 index	–0.077*** (0.020)	0.926	0.890	0.963
Gender (dummy): 1 – female, 0 – male	0.078 (0.187)	1.081	0.750	1.558
BMI	–0.020* (0.012)	0.980	0.958	1.003
Living with a partner (dummy): 1 – no, 0 – yes	–0.049 (0.243)	0.952	0.591	1.533

Source: Own elaboration based on SHARE data (7th Wave, 2017).

Notes: Asterisks denote significance levels: *** – 0.01, ** – 0.05 and * – 0.1. Standard errors are reported in parentheses.

odds ratios could not be compared across groups (Mood, 2010). Nevertheless, given the complexity of retirement preferences, problems with precise measurements are almost insuperable, and we believe that logistic regression might be useful for merely explorative purposes. The results clearly show that lower scores on CASP-12 scale (i.e. lower quality of life) as well as lower subjective health assessment increase the probability of looking for early retirement. Those results are generally very similar to results for Western European countries (Wahrendorf, Akinwale, Landy, Matthews, & Blane, 2017). Interestingly, the variable concerning gender is not statistically significant. Contrary to our expectations derived from observation of the analysis macro-context, and somewhat surprisingly, we cannot say whether women would like to leave the labour market as early as possible. This argument is important in the context of a unique treatment of gender in pension systems in our two cases, which we elaborate on in the following section.

Pensions systems in the Czech Republic and Poland

While the Czech Republic and Poland are similar in terms of the initial conditions (departure from state socialism), they differ in terms of the transition style (shock therapy in Poland and a gradualist approach in the Czech Republic), developments in the labour market (very fast growth of unemployment in Poland and delayed increase of unemployment by a significantly smaller magnitude in the Czech Republic), as well as pension reforms (radical, paradigmatic change from a defined benefit to a defined contribution system in Poland and parametric reform of the defined benefit system in the Czech Republic). However, they share one important feature: in both countries, the governments have extensively used the pension schemes as a way of influencing labour utilisation (for an overview of these processes see Barr, 2005). In this respect, the regulations concerning retirement age, statutory as well as early retirement, have been central in controlling the levels of employment and unemployment. While in the early years of the transition, early retirement had been used extensively, around the mid-2000s, the routes to retirement have been restricted.

The recent publication by Börsch-Supan and colleagues (2019) emphasises the role of early retirement schemes and other policies and practices apart from statutory retirement regulations in employment of older cohorts of workers. The authors found a correlation between the existence of such policy instruments and labour force participation. In a crude way, our empirical analysis suggests that these factors indeed affect employment in the Czech Republic and Poland when it comes to older workers.

Nevertheless, we should remember that, as pension systems are 'slow-moving objects', pension reforms operate on long phasing-out and phasing-in periods principles. Further, in some instances, policy changes in the pensions field are offset by other compensatory measures, which means that in fact isolating the effect of such reforms is particularly troublesome. Given these two points, in some instances the analysis goes beyond a narrow understanding of retirement age reforms.

From the perspective of labour utilisation, one may argue that the reforms presented in what follows were moderately successful. In both countries, the average effective age of retirement was fluctuating, which can be associated with changes in retirement rules but also the economic situation. A specific, unintended consequence of removing early retirement options was the 'retirement run' preceding policy change – individuals who were eligible to use such options did so. This is why, in Figure 10.2, we see drops in the retirement age followed by steep increases (especially in the case of Polish women). Also, what we note is the closing but still existing gap in the retirement age between men and women in both our cases. The gap is still bigger compared to the 'old' EU Member States average.

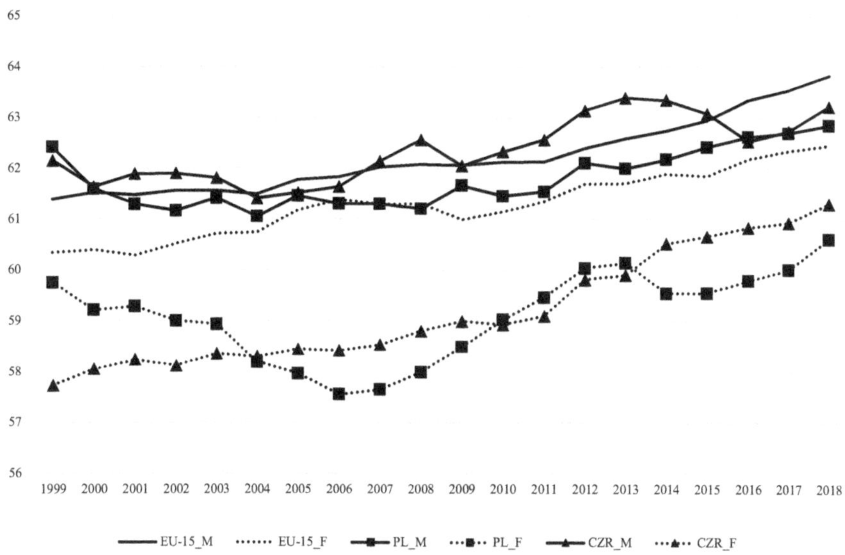

Figure 10.2 Average effective age of retirement between 1999 and 2018

Source: Own elaboration based on OECD (2020).

Notes: M denotes men, F denotes women. Averages for EU-15 computed by the authors.

The Czech Republic

Like many other socialist states, Czechoslovakia had a pension system which operated on different principles depending on the occupation group or sector of the economy. One of the first changes in the pension system after 1990 was to merge all three occupational categories into one which, meant the unification of eligibility rules (Müller, 1999). However, the low statutory retirement age (60 years for men and 55 years for women) remained unchanged. A peculiarity of the Czech system has been the retirement age for women depending on the number of children born.

The major parametric reform was introduced in 1995 (OECD, 1996). As a part of it, the retirement age increase was introduced (Bezdek, 2005). For men the increase of the retirement age was from 60 years in 1995 to 62 in 2000; while for women, a very firm increase of the age from 53 to 57 in 1995 to 57 and 61 in 2007 (depending on the number of children she had birthed). As in other reforms of this type in CEE of that period, the increase in the retirement age was accompanied by an introduction of favourable early retirement schemes (Polakowski, 2010). However, it turned out that the temporary measure provided a much more generous provision than the regular one due to small decreases in the benefits. The result of this reform was a wave of retirement based on early retirement principles in the period of 1997 to 2000 (in 2000, almost 59% of all new retirees used the early retirement path; OECD, 2001). There were two general categories of early retirement benefits. The difference between them was that the first type of benefit could be temporarily reduced for those in employment and meeting eligibility conditions and who retire up to 2 years early before the statutory retirement age. Upon reaching this age, the benefit would be paid in full. The second option concerned early retirement 3 years before the statutory retirement age when standard pension qualifying conditions were met. In this case, the benefit would be reduced permanently (Bezdek, 2005).

The role of early retirement schemes was constantly growing in the late 1990s,[6] and eventually, in the year 2000, 2.5% of the Czech working-age population was drawing early retirement benefits (2.2% permanently reduced and 0.3% of temporarily reduced; OECD, 2001). This is why in June 2001 the government introduced a reform which reduced the early retirement benefits of the permanently reduced category in a manner which would be more proportional (Vylitova, 2002). However, no change for the temporarily reduced benefits was introduced. A year later the share of early retirement in all newly granted benefits declined to 32%. The main channel of exit from the labour market was through the disability pensions: in 2000, 7.54% of the working-age population participated in such schemes (OECD, 2001). Nonetheless the share of working age population receiving early retirement increased to 3.1% in 2002.

In the end of 2003, the Czech government introduced a slight increase in the retirement age. Between 2007 and 2013 the retirement age was increased by 1 year for men and by 2 years for women. This meant that men and women without children could have retired at the age of 63. However, the child-related reductions of the retirement age were maintained (Bezdek, 2005). The same reform banned the possibility of early retirement based on temporarily reduced benefits (that is a possibility of retirement 2 years before the statutory retirement age). This change was partially offset by the introduction of a special unemployment benefit for individuals with at least 25 years of participation in pension insurance (with a benefit duration of 9 months) or 30 years (benefit duration of 12 months) and registered as unemployed. Nonetheless the possibility to retire 3 years earlier before reaching the statutory age with permanently reduced benefit was maintained. It should be mentioned that the age-related unemployment benefit did not allow retirees to work. The plan of the government was to phase out this possibility by 2006 (OECD, 2004).

Another reform to the pension system was introduced in 2008 (OECD, 2010). First, again, the retirement age was increased with the phase-in period until 2030. Further, the principles regarding combining retirement at work were changed. Importantly from the perspective of this chapter, the legislation stipulated that an early retirement can be taken only in the case of a full, 35-year contributory history. However, as the retirement age was being increased, the early retirement period (3 years) would be extended to 5 years to keep up with the retirement age of 65. Importantly, the penalties for taking early retirement would be increased from 3.6% per year to 6% per year for those individuals retiring 5 years early.

This took place from 2010 onwards and was seen as a measure which reduced the benefit level more than required by the actuarial calculations (OECD, 2011b).

In 2011 an interesting phenomenon could be noted where a peak in early retirement occurred. Accordingly, in this single year, a double of the normal number of individuals went for the early retirement path. This peak occurred shortly after the economic slowdown that took place in the Czech Republic at that time. Figure 10.3 illustrates the scale of this change. After this year another significant drop could be observed for both women and men.

The reform introduced in 2011 was a major change to the pension system, as it introduced a multi-pillar pension system with the mandatory funded component (Loužek, 2014). More importantly from the perspective of this chapter, the reform consisted of another increase in the statutory retirement age. Accordingly, in 2044 the mandatory retirement age will be 67. After 2041, the retirement age will be increased by two months every year.

To sum up the dynamics of the retirement age, the Czech old-age pension system has undergone significant changes. The statutory retirement change has been increased over the last two decades and will increase further in the coming decades. It should be emphasised, nonetheless, that changes in the statutory retirement age are only a part of the picture. In many respects the early retirement options should be seen as a crucial way of exiting the labour market by

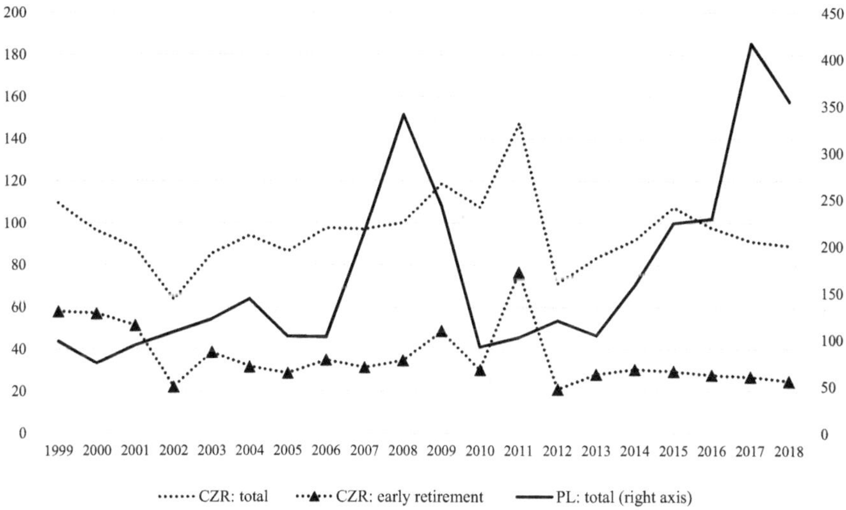

Figure 10.3 The number of newly granted old-age pensions, in thousands

Source: Own elaboration based on data of the Ministry of Labour and Social Policy in the Czech Republic and the Social Insurance Institution in Poland.

Notes: CZR total denotes the number of newly granted old-age pension in the Czech Republic in a given year. CZR early retirement refers to the number of those who were granted an early pension of various kinds. PL total denotes the number of newly granted old-age pension in Poland in a given year.

both the workers and unemployed but also by policymakers. The impact of early retirement cannot be established in a robust way, as there have existed other exit options from the labour market such as disability pensions and unemployment benefits. The hint that early retirement operates as a labour market safety net can be confirmed by the fact that this policy option was used by many individuals in the periods of worsening situations in the labour market. This led to a situation in which the unemployment rates were systematically higher in the 50- to 55-year-old age group than in the 55–64 group over the 1993–2005 period. It can be explained by the very presence of early retirement which contributed to the reduction of the oldest workers' unemployment. Finally, the government, knowing that in certain periods of time more individuals retired on preferential basis as compared to regular retirement, enforced the reduction of the early retirement option and increased the statutory retirement age.

Poland

Poland entered the transition with a highly fragmented pension system. It consisted of several sub-components: the general system for workers accompanied by a number of special retirement schemes for certain professions or occupations, as well as several clauses allowing early retirement. This means that, unlike in the Czech Republic, the early retirement schemes were well embedded in the pension system's institutional architecture already before 1989.

The period before the major paradigmatic change, introduced in the late 1990s, was characterised by extensive discussions regarding low retirement age (resulting largely from early retirement), but in practice actions were targeted mostly at the benefit calculation formula as well as the pension financing model (Polakowski, 2010). The 1999 reform did not alter the retirement age significantly when it comes to general categories of workers. In the discussions regarding the reform blueprint there was a proposal of the retirement age equalisation to 62 years for both genders. However, one of the trade unions successfully blocked it (Polakowski, 2010). Nonetheless, the reform dealt with early retirement possibilities to a larger extent than previous efforts, assuming they would be completely phased out by the end of 2006 and replaced by the so-called 'bridging pensions', which would smooth out the transition to retirement for older workers in specific instances (Chłoń-Domińczak, 2016a).

Early retirement possibilities were retained for all workers born before 1949 as well as some workers born before 1968. Early retirement was largely removed only in 2008 with the bridging pensions introduced. It should be noted that the announcement of the change resulted in a 'run for early retirement'. Therefore, instead of smoothing the impact of the early retirement removal over the years, in 2008 one could see a massive wave of retirement cumulated over a short period in time (see Figure 10.3). The main difference between early retirement and the bridging pensions is that in the case of the latter, the number of eligible workers is significantly smaller (OECD, 2015). The president vetoed the bill on the grounds of its being too narrowly focused. In the veto statement it was emphasised that early retirement applied to approximately 1.1 million workers while the bridging pensions scheme applied only to 250-thousand workers. However, the president's veto was rejected by the parliament (Chłoń-Domińczak, 2016a).

An important but very short-lived change dealt with the early retirement of men based on the judgement of the Constitutional Tribunal, which stated that the conditions for early retirement for men are in conflict with the gender equality principle. Whereas in the case of women, the only criterion was age, in the case of men, an additional requirement – disability – had to be met (Antonów, 2011). The judgement opened the pathway for early retirement for all men with the contributory period of 35 years and the age of at least 60 years. This single change contributed to a massive inflow to the retirement. In 2008 alone approximately 50% more individuals decided to retire, compared to the previous years.

In May 2012 an increase to the retirement age to 67 years for men and women was decided by Parliament. The implementation of the reform started at the beginning of 2013 and the period of increasing the retirement age was different for men and women. Accordingly, for men the retirement age was to be increased until 2020, while for women, until 2040 (OECD, 2013). An option was left to retire early via so-called 'partial pensions' (Chłoń-Domińczak, 2016b). The basic eligibility criterion for partial benefits was reaching 62 years of age for women (and having paid the contributions for at least 35 years) and 65 years of age for men and 40 years of contributions. The level of the benefit was to be 50% of the full amount of the benefit calculated according to the pension formula.

Increasing the retirement age starting in 2013 was a major political issue. This was why it was so extensively used in electoral campaigns by different political parties. The reversal of the retirement age took place in October 2017, and since then, it has been possible to retire at the age of 65 (men) and 60 (women) (Chłoń-Domińczak, 2016b). Indeed, Poland, together with Austria, is currently characterised by the lowest statutory retirement age in Europe for women, being also a very rare example of an OECD country that will maintain a (substantial) gender gap in the retirement age.

As a way of summarising, it should be stated that the developments regarding the retirement age which have taken place since 1989 were heavily influenced by the legislation introduced earlier. The different categories of early retirement lasted long after 1989. As in other countries, they served as a way of managing labour utilisation, especially in the sectors affected greatly by the transition – in industry in particular. The other category was women. The reform introduced in 1999 aimed at increasing labour utilisation by introducing two important components. First, it was narrowing the exit via early retirement schemes. Second, it was the introduction of the defined contribution pension formula (Polakowski & Hagemejer, 2018). In the defined contribution formula, the changes in the retirement age affect the level of benefits in a twofold way. First, it is the shorter contributory period, which translates into lower amount of contributions. Second, the retirement moment affects the length of a period over which the benefit would be paid out. Given the fixed amount of contributions paid to the pension system, the longer periods of drawing benefits translate into lower annuities.

In Poland, even after the introductions of the defined contribution formula, the discussions on the statutory retirement age did not stop. For many policymakers and experts, the statutory retirement age remained too low, even though the links between the amount of contributions, retirement moment and longevity are straightforward.

Discussion

Comparing our two cases, one can draw several conclusions. First, already during the socialist period, the governments influenced the labour supply, especially in the periods of economic slowdowns. This was the case in Poland more than in the Czech Republic, where old-age pension benefits were used to deactivate women and prioritise the employment of men. Second, during the first decade of the transition, several measures related to early retirement that either were already present, like in Poland, or newly introduced, as in the Czech Republic, were used to allow older workers to transit to inactivity. Third, since the beginning of the twenty-first century, there have been numerous attempts to retain older workers in the labour market. This was done by increases to the statutory retirement age and phasing out the early retirement schemes. At least two sets of reasons were given by policymakers to justify such reforms: the costs of retirement on the public pension systems and a shrinking labour force.

The analysis provided suggests that reforming the retirement age is not an easy task. In both countries, a number of piecemeal reforms aimed at curbing the extent of early retirement. However, in the short term such reforms were moderately successful, as they were accompanied by 'retirement runs' of those who were eligible and could lose the early retirement right. Also, reforming retirement age entails several political and social trade-offs. Pension rights are a highly salient issue for voters and social partners, as they provide income security. This is why when policymakers decide to reform retirement age, they often propose some compensatory measures, such as unemployment benefits or pre-retirement benefits for older workers. Also, some other functional equivalents, such as disability schemes, were available.

Conclusion

The general aim of this chapter was to assess whether the pension systems in two countries under study facilitate the keeping of labour utilisation of older people at high level. We started our considerations by formulating the hypothesis that an increase to a statutory retirement age brings about an immediate increase in labour market participation of older workers in both countries. While this hypothesis has been partially confirmed, we draw the attention of the reader to the role of the early retirement schemes – it is due to their reforms, the gains in the labour utilisation are fast. When it comes to increases to the statutory age, they are usually phased in over a longer period of time. Therefore, an increase of the labour market exit age should be seen as a joint effect of and increases in the retirement age and early retirement removal. When these two policies are developed simultaneously, we can see a positive result in the short term. This is visible more clearly in the Czech Republic rather than in Poland. Thus, the pension system in the former country may be assessed as a greater facilitator of labour utilisation of older people than the pension system in the latter case.

To a large extent our analysis confirms the results presented recently by Börsch-Supan and colleagues (2019): the retirement age and especially specific regulations which allow for the withdrawal from the labour market before reaching statutory retirement age (early retirement). are one of the most important aspects affecting labour utilisation of older workers. As the authors argue, quick increases to the statutory retirement age benefit reductions in the situation of early retirement and the universality of pension provisions all contribute to a lower attractiveness of early labour market withdrawal. Conversely, the lack of a mandatory retirement requirement, no earnings limits or increases of benefits when working past the statutory age are seen as influencing the attractiveness of later retirement. Therefore, it seems that the recommendations are quite universal and may be put forward with respect to the CEE region.

Looking at our two case studies from the perspective of labour utilisation, reducing the role of early retirement should be seen as equally important as increasing the statutory age. However, as the quantitative part of our analysis indicates, the willingness to retire early is associated with a lower quality of life, which points to other aspects of social policy as the conditions for increasing social acceptance for retiring later. Also, one might speculate that the economic hardship of the transition, but also earlier experience, might influence these results. We think that this argument should be considered with regard to other CEE countries as well. On a practical note, by adopting a broader perspective and following the lines of the life-cycle approach, it can be recommended that policies supporting later retirement should go beyond older cohorts and continuously improve the quality of individuals' lives from early on. Publicly financed, high-quality education, healthcare, care services, review of qualifications, access to up-skilling and re-skilling, and income protection should be backbones of this strategy. At the same time, workplace practices such as adjustment of jobs to individual capacities and abilities should be integral parts of it.

Finally, and more generally, we do not over-emphasise the positive aspects of increasing the statutory retirement age in the CEE region. Although there are many reasons to believe that prolonging careers of older workers could be considered a good policy choice, the actual benefits and costs (measured at individual, firm and society levels) of increasing labour utilisation of seniors are largely contingent on the availability of good-quality jobs that are suited to older people's preferences.

Acknowledgements

This paper uses data from SHARE Wave 7 (doi:10.6103/SHARE.w7.700), see Börsch-Supan et al. (2013) for methodological details. The SHARE data collection has been funded by the European Commission through FP5 (QLK6-CT-2001–00360), FP6 (SHARE-I3: RII-CT-2006–062193, COMPARE: CIT5-CT-2005–028857, SHARELIFE: CIT4-CT-2006–028812), FP7 (SHARE-PREP: GA N°211909, SHARE-LEAP: GA N°227822, SHARE M4: GA N°261982) and Horizon 2020 (SHARE-DEV3: GA N°676536, SERISS: GA N°654221) and by DG Employment, Social Affairs & Inclusion. Additional funding from the German Ministry of Education and Research, the Max Planck Society for the Advancement of Science, the U.S. National Institute on Aging (U01_AG09740–13S2, P01_AG005842, P01_AG08291, P30_AG12815, R21_AG025169, Y1-AG-4553-01, IAG_BSR06–11, OGHA_04–064, HHSN271201300071C) and from various national funding sources is gratefully acknowledged (see www.share-project.org).

Michał Polakowski's work is part of research project UMO-2016/20/S/HS5/00452, financed by the National Science Centre of Poland.

Notes

1 We restrict our attention only to a public pension system.

2 In 2015 for people at age 30 such differences were exceptionally high, given OECD standards – for males (10.6 years for the Czech Republic and 11.8 years for Poland – while the OECD average was 7.1 years). Interestingly, those gaps for Czech women (2.7 years) is lower than the OECD average (4.2 years), while for Polish women is higher than the average by only less than one year (OECD, 2017).

3 At the beginning of the twenty-first century in the Czech Republic, the share of people aged 55–64 who had only lower-secondary education or less (ISCED 0–2) was markedly the lowest among all transition countries, amounting to 20% (for Poland more than 40%) and was also more than two times lower than the EU-15 average (Kogan et al., 2008).

4 Retention rate growth in the Czech Republic was at 12.3% and at 11.9% in Poland.

5 For the Czech Republic it was 0.97 in 2008 and 0.98 in 2018, while for Poland this measure was 1.12 and 0.95, respectively.

6 In 1996, 18% of all new pensioners were receiving early retirement pensions. In terms of early retirement as a share of working-age population, it grew from 0.2% in 1996 to 1.1% in 1998 (OECD, 2000). As for the permanently reduced pension beneficiaries, their share equalled 0.1% of the working-age population in 1996 and then increased to 0.6% in 1998. In the case of temporarily reduced benefit, the recipients constitute 0.1 of the working-age population in 1996 and 0.9% in in 1998.

References

Ardito, C. (2017). *Rising pension age in Italy: Employment response and program substitution* (Collegio Carlo Alberto, Working Paper No. 115). Retrieved from www.laboratoriorevelli.it/sites/default/files/documents/papers/wp155.pdf

Antonów, K. (2011). Ewolucja systemu emerytalnego. In *Ewolucja ubezpieczeń społecznych w okresie transformacji ustrojowej*. Bydgoszcz: Polskie Stowarzyszenie Ubezpieczenia Społecznego.

Atalay, K., Barrett, G. F., & Siminski, P. (2019). Pension incentives and the joint retirement of couples: Evidence from two natural experiments. *Journal of Population Economics, 32*(3), 735–767. Doi:10.1007/s00148-018-0725-9

Barr, N. (Ed.). (2005). *Labor markets and social policy in Central and Eastern Europe: The accession and beyond.* Washington, DC: The World Bank.

Bezdek, V. (2005). *The public pension system in the Czech Republic from the point of view of public finance* (No. 257). Retrieved from Center for Intergenerational Studies, Institute of Economic Research, Hitotsubashi University website: https://ideas.repec.org/p/hit/piedp1/257.html

Blundell, R., French, E., & Tetlow, G. (2016). Retirement incentives and labor supply. In J. Piggott & A. Woodland (Eds.), *Handbook of the economics of population aging* (Vol. 1, pp. 457–566). North-Holland: Elsevier.

Boeri, T., & Van Ours, J. (2013). *The economics of imperfect labor markets.* Princeton: Princeton University Press.

Börsch-Supan, A., Brandt, M., Hunkler, C., Kneip, T., Korbmacher, J., Malter, F., . . . Zuber, S. (2013). Data resource profile: The Survey of Health, Ageing and Retirement in Europe (SHARE). *International Journal of Epidemiology, 42*(4), 992–1001.

Börsch-Supan, A., Bucher-Koenen, T., Kutlu-Koc, V., & Goll, N. (2018). Dangerous flexibility – Retirement reforms reconsidered. *Economic Policy, 33*(94), 315–355. doi:10.1093/epolic/eiy002

Börsch-Supan, A., Hanemann, F., Beach, B., Halimi, D., Harding, S., Van Der Waal, M., & Staudinger, U. M. (2019). Older adults' integration in the labour market: A global view. *Ageing and Society*, 1–19. doi:10.1017/S0144686X19001454

Botev, N. (2012). Population ageing in Central and Eastern Europe and its demographic and social context. *European Journal of Ageing, 9*(1), 69–79. doi:10.1007/s10433-012-0217-9

Chawla, M., Betcherman, G., & Banerji, A. (2007). *From red to gray: The "third transition" of aging populations in Eastern Europe and the former Soviet Union.* The World Bank. Retrieved from http://documents.worldbank.org/curated/en/185581468034762694/From-red-to-gray-the-third-transition-of-aging-populations-in-Eastern-Europe-and-the-Former-Soviet-Union-overview

Chłoń-Domińczak, A. (2016a). *ESPN Thematic Report on retirement regimes for workers in arduous or hazardous jobs Poland.* Brussels: European Commission.

Chłoń-Domińczak, A. (2016b). *Reversing the 2013 retirement age reform in Poland. ESPN flash report 2016/7.* Brussels: European Commission.

Conde-Ruiz, J. I., & Galasso, V. (2004). The macroeconomics of early retirement. *Journal of Public Economics, 88*(9–10), 1849–1869. doi:10.1016/j.jpubeco.2003.12.005

D'Addio, A. C., Keese, M., & Whitehouse, E. (2010). Population ageing and labour markets. *Oxford Review of Economic Policy, 26*(4), 613–635. doi:10.1093/oxrep/grq035

De Preter, H., Van Looy, D., & Mortelmans, D. (2013). Individual and institutional push and pull factors as predictors of retirement timing in Europe: A multilevel analysis. *Journal of Aging Studies, 27*(4), 299–307. doi:10.1016/j.jaging.2013.06.003

Domański, B. (2003). Industrial change and foreign direct investment in the postsocialist economy: The case of Poland. *European Urban and Regional Studies, 10*(2), 99–118. doi:10.1177/0969776403010002001

Dorn, D., & Sousa-Poza, A. (2010). "Voluntary" and "involuntary" early retirement: An international analysis. *Applied Economics, 42*(4), 427–438. doi:10.1080/00036840701663277

Ebbinghaus, B. (2006). *Reforming early retirement in Europe, Japan and the USA*. New York, NY: Oxford University Press.

Etgeton, S. (2018, May). The effect of pension reforms on old-age income inequality. *Labour Economics*, *53*, 146–161. doi:10.1016/j.labeco.2018.05.006

Eurostat. Retrieved from https://ec.europa.eu/eurostat/data/database

Geppert, C., Guillemette, Y., Morgavi, H., & Turner, D. (2019). *Labour supply of older people in advanced economies: The impact of changes to statutory retirement ages* (p. 1554). doi:10.1787/b9f8d292-en

Ginter, E., & Simko, V. (2012). Dramatic decline of ischaemic heart disease mortality in post communist Central Europe: Recovery from totality. *Central European Journal of Public Health*, *20*(2), 101–103. doi:10.21101/cejph.a3658

Golinowska, S. (2009). The national model of the welfare state in Poland. In S. Golinowska, P. Hengstenberg, & M. Żukowski (Eds.), *Diversity and commonality in European social policies: The forging of a European social model* (pp. 213–260). Warszawa: Wydawnictwo Naukowe Scholar.

Góra, M. (2019). Redesigning pension systems. *IZA World of Labor* (April 2019), 1–10. doi:10.15185/izawol.51.v2

Hardy, W., Kiełczewska, A., Lewandowski, P., & Magda, I. (2018). Job retention among older workers in Central and Eastern Europe. *Baltic Journal of Economics*, *18*(2), 69–94. doi:10.1080/1406099X.2018.1514562

Kogan, I., Gebel, M., & Noelke, C. (2008). *Europe enlarged: A handbook of education, labour and welfare regimes in Central and Eastern Europe* (pp. 1–390). Bristol: The Policy Press.

Lacomba, J. A., & Lagos, F. (2009). Defined contribution plan vs. defined benefits plan: Reforming the legal retirement age. *Journal of Economic Policy Reform*, *12*(1), 1–11. doi:10.1080/17487870802677668

Lalive, R., & Parrotta, P. (2017). How does pension eligibility affect labor supply in couples? *Labour Economics*, *46*(October 2016). 177–188. doi:10.1016/j.labeco.2016.10.002

Lewandowski, P. (2017). Employment in Poland – Old is the new young. In P. Lewandowski & J. Rutkowsi (Eds.), *Population ageing, labour market and public finance in Poland* (pp. 23–28). Warsaw: European Commission Representation in Poland. doi:10.2775/9

Loužek, M. (2014). Pension reform in the Czech Republic after 2010. *Post-Communist Economies*, *26*(1), 89–102. doi:10.1080/14631377.2014.874657

Lutz, W., Amran, G., Bélanger, A., Conte, A., Gailey, N., Ghio, D., . . . Stonawski, M. (2019). *Demographic scenarios for the EU-migration, population and education*. Luxembourg: Publications Office. doi:2760/590301

Lux, G. (2018). Reintegrating economic space: The metropolitan – provincial divide. In G. Lux & G. Horvath (Eds.), *The Routledge handbook to regional development in Central and Eastern Europe* (pp. 15–28). London: Routledge.

Michael, K., Kogan, I., & Gebel, M. (2012). Educational systems and inequalities in educational attainment in Central and Eastern European countries. *Studies of Transition States and Societies*, *4*(1), 69–83.

Mood, C. (2010). Logistic regression: Why we cannot do what we think we can do, and what we can do about it. *European Sociological Review*, *26*(1), 67–82. doi:10.1093/esr/jcp006

Müller, K. (1999). *The political economy of pension reforms in Central Eastern Europe*. Cheltenham and Northampton: Edward Elgar.

Müller, K. (2002). Beyond privatization: Pension reform in the Czech Republic. *Journal of European Social Policy, 12*(11), 293–306. doi:10.1177/a028429

OECD. (1996). *OECD economic surveys: The Czech Republic 1996.* Paris: OECD Publishing. doi:10.1787/eco_surveys-cze-1996-en

OECD. (2000). *OECD economic surveys: Czech Republic 2000.* Paris: OECD Publishing. doi:10.1787/eco_surveys-cze-2000-en

OECD. (2001). *OECD economic surveys: Czech Republic 2001.* Paris: OECD Publishing. doi:10.1787/eco_surveys-cze-2001-en

OECD. (2004). *OECD economic surveys: Czech Republic 2004.* Paris: OECD Publishing. doi:10.1787/eco_surveys-cze-2004-en

OECD. (2010). *OECD economic surveys: Czech Republic 2010.* Paris: OECD Publishing. doi:10.1787/eco_surveys-cze-2010-en

OECD. (2011a). *Pensions at a glance 2011: Retirement-income systems in OECD and G20 countries.* Paris: OECD Publishing. doi:10.1787/pension_glance-2011-en

OECD. (2011b). *Economic surveys: Czech Republic 2011.* Paris: OECD Publishing. doi:10.1787/eco_surveys-cze-2011-en

OECD. (2013). *Pensions at a glance 2013: OECD and G20 indicators.* Paris: OECD Publishing. doi:10.1787/pension_glance-2013-en

OECD. (2015). *Ageing and employment policies: Poland 2015.* Paris: OECD Publishing. doi:10.1787/9789264227279-en

OECD. (2017). *Health at glance.* Paris: OECD Publishing. doi:10.1787/health_glance-2017-en

OECD. (2019a). *Working better with age, ageing and employment policies.* Paris: OECD Publishing. doi:10.1787/c4d4f66a-en

OECD. (2019b). *Pensions at glance: Retirement-income systems in OECD and G20 countries.* Paris: OECD Publishing. doi:10.1787/b6d3dcfc-en

OECD. (2020). *Average effective age of retirement in 1970–2018 in OECD countries (time series)* [xls]. Retrieved from www.oecd.org/els/emp/average-effective-age-of-retirement.html

Polakowski, M. (2010). *The institutional transformation of social policy in East Central Europe. Poland and Hungary in comparative and historical perspective.* Maastricht: Boekenplan.

Polakowski, M., & Hagemejer, K. (2018). Poland. In I. Ortiz & F. Durán-Valverde (Eds.), *Reversing pension privatizations: Rebuilding public pension systems in Eastern Europe and Latin America.* Geneva, Switzerland: ILO.

Qi, H., Helgertz, J., & Bengtsson, T. (2018). Do notional defined contribution schemes prolong working life? Evidence from the 1994 Swedish pension reform. *Journal of the Economics of Ageing, 12*, 250–267. doi:10.1016/j.jeoa.2016.11.001

Vylitova, M. (2002). *Old-age pension system and its place in the Czech welfare state* (Discussion Paper No. 62).

Wahrendorf, M., Akinwale, B., Landy, R., Matthews, K., & Blane, D. (2017). Who in Europe works beyond the state pension age and under which conditions? Results from SHARE. *Journal of Population Ageing, 10*(3), 269–285. doi:10.1007/s12062-016-9160-4

11

HOW ACTIVE LABOUR MARKET POLICY HELPS THE MOST DISADVANTAGED

Evidence from the Czech Republic

Ondřej Hora and Tomáš Sirovátka

Introduction

The current labour market exhibits remarkable growth of employment and wages and a decrease of unemployment in the Czech Republic to a level that has not been seen for a decade (general unemployment rate at 2.9% in 2018). Despite this, there are still groups of people who have been unemployed for a long time or who have already accumulated several substantial unemployment spells. Inclusion of at least a part of this heterogeneous group to the employment pool could increase labour utilisation in the conditions of an ageing society and help to meet EU employment targets. Such an objective presupposes an effective usage of active labour market policies (ALMPs) and services in general and in post-communist countries in particular given their limited scope and resources available.

This chapter addresses the question: 'How successful has the Czech public employment service been in including the long-term unemployed into the labour market in times after the crisis (2014–2016)?'[1] When conducting the national case study, we examined the following issues:

- i Targeting and impacts of the key active labour market policy instruments (vocational training, subsidised jobs and public works), which are the most widespread types of ALMP programs in the Czech Republic within the heterogeneous group of the unemployed. The analysis is based on administration data from Public Employment Services (PES). The measurement of the impacts is done using quasi-experimental evaluation based on matching or propensity scores in combination with exact matching.
- ii Some conditions of ALMP programs delivery that influence targeting of the programs. Assessment of the implementation of ALMPs conditions is based

on a secondary analysis of various policy documents, implementation studies, and statistics.

The examination of the heterogeneity of the effects of ALMP measures among the different groups of unemployed and the link between targeting and net effects of ALMP measures represent the original contribution to this study.

Our findings indicate that, despite rather modest numbers of participants in ALMP measures, the disadvantaged unemployed (those with low education, of older age and worsened health status) are underrepresented in the ALMP measures. At the same time, the analysis of net effects of the ALMP measures show very good outcomes, especially in the medium-term horizon and in the case of long-term unemployed. The findings are consistent with the other studies on ALMP carried out in CEE countries. Although there is an apparent improvement in targeting Czech ALMP when comparing the current situation with the situation ten years ago, there are indications that selection of the most employable participants into ALMP measures (creaming off) within the target group of the long-term unemployed is considerable, in favour of the better-educated, younger and those with good health status. The reasons of the creaming-off within the group of the long-term unemployed are manifold: the limited resources and unstable financing and selection mechanisms.

In the next section, we discuss the theoretical considerations on the role of targeting ALMP measures in general and on targeting ALMP measures in CEE countries. In the third section, we present the findings on targeting and net effects of ALMP measures and how they are affected by the conditions of the implementation process. In the last section, we conclude. The findings are compared with the reference to other studies dealing with the effects of active labour market policies enacted in CEE countries.

Theoretical considerations

The Czech Republic as an example of a 'Central-East Europe labour market regime'?

Czech active labour market policy represents an example of a specific labour market regime, which seems different when compared to the other countries in Western Europe (see Hora, Horáková, & Sirovátka, 2019). When looking at this regime from the perspective of effort (and generosity) provided to the unemployed in both passive and active labour market policies as indicated by the level of expenditure, this regime scores lower than most of the other regimes; the universalist/Nordic regime scores highest, followed by continental/dualist regime, liberal regime and southern/sub-protective regime. The ALMPs are generally less developed. For this reason, this labour market regime was classified as a 'transitional labour market regime' and considered to be an extreme version of the sub-protective regime (Gallie, 2013).

Yet several studies (e.g. Bánociová & Martinková, 2017; De la Porte & Jacobsson, 2012; Vanhuysse, 2014) document the limited scope of ALMPs measured as expenditure and/or the numbers of participants in post-communist countries and label their approach as 'lenient activation' (Csillag, Samu, & Scharle, 2013). In consequence of the continuous pressures of tight public budgets that emerged due to transitional restructuring, due to fiscal discipline during accession to the EU later and due post-crisis excessive budget procedure recently, ALMPs' expenditures are also to a great extent dependent on European structural funds. Hora et al. (2019) documented that a 'transitional labour market regime' is characterised by a limited scope of ALMP measures in the Czech Republic and Poland in 2013: expenditure on ALMP measures per 1% of unemployment were at most 0.05% of GDP when a similarly low level of ALMP expenditure was found only in Greece, however, in conditions of much higher unemployment rates. A work-first approach strongly prevails over human capital development. The approach to the unemployed is based on switching the responsibility for job searching on the unemployed themselves while the PES capacity for job-search assistance is clearly limited.

More recent data, however, document some divergent developments and that ALMP policy effort is not identical in CEE countries. In 2017, expenditure on ALMPs (job mediation and other PES services including) was low in Slovakia (0.22% of GDP), close to the OECD average 0.52% in the Czech Republic and Poland (0.43% and 0.42% of GDP respectively) and relatively high in Hungary (0.86% of GDP). Similarly, the number of ALMP participants as a percentage of labour force was low in the Czech Republic and Slovakia (1.31% and 2.37% respectively) but above the OECD average (3.81%) in Poland (3.72%) and in Hungary (4.82%) (OECD, 2019). Still, no CEE country belongs among the leaders in ALMP effort.

On top of that, there are some similar problems observed in the ALMP policy implementation process. There are high caseloads of the unemployed per PES front-line staff in post-communist countries, higher when compared to countries like Germany, Sweden, and Belgium and similar to countries like Greece, Portugal, and Ireland (Eichhorst, Neder, Tobsch, & Wozny, 2015). Not only understaffing of PES but also a burden of excessive bureaucracy is mentioned (Bouhol, 2014).

Studies also refer to governance failures and political constrains on ALMPs in CEE countries. Government decision making does not follow the best practice of Scandinavian or British governments, where policymakers rely on monitoring results and impact evaluation of past measures. Also, the procedures for consulting government experts across ministries, social partners, and other stakeholders tend to be weak, making it difficult to implement complicated reforms. The governments also face a temptation to play on the strong anti-unemployed prejudice of middle-class voters and use disadvantaged groups as a scapegoat for the recession (Scharle, 2014). Large Roma minorities in the Czech Republic, Hungary, and Slovakia tend to increase this temptation.

Targeting and effectiveness of ALMP measures

With the shift towards activation in the labour market policies that have prevailed from the 1990s (Lødemel & Trickey, 2000; Van Berkel, de Graaf, & Sirovátka, 2011), accompanied with the neoliberal policy governance concerned with welfare dependency, the new target groups have become the subject of activation measures (e.g. Van Berkel et al., 2017). In CEE countries, during the transition to market economies in the 1990s, an emphasis was put on the protection of the 'regular' labour force affected by processes of the economic restructuring more deeply than the labour force in advanced market economies are typically affected by the fluctuations of the business cycle (see Lehmann & Kluve, 2010; Sirovátka & Hora, 2011). The 'activation turn' that arrived with some delay around 2000 in CEE countries (e.g. Lødemel & Moreira, 2014) brought about the need to address the heterogeneous group of the vulnerable, mostly the long-term unemployed with multiple barriers to labour market participation.

The arguments for targeting ALMP measures towards disadvantaged groups of the unemployed are mainly based on the grounds of efficiency (the economic view) and equity (the social view). In terms of efficiency, targeted measures are expected to be more effective, because of their assumed role in minimising the deadweight loss effects, substitution effects and displacement effects (e.g. Brown & Koettl, 2015; Calmfors, Forslund, & Hemström, 2002). The arguments for targeted policies based on the grounds of equity recognise both the value of providing access to jobs to those who are in some way disadvantaged and the value of reducing social exclusion of vulnerable groups. Participation in a programme can lead to the enhancing, transition or springboard effects (Brown, 2015; Brown & Koettl, 2015). As stated in European Commission (2016), in order to avoid deadweight losses as much as possible, ALMPs should best be targeted at those most detached from the labour market, i.e. mainly the long-term unemployed.

Proper targeting of ALMP measures presupposes a more individual approach at the front-line level in order to meet the heterogeneous individual needs of the disadvantaged groups with use of the tailored measures (e.g. Lødemel & Moreira, 2014; Van Berkel & Valkenburg, 2007). Often, individual case work is also necessary that aims to change attitudes and behaviour (Caswell, Larsen, van Berkel, & Kupka, 2017; Van Berkel et al., 2017).

Failures in targeting

Targeting, however, is a difficult exercise for PES. There are several reasons targeting fails. In his seminal book, Lipsky (2010) considers resource inadequacy as a common problem, indicated by the ratio of the clients to front-line workers (high caseloads), lack of time, lack of competencies and training. Van Berkel et al. (2017) emphasise not only the lack of time for the clients but also the lack of communication skills of front-line workers and conflict of the aspirations to meet the needs of the clients and the standardisation of their work.

The second common reason is the governance framework, in particular the inadequacy of the organisational goals and performance measures that may go against client-centred goals. Van Berkel et al. (2017) argue that the dominant welfare-to-work philosophy forms the values and norms of front-line workers that are not respectful to the real worlds and needs of the clients.

Besides, there are several obstacles and mechanisms in the governance and implementation process. Creaming off is a very common cause of failures in targeting considering that unemployed people who are better equipped with human and social capital tend to enter ALMPs more frequently than those who are less equipped (self-selection), while PES face recruitment difficulties with those less equipped and/or they do not meet eligibility criteria (e.g. Nicaise et al., 1995). Sometimes, PES distinguish between cooperative/compliant clients who deserve help and non-cooperative/non-compliant clients who do not deserve help, and the latter group is given lower priority in the programmes (e.g. Wright, 2013). Last but not least, the selection criteria and procedures applied by employment agency officers are typically based on the objective of outcome efficiency rather than on needs or risk assessment (Brown & Koettl, 2015).

Targeting ALMPs in CEE countries

Some studies discuss targeting of ALMPs in post-communist countries. Boeri (1997, p. 370) assumes that substitution effects of these policies are likely to be even more significant in heavily contested labour markets of Central and Eastern Europe. However, some substitution of unemployed for employed may be desirable on equity grounds and may not necessarily involve efficiency losses. This consideration underlines the necessity of targeting ALMPs at the disadvantaged groups of the (long-term) unemployed. At the same time, some studies warn that addressing the programme mostly to people in a particularly difficult situation may lower the final results, as many of these people will have problems finding employment despite participation (e.g. Dahlke, 2016). Lehmann and Kluve (2010) argue that targeting the least capable among the unemployed might be an extremely inefficient way to spend the very scarce resources that the transition (e.g. CEE) government has. Given the relatively high ‘quality’ of the average unemployed in transitional economies, even if human capital of marginal persons is increased, this increase might not be sufficient to enable these persons to compete with those potentially very productive unemployed. At the same time, the authors point out that actually, the findings show that in many transition countries the training measures are targeted at the best among the unemployed: these ‘creaming effects’ might, however, also be an expression of inefficiency, since the targeted persons might have found regular employment even without participation.

The role of adequate staffing of PES that enables effective individual work and proper distribution (targeting) of ALMPs is also emphasised. Boeri (1997, p. 383) documented that the impact of ALMPs on outflows from register is higher in districts with larger PES staff per unemployed in the country with the lowest unemployment rate (the Czech Republic), although generally differences in staffing PES could not explain the impacts of ALMPs in CEE countries.

Hypotheses

Based on this discussion we hypothesise that targeting of ALMP measures is an effective strategy that underpins effectiveness of ALMPs. This assumption is increasingly relevant for CEE countries, where the labour market inclusion of the disadvantaged groups of the unemployed becomes more important for an effective labour utilisation with their increasing share among the unemployed and heterogeneity and with the increasing focus on activation objective.

Second, we hypothesise that targeting the measures at the disadvantaged groups of the unemployed may depend on various implementation conditions and may fail if these are deficient. We examine these hypotheses in accord with the research questions (as outlined in the Introduction).

Evidence on the interrelations between targeting, effects, and implementation conditions of ALMPs in the Czech Republic

In the next sections we provide evidence about targeting and impacts of main Czech ALMP programmes that operated in 2014–2015. These programmes are briefly characterised in the following table.

Disadvantaged target groups of ALMP in the Czech Republic

The policy practice of distinguishing people who are potentially disadvantaged on the labour market (i.e. risk groups) has been used in Czech ALMP for a long time. The typical target groups addressed by ALMP measures usually include:

- i People who are currently long-term unemployed or who have substantial unemployment history during their previous unemployment spells.
- ii People who have attained only primary levels of qualification (ISCED 1–2).[2]
- iii People who are social assistance claimants.
- iv Other people who are included in so-called risk groups including school graduates, parents after parental leave, older workers and people with disabilities (see e.g. MPSV, 2014).

Table 11.1 Brief description of main ALMP tools in the Czech Republic

Type of program	*Brief description*
Standard training	Training programs in the Czech Republic mostly (with some exceptions) are characterised as rather short-term (only few weeks) training courses leading to manual jobs and some administrative skills and positions (like accounting, computers). There is also a special program for the new (potential) self-employed. Some of the training ends with recognised certifications for a specific profession such as a driving licence and electro-technic or welding certification.
Chosen training	A new program, 'chosen training', was introduced in the Czech Republic in 2012 that represents an alternative to the traditional training organised by PES. It allows retraining in the programs chosen by the unemployed themselves, including training in the specific infrequent/rare professions which are not offered in the standard training courses.
Subsidised workplaces	Subsidised workplaces (SW) are temporarily provided wage subsidies to previously unemployed workers placed in private firms. In the Czech Republic these subsidies are usually provided for one year.
Public works	Public works (PW) are temporary placements in the public sector. Temporary work contract and salary at the level set by the minimum wage (or slightly above) is provided. Public works are usually provided to people whose chances on the labour market are considered to be the poorest, including people living in rural areas with bad public transport connections. Mayors in small municipalities typically use the subsidies available to hire these unemployed for various manual jobs, including cleaning of public space and gardening. The maximum supported period for public works has been prolonged from 12 months to 24 months in 2015 (Hora, Suchanec, Horáková, Rákoczyová, & Sirovátka, 2018), but in practice they mostly last from 6 to 12 months.

Source: Own elaboration based on information from MPSV (2019) and Hora et al. (2018).

In the Czech Republic, quantitative empirical results based on PES data show that men, people with primary education, older people and former unemployed (with previous unemployment spells) are significantly overrepresented among the long-term unemployed (see Hora et al., 2018, p. 43). Less pronounced is the fact that some of the unemployed are ethnic Roma – some of whom live in socially excluded localities. This is neither as much officially reflected nor included in commonly published statistics.

There is substantial overlap between groups of the long-term unemployed, low-skilled people and social assistance claimants (Hora & Vyhlídal, 2016). In other words, most social assistance claimants are registered unemployed, often with their other family members. Hora and Vyhlídal (2016) have found that subsidised workplaces have (short-term) potential to terminate social assistance benefit claiming in a two- to three-month period. This means that from the perspective of public budgets, it may be advantageous to provide job subsidies to these people instead of social assistance benefits.

Hora and Suchanec (2014) assessed the chances of unemployed people to leave the PES register without the programme. They found that specific combinations of such characteristics (e.g. simultaneous low education, health problems and high age) led to substantial decreases of their chances. Such characteristics accumulate and create (in the statistical perspective) multiple barriers to enter the labour market.

Developments in the Czech Labour Market and ALMPs

The labour market situation in the Czech Republic started to improve in the first half of 2014. Changes in the labour market like more vacancies available and substantial reduction of unemployment allowed PES to reduce the overall scope of ALMP and to focus on more difficult cases.

However, despite a decrease in the total unemployment level, some categories of the unemployed remained in the PES register longer. The share of long-term unemployed among unemployed increased as a consequence of their worse chance to leave unemployment and, similarly, the share of other (heterogeneous) vulnerable groups (Hora et al., 2018).

The scope/effort of Czech ALMP

The policy effort is here mostly defined simply as a scope of realised ALMP programmes indicated by expenditure and/or number of participants in the main ALMP programmes. 'Crude ratio of programme effort' is counted here as the number of selected programme participants divided by the average number of unemployed in given year (see Table 11.2). Not all programmes are included here (and among them, the support for the disabled is the most important). In the Czech case, the policy effort is relatively unstable and unpredictable, as indicated by the level and year-to-year fluctuations in ALMP expenditure.

The scope of ALMP was relatively low since 2011 (at most 16% of the average unemployment stock). It dropped considerably in 2012 compared to the previous years and increased during 2013–2015. The changes were not so much due to the business cycle and the need of an anti-cyclical policy response but rather due to the political factors: centre-right government retrenchment reforms of 2011 and a restoration effort by the caretaker government established in 2013 and centre-left government of 2014. ALMP effort culminated in 2015 when 26% of average unemployment stock was included in ALMP measures. The scope of ALMP was substantially reduced again after 2015 because the situation on the labour market was quickly improving. A switch from training to subsidised workplaces has been evidenced (Hora et al., 2018). Due to high placements of unemployed to subsidised workplaces (especially in 2015) connected to ending PES registration (and impacts of other programs), ALMP was able to reduce level of registered unemployment (see Table 11.2).

Table 11.2 Development of number of program participants in public works, subsidised workplaces and training (total for years 2011–2018)

Year	*2011*	*2012*	*2013*	*2014*	*2015*	*2016*	*2017*	*2018*
PW (national)	9 830	5 279	5 232	4 263	940	6 133	12 258	6 222
PW (ESF)	11 492	3 447	16 607	18 704	34 236	16 142	7 001	10 057
SW (national)	9 030	7 933	8 858	8 087	4 472	5 895	5 060	2 656
SW (ESF)	4 380	7 554	12 885	24 994	48 146	20 864	12 377	9 524
TC ST (total)	45 521	17 606	27 877	25 849	20 437	12 847	11 487	7 231
TC ST (national)	n. d.	n. d.	n. d.	n. d.	4 087	2 910	698	107
TC ST (ESF)	n. d.	n. d.	n. d.	n. d.	16 350	9 937	10 780	7 124
TC CHOSEN (total)	d. n. e.	6 568	13 561	20 605	17 641	9 701	6 696	6 010
TC CHOSEN (national)	d. n. e.	n. d.	n. d.	5 531	4 891	3 348	1 027	213
TC CHOSEN (ESF)	d. n. e.	n. d.	n. d.	15 074	12 750	6 353	5 669	5 797
Average number of unemployed	507 779	504 381	564 448	561 437	478 875	405 957	317 612	241 921
Crude ratio of program effort	0.16	0.10	0.15	0.18	0.26	0.18	0.17	0.17

Source: Own elaboration based on MPSV (2011–2018a) and MPSV (2011–2018b).

Notes: PW – public works, SW – subsidised workplaces, TC ST – standardised training courses, TC CHOSEN – chosen training courses, ESF – programs paid from European social fund, national – programs paid from national financial sources, n. d. – no data available, d. n. e. – did not exist.

Targeting of the Czech ALMP programmes towards the long-term and repeatedly unemployed

Data on targeting for ALMP programmes realised in 2014 and 2015 (Table 11.3) focus on the categories of the unemployed we are mostly interested in (with the highest probability of employment problems). The first three columns show targeting ALMP on the specific categories of the unemployed depending on (a) length of current (last) unemployment spell, (b) whether and how many times the unemployed were registered before their last unemployment spell and (c) total length of previous unemployment spells. The last three columns show the categories of the unemployed characterised by (d) low level of education, (e) age over 50 years and (f) changed health status. Actually, the data show in the odd columns the share of specific vulnerable groups among programme participants. Targeting indices (even columns) compare the share of people from risk groups in ALMP programmes with their share in the population of the unemployed. Values over 1 mean a higher-than-average level of targeting, while values below 1 mean a lower-than-average level of targeting.

Table 11.3 Share of chosen groups in ALMP programs and indexes of targeting

	(a) Long term unemployed in last spell		*(b) Repeatedly unemployed (3 or more previous spells)*		*(c) Cumulated previous registration (more than one year)*		*(d) Low education (ISCED 1–2)*		*(e) 50+ years*		*(f) Health limits or disability*	
2014	SHARE	TAR IND	SHARE	TAR IND	SHARE	TAR IND	SHARE	TAR IND	SHARE	TAR IND	SHARE	TAR IND
Chosen training	21.3	0.7	47.7	1	47.4	1	13.8	0.6	16.9	0.7	13.9	0.7
Standard training	30.7	0.9	46.5	1	46.5	1	13.2	0.6	25.5	1	17.9	1
Subsidised Workplaces	30.8	0.9	36.9	0.8	39.5	0.8	9.4	0.4	17.8	0.7	11.6	0.6
Public works	20.1	0.6	69.5	1.5	75.5	1.5	35.6	1.5	36.9	1.5	20.4	1.1
2015	SHARE	TAR IND	SHARE	TAR IND	SHARE	TAR IND	SHARE	TAR IND	SHARE	TAR IND	SHARE	TAR IND
Chosen training	n. d.	n. d.	45.1	1	45.4	0.9	12	0.5	14.7	0.6	13.8	0.7
Standard training	n. d.	n. d.	47.9	1	52.7	1	13.8	0.6	25.7	1.1	23.5	1.2
Subsidised Workplaces	n. d.	n. d.	40.3	0.9	44.6	0.9	11	0.5	20.9	0.9	15.5	0.8
Public works	n. d.	n. d.	71.6	1.5	78.8	1.6	36.9	1.7	37.5	1.6	27.9	1.4

Source: Own elaboration based on Hora et al. (2018) and Horáková and Sirovátka (2018).

Notes: SHARE – share of particular group among program participants, TAR IND – targeting index.

The first issue of targeting is the timing of the programmes. The greatest share of the unemployed (about 50%) entered ALMP programmes in a period of 3 to 12 months since the start of their current unemployment spell (Hora & Suchanec, 2014; Hora et al., 2018). Public works were more often provided earlier in an unemployment spell than other programmes (this may indicate a repetition of the programme and other forms of unemployment prevention). Long-term unemployed in their last spell (a) are not overrepresented among programme participants in any of the ALMP programmes in focus. However, a longer unemployment history is more relevant for an assignment of the unemployed to the programme than the length of the current unemployment spell. Previously the long-term (c) and repeatedly unemployed (b) often constituted about 50% of programme participants. Surprisingly, they are substantially represented in both the 'chosen' and standard training programmes. Subsidised workplaces were provided more often to the currently long-term unemployed than the other programmes, but otherwise they less often included people with other characteristics of low employability; this finding may indicate the creaming off within the long-term unemployed. From all ALMP programmes, only public works served the specific target group with a high share of people with cumulative, previous unemployment spells and with the highest shares of low educated, older workers and people with health problems and disabilities.

When comparing the results with the results of the study that capture the situation in 2007 (Hora & Sirovátka, 2012), Hora et al. (2018) found that the share of participation of the long-term and repeatedly unemployed among ALMP participants has substantially increased in 2014–2015. This may be, however, a result of both the change in the structure of the unemployed and better targeting of the programmes.

We may conclude that in the last decade, the Czech ALMP was usually (with exception of public works) targeted to people with a medium to high level of potential labour market problems.[3] On the other hand, targeting indices clearly show that the substantial portion of the unemployed with the most severe labour market problems was not included in ALMP in both years. The factors that contribute both to long-term unemployment and low ALMP programme participation include low education, older age and worsened health status (see Hora et al., 2018). In other words, people who are most distanced from the labour market and overrepresented among the unemployed are underrepresented in ALMP programmes, although the long-term and repeatedly unemployed appear sufficiently represented. This indicates a creaming-off effect within the group of long-term and repeatedly unemployed.

Impacts of ALMP in the Czech Republic

We used a contra-factual approach for assessing the impacts of programmes realised in 2014 using administrative data manufactured by street-level workers at employment offices. We compare the outcomes of programme participants with paired people from the pool of the unemployed who did not partake in any ALMP programme during 2014. The outcomes of the programmes are measured as the presence of the unemployed in the PES register in the period after the start of the programme (or corresponding period for the control group since their registration) for following more than two years (including 2014–2016 and the first quarter of 2017). Information about reasons people left the register is available only for the moment of leaving PES register, and on top of that, this information is incomplete. This is because some unemployed refused to state the actual reasons why they left the register ('upon their own request' is used in their case) or they just stop contacting the employment office. Linking data from the PES registers with data from social security records is not allowed (with few exceptions given by law).[4]

Programme participants and people in the control group were paired on a one-to-one basis (K-to-K) using propensity score matching in combination with exact matching on 'the period of entering PES register' and 'duration of pre-event unemployment spell'. We used the nearest neighbour matching technique with randomly chosen cases from the control group that were in calliper of a maximum 0.15 standard deviation of logit of propensity score. Variables used for matching included 'region of employment office', 'local unemployment rate', 'number of locally offered workplaces', 'gender', 'age', 'health status', 'nationality', 'number of children', 'level and field of education', 'preferred profession' and information about the history of unemployed people including 'previous employment and unemployment records' and 'former self-employment' (see Hora et al., 2018 for more details). We were able to pair 84.5% of programme participants of training courses, 87.5% of public works and 79.6% of subsidised workplaces. We present the number of paired cases in the last column of Table 11.4 for the first spell.

Table 11.4 Stated reasons to leave PES register for program participants and control groups

	Spell	*Found work*	*Personal reasons*	*Sanction*	*Unknown*	*Subsidised workplace*	*Stayed in register*	*Aver. N*
Chosen training	1	62.7	0.6	8.8	7.7	17.4	2.9	5 049
	2	–	–	–	–	–	–	
Standard training	1	52.9	0.8	7.9	9.6	23	5.8	18 121
	2	–	–	–	–	–	–	
All training	1	55	0.7	8.1	9.2	21.8	5.2	22 948
	2	58.3	1.6	8.7	7.4	6.9	17	5 005
Control training	1	44.9	1.9	13.7	21.2	8.4	9.9	22 948
	2	53.7	1.6	11.3	8.7	5.3	19.4	4 347
Subsidised workplace	1	6.3	0	0.4	0.3	92.6	0.3	22 993
	2	57	1.8	7.9	8.4	9.5	15.4	4 877
Control for SW	1	44.8	2.4	14.6	19.9	10	8.2	22 993
	2	50.5	2.2	12.9	8.4	5.6	20.4	4 102
Public works	1	3.6	0.1	0.6	0.5	94.1	1.1	14 646
	2	24	1.2	5.3	5.9	50.1	13.6	8 782
Control for PW	1	37.8	2.2	19.2	18.2	10.5	11.5	14 646
	2	43.5	1.8	15.8	7.5	8.1	23.4	3 659

Source: Hora et al. (2018).

Figures presented in the next sections show the presence of unemployed in the PES register in 30-day intervals (N30–N720), approximating months. This includes all their (current and following) unemployment spells after the start of the measurement. On the left axis is the proportion (in percent) of people who were in the PES register in the concrete time points (days) of the measurement. At the start of the measurement, all people were in the register, but the proportion naturally decreased in following time. The impact is assessed as the difference between programme participants and people in the control group when controlling for the potential impact of other factors included in the matching model. Programme participants (and people in the control group) are in the figures further divided into three sub-groups. These are based on the pre-program unemployment spell duration (SH – registered in the PES register for a short time, i.e. no longer than 90 days, ME – registered for a duration of 91 to 365 days, LO – registered for more than one year). This is relevant also for the control group, because the pairs are exactly matched on this characteristic.

Impacts of training programmes

Within the category of training programmes, the standard training and the chosen training are distinguished. In the study of Hora et al. (2018), the chosen training programmes exhibited better outcomes than standardised training, but this could be caused by a different composition of programme participants, as impacts of both sub-types were not estimated separately.

For participants in training programmes, participation resulted in their leaving the PES register earlier than for comparable people in the control group. This effect was most pronounced in the case of people with long pre-programme PES registration – 22.8% of programme participants were in the register at the time of the last measured day point comparing to 33% of people in the control group (see Figure 11.1). This is because the long-term unemployed without the programme had a substantially worse chance to leave the PES register than people in the control group with shorter, previous PES registration. In Table 11.4, we present concrete reasons evidenced in the administration system as reasons for leaving the PES register for the first two spells lasting after the start of the programme. The program effects were present even after considering concrete reasons to leave the register, including cases of unknown reasons of outcome (see Table 11.4.). The effect of training is to some extent enhanced by later placement of trained people into a subsidised workplace and by people in the control group going out of the labour market (mainly due to sanctions induced on them by PES staff).

A locking-in effect is not typical for Czech training programmes, because most of the programmes are very short, and a minority of specific, longer programmes (typically training for health care) was able to compensate well for the locking-in effect (see Hora et al., 2018).

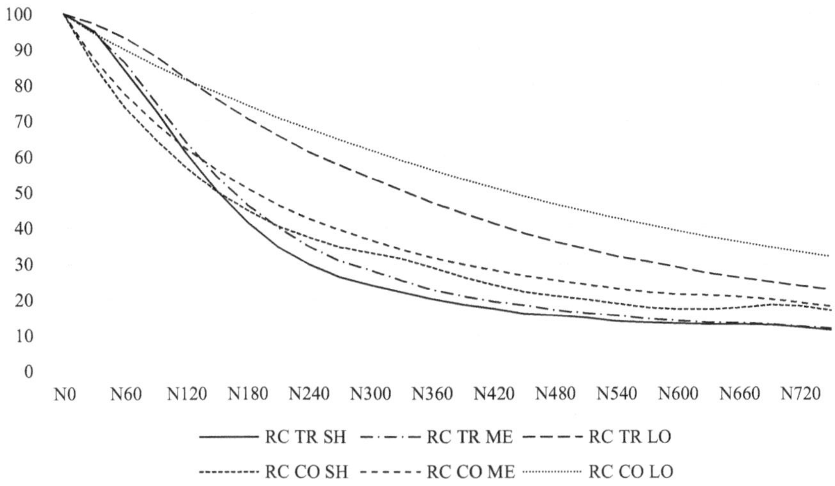

Figure 11.1 Presence of training programs' participants and people in the control group in PES register in 750 days after the start of the program

Source: Own elaboration based on data from OKPráce (2014–2017).

Notes: T-C – Training Courses; TR – Programs participants; CO – control group; SH – pre-program PES registration 0–90 days; ME – pre-program PES registration 91–365 days; LO – pre-program PES registration 366+ days.

Impacts of 'subsidised workplaces'

Subsidised workplaces enable the unemployed to be placed in jobs. This automatically leads to the termination of their registration at PES (and thus reduces the level of unemployment). Most programme participants did not return to the PES register during the period of more than 2 years since the start of the programme. When they did return, they left quickly again, with a higher probability of finding another job than people in the control group. Placement length was in almost all cases no more than 1 year (and we followed the participants' entries and exits for more than 2 years). The impact of the programme is better for the long-term unemployed because the chances of people in the control group are worse than for the short-term unemployed. In other words, subsidised workplaces were able to end long-term unemployment for most programme participants (see Figure 11.2).

Impacts of 'public works'

Placement to public works (see Figure 11.3) leads to leaving the PES register. When comparing to subsidised workplaces (above), more people are after the start of the programme in the PES register and their PES registration is more directly connected with the termination of subsidised job placement (which can

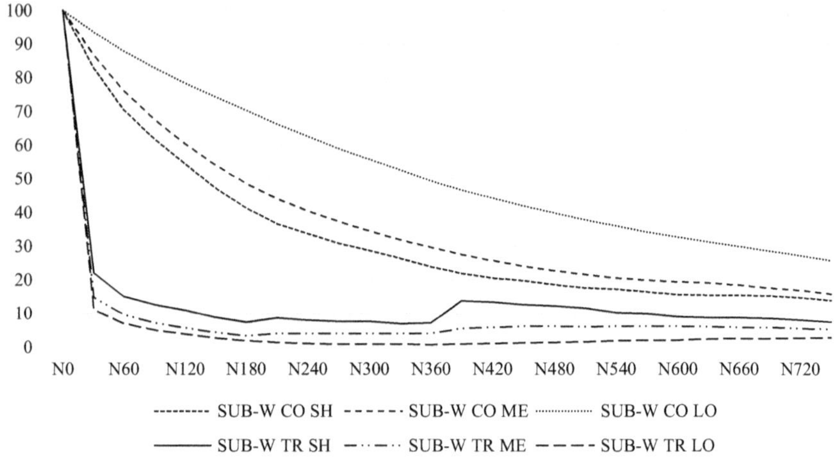

Figure 11.2 Presence of subsidised workplaces' participants and people in the control group in PES register in 750 days after the start of the program

Source: Own elaboration based on data from OKPráce (2014–2017).

Notes: SUB-W – Subsidised Workplaces; TR – Programs participants; CO – control group; SH – pre-program PES registration 0–90 days; ME – pre-program PES registration 91–365 days; LO – pre-program PES registration 366+ days.

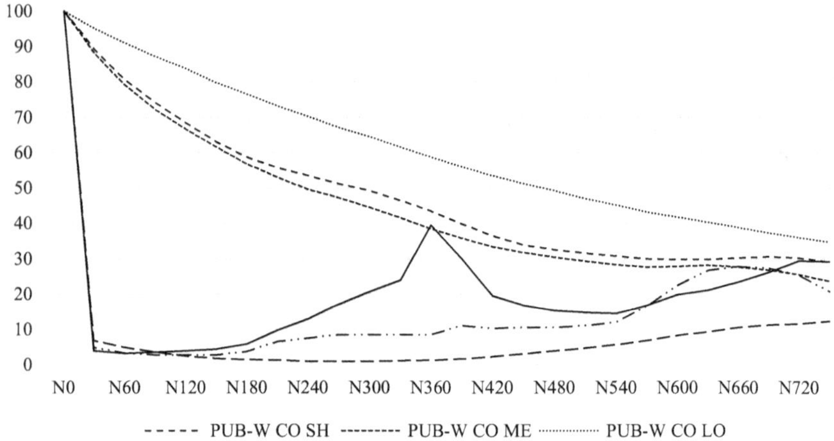

Figure 11.3 Presence of public works' participants and people in the control group in PES register in 750 days after the start of the program

Source: Own elaboration based on data from OKPráce (2014–2017).

Notes: PUB-W – Public Works; TR – Programs participants; CO – control group; SH – pre-program PES registration 0–90 days; ME – pre-program PES registration 91–365 days; LO – pre-program PES registration 366+ days.

be as short as half a year). A substantial share (50%) of public works participants who returned after the programme to the register repeated participation in this programme and got another public-works placement. When compared to people in the control group, their chances to get a non-subsidised job were lower even after public-works participation. Some stakeholders are concerned with a temporal character of the placement leading to repeated unemployment and problematic or repeated placements of people into the same PW job – effectively working as 'parking places'. Other stakeholders raise the argument that for some people these constitute the only work option or the only possibility to get work experience.

Lessons learned from the evaluation of Czech ALMP

A study by Hora et al. (2018) has shown that ALMP has some impacts both on PES registration and to some extent on the reason for which the unemployed leave the register (see Table 11.4). Subsidised workplaces had almost marvelous outcomes, because their participants are in the PES register only sporadically following more than a 2-year period after starting the programme. This means that the outcome of subsidised workplaces really is prevention of PES registration. The corresponding risk is that these programmes are not so well targeted (risk of deadweight), but when they are, their results are promising. The impacts of training programmes are rather modest. However, most of these programmes are relatively short and cheap comparing to their job placement alternatives. Although public works seem to bring the worst results, when we consider the target group of this programme, such a result is hardly surprising. This issue was further addressed by workers of MLSA, who proposed the possibility of having two different types of these jobs: 'maintaining' (help most disadvantaged to get job, do something for the country and have at least some income) and 'bridging' (this is using public works more as springboards to jobs or other programmes).

We can conclude that ALMP programmes do reduce unemployment. However, short-term and medium-term outcomes and impacts are usually very different. When we consider the longer period (more than 2 years), usually impacts on presence in the register are smaller since most people in the control group leave the register in such a time period as well. On the other hand, people in control groups substantially more often leave due to reasons that lead to economic inactivity, or it is unclear where they actually left (as in the case of 'their own request' and due to sanctions). Next, programme participation in most ALMP programmes led to a more frequent return of programme participants to the PES register than in the control group. However, for some programmes it does not matter much, because this return is only temporal and the unemployed quickly leave the PES register again.

The main advantage of the Czech ALMP is that its outcomes are more often 'to work' and not for other reasons (e.g. inactivity). Parking and locking in is not apparent (except for public works) because the policy measure is of reasonable length and leading mostly to an open labour market.

On the other hand, direct work with the unemployed (job search assistance) is not included here because we do not have sufficient data. However, the unemployed often consider the general approach and the direct help of PES workers in their job search the main factor in their (often negative) assessment of employment offices (see e.g. Trlifajová, Musil, Kovářová, & Hurrle, 2015). Job search assistance is also substantial for effective programme targeting.

In spite of these limitations, the results/outcomes of ALMP programmes seem to be plausible, in the case of LTU in particular. However, it seems that the most vulnerable unemployed (by human capital characteristics) were less represented among LTU participants of ALMPs. This failure in targeting seems to be an obstacle to better effectiveness of ALMPs.

Implementation of ALMPs and targeting failures

Paradoxically, while the disadvantaged groups of the unemployed, like the long-term unemployed and others, benefit from ALMP measures the most, targeting of ALMP measures towards these groups is not strong and if we consider those most disadvantaged, it is rather weak. These failures are due to several implementation problems and implementation deficits. We can identify them with the help of these recent studies:

i The study by VÚPSV (2013) is a study that summarised the experiences of staff of regional employment offices with the implementation of ALMP measures.
ii Rákoczyová et al. (2019) focused their study also on the implementation of ALMPs and collected 1,339 online questionnaires from employment office (mainly front-line) workers and also carried out focus groups with staff as well as individual interviews with the directors at 14 regional employment offices.

The distribution of ALMP programmes to the unemployed is guided by the methodological instruction by the General Directorate of Employment Office, where preference for the disadvantaged unemployed is emphasised, long-term unemployed in the first place. Also, room is provided to the front-line workers for individual assessment of the cumulated handicaps. The definition of target groups is, however, broad and makes the selection of more employable candidates within the target groups rather easy. As suggested by Rákoczyová et al. (2019), in practice, employment office staff prefer more employable candidates when following two objectives at the same time. First, it is the objective to fulfil the ‘numbers’ required in the projects supported from ESF in order to reach a timely implementation of these projects. The second objective is to achieve a better result of the projects which are defined as job placements (gross effects based only on outcomes). At the same time, in the case of subsidised jobs in the private sector, and to some extent also in the case of public works, the candidates are pre-selected or recommended by the employment office for a specific employer. However, the final selection of the candidates is done by the employer or municipality in the case of public works. This means that creaming-off due to self-selection and selection by employers is not sufficiently prevented. Second, the real/actual objectives of employment offices are supportive to the 'reversed targeting' of ALMPs towards more employable candidates. Actually, the front-line workers perceive the following as a barrier for participation in the programme: low motivation to work, poor health status, complicated social/family situation, addictions, seizures, problematic individual traits, low/obsolete qualification, lack of work experience, language barrier and refusal by employers (Rákoczyová et al., 2019).

The unmet need of support for competences for individual work plays a significant role as well for targeting. In the Czech Republic, front-line staff performing individual work (job mediators and counsellors of employment offices) are not required to be qualified in social work. Any type of education at the secondary level is required for the positions of mediators (ISCED 4); higher school (ISCED 5), for the positions of counsellors. There is no systemic training provided to the front-line workers in individual work. They are required to follow the standard courses for public servants (mainly focused on legislation like the Employment Act and Administrative Rules).

The other problem is work overload. The findings by Sirovátka, Rákoczyová, and Šimíková (2019), for example, document that staffing of front-line work is not corresponding to the need of individual casework with clients who face multiple barriers to access employment; in 2015 there were on average 311 clients/job-seekers per front-line worker at the local employment offices.

Finally, there are some governance problems that make targeting the ALMP measures at the disadvantaged clients difficult. The tenders for vocational training courses stipulate the price of the courses as a ground for the decision about the winner: in consequence, tailored-made, small-scale programmes are insufficiently available (for example the offer of the courses for the low-skilled unemployed is very limited), and their quality is variable. Second, a major share of ALMP measures is financed from ESF, but the continuity of financing is affected by several unpredictable factors like the regularity in the announcement of the calls (that depends on the administrative capacity), sufficient fulfilment of the indicators prescribed and others. Training courses 'by choice' by the client, which are not required to be contracted based on tender, represent a certain solution to overcome the obstacles associated with the preference for a price and irregularity of the calls. On the other hand, this type of training is leading to a more significant effect of creaming-off due to self-selection of more motivated and better-equipped candidates as well as due to the selection of the candidates by the employers (for detail see Rákoczyová et al., 2019).

Conclusion

In the long run, with the increasing activation effort that aims at groups of people more detached from the labour market, and in the short run, with the economic recovery and decrease of unemployment, these more disadvantaged groups (like the long-term unemployed, low-skilled, disabled, older workers and those with social problems) represent the lion's share of unemployment and the policy target at the same time. For effective labour utilisation of these groups, an important question arises: How successful are employment services in including them into the labour market, and what are the factors that affect this, like targeting of ALMP programs and some implementation conditions? We examined these questions on the case of Czech active labour market policy, which is a representative of a CEE country labour market regime characterised by a limited scope/effort of ALMP measures and PES capacity and work-first approach.

Our findings indicate, that despite a rather modest volume of the measures, the disadvantaged unemployed (those with low education, of older age and worsened health status) are underrepresented in the ALMP measures, although the long-term unemployed are targeted similarly as medium- and short-term unemployed in most ALMP measures. At the same time the analysis of net effects of the ALMP measures shows that subsidised workplaces achieve very good outcomes and similarly the training measures, especially on a medium-term horizon, and in the case of long-term unemployed. The programme of public works which is most often targeted at the most disadvantaged groups does not exhibit such promising results. However, in the two-year time horizon the net effects for the long-term unemployed are also better than in the case of the other groups of unemployed, even in the case of public works.

The findings are consistent with the other studies on ALMP carried out in CEE countries. Spevacek (2009) summarised, based on several studies, namely by Betcherman, Olivas, and Dar (2004), Luboyva and Van Ours (1999), O'Leary (1998), Rutkowski and Scarpetta (2005), Van Ours (2002) and Vodopivec (1999), that most of ALMP measures (employment services, training, job subsidies and self-employment) bring consistently positive outcomes, but the public works scheme is less successful. Lehmann and Kluve (2010) also found job brokerage, training and retraining programmes the most promising while public works have a negative impact on labour market outcomes, based on a review of methodologically more-rigorous studies: Boeri and Lehmann (1999), Kluve, Lehmann, and Schmidt (2008), Micklewright and Nagy (2005), van Ours (2002), Vodopivec (1999).

In our case, however, similarly as in the cited studies, the positive (net) effects of ALMP measures in the case of the long-term unemployed might be a reason for targeting the programmes mainly at this group. This is not actually the case – as we have shown and as some other studies also recognised (see section on targeting in CEE countries).[5] We hypothesise that it appears more rational for PES to concentrate, with the aim to reduce the level of unemployment, on cases with a medium level of perceived problems than to invest in the most disadvantaged, who present an unsure outcome. PES workers often complain that they are unable to find 'suitable candidates' for the programmes. At the same time, public works are mostly used as an ALMP measure suitable for the disadvantaged groups, although they are often criticised as ineffective tools. However, since 2014 PES has been deliberately aiming to include the disadvantaged groups into ALMP more systematically, as documented by the methodical instruction by the employment office. Still, there are indications that the creaming off within the target group of the long-term unemployed is considerable, in favour of the unemployed who are better educated, younger, with good health status.

The reasons of the creaming off within the group of the long-term unemployed are manifold. We explain them by the interaction of the following circumstances: the limited resources and unstable financing, high dependence on ESF resources are the first, leading to a limited scope of ALMP measures and high workloads/overload of front-line staff. In such circumstances, self-selection of the better-equipped unemployed is common in training measures and selection by employers in the case of subsidised job measures. The governance principles and related selection criteria to ALMP measures are another reason when the gross effects are prioritised by PES staff. Third, PES front-line staff often lack competences and systemic training for individual casework. Last but not the least, there is a lack of good-quality training programmes tailored for the most disadvantaged that would improve their employability, since the price is the key selection criterion in the tenders. The similar design, governance, and implementation circumstances of ALMP measures seem to be typical in the case of the other CEE countries; see e.g. Bánociová and Martinková (2017), Bouhol (2014), Csillag et al. (2013), Eichhorst et al. (2015) and Scharle (2014).

All in all, in spite of the problems identified with respect to implementation and targeting, the findings indicate that the ALMP programmes contribute to better labour utilisation because of positive impacts on outflows from unemployment registers, most often into employment. These positive impacts are particularly strong in the case of the participants that are more disadvantaged like long-term unemployed. At the same time, targeting the more disadvantaged unemployed has been improving over time.

Acknowledgement

This work was supported by the EU and Czech funding within the project Evaluating the Efficiency and Effectiveness of ALMP Implementation, the ESF OPZ project, Grant No. CZ.03.1.54/0.0/0.0/15_122/0006089.

Notes

1 There was a drop of GDP in 2012 and 2013 (-0.8% and -0.5% of GDP), unemployment rate was 6.1% in 2014, long-term unemployment rate 2.7%.

2 The International Standard Classification of Education (ISCED) is the reference international classification for organising education programmes and related qualifications by levels and fields.

3 For older results see e.g. Hora and Suchanec (2014), Table 4.4 (data for year 2010).

4 However, it is important to note that this may conceal some key aspects of the evaluation results. For some groups of the unemployed, some types of withdrawal from the PES

register are more prevalent (e.g. young people without a finished formal education more often return to school; older people more often go on premature pension). One of the important reasons for the ending of PES registration is also expulsion (sanction). Between 10% and 16% of unemployed are, according to data for 2014 and 2016, generally expelled from the register. The share of the expelled is similar or sometimes even higher in paired control groups or programme participants (see Table 11.4.). In other words, the direct 'effect' of expulsion on the level of unemployment may be, in the Czech context, of comparable magnitude as an effect of ALMP programmes. We consider low ability to control for types of outcome more precisely and reliably on a longer time horizon after the unemployed left the register as a great limit of current evaluation potential in the Czech Republic.

5 Anyway, there is an apparent improvement in the targeting of Czech ALMP when comparing the current situation with the situation ten years ago, as a substantial part of people with the most severe problems is now included in ALMPs.

References

Bánociová, A., & Martinková, S. (2017). Active labour market policies of selected European countries and their competitiveness. *Journal of Competitiveness*, *9*(3), 5–21.

Betcherman, G., Olivas, K., & Dar, A. (2004). *Impacts of active labor programs: New evidence from evaluations with particular attention to developing and transition countries* (Social Protection Discussion Paper No. 402). Washington, DC: The World Bank.

Boeri, T. (1997). Learning from transition economies: Assessing labor market policies across & Central and Eastern Europe. *Journal of Comparative Economics*, *25*(3), 366–384.

Boeri, T., & Lehmann, H. (1999) Introduction: Unemployment and labor market policies in transition countries. *Journal of Comparative Economics, 27*(1), 1–3.

Bouhol, H. (2014). *Making the labour market work better in Poland* (OECD Economics Department Working Papers No. 1124). Paris: OECD.

Brown, A. J. G. (2015). Can hiring subsidies benefit the unemployed? *IZA World of Labor*, *163*. doi:10.15185/izawol.163

Brown, A. J. G., & Koettl, J. (2015). *Active labour market programmes: Employment gain or fiscal drain?* Bonn: The Institute for the Study of Labor (IZA). doi:10.1186/s40172-015-0025-5

Calmfors, L., Forslund, A., & Hemström, N. (2002). *Does active labour market policy work? Lessons from the Swedish experiences* (Working Paper No. 4; CESIFO Working Paper Series No. 675; IFAU Working Paper No. 2002:4). SSRN. Retrieved from https://ssrn.com/abstract=305360

Caswell, D., Larsen, F., van Berkel, R., & Kupka, P. (2017). Conclusions and topics for future research. In R. Van Berkel, D. Caswell, P. Kupka, & F. Larsen (Eds.), *Frontline delivery of welfare-to-work policies in Europe. Activating the unemployed* (pp. 181–200). London: Routledge.

Csillag, M., Samu, F., & Scharle, A. (2013). *Job search and activation policies in Central and Eastern Europe*. GRINCOH project (7.RP EU). Retrieved from www.grincoh.eu

Dahlke, M. (2016). Efficiency of active labour market policies in Poland. In *Conference proceedings compilation: Proceedings of FIKUSZ '16 symposium for young researchers* (pp. 31–40). Obuda: University Keleti Faculty of Business and Management. Retrieved from http://kgk.uni-obuda.hu/fikusz

De la Porte, C., & Jacobsson, K. (2012). Social investment or recommodification? Assessing the employment policies of the EU member states. In N. Morel, B. Palier, & J. Palme

(Eds.), *Towards a social investment welfare state*? (pp. 117–149). Bristol and Chicago: The Policy Press.

Eichhorst, W., Neder, F., Tobsch, V., & Wozny, F. (2015). *A European perspective on long-term unemployment* (IZA Discussion Paper No. 9321). Retrieved from http://ftp.iza.org/dp9321.pdf

European Commission. (2016, November 11). *European semester thematic factsheet: Active labour market policies*. Retrieved from https://ec.europa.eu/info/sites/info/files/european-semester_thematic-factsheet_active-labour-market-policies_en_0.pdf

Gallie, D. (2013). *Economic crisis, quality of work, and social integration*. Oxford: Oxford University Press.

Hora, O., Horáková, M., & Sirovátka, T. (2019). Policy adaptation to address early job insecurity in Europe. In B. Hvinden, C. Hyggen, M. A. Schoyen, & T. Sirovátka (Eds.), *Youth unemployment and job insecurity in Europe: Problems, risk factors and policies* (pp. 158–183). Cheltenham: Edward Elgar Publishing.

Hora, O., & Sirovátka, T. (2012). *Srovnání efektů aktivní politiky zaměstnanosti v České Republice v období růstu (2007) a během první fáze krize (2009)*. Praha: VÚPSV.

Hora, O., & Suchanec, M. (2014). Zhodnocení programů aktivní politiky zaměstnanosti realizovaných v České republice v období krize. In T. Sirovátka, M. Horáková, & P. Horák (Eds.), *Česká politika zaměstnanosti v době krize a po krizi* (pp. 143–182). Brno: Muni Press.

Hora, O., Suchanec, M., Horáková, M., Rákoczyová, M., & Sirovátka, T. (2018). *Zhodnocení krátkodobých a střednědobých dopadů vybraných programů APZ realizovaných v roce 2014 s důrazem na situaci dlouhodobě nezaměstnaných*. Praha: VÚPSV.

Hora, O., & Vyhlídal, J. (2016). *Hodnocení ochranné, pobídkové a integrační funkce sociální politiky pro osoby v hmotné nouzi*. Praha: VÚPSV.

Horáková, M., & Sirovátka, T. (2018). *The low skilled unemployed in the main ALMP tools in 2014 and 2015*. Praha: VÚPSV.

Kluve, J., Lehmann, H., & Schmidt, C. M. (2008). Disentangling treatment effects of active labor market policies: The role of labor status sequences. *Labor Economics*, *15*(6), 1270–1295. doi:10.1016/j.labeco.2007.12.002

Lehmann, H., & Kluve, J. (2010). Assessing active labour market policies in transition economies. In F. Caroleo & F. Pastore (Eds.), *The labour market impact of the EU enlargement. AIEL Series in Labour Economics* (pp. 275–307). Heidelberg and Berlin: Physica-Verlag HD. doi:10.1007/978-3-7908-2164-2_11

Lipsky, M. (Ed.). (2010). *Street-level bureaucracy: Dilemmas of the individual in public services* (2nd ed.). New York: Russell Sage Foundation.

Lødemel, I., & Moreira, A. (Eds.). (2014). *Activation or workfare? Governance and the neo-liberal convergence*. Oxford: Oxford University Press. doi:10.1093/acprof:oso/9780199773589.001.0001

Lødemel, I., & Trickey, H. (Eds.). (2000). *An offer you can't refuse: Workfare in international perspective*. Bristol: The Policy Press.

Luboyva, M., & Van Ours, J. (1999). Effects of active labor market programs on the transition rate from unemployment into regular jobs in the Slovak Republic. *Journal of Comparative Economics*, *27*, 90–112. doi:10.1006/jcec.1998.1571

Micklewright, J., & Nagy, G. (2005). *Job search monitoring and unemployment duration in Hungary: Evidence from randomised control trial* (IZA Discussion Paper No. 1839). Retrieved from http://ftp.iza.org/dp1839.pdf

MPSV. (2011–2018a). *Statistická ročenka trhu práce v České republice* [Statistical yearbooks of labour market for years 2010–2017]. Praha: MPSV.

MPSV. (2011–2018b). *Statistická ročenka z oblasti trhu práce a sociálních věcí* [Statistical yearbooks from fields of labour market and social affairs for years 2010–2017]. Praha: MPSV.

MPSV. (2014). *Strategie politiky zaměstnanosti do roku 2020*. Praha: MPSV.

MPSV. (2019). *Služby* [Services]. Retrieved from www.mpsv.cz/web/cz/sluzby

Nicaise, I., Bollens, J., Dawes, L., Laghaei, S., Thaulow, I., Verdié, M., & Wagner, A. (1995). Labour market programmes for the poor in Europe: Pitfalls, dilemmas and how to avoid them. *Journal of European Social Policy*, *5*(3), 199–217. doi:10.1177/095892879500500302

OECD. (2019). *OECD Statistics – labour*. Retrieved from https://stats.oecd.org/

OKPráce. (2014–2017). *Database of individual anonymised data from public employment created by company OKsystem for needs of Research Institute of Labour and Social Affairs* [for more information about OKsystem see www.oksystem.com/en; www.oksystem.com/downloads/OKsystem_Annual_Report_2018.pdf]

O'Leary, C. (1998). *Evaluating the effectiveness of active labor programs in Hungary* (Upjohn Institute Technical Report No. 98-013). Michigan: W.E. Upjohn Institute for Employment Research. Retrieved from https://research.upjohn.org/cgi/viewcontent.cgi?article=1016&=&context=up_technicalreports

Rákoczyová, M., Kotrusová, M., Horák, P., Kubát, J., Marešová, H., Schebelle, D., . . . Váňová, J. (2019). *Realizace vybraných programů aktivní politiky zaměstnanosti a hodnocení jejich efektivity a účinnosti perspektivou zaměstnanců ÚP ČR v roce 2017. Dílčí podkladová studie I.* Praha: VÚPSV. Retrieved from http://praha.vupsv.cz/Fulltext/vz_454.pdf

Rutkowski, J., & Scarpetta, S. (2005). *Enhancing job opportunities: Eastern Europe and the former Soviet Union*. Washington, DC: International Bank for Reconstruction and Development (IBRD)/The World Bank. Retrieved from https://openknowledge.worldbank.org/handle/10986/7408

Scharle, A. (2014). *True and false remedies for long time unemployment in Visegrad countries* (CASE Network Studies & Analyses 475). Retrieved from www.slideshare.net/economics10/sa-475

Sirovátka, T., & Hora, O. (2011). The Czech Republic: Activation, diversification, and marginalisation. In J. Clasen & D. Clegg (Eds.), *Regulating the risk of unemployment* (pp. 255–277). Oxford: Oxford University Press.

Sirovátka, T., Rákoczyová, M., & Šimíková, I. (2019). *Vyhodnocení indikátorů Strategie sociálního začleňování České republiky na roky 2014–2020*. Praha: VÚPSV.

Spevacek, A. M. (2009). *Effectiveness of active labor market programs: A review of programs in Central and Eastern Europe and the Commonwealth of Independent States*. Washington, DC: USAID Knowledge Services Center.

Trlifajová, L., Musil, P., Kovářová, L., & Hurrle, J. (2015). *Mezi dávkami a prací, která není? Analýza motivace k zaměstnání u osob, které se pohybují na hraně mezi dávkovým systémem a přijetím nízce-hodnoceného zaměstnání*. Praha: Multikulturní centrum Praha a SPOT.

Van Berkel, R., Caswell, D., Kupka, P., & Larsen, F. (Eds.). (2017). *Frontline delivery of welfare-to-work policies in Europe: Activating the unemployed*. London: Routledge.

Van Berkel, R., de Graaf, W., & Sirovátka, T. (Eds.). (2011). *The governance of active welfare states in Europe*. Houndmills, Basingstoke: Palgrave Macmillan.

Van Berkel, R., & Valkenburg, B. (Eds.). (2007). *Making it personal: Individualising activation services in the EU*. Bristol: Bristol University Press. doi:10.2307/j.ctt9qgz1t
Van Ours, J. C. (2002). *The locking-in effect of subsidized jobs* (William Davidson Working Paper No. 474). Ann Arbor, MI: The William David Institute at the University of Michigan Stephen M. Ross Business School.
Vanhuysse, P. (2014). *Workers worries and labour market policies* (Policy Brief June 2014). Vienna: European Centre.
Vodopivec, M. (1999). Does the Slovenian public work program increase participants' chances to find a job? *Journal of Comparative Economics*, *27*, 113–130.
Výzkumný ústav práce a sociálních věcí/VÚPSV. (2013). *Zpráva z šetření realizovaného v rámci projektu MIKOP. Oblast trhu práce*. Unpublished.
Wright, S. (2013). On activation workers' perceptions: A reply to Dunn (2). *Journal of Social Policy*, *42*(4), 829–837. doi:10.1017/S0047279413000494

12

ERODING COLLECTIVE BARGAINING IN CEE COUNTRIES AS A COUNTERPRODUCTIVE FACTOR IN THE PROCESS OF LABOUR UTILISATION

The cases of Bulgaria and Poland

Jan Czarzasty and Vassil Kirov

Introduction

More than 30 years after the fall of the Berlin Wall and 15 years after the 2004 European Union (EU) enlargement, Central and Eastern European (CEE) countries have not been able to catch up with Western European countries economically (wages and incomes included). Although the wage gap has been narrowing over the years and this catching-up process has been accelerating since 2014 (Dorbec, 2017), in general, the CEE economies still benefit from the advantages of low-cost labour, and the wage gap has been qualified as persistent (Myant, 2018).

The subject of the chapter is collective bargaining and how its on-going deterioration as a key wage determination mechanism negatively affects the process of wage formation. The lower pay in CEE cannot be explained by different labour-force skill structures or by the different sectoral structures of economies (Drahokoupil & Piasna, 2019). The weak collective bargaining weight certainly exercises pressure on wage coordination, together with the dependence from multinational corporations (MNC) and the disconnection from productivity (Myant, 2018). The chapter compares two country-level cases, Bulgaria and Poland, representing two waves of the post-2004 EU enlargement and two types of transitional development, i.e. the Visegrad countries, and the South-Eastern European. The examined period is from 2004/2007 on, when the two countries joined the European Union respectively.

Our key argument is that the marginalisation of collective bargaining triggered inter alia by trade union weakness has played a vital role in moderating the wage growth in the two countries in focus, thus preserving their competitive advantage made of relatively cheap labour. As a consequence, labour utilisation in the two countries in focus is distorted. Wage coordination resulting from faulty bargaining is a factor hampering economic modernisation and, as such, preventing the creation of better-quality jobs. We further argue that the chance for breaking away from the model, which seems to have opened in the 2010s, has not been taken. Specifically speaking, the deepening undersupply of skilled workforce entailed by outward migration in both countries and a political shift of 2015 in Poland, accompanied by rhetoric stressing the risks of 'the middle-income trap' (SOR, 2017), suggested there was ground for a macroeconomic policy focused on boosting labour productivity by promoting high-value-adding sectors. Instead, the policy of turning a blind eye to increasing inward (cheap) labour migration not only from neighbouring countries but also from more distant locations (Asia) filling the gaps on the supply side of the labour market appears to have prevailed. Ultimately, the semi-peripheral status of the two economies seems to be solidified. The chapter relies on original empirical evidence collected within various research projects on collective bargaining in which the authors participated in the last decade (e.g. Czarzasty, 2019; Kirov, 2019; Delteil & Kirov, 2016) and secondary data sources. We employ data delivered by public statistics (national statistical office in Bulgaria, Poland, and Eurostat) and other central administration bodies (labour inspectorates and labour administration in particular), on industrial relations (number of collective agreements, union and employer organisations' density), wage dynamics and migration flows (in and out).

As we have established, the state of collective bargaining in both countries in focus is weak (in quantitative terms), and its role in wage determination insignificant, which is manifested by a de facto absence of multi-employer collective agreements. This is a direct result of low union and employer organisation density. Even though the pay dynamics (rapidly rising minimum wages serve as the benchmark) have accelerated in the 2010s as both economies recovered after the 2008+ crisis, largely due to an undersupply of a skilled workforce, the growth has been mitigated by incoming migration. Labour productivity has increased, albeit the gap remains wide.

The chapter is structured as follows. First, we introduce the theoretical frame of our analysis, followed by the two country cases presenting the data on all relevant dimensions of analysis (industrial relations indicators, wages, labour productivity, migration). Next we move on to a discussion part, where we present our key arguments in a more detailed way. The last part concludes.

Theoretical background

The theoretical frame of the chapter builds on the research streams of Eastern European capitalism and the development of industrial relations in the post-communist world in the context of the overall decentralisation of collective bargaining in Europe.

The downfall of communism opened the way for a re-introduction of a market-coordinated economy in Eastern Europe. Devoid of own capital resources and a domestic bourgeoisie, the post-socialist countries of the Central-Eastern region began to build 'capitalism without capitalists' (Eyal, Szelenyi, & Townsley, 1998) relying heavily on foreign direct investment (FDI) as the main engine for economic development. As a consequence, those economies evolved into 'dependent market economies' (DME) dominated by foreign capital, represented mainly by transnational enterprises (Nölke & Vliegenthart, 2009, p. 680). However, Bulgaria initially followed a different path than Poland and other Visegrad countries. King and Szelenyi (2005, p. 213) contrasted Poland (the Czech Republic and Hungary too) as the case of 'liberal dependent capitalism' with South-Eastern Europe or SEE (e.g. Romania, Bulgaria not named explicitly but bearing close resemblance) representing 'patrimonial capitalism' built 'from above', similar to Ukraine. The 'slow-trackers' from the SEE (Iankova, 2002) began to drift away from 'patrimonial capitalism' towards the neoliberal model as the EU-accession process was accelerating, turning more similar to Baltic states than to Visegrad countries, representing the 'embedded neoliberal' model in the words of Bohle and Greskovits (2012). The illiberal turn of the 2010s has had some effects on the model of capitalism, with signs of 'capitalism from above' and more active involvement of the state emerging (Szelenyi & Csillag, 2015), yet in the case of Poland it remains to be seen whether the shift will go beyond mere rhetoric. As outlined in the introduction and subsequent sections of the chapter, we remain sceptical about the capacity of the two economies in focus to break away from the dependent model of economic development towards a model that could be described in terms of a 'state-permeated' one (Nölke, 2018). Our scepticism relates mainly to a fairly low level of 'knowledge system' indicators such as R&D employment, employment in high- and medium-high-technology manufacturing and knowledge-intensive sectors, high-tech exports (see Tables 12.1 to 12.3), which, combined with fairly high levels of education, place both countries in the 'aspiring' cluster (Karbowski, 2019).

The second stream of literature refers to industrial relations. The construction of a new system of industrial relations (IR) took place within the delicate context of the transition to democracy and the difficult international reintegration of poorly competitive economies (Delteil & Kirov, 2016). Already in the second half of the 1990s, the weakness of the trade union movement in the region was attracting research interest, e.g. from the perspective of eventual union revival. However, as Ost (2009) argued, there were strong factors playing against this revival, namely ideological (continued distrust of unions), organisational (plethora of small firms), and structural (location in the global economy). Unlike in Western Europe, one of the most striking features of industrial relations in Central and South-Eastern Europe, considered as a whole, has been the near-total absence

Table 12.1 Labour productivity per person employed and hour worked

Indicator	*Nominal labour productivity per person*													
Year	*2005*	*2006*	*2007*	*2008*	*2009*	*2010*	*2011*	*2012*	*2013*	*2014*	*2015*	*2016*	*2017*	*2018*
EU (27 countries)	100	100	100	100	100	100	100	100	100	100	100	100	100	100
EU (including UK)	101.6	101.5	101.2	101.0	100.7	100.7	100.4	100.6	100.5	100.5	100.5	100.3	100.2	100.1
Euro area	110.5	110.4	110.0	109.3	108.9	108.1	107.7	107.5	107.5	107.6	107.3	107.2	106.9	106.3
Bulgaria	37.0	36.9	38.0	39.7	39.7	41.2	42.1	43.7	42.9	44.0	44.5	45.8	46.1	47.4
Poland	62.0	61.2	62.0	62.5	65.6	70.4	72.6	74.2	74.1	73.8	74.0	74.0	75.4	77.3
Indicator	*Nominal labour productivity per hour*													
Year	*2005*	*2006*	*2007*	*2008*	*2009*	*2010*	*2011*	*2012*	*2013*	*2014*	*2015*	*2016*	*2017*	*2018*
EU (27 countries)	100	100	100	100	100	100	100	100	100	100	100	100	100	100
EU (including UK)	101.7	101.7	101.3	101.3	100.9	101.0	100.6	100.5	100.3	100.2	100.3	100.0	99.9	99.8
Euro area	114.1	113.8	113.3	112.8	112.6	111.8	111.3	111.2	111.4	111.5	111.2	111.2	110.7	110.0
Bulgaria	37.6	37.5	38.7	39.5	40.0	41.7	42.6	43.8	42.6	43.8	44.3	45.7	45.8	46.9
Poland	50.2	49.5	50.3	50.9	53.0	57.1	59.1	59.9	59.5	59.1	59.5	59.1	60.6	62.8

Source: Own elaboration based on Eurostat.

Notes: The reference group of 27 EU countries does not include the United Kingdom (UK). Among the Euro area group all its current 19 members have been included.

Table 12.2 Total R&D personnel and researchers by sectors of performance, as a percentage of the total labour force and total employment

Year	*2004*	*2005*	*2006*	*2007*	*2008*	*2009*	*2010*	*2011*	*2012*	*2013*	*2014*	*2015*	*2016*	*2017*	*2018*
EU (including UK)	1.044	1.057	1.08	1.096	1.126	1.158	1.199	1.232	1.267	1.290	1.307	1.34	1.35	1.403	1.459
Euro area	1.119	1.128	1.163	1.187	1.228	1.27	1.313	1.349	1.393	1.411	1.425	1.461	1.476	1.528	1.563
Bulgaria	0.544	0.538	0.531	0.528	0.521	0.569	0.546	0.580	0.579	0.607	0.661	0.756	0.848	0.758	0.838
Poland	0.580	0.555	0.513	0.502	0.48	0.471	0.537	0.557	0.591	0.612	0.669	0.691	0.703	0.896	1.004

Source: Own elaboration based on Eurostat.

Notes: The same as Table 12.1.

Table 12.3 Exports of high-technology products as a share of total exports

Year	*2007*	*2008*	*2009*	*2010*	*2011*	*2012*	*2013*	*2014*	*2015*	*2016*	*2017*	*2018*
EU (including UK)	16.1	15.4	17.1	16.1	15.4	15.7	15.3	15.6	17.0	17.8	17.8	17.9
Bulgaria	3.5	3.6	4.6	4.1	3.7	3.8	4.0	3.9	4.4	5.1	5.4	5.9
Poland	3.0	4.3	5.7	6.0	5.1	6.0	6.7	7.9	8,5	8.5	8.4	8.4

Source: Own elaboration based on Eurostat.

Notes: The values are based on the 4th revision of Standard International Trade Classification (SITC Rev. 4).

of strong branch-level systems of negotiation (Bafoil, 2016). In the context of continuous decentralisation of collective bargaining in the old member states (cf. Baccaro & Howell, 2011), trade unionism in Central and Eastern Europe recorded a continuous decrease of trade union density and collective bargaining coverage (Kohl, 2015).

In these complex dynamics of transformation, the processes of EU economic integration and EU regulation have been an ambivalent force for change increasingly playing against a ‘high road’ convergence and Europeanisation process (Delteil & Kirov, 2016, p. 1). As shown first by Meardi (2013), the Eastern enlargement is far from a success on the basis of migrants, investigated in two large European economies: the UK and Germany. In the context of the outward migration, there have been scholars arguing that this could be a factor prompting unions in CEE countries to push for higher wages (e.g. Hardy, Calveley, Kubisa, & Shelley, 2014). However, Stan and Erne (2016) show how austerity policies in the region have played against this eventual revival of collective bargaining, thus favouring individual wage arrangements.

Decentralised wage determination is coupled with persistence of low wages as the recent data on six CEE countries, Visegrad (the Czech Republic, Hungary, Poland, and Slovakia), Bulgaria, and Romania suggest. Slovakia pays the highest wages, at EUR 7.8 per hour in 2016 on average, but wage costs there are only 30% of the EU average. In Bulgaria, wages are still the lowest, with average hourly wages of EUR 3.7, which is only 14% of the European average (EUR 25.9 in 2016) (Dorbec, 2017). According to Eurofound (2019a), all CEE countries except Slovenia are classified as low-range countries with minimum wage rates of mostly below 500 euros. From that perspective, the still-missing pay convergence deserves a thorough analysis in order to see what the causes behind it are.

It is a plausible claim that employers are inclined to maintain low-wage competition, because the innovation capacity of national economies in focus remains inadequate to upshift and move on to production of high-value-added goods and services. The data for labour productivity, employment in high- and medium-high-technology manufacturing, R&D personnel and researchers or high-tech exports serve as a signpost (see Tables 12.1–12.3).

National case: Bulgaria

Economic and political background

Bulgaria is the poorest member of the European Union (EU). It had a difficult economic and political transition and faces substantial demographic challenges. During the post-communist transition industrial relations and collective bargaining practices developed in the context of a dynamic political, economic, and social environment. The Bulgarian state could be characterised as weak, in Bohle and Greskovits' typology (2012), postponing or imposing reforms without domestic consent and locking the fragile economy into 'low-road' competitiveness policies and dependent capitalism (Delteil & Kirov, 2016).

After painful reforms and complex political and economic development during the 1990s, Bulgaria experienced solid economic growth in the first decade of the 21st century. In 2007 the country joined the EU, a long-term goal for Bulgarian political actors and society as a whole. From the beginning of the financial crisis, however, the economic situation in Bulgaria was deteriorating and then resumed growth in 2010 (see data in Table 12.4). During the last few years employment rose and in 2018 is equal to 72.4% (exactly the same as the EU-28 average, according to Eurostat) while the unemployment rate decreased to about 5% in 2019.

Industrial relations: general outlook

Bulgaria's industrial relations system includes various tripartite structures (Iankova, 2000; Kirov, 2019) for national and sectoral social dialogue and collective bargaining structures at the sectoral, industry, and enterprise levels and, in some cases, also at the territorial level (municipalities). National tripartite cooperation takes place within the National Tripartite Cooperation Council (since 1993), the

Table 12.4 Main economic indicators for Bulgaria and Poland

Year	*2008*	*2009*	*2010*	*2011*	*2012*	*2013*	*2014*	*2015*	*2016*	*2017*	*2018*
Real GDP growth rate – PL	4.2	2.8	3.6	5.0	1.6	1.4	3.3	3.8	3.1	4.8	5.1
Real GDP growth rate – BG	6.0	–3.6	1.3	1.9	0.0	0.5	1.8	3.5	3.9	3.8	3.1
Employment rate (20–64) – PL	65.0	64.9	64.3	64.5	64.7	64.9	66.5	67.8	69.3	70.9	72.2
Employment rate (20–64) – BG	70.7	68.8	64.7	62.9	63.0	63.5	65.1	67.1	67.7	71.3	72.4
Unemployment rate – PL	7.1	8.1	9.7	9.7	10.1	10.3	9.0	7.5	6.2	4.9	3.9
Unemployment rate – BG	5.6	6.8	10.3	11.3	12.3	13.0	11.4	9.2	7.6	6.2	5.2

Source: Own elaboration based on Eurostat.

Economic and Social Council (since 2001), and various tripartite governing or supervisory bodies within the employment and social security administration. Industrial tripartite cooperation takes place at (sub-)industrial councils under the umbrella of the respective ministries (in about 50 councils). Although trade union density and the impact of collective bargaining have been decreasing since the 1990s, bargaining coverage is still substantial in a number of industries and companies.

During the transition the Bulgarian trade union movement was dominated by two large confederations (Kirov, 2019). The main actors in the development of industrial relations on the trade union side were the reformed old social partners' structures and the newly created organisations. Two trade union confederations are of enduring importance. The Confederation of Independent Trade Unions of Bulgaria (*Konfederatziata na nezavisimite sindikati v Balgaria, KNSB*) is the largest confederation in Bulgaria. The membership of the confederation stood at 271,312 in 2016 (Eurofound, 2019b, on the basis of self-reporting). The Confederation of Labour (CL) 'Podkrepa' (*Konfederatziata na truda 'Podkrepa'*) was formed on 8 February 1989 by a small group of dissidents. After the political changes in 1989, CL Podkrepa rapidly became the second largest trade union confederation in Bulgaria with a strong presence in all sectors and regions. According to the latest available data CL Podkrepa had 79,567 members in 2016 (Eurofound, 2019b, on the basis of self-reporting).

KNSB was established on the basis of the former communist union *Balgarski profesionalni sauizi (BPS)* (see Petkov & Thirkell, 1991). It emancipated itself from the former Communist Party at the beginning of the transition and stood politically neutral, with a few exceptions, when particular centrist political coalitions were supported. In late 1989, the membership of BPS was about 4 million (about 98% of the labour force) because membership was quasi-obligatory (Gradev, 2001). In February 1990, when KNSB was established, BPS's membership was already declining as many employees cancelled their membership. In 1993 KNSB still had 1,426,057 members organised in 79 industrial federations and unions, which corresponded to 70% union density. Four years later, in 1997, its membership had almost halved to 850,000 in 53 industrial federations with more than 11,000 trade union company sections (Kirov, 2005). According to national census figures membership decline continued in the following years from 607,883 in 1998 to 380,000 in 2003 to reach 275,762 in 2012 (Eurofound, 2019b; Kirov, 2019). CL Podkrepa, the second-largest trade union confederation, was initially part of the democratic opposition in Bulgaria and one of the founders of the Union of Democratic Forces (*Saiuz na demokratichnite sili, SDS*). Since 1992 CL Podkrepa has been politically neutral or has supported centrist parties. According to CL Podkrepa leaders, at the time of its creation the laws were very 'liberal' with regard to trade unions (Kirov, 2005), and it was able to obtain official status and operate legally. During the initial period of CL Podkrepa (1989–1991) it was very difficult to distinguish its trade union activities, as it functioned rather as a political movement. Even its initial demands were more political (free movement of persons within the country) than trade unionist. The membership of CL Podkrepa was fairly limited before 11 November 1989. It started to grow rapidly at the end of 1989 to reach about 250,000 members in 1992. After 1992, CL Podkrepa membership began to decrease. One of the explanations given by the leaders of the organisation was that in its first years CL Podkrepa had been also a strong political movement, and the decrease started when it turned into an 'authentic' union (Kirov, 2005). In 1998, CL Podkrepa had 154,894 members. Subsequently, membership declined further, to 120,000 members in 2003 and 91,738 in 2012 (Kirov, 2019; Eurofound, 2019b).

Trade union membership declined significantly in the early years of transition. The decline continued at the beginning of the 21st century for various reasons, including high unemployment, privatisation followed by restructuring, employers' anti-union behaviour, especially in private companies, where union leaders were sacked, and lack of trust in trade unions (Kirov, 2005). In addition, unions are rarely present in the huge number of small and medium enterprises that came into being (Illessy, Makó, Kirov, & Stoeva, 2007; Kirov, 2019). There are different explanations of why membership temporarily stabilised in the decade of 2000. Large-scale privatisation and restructuring ended in the 1990s, while the economic boom in the mid-2000s led to labour shortages, thereby boosting trade union bargaining power. At the same time trade unions started to develop more successful unionisation strategies (Kirov, 2019; Tomev, 2017). Trade union membership resumed its decline from 2010–2012. However, according to ILO data, overall trade union density has been decreasing continuously since then. Whereas in the early transition period union density was very high, figures from the ILO Industrial Relations database suggest that it was only 13.7% in 2012 and 14% in 2016. Behind the overall density figures, however, there are major differences between industries. In general, trade union presence is higher in the public sector (education and health care) and in a few manufacturing industries, such as metal, chemicals, and mining, where existing companies were privatised, but very low in the rest of manufacturing, services, and construction (Kirov, 2019).

Compared with the trade union movement, pluralism is much more prominent on the employers' side. Since the last social partners Census of 2016, five organisations have been nationally representative (Eurofound, 2019b). The successors of the old structure of managers of state-owned companies, the Bulgarian Industrial Association (*Balgarskata stopanska kamara, BSK*) and the Bulgarian Chamber of Commerce and Industry (*Balgarskata targovskopromishlena palata, BTPP*) coexist with the more recently established organisations, such as the Confederation of Employers and Industrialists in Bulgaria (*Konfederaziata na rabotodatelite i industrialzite v Balgaria, KRIB*), claiming to represent a significant part of GDP and employment, or the Association of Industrial Capital in Bulgaria (*Assoziaziata na industrialnia capital v Balgaria, AIKB*), representing the former mass privatisation funds. From early 1990 until 2012, two organisations of small businesses, the Union for Economic Initiative (*Saiuzat za stopanska initziative, SSI*) and the Union of Private Employers 'Renaissance' (*Saiuzat na chastnite predpiremachi*

'Vazrajdane') were active employers' organisations and recognised as nationally representative. Since 2016, SSI has again been recognised as nationally representative. Until 2012 a company could be a member of more than one employer's organisation, but the rules were changed, and now only one membership is permissible (Eurofound, 2019a).

Collective bargaining

At the industry level both the organisational structure and the attitude of employers' organisations make collective bargaining difficult. This is because, in some industries, there are no employers' organisations with which trade unions can negotiate. In other cases, employers' organisations exist at the industry level but are not willing to negotiate, and, as in other countries in the region, their role is limited to business representation and lobbying. In recent years, the prevailing attitude of employers has been to skip joining employers' associations or not to authorise them to conclude sectoral/industry agreements. The latter is the case not only among local employers but also large multinational companies, often from countries with a strong bargaining tradition, such as Germany or Belgium (Kirov, 2019).

Collective bargaining in Bulgaria takes place between trade unions and employers' organisations at the industry and company level. The most important bargaining level, however, is the company level. Even though in the ten years between 2002 and 2012, collective bargaining coverage decreased by 11 percentage points, at 29% it is still fairly high compared with other CEE countries. An important factor explaining the decline in collective bargaining coverage is the decreasing union density from 26% in 2002 to about 14% to 15% in 2012. For the employers' side there are no figures available for 2000, but in 2012 employer organisation density was about 50%. Overall collective bargaining coverage is fairly low in

Table 12.5 Single-employer collective agreements in Bulgaria registered annually

Year	*No. of new agreements*	*Additional protocols to existing collective agreements*	*No. of employees covered*
2010	1 138	275	–
2011	1 274	316	311 661
2012	1 353	354	351 186
2013	1 163	300	338 318
2014	1 204	284	336 958
2015	1 055	292	328 267
2016	1 113	239	326 401
2017	974	264	331 247
2018	941	189	315 954

Source: Own elaboration based on the data form the National Institute for Conciliation and Arbitration, Bulgaria.

Bulgaria compared with the EU average or yet the EU-15 (Visser, 2019), but it still stands among the highest in Central and Eastern Europe. There are different estimations of bargaining coverage, between 20% and 30% (ETUI, 2016), for recent years. Probably the most reliable data come from the Structure of Earnings Survey for 2014 (NSI, 2017), which estimates collective bargaining coverage for this year at 27.55% for 2014. The latest data provided by the National Institute for Conciliation and Arbitration suggest that not only the coverage but the number of collective agreements has been slowly decreasing in recent years. In 2016, there were 1,658 active collective agreements at the company level covering a total of 247,426 employees, which amounts to coverage of approximately 11%. Most agreements were signed in the public sector. Only 12.2% of all collective agreements active in 2016 were in the private sector, covering 32.1% of all covered employees.

The continuous decrease of collective bargaining coverage in Bulgaria reflects the gradual decrease of trade union and employer organisation density rates. As in other CEE countries, the reason for weak sectoral/industry bargaining is the increasing organisational weakness of the industry-level organisations. Within trade unions, industry-level federations are often badly funded and staffed, unable to mobilise employees in the industry as a whole. At company level, collective bargaining can be hindered by anti-union activities of specific employers.

According to the Labour Code, collective agreements in Bulgaria are concluded at the enterprise, industrial/sectoral, and municipal levels. At the first two levels, only one collective agreement can be concluded. Industry-level agreements usually only provide a general minimum floor, which in most cases is not higher than the legal provisions. The social partners at the company level can negotiate more favourable clauses for better working conditions in a company-level collective agreement. At the municipality level, collective agreements are concluded in areas financed from municipal budgets, such as education, health care, and social services (Kirov, 2019).

If a collective agreement is concluded at the sectoral or industry level between all representative organisations of employees and employers within the sector/industry, since 2001 the Labour Code provides that, upon their joint request, the Minister of Labour and Social Policy can extend the agreement or certain individual provisions thereof to all enterprises in the sector or industry. Between 2001 and 2011 the option to extend collective agreements was not used because of employer-induced government opposition to the principle of extension. This situation changed in 2011 when the trade unions campaigned to promote extension in anti-crisis agreements. Hence, after May 2011 five agreements were extended in industries such as mining, beer brewing, and water supply (Kirov, 2019). Since 2016, however, the extension mechanism has not been used.

In the case of Bulgaria at the national level, the wage bargaining takes place only for the setting of the minimum statutory wage. The monthly minimum statutory wage is set by administrative decision of the government, after consultations with social partners within the National Council for Tripartite Cooperation (see more about the mechanisms, debates, and developments in Kahancova & Kirov, 2020). According to the Eurofound (2018) Report on Statutory Minimum Wages, the share of minimum wage earners (%) in the country is about 17.7% (or 403,000 employees). Statutory Minimum Wages in Bulgaria recorded a significant increase during the last ten years, in line with the development in the region. The minimum wage increase has been impacted recently more by the positive push from the government rather than by collective bargaining. More precisely, the medium-term budget plans of the current government included increasing the minimum wage to BGN 510 (€260) in 2018 and to a minimum of BGN 610 (€311) in 2020, still being the lowest in the CEE region. Although there has been a continuous push from the European Commission (Kirov & Markova, 2020) for setting a clear and transparent mechanism for SMW setting, for the time being social partners were not able to reach an agreement, particularly on the lower threshold of the minimum wage. Consequently, the unilateral setting of SMW under the government's discretion has not yet been replaced with a more transparent mechanism. Finally, the meaningfulness of the SMW for collective bargaining is limited. Despite a few exceptions, real wage bargaining at the sector level is not practiced, and sectoral collective agreements often replicate Labour Code provisions. Nevertheless, the SMW remains relevant for low-wage workers, including those working in the public sector (Kirov, 2019). At the same time, in the country there is no official information about collectively agreed pay. According to observation on collective agreements, there are few sectoral collective agreements (metal industry, construction, and mining) that define higher starting pay than the minimum for the country statutory minimum wage. Company-level collective agreements also could negotiate higher pay, but there is no data available about the wage developments, and what is evident, as explained earlier, is that the segment of companies with collective bargaining coverage is continuously decreasing.

Labour market situation and migration flows

In Bulgaria, the unemployment level was more than 15% in 2003 but fell down to 5.6% in 2008. Yet as the global crisis hit, the tendency was reversed, and in 2013 unemployment reached 13.0%. Since then the economic recovery contributed to a sharp decrease of unemployment to 4.1% of the fourth quarter of 2019 (NSI, 2020).

According to a recent report, the total number of people born in Bulgaria and living abroad is about 1.1 million people, out of whom 600 thousand to 700 thousand left the country for economic reasons. They live mainly in the EU, Turkey, and the USA (Angelov & Lessenski, 2017). Actually, for the entire period from 1985 to 2016, the population of Bulgaria decreased by 1.85 million people. According to NSI, more than half (over 52%) is due to the negative natural growth (the difference between birth rate and mortality rate), while 48% is due to net migration (Angelov & Lessenski, 2017).

While Bulgaria entered the EU in 2007, the labour market restrictions for its citizens have been removed in most of the EU countries in 2014. In the last ten years, since Bulgarians have the right to move freely in the EU, the percentage of citizens who have benefited from living and working in another country has doubled. Hence, in 2018 about 13.3% of the working-age population of the country (20–64 years) is mobile (Ivanova, Stoilova, & Santova, 2019). But this data should be treated with caution, as Bulgarian labour migrants heading for EU Member States have no formal obligation to inform the state authorities about their moves (see Kalfin, 2018). There are documented cases of a significant number of circular and temporary migrants, many of them low skilled (Velizarova & Kirov, 2018).

National case: Poland

Economic and political background

Poland is the largest of the New Member States of the EU (NMS), with the biggest population, economy (in terms of the aggregated GDP) and the labour market (in terms of the number of people in employment). Outward (the post-2004 wave) and inward (visible since about 2006 and accelerating visibly from mid-2010s onwards) migration seem to be a manifestation of weak economic (and specifically wage) coordination, which is confirmed by manifold studies on Polish capitalism in a comparative perspective (e.g. Bohle & Greskovits, 2012; Mykhnenko, 2007; Nölke & Vliegenthart, 2009).

Industrial relations: general outlook

Poland's system of industrial relations has been generally described as hybrid. Bechter, Brandl, and Meardi (2012) noticed that industrial relations models differed between the public and private sectors: in the former it is labelled 'state-centred', while in the latter it is said to be 'mixed' or 'empty' (that is, largely devoid of institutional representation of collective interests). Just like in all NMS with post-communist background, tripartite institutions of social dialogue have been established in Poland (yet introduced relatively late). Between 1993 and 2015 tripartite social dialogue at the national level was conducted within the Tripartite Commission for Social and Economic Affairs and, following its de facto paralysis (2013–2015), was relaunched with the formation of the Social Dialogue Council (Czarzasty & Mrozowicki, 2018).

All these analyses point to advanced and persistent decentralisation of industrial relations. Its main root is enterprise-level union movement, which had originated in the 1980–81 period of the 1st Solidarity. Even the brutal crushing of the opposition in 1981 did not lead to reinstatement of a centralised model of trade unionism. Solidarity was banned, but the new 'official' trade unions established in the early 1980s took the form of a loosely coupled confederation named All-Poland Alliance of Trade Unions (*Ogólnopolskie Porozumienie Związków*

Zawodowych, OPZZ). OPZZ was built in a bottom-up (yet administered from above by the government) manner, with company-level organisations called into existence first, followed by creation of sectoral unions (autonomous organisations and federations) and only in the final step assembled into a national-level association. The rationale behind such a project was the fear that the authoritarian government would have to face another working-class rebellion (Gardawski, Mrozowicki, & Czarzasty, 2012).

Although collective agreements, including branch agreements (multi-employer), had existed in Poland prior to 1989, collective bargaining in a usual form – that is, typical for market economies, regardless of their specific model to be defined in line with the Varieties of Capitalism framework (Hall & Soskice, 2001) – never existed. It was rather a different type of wage bargaining, in which employees and so-called employers (de facto appointees of the government charged with supervisory tasks) would frequently join their forces vis-à-vis the government (at the level of ministries responsible for respective industries) to negotiate better pay and additional bonuses (Naishul, 1991).

The socialist model of sectoral bargaining broke down in 1989, triggered by the overall political change, but the radical marketisation route was initially not an absolutely inevitable option. There was at least one viable alternative, combining the internal factor (tradition of the worker participation of the 1st Solidarity) and external one (social market economy of German ordoliberal style). The scenario was rejected in favour of a neo-liberal pattern, to which the scattered, pluralistic model of industrial relations would fit perfectly, as no institutional barriers potentially obstructing the top-down reforms applied in an 'imperative and revolutionary' manner (Morawski, 2001) such as strong sector-level trade unions and corresponding autonomous regulations in a form of sectoral (or multi-employer) collective agreements would exist.

Ironically, petrification of trade union pluralism was a consequence of strategic decisions taken by major trade unions. While negotiating the political contract between the communist government and the democratic opposition which laid down the foundations for systemic transition in 1989, two concepts of union movement clashed. OPZZ (part of the government camp) favoured the 'one union per workplace', Anglo-Saxon model (representative trade union elected by workers in a general ballot), while 'Solidarity' (the core of the opposition camp) pushed for the pluralistic model and would eventually prevail. It is likely that had the OPZZ concept won, there would have been only 'Solidarity' left in workplaces, given anti-communist moods in the entire society, which manifested in the early years of transition (Gardawski, 2009).

Nevertheless, OPZZ not only survived but would dominate along with Solidarity the national industrial relations scene until 2002. High politicisation of unions directly and indirectly remained involved in the party politics led to growing frustration in the union movement and ultimate establishment of Trade Unions Forum (Forum Związków Zawodowych, FZZ). 'Solidarity' and OPZZ have approximately the same number of members, with some 560,000 (2016) each

Table 12.6 Trade union density in Poland (%): survey data

Year	*1987*	*1991*	*2000*	*2010*	*2015*	*2016*	*2017*	*2018*	*2019*
Trade union density (%)	38	28	20	15	11	–	11	11	13

Source: Wenzel (2009, p. 540) and the reports of the Public Opinion Research Centre (CBOS) in Poland.

(authors' assessments), while FZZ gathers just above 300,000 members (official data, 2018) (Eurofound, 2019c).

Union density in Poland is low, but the long trend can be drawn based only on survey data, as administrative data by trade unions themselves is insufficient. The process of de-unionisation proceeded continuously since early 1990 (see Table 12.6), with two noticeable dips (in the early 1990s) and on the verge of the 20th and 21st centuries. Interestingly, in 2019 there was an increase registered. While this may be just an anomaly, not a reverse in trend or a matter of statistical measurement error (+/– 3%), it might also be an effect of extending the right to association from 1 January 2018 to all people in employment.

Employer organisations are weak as well, with a density of only 20% (Czarzasty, 2019). Unlike trade unions, the law allows for multiple membership in employer's organisations, which further complicates the picture. In general, only rounded-up, self-reported figures are disclosed by the five nationwide organisations (all figures obtained from the respective organisations' websites as of 2020). The Business Centre Club (BCC) claims to have some 400,000 employees working for their member enterprises, Confederation Lewiatan *(Konfederacja Lewiatan)* about 1 million; Employers of Poland *(Pracodawcy Rzeczypospolitej Polskiej*, Pracodawcy RP) – more than 5 million, Union of Entrepreneurs and Employers (*Związek Przedsiębiorców i Pracodawców*, ZPP) – more than 0.5 million, while Polish Crafts Association *(Związek Rzemiosła Polskiego*, ZRP) reports a number of associated companies only, with about 300,000. It is not just the low density that matters. The key point is that employer organisations are virtually absent from collective bargaining at the supra-enterprise level (Czarzasty, 2019).

Collective bargaining

Collective bargaining is highly decentralised and rests on single-employer collective agreements, with sectoral-level bargaining de facto absent. By 2018, 9,908 single-employer collective agreements were registered, covering little more than 1.8 million workers, of whom approximately 1 million represented the public sector and about 800 thousand private sectors. According to the National Labour Inspectorate reports, a vast part of newly concluded single-employer collective agreements simply replicates the content of the Labour Code.

Table 12.7 Single-employer collective agreements in Poland registered annually

Year	*No. of new agreements*	*Additional protocols to existing collective agreements*	*Accords on application of collective agreements*	*No. of employees covered by new agreements*
2004	328	2 193	21	166 661
2005	220	1 792	12	119 601
2006	177	1 646	6	68 000
2007	168	1 961	15	121 454
2008	155	1 732	4	62 802
2009	123	1 688	2	62 572
2010	130	1 396	1	172 425
2011	136	1 291	3	49 407
2012	92	1 265	3	61 109
2013	109	1 131	1	43 800
2014	88	1 030	1	43 576
2015	69	909	0	101 473
2016	79	896	–	38 227
2017	50	845	–	28 230
2018	54	945	–	21 067

Source: Own elaboration based on National Labour Inspectorate of Poland.

Notes: all the figures in rows reported annually; additional protocol to existing collective agreements is a formal amendment to a collective agreement in place, the parties are required to notify labour inspectorate of the conclusion.

According to the Ministry of Labour the multi-employer collective agreements' (whose official number is 86) coverage is just 390,000 employees (in large part from the public sector). Therefore, employer organisations cannot be considered anything more, but business associations mainly engaged in lobbying activities. The overall coverage of collective bargaining can be estimated at 20%. The wrecked state of collective bargaining is also a result of an obsolete and dysfunctional legal environment. Polish labour law prefers the 'managerial concept' of employer over the 'ownership concept' (Czarzasty, 2019). In other words, it does not matter if the 'employer' owns the enterprise or not. For the employee side it is certainly a factor undermining legitimacy of their negotiating partner (management contracted by the actual owner who are not involved in the process) and credibility of accords to be achieved in the course of bargaining.

Although the 'social market economy' faction (existing above political party divisions due to historical 'post-communist cleavage') retained some influence which would translate into the 1995 reform of the labour law intended to boost autonomous regulation of the labour relations, no significant correction to the trend set at the eve of the political and socio-economic transformation occurred. Two ambitious attempts of labour law modernisation undertaken in 2005 and between 2016 and 2018 aiming at introducing separate codes for individual and collective labour relations (the latter seen as a potential cure for collective bargaining) failed. So despite the political and legal attempts to reinvigorate collective bargaining, it has been continuously deteriorating to the point of 'near-death' (Czarzasty, 2019).

With the absence of autonomous wage coordination, the responsibility for pay setting falls on the state and individual employers. Acting within its capacities, the state via government can only determine wages through legal regulation. In the Polish context this is practically limited to two instances: the public sector or, precisely speaking, the state budgetary sphere and the national minimum wage. In the case of the former, the notion refers to all entities financed by the central budget (central administration, public services). In the case of the latter, negotiating the minimum wage is a prerogative of the central-level tripartite body, yet it has rarely been able to fix it in a consensual way. As a result, it is the government which has usually had the last word. After 2015, the government twice (2016 and 2019) outbid the trade unions' joint proposal regarding the minimum wage raise the following year. Especially, in 2019 the government's move was shocking, because the level of minimum wage for 2020 actually set was not only exceeding the unions' bid but also considerably higher than the government's original offer (by 6%), which triggered claims that it was intended to undermine not only institutional but societal (symbolic) power of trade unions (using the language of power resources, e.g. Schmalz, Ludwig, & Webster, 2018).

At the level of enterprise, the fluctuation of wages has been for years determined by the supply and demand of labour interplay. In the popular discourse (also becoming a part to the academic debate) the terms 'employer-dominated labour market' and 'employee-dominated labour market' have been used. High unemployment persistent over the period of 20 years had facilitated the rise of the former (characterised by low level of wages), which in turn triggered a huge wave of outward migration (Meardi, 2013). A shrinking labour supply combined with a high pace of GDP growth in the post-crisis years (after 2013), marked the shift towards the latter, which stimulated a brisk wage growth but also opened a gap to be filled by incoming migration.

Labour market situation and migration flows

In Poland, on the eve of EU accession the unemployment rate was 19.1%, slumping to 7.1% in 2008. However, after the arrival of the crisis (in the case of Poland there was no recession but a noticeable slowdown) the trend was reversed, with 2013 proving to be the worst after the global recession hit and unemployment reaching 10.3%. Economic recovery contributed to a sharp fall in unemployment which reached 3.4% at the end of 2019. In 2018 more than 2.4 million citizens resided abroad, with Germany (700 thousand), UK (700 thousand), the Netherlands (123 thousand), and Ireland (113 thousand) being the most popular destinations (GUS, 2019). The great exodus of domestic labour began after EU accession, and even the impact of the global recession on the major receiving countries in 2008/2009 did not reverse the trend. Only the Brexit-related fears have recently affected the number of Poles in the UK, which fell by 100 thousand between 2018 and 2019 (GUS, 2019).

An incoming labour migration in Poland has been on the rise. The number of work permits issued increased by ten times only between 2014 and 2019 (up to some 400 thousand), 80% of which were to Ukrainians. The highest number of work permits issued concerns activities in road transport and construction. There is also a 'special route of entry' available since 2006 to citizens of selected non-EU member countries (Armenia, Belarus, Georgia, Moldova, Russia, and Ukraine), who can undertake employment without a work permit. The only requirement is a 'declaration of intent to employ a foreign citizen' issued by a potential employer. This route is grounds for receiving a visa entitling legal work for half a year within 12 consecutive months. Between 2010 and 2017 the number of such documents issued grew by ten times (from 180 thousand to 1.8 million), heavily accelerating after 2014 (GUS, 2019; Ministry of Family, Labour and Social Policy, 2019).

Discussion

As signalled in the opening part, our key argument is that collapsed collective bargaining has led to inefficient wage coordination, which in turn undermines economic development, labour market instability being one of the main consequences manifested *inter alia* with wide migration flows, both in- and outward.

As both national case studies demonstrate, there are a number of similar trends illustrating degradation of the industrial relations system and an erosion of collective bargaining during the post-communist period. During the examined period in both countries collective bargaining coverage decreased continuously, from 25% to about 20% in Poland and from almost 40% to less than 30% in Bulgaria (based on Visser, 2019). That decrease has been parallel to the trade union density decrease. Trade union pluralism, confirmed logically as a political choice at the very beginning of the post-communist transition, led to further fragmentation and the weakening of the trade union movement in both countries. In both countries trade unions succeeded in preserving some strongholds, mainly in the public sector and in some large manufacturing companies, leaving the wage setting in the rest of the labour market outside of the reach of collective bargaining institutions. The existing collective agreements at the sectoral level in Bulgaria not only decreased but in many cases became meaningless, as they were just copying the minima from the labour legislation. In addition, the lack of extension collective agreements in both countries further undermined collective bargaining power.

In this context, the shrinking collective bargaining further undermines economic development and contributes to the labour market instability (of supply and demand) in both countries and in general in the whole CEE region with the exception of Slovenia (for Slovenia see Stanojević, Mrčela, & Breznik, 2016). In general, the labour market instability has been persistent, firstly, because of the continuous and massive post-communist restructuring. During the 1990s, the de-monopolisation, the liberalisation, and the privatisation profoundly changed the labour markets in the former communist states. Despite the fact the large post-socialist restructuring took place mainly in the 1990s and in the beginning of the 2000s, labour market instability has been observed persistently also since the years 2004–2007. Data about employment and unemployment confirms this statement.

As data in Table 12.4 reveal, there has been no clear-cut correlation between economic growth and unemployment. Furthermore, there are significant variations of unemployment and employment rates during the examined period. As Astrov et al. (2019, p. 34) write, 'it can be said that – unlike in Germany or Austria – the transmission mechanism underlying the Phillips curve is hardly present in most CEE countries'.

But the more eminent manifestation of the labour market instability is related to the migration trends, affecting the demand and supply for labour. Despite the limits of the data available (difficulties to report internal EU migration, temporary and circular migration, and so on), it clearly indicates that throughout the examined period the net migration is negative, even if decreasing. Net migration has been decreasing in the Bulgarian case during the last years, but still more people leave the country than return (see Table 12.8). In Poland during the same period net migration has been also negative. In the literature there is an understanding that the 'negative consequences of emigration for the labour market of the sender country are most directly visible when it comes to the issue of losing labour resources, of people with specific professional skills and professions' (Beleva, 2016).

As a result of the negative net migration and continuous labour emigration, Bulgaria is experiencing a lack of a qualified labour force (or a labour force in general), and multiple studies and analyses concluded that several sectors in the country lack a qualified labour force (see Kalfin, 2018).

In order to respond to this challenge, Bulgarian employers have continuously pushed for the imports of cheap labour from abroad. However, for the moment this is not the case, except for particular cases of seasonal employment, for example in tourism. According to some sources (Cheresheva, 2017), nationals from Ukraine and Moldova, which have large ethnic Bulgarian communities, as well as Macedonia and Belarus, are engaged most frequently at summer jobs at Bulgaria's seaside resorts during the last years. In general, the conclusion of a recent report shows that Bulgaria has no comprehensive policy to regulate labour migration (Kalfin, 2018).

The lack of qualified personnel has also motivated Bulgarian authorities to promote the return of Bulgarian professionals in the country. However, the pace of the process is slow, and the administration actions have limited results. Similar initiatives undertaken in Poland have also proved inconclusive: the recent data (e.g. Narodowy Bank Polski, 2019) suggest that the main factors considered by migrants pondering return are the good shape of the economy and Brexit-induced uncertainty, while re-adaptation to the domestic labour market is often difficult (e.g. Coniglio & Brzozowski, 2018).

Table 12.8 Emigration and immigration in Bulgaria and Poland

Country	*2008*	*2009*	*2010*	*2011*	*2012*	*2013*	*2014*	*2015*	*2016*	*2017*
Bulgaria emigration	–	–	–	–	16 615	19 678	28 727	29 470	30 570	31 586
Bulgaria immigration	–	–	–	–	14 103	18 570	26 615	25 223	21 241	25 597
Net migration	–	–	–	–	–2 512	–1 108	–2 112	–4 247	–9 329	–5 989
Poland emigration	30 140	229 320	218 126	265 798	275 603	276 446	268 299	258 837	236 441	218 492
Poland immigration	15 275	189 166	155 131	157 059	217 546	220 311	222 275	218 147	208 302	209 353
Net migration	14 865	–40 154	–62 995	–108 739	–58 057	–56 135	–46 024	–40 690	–28 139	–9 139

Notes: All values in thousands of people.

Source: Own elaboration based on Eurostat.

The Posting of Workers debate has been placed high on the political agenda in both Bulgaria and Poland. For the sake of our argument it is relevant to focus on the debate as it perfectly captures the attitudes of the governments and a significant part of the business community in both countries towards the competitive advantage vis-à-vis the 'old' Europe (see: Adamski, 2018). In Poland, once the process of revising the Posting of Workers Directive took off, there was a split in the domestic public debate between the government and employers on the one side and trade unions on the other. The former opposed the process; the latter were generally supportive, albeit not without reservations. Especially noteworthy was the campaign of employers under the banner 'End of Polish services in Europe', implicitly stating that it is the right of the 'poor' MS from the CEE to compete by maintaining low wages. The governments of nine 'low-wage' countries united in their resistance issuing the Letter of Nine Labour Ministers. In Bulgaria, the Posting of Workers debate has been especially active in 2018 and 2019 to oppose the so called 'Macron' law. The estimations in media suggest that about 100,000 Bulgarian truck drivers work in the EU and could lose their jobs because of the new regulations. During the spring of 2019 many Bulgarian truck drivers protested, both in Strasbourg and in Sofia, supported by the government and the majority of the political forces (Stancheva, 2019).

Conclusion

In the beginning of the post-communist transition there were strong beliefs that the former socialist countries would quickly catch up to Western European countries. However, more than 30 years after the fall of the Berlin Wall, CEE countries are still laggards in terms of wages and incomes, contributing to a diversified picture in the enlarged European Union. The analysis, based on the national cases of Poland and Bulgaria, shows that the region is still counting on low wages in order to develop its competitiveness. This has been facilitated by the continuous erosion of collective bargaining. Despite the heterogeneity of transformational paths, Poland, being part of the Visegrad countries, and Bulgaria, of the South-Eastern European cluster, both have not succeeded in fully mobilising labour utilisation. In this perspective, one of the particular contributions of this chapter was the emphasis on the relation between the collective bargaining erosion and the particular emigration trends, something that has not been featured in the socio-economic literature.

The persisting wage gap between Bulgaria and Poland on the one hand and the EU-15 wages on the other contributes to significant labour force mobility in both countries. After joining the EU, the emigration from both countries continued to expand, not being compensated by immigration. In the situation of negative net migration, both countries have attempted to react through different measures.

In this situation, the persisting wage gap, on the one hand between Bulgaria and Poland and the old member states, and on the other, non-EU countries, would further trigger the 'potential for emigration of workers to the core of the EU, given the persisting large difference in wages and income between Bulgaria and 'old' Europe, as well as immigration to Bulgaria as an EU member state' (Kalfin, 2018, p. 18). Very much the same can be said about Poland (White, Grabowska, Kaczmarczyk, & Slany 2018).

The rate of return could be increased, only if there were high economic growth, growing employment, and a decrease in the differences in incomes and standards of living between Bulgaria and the countries of Western Europe (Angelov & Lessenski, 2017). The wage gap is cited as the main economic factor weighing on decisions to return to Poland (Narodowy Bank Polski, 2019, p. 38). Most probably, this is already taking place in some particular sectors, e.g. ICT in Bulgaria. However, in order to close the income gap between Bulgaria and Poland on the one hand and the old EU member states on the other, the strengthening of wage coordination (based on the relaunch of collective bargaining) is the key precondition for breaking the vicious circle of low wage–low income–low productivity.

References

Adamski, D. (2018). *Redefining European economic integration.* New York: Cambridge University Press.

Angelov, G., & Lessenski, M. (2017). *10 years in the EU: Migration trends in Bulgaria.* Sofia: Open Society Institute.

Astrov, V., Holzner, M., Leitner, S., Mara, I., Podkaminer, L., & Rezai, A. (2019). *Wage developments in the Central and Eastern European EU member states* (Research Report No. 443). Vienna: Wiener Institut für Internationale Wirtschaftsvergleiche.

Baccaro, L., & Howell, C. (2011). A common neoliberal trajectory: The transformation of industrial relations in advanced capitalism. *Politics & Society, 39*(4), 521–563.

Bafoil, F. (2016). The limits of Europeanization in Central Europe: A critical perspective on property rights, banking capital, and industrial relations. In V. Delteil & V. Kirov (Eds.), *Labour and social transformation in Central and Eastern Europe* (pp. 37–55). London and New York: Routledge.

Bechter, B., Brandl, B., & Meardi, G. (2012). Sectors or countries? Typologies and levels of analysis in comparative industrial relations. *European Journal of Industrial Relations, 18*(3), 185–202.

Beleva, I. (2016). *Labour market policies for encouraging economic activity and labour productivity in Bulgaria* (MPRA Paper No. 73184). Munich: University Library of Munich.

Bohle, D., & Greskovits, B. (2012). *Capitalist diversity on Europe's periphery.* Ithaca, NY: Cornell University Press.

Cheresheva, M. (2017, May 23). *Bulgaria imports cheap regional labour to save tourism boom.* Retrieved from https://balkaninsight.com/2017/05/23/bulgaria-seeks-foreign-workers-to-save-tourist-season-05-22-2017/

Coniglio, N. D., & Brzozowski, J. (2018). Migration and development at home: Bitter or sweet return? Evidence from Poland. *European Urban and Regional Studies, 25*(1), 85–105.

Czarzasty, J. (2019). Collective bargaining in Poland: A near-death experience. In T. Mueller, K. Vandaele, & J. Waddington (Eds.), *Collective bargaining in Europe: Towards an endgame* (Vol. 2, pp. 465–481). Brussels: ETUI.

Czarzasty, J., & Mrozowicki, A. (2018). Industrial relations in Poland. *Employee Relations*, *40*(4), 674–691.

Delteil, V., & Kirov, V. (Eds.). (2016). *Labour and social transformations in Central and Eastern Europe: Europeanization and beyond*. London and New York: Routledge.

Dorbec, A. (2017, September). *The Eastern members of the EU: Catching up fast. Conjoncture*. Paris: BNP Paribas.

Drahokoupil, J., & Piasna, A. (2019). Dependent market economies and wage competition in Central and Eastern Europe. In T. Gerőcs & M. Szanyi (Eds.), *Market liberalism and economic patriotism in the capitalist world-system*. Cham: Springer, 43–66.

ETUI. (2016). *National industrial relations: Bulgaria*. Brussels: ETUI.

Eurofound. (2018). *Developments in collectively agreed pay 2000–2017*. Dublin: Eurofound.

Eurofound. (2019a). *Minimum wages in 2019: Annual review*. Dublin: Eurofound.

Eurofound. (2019b). *Living and working in Bulgaria*. Dublin: Eurofound.

Eurofound. (2019c). *Poland: Latest working life developments Q4 2018*. Dublin: Eurofound.

Eyal, G., Szelenyi, I., & Townsley, E. R. (1998). *Making capitalism without capitalists: Class formation and elite struggles in post-communist Central Europe*. London: Verso.

Gardawski, J. (Ed.). (2009). *Polacy pracujący a kryzys fordyzmu*. Warszawa: Scholar.

Gardawski, J., Mrozowicki, A., & Czarzasty, J. (2012). *Trade unions in Poland* (Report 123, pp. 465–481). Brussels: ETUI.

Gradev, G. (2001). Bulgarian trade unions in transition: The taming of the hedgehog. In S. Crowley & D. Ost (Eds.), *Workers after workers' states: Labor and politics in postcommunist Eastern Europe* (pp. 121–140). Oxford: Rowman & Littlefield.

GUS. (2019). *Informacja o rozmiarach i kierunkach czasowej emigracji z Polski w latach 2004–2018*. Warszawa: GUS.

Hall, P. A., & Soskice, D. (Eds.). (2001). *Varieties of capitalism: The institutional foundations of comparative advantage*. Oxford: Oxford University Press.

Hardy, J., Calveley, M., Kubisa, J., & Shelley, S. (2014). Labour strategies, cross-border solidarity and the mobility of health workers. *European Journal of Industrial Relations*, *20*(1), 1–19.

Iankova, E. A. (2000). Multi-level bargaining during Bulgaria's return to capitalism. *Industrial and Labor Relations Review*, *54*(1), 115–137.

Iankova, E. A. (2002). *Eastern European capitalism in the making*. New York: Cambridge University Press.

Illessy, M., Makó, C., Kirov, V., & Stoeva, S. (2007). Labour relations, collective bargaining and employee voice in SMEs in Central and Eastern Europe. *Transfer*, *13*(1), 95–113.

Ivanova, Y., Stoilova, Z., & Santova, A. (2019, September 10). *How many Bulgarians live in Europe? And what are the trends in their mobility?* Retrieved from www.europeandatajournalism.eu/eng/News/Data-news/How-many-Bulgarians-live-in-Europe-And-what-are-the-trends-in-their-mobility

Kahancova, M., & Kirov, V. (2020). Shaping minimum wages in Central and Eastern Europe: Giving up collective bargaining in favour of legal regulation? In I. Dingeldey, T. Schulten, & I. Grimshaw (Eds.), *The interplay between minimum wage and collective bargaining – Actors and institutions in different sectors and regions of the world*. London and New York: Routledge (Forthcoming).

Kalfin, I. (Ed.). (2018). *The impact of labour migration on the Bulgarian economy* (Report). Sofia: Friedrich-Ebert-Stiftung and Economics and International Relations Institute.

Karbowski, A. (2019). Knowledge system. In R. Rapacki (Ed.), *Diversity of patchwork capitalism in Central and Eastern Europe* (pp. 146–164). London and New York: Routledge.

King, L., & Szelenyi, I. (2005). *Varieties of post-communist capitalism: Patrimonial and liberal regimes*. Paper presented at the Department of Sociology, University of Gothenburg.

Kirov, V. (2005). Facing EU accession: Bulgarian trade unions at the crossroads. In D. Dimitrova & J. Vilrokx (Eds.), *Trade union strategies in Central and Eastern Europe: Towards decent work* (pp. 111–151). Budapest: International Labour Office.

Kirov, V. (2019). Bulgaria: Collective bargaining eroding, but still existing. In T. Mueller, K. Vandaele, & J. Waddington (Eds.), *Collective bargaining in Europe: Towards an endgame* (Vol. 1, pp. 77–92). Brussels: ETUI.

Kirov, V., & Markova, E. (2020). *Channels for trade union involvement in the European semester* (Analytical Report Work Package 5, OSE Working Paper Series, Research Paper). Brussels: European Social Observatory.

Kohl, H. (2015). Convergence and divergence – 10 years since EU enlargement. *Transfer, 21*(3), 285–311.

Meardi, G. (2013). *Social failures of EU enlargement: A case of workers voting with their feet*. London and New York: Routledge.

Ministry of Family, Labour and Social Policy of the Republic of Poland. (2019). *Informacje o zatrudnieniu cudzoziemców w Polsce*. Retrieved from: https://psz.praca.gov.pl/web/urzad-pracy/-/8180234-informacje-o-zatrudnieniu-cudzoziemcow-w-polsce

Morawski, W. (2001). *Socjologia ekonomiczna: problemy, teoria, empiria*. Warszawa: PWN.

Myant, M. (2018). *Why are wages still lower in Eastern and Central Europe?* (Research Paper-Working Paper). Brussels: ETUI.

Mykhnenko, V. (2007). Strengths and weaknesses of 'weak' coordination: Economic institutions, revealed comparative advantages, and socio-economic performance of mixed market economies in Poland and Ukraine. In B. Hancké, M. Rhodes, & M. Thatcher (Eds.), *Beyond varieties of capitalism: Conflict, contradictions, and complementarities in the European economy* (pp. 351–378). Oxford: Oxford University Press.

Naishul, V. A. (1991). *The supreme and last stage of socialism: An essay*. London: Centre for Research into Communist Economies.

Narodowy Bank Polski. (2019). *Polacy pracujący za granicą w 2018 roku*. Warszawa: Narodowy Bank Polski.

National Labour Inspectorate of Poland (PIP). *Annual reports 2004–2018*. National Labour Inspectorate of Poland.

National Statistical Institute (NSI). (2017). *Structure of earnings survey 2014*. Sofia: National Statistical Institute.

National Statistical Institute (NSI). (2020). *Unemployed and unemployment rates – National level; statistical regions*. Sofia: National Statistical Institute. Retrieved from https://www.nsi.bg/en/content/6481/unemployed-and-unemployment-rates-national-level-statistical-regions

Nölke, A. (2018). Dependent versus state-permeated capitalism: Two basic options for emerging markets. *International Journal of Management and Economics, 54*(4), 269–282.

Nölke, A., & Vliegenthart, A. (2009). Enlarging the varieties of capitalism: The emergence of dependent market economies in East Central Europe. *World Politics*, *61*, 670–702.

Ost, D. (2009). The consequences of postcommunism: Trade unions in Eastern Europe's future. *East European Politics and Societies*, *23*(1), 13–33.

Petkov, K., & Thirkell, J. (1991). *Labour relations in Eastern Europe*. London and New York: Routledge.

Schmalz, S., Ludwig, C., & Webster, E. (2018). The power resources approach: Developments and challenges. *Global Labour Journal*, *9*(2).

SOR. (2017). *Strategia na rzecz Odpowiedzialnego Rozwoju*. Ministry of Development of the Republic of Poland. Retrieved from https://www.gov.pl/documents/33377/436740/SOR.pdf

Stan, S., & Erne, R. (2016). Is migration from Central and Eastern Europe an opportunity for trade unions to demand higher wages? Evidence from the Romanian health sector. *European Journal of Industrial Relations*, *22*(2), 167–183.

Stancheva, G. (2019, May 8). *Bulgarian truck drivers to protest in Brussels against mobility package*. Retrieved from www.euractiv.com/section/transport/news/bulgarian-truck-drivers-to-protest-in-brussels-against-mobility-package/1302842/

Stanojević, M., Mrčela, A. K., & Breznik, M. (2016). Slovenia at the crossroads: Increasing dependence on supranational institutions and the weakening of social dialogue. *European Journal of Industrial Relations*, *22*(3), 281–294.

Szelenyi, I., & Csillag, T. (2015). Drifting from liberal democracy: Neo-conservative ideology of managed illiberal democratic capitalism in post-communist Europe. *Intersections*, *1*(1), 18–48.

Tomev, L. (2017). Innovative trade union practices in Bulgaria: A remedy for falling membership and declining institutional power? In M. Bernaciak & M. Kahancová (Eds.), *Innovative union practices in Central-Eastern Europe* (pp. 21–38). Brussels: ETUI.

Velizarova, M., & Kirov, V. (2018). Labour exploitation of Bulgarian migrants in Europe: Coping mechanisms. *Przegląd Socjologiczny*, *67*(3), 63–84.

Visser, J. (2019, November). *ICTWSS database* (version 6.1). Amsterdam: Amsterdam Institute for Advanced Labour Studies (AIAS), University of Amsterdam.

Wenzel, M. (2009). Związki zawodowe w badaniach CBOS 1980–2008. In J. Gardawski (Ed.), *Polacy pracujący a kryzys fordyzmu* (pp. 533–550). Warszawa: Scholar.

White, A., Grabowska, I., Kaczmarczyk, P., & Slany, K. (2018). *The impact of migration on Poland: EU mobility and social change*. London: UCL Press.

CONCLUSIONS

Beata Woźniak-Jęchorek and Michał Pilc

More than 15 years after the first post-socialist countries entered the European Union a question may be posed whether it is still justified to analyse the labour markets of Central and Eastern Europe (CEE) as a distinguished group from the Western European (EU-15) markets. One might expect that such factors as the freedom of movement within the EU, decreasing dissimilarities in the accumulated wealth, the necessity to implement the EU law, or the encouragement to follow the common economic policy principles should have left limited space to identify meaningful differences between CEE and EU-15 countries. The presented book gives evidence that such differences still exist and argues that in terms of labour utilisation and labour market institutional framework the convergence process is still not fully completed.

To a large extent the differences between CEE and EU-15 countries are rooted in the process of transition from the centrally planned to a market economy that was initiated in Central and Eastern Europe almost 30 years ago. The post-socialist economies entered this period with a large excess supply of low-skilled workers, employed predominantly in non-competitive state-owned companies, and an insufficient supply of highly skilled employees that were needed in the consumer market-oriented economy. The quickly initiated process of privatisation and restructuring decreased the quantitative aspect of labour utilisation by forcing many of these low-skilled workers to become unemployed or economically inactive but improved the qualitative aspect of labour utilisation and raised the labour productivity. Moreover, the initiation of the transition process forced the CEE governments to redefine the labour market institutional framework and reform it many times in the subsequent years in order to adjust it to largely unanticipated consequences of the introduced reforms and external shocks.

As a result, the literature identified at least three divergent models of the labour market institutional framework in this relatively small group of countries: neoliberal, embedded neoliberal, and neo-corporatist models. The neoliberal type is characteristic for the Baltic States, Bulgaria, and Romania. It is defined by a very limited role of government, fragmentary forms of the welfare state, and strong dependence on foreign direct investments. However, there are internal differences in terms of collective bargaining and the power of union movement in this group. In Estonia, Latvia, and Lithuania collective agreements and the trade union density are at their lowest level in Europe, and labour organisations are rather excluded from the process of creating policy. In contrast to these countries, Romania and Bulgaria have greater labour mobilisation and higher collective bargaining coverage and conclude the agreements widely at sectoral or industry levels. In turn, Visegrad countries (the Czech Republic, Hungary, Poland, and Slovakia) rather belong to the embedded neoliberal model. Here also, there is a significant position of foreign investments, a flexible labour market, however with a more generous welfare state. Collective agreements are held here mainly at the level of the enterprise (except Slovakia), and trade unions, even though still relatively weak in comparison to EU-15, are stronger than in Baltic countries. Finally, the only CEE country which is included in the neo-corporatist model is Slovenia. The model is characterised by a generous welfare state and a regulated labour market as well as the highest among CEE countries indicators of trade union density and collective bargaining coverage.

Although it is not justified to treat the CEE countries as a homogenous group of states as far as the labour market institutional framework is concerned, the results presented in this book indicate that there are some common patterns among the CEE countries that distinguish this group from Western European states in the way the labour supply is utilised. Furthermore, the legacy of transition reforms and a centrally planned past is still relevant in explaining these patterns. One of such a common pattern, identified by Beata Woźniak-Jęchorek and Sławomir Kuźmar in the first chapter, is the lower labour force participation rate in CEE countries than in EU-15. The roots of this pattern can be traced to the period of economic transition when the governments in CEE, in an attempt to increase the support of the low-skilled workers for the conducted reforms, decided to increase statutory minimum wages and introduced various early retirements programmes, which reduced the labour force participation rate in the subsequent years. Suzana Laporšek, Matija Vodopivec, Paweł Łuczak, and Michał Polakowski documented examples of such reforms in the Czech Republic, Poland, and Slovenia in the ninth and tenth chapters. At the same time, largely as a result of the lower level of accumulated wealth, part-time employment still remains less common in CEE than in EU-15 countries, what is documented by Kamila Fialová in the fifth chapter. It translates to a greater number of hours worked per an average employed person during a year in CEE than in EU-15. As a result, it counterbalances the negative impact of the lower labour force participation rate on the quantitative aspect of labour utilisation (measured by the average hours worked per capita) and helps to keep this aspect of labour utilisation in CEE at a slightly higher level than in EU-15.

The other common pattern is a relatively weak position of trade unions (in a comparison to Western European countries), which is a consequence of deterioration in the trade union membership resulting from the process of privatisation and restructuring of the state-owned companies. Jan Czarzasty and Vassil Kirov have documented this process in detail for Bulgaria and Poland in the twelfth chapter.

Its direct consequence is the process of work precarisation which affected labour markets in CEE countries to a greater extent than EU-15 states, as is indicated by Adam Mrozowicki in the sixth chapter. However, the deterioration of trade union membership has also indirect consequences. The theory of power resources argues that the political strength of trade unions, understood as a key player in the process of public choice concerning the labour market policy, has a decisive impact on the level of expenditure on that policy. As a result, it is not surprising that the generosity of both the active and the passive labour market policy in CEE countries still remains generally lower than in Western European countries, as is evidenced by Monika Banaszewska and Michał Pilc in the fourth chapter and corroborated by the Ondřej Hora's and Tomáš Sirovátka's case study analysis in the eleventh chapter. However, it is difficult to assess to what extent these tendencies translate to differences in the level of labour utilisation between CEE and EU-15 regions, because the impact of labour market policy generosity on labour utilisation remains equivocal: it is generally beneficiary in the case of active policy but may be strongly negative in the case of passive policy.

Much more unequivocal dissimilarity can be noticed in the level of labour productivity (as measured, for instance, by GDP per hour worked), which remains substantially lower in CEE than in EU-15 countries. To a large extent this is a consequence of the difference in the level of accumulated capital between these two groups of countries. However, the difference in this respect would have been smaller if the utilisation of workers' skills in CEE states had been greater. What is important is that this qualitative aspect of labour utilisation can be still significantly improved, as it is indicated by the results obtained by Dominik Buttler, Magdalena Andrałojć, Kea Tijdens, Maryna Tverdostup, Egidijus Barcevičius, Luka Klimavičiūtė, and Lukas Pukelis, in the second, third, seventh, and eight chapters of the book, respectively. Moreover, increasing the stock of skills accumulated by the employed and improving utilisation of these skills seems to be the first-best solution to one of the main challenges of the contemporary labour market, which is the increasing pace of task automation and the substitution of human labour by robots and artificial intelligence. This recommendation applies not only to the highly developed countries but also to the CEE states, which face the risk of freezing the differences in the achieved welfare between them and Western European countries if the latter group were able to better adjust the skills of their population to new technologies. Moreover, creating more highly productive job matches between skilled workers and technologically advanced employers should also translate into greater job satisfaction, longer employment spells, and higher labour force participation rate in CEE. Thus, improving the skills of the employed and increasing their utilisation seems to be a crucial ingredient in achieving the aim of 30 years ago that was expected from the process of economic transition: to reach the level of economic development characteristic for the Western European states.

INDEX

Note: Page numbers in *italic* indicate a figure and those in **bold** indicate a table on the corresponding page.

active labour market policy (ALMP) 260–283, 311; creaming off 264, 270, 277, 279; Czech ALMP evaluation 275–276; Czech labour market and ALMPs 267–270; Czech Republic, impacts of ALMP in 270–276; Czech Republic as labour market regime 261–262; disadvantaged target groups in Czech Republic 265–267; disadvantaged unemployed 261, 263, 276; key instruments of 5, 260; Public Employment Services (PES) 260, 264, 265, 271, 278; public works **266**, 270, 273, *274*, 275, 277, 278; subsidised workplaces **266**, 270, 273, *274*, 278; targeting ALMPs in CEE countries 264–265; targeting and effectiveness of ALMP measures 263; targeting failures 263–264, 276–277; training programmes **266**, 270, 272–273, 278

automation in jobs, education for 86

Belarus, occupational matrix of **62**, *73*

Belgium, occupational matrix of **62**, *77*

brain drain, in Lithuania 191

bricoleurs, and precarious employment in Poland 156, 157–158

bridging pensions in Poland 252–253

Bulgaria *see* collective bargaining

business cycle, and part-time employment 126, **129**, 130, **131**

capitalism, in Poland 145, 148, 286

Central and Eastern Europe (CEE): geographical scope of study 1; *see also* European Union, comparisons with CEE countries

collective agreements 285, 301, 310; in Bulgaria **293**, 294–295; in Poland 297, 298, **299**

collective bargaining 284–308; argument and discussion 284–285, 301–304; in Bulgaria 290–296; industrial relations 40, 285, 290–292, 296–297, 301; in Poland 296–301; theoretical background 285–289; tripartism 290–291, 296, 300

collective bargaining coverage 48, 289, 293–294, 301, 310

creativity, and precarious employment in Poland 156–157, 158

Croatia, minimum wage effects 215

Czech Republic: minimum wage effects 215, 220; occupational matrix of **62**, *73*; pension systems in 241–242, 248–252; *see also* active labour market policy (ALMP); pension systems

defined benefit and defined contribution systems 241, 248, 253–254

Denmark, occupational matrix of **62**, *77*

descriptive databases for labour market regulations 10, 14–17, 28n1

discrimination, in Estonia, and gender gap 167, 183

dualist employment regimes 36, 261

economic conditions, and employee training 50, *51*

Economic Freedom around the World database 14

education systems: and employee training 38, 39–40, **42**, **45**, 49–50, *50*, **52**; in Estonia, and gender gap 167, 175; in Poland, and precarious employment 147, 149
embedded neoliberal model 286, 310
employee training 34–58; cross-country variation 35, 47–48, 53–56; economic conditions 50, *51*; education systems 38, 39–40, **42**, **45**, 49–50, *50*, **52**; empirical results of study 41; empirical strategy 42–46; employment protection 40, **45**, 50, *51*, **52**; employment regimes 36; labour market policies 40, **42**, **45**, 49, *49*, **52**; results, macro-level determinants 47–55; results, micro-level determinants **46**, 46–47; skill development and employment quality 35; trade union strength 40, **42**, **45**, 48, *48*, **52**; transition regimes 34, 36–39, 47–48, 53–55; two-level random intercept logit model 51, **52**; *see also* training programmes
employer organisations 298–299
employment, minimum wage effects 212–215, 226–228, 228–230
employment centred transition regimes 34, 36–39, 47, 53–55
employment protection, and institutional determinants of employee training 40, **45**, 50, *51*, **52**
Employment Protection Legislation (EPL) index 14, 17–20, *18*, 28n2
employment protection rules/regulations 10–11; effect on part-time employment 119–120, 130, 134; impact on labour utilisation 12–13; indicators, relation with labour utilisation measures 23–26; Labour Code and employment contracts in Poland 147, 149–150, 156–157, 298–300
employment quality 34–35
employment regimes 36
entrepreneurship, and precarious employment in Poland 150–151, 156–158
Estonia: minimum wage effects 215, 216, 220; *see also* gender and skills utilisation in Estonia
European Social Survey (ESS) 34, 43
European Union, comparisons with CEE countries 309–311; collective bargaining **287–289**; employment protection regulations and labour utilisation 11, 15, **16**, 17–20, **21–22**; firm-sponsored training 35, 47–48, 53–56; minimum wage 213, 216, 219–221; part-time employment 116, 121, 123–124, 134; pension systems 243, **244**, **246**, **249**; skills utilisation and gender gap 168–169; skills utilisation and occupational matrix 62, 65, **66–70**, 71–72, *77–80*, 82–85; skills utilisation and return migration 191; trade unions 310–311; unemployment benefits 91, 95–99, **104–107**
Eurostat Labour Force Survey 127–128

field of study mismatch, of skills 61
firm performance, and minimum wage effects 213, 216–217, 227
firm-sponsored training of employees *see* employee training
foreign direct investments (FDIs) 145, 148, 242, 286

GDP per capita: and employee training 50, *51*; labour utilisation and labour productivity 20, **21–22**; in Lithuania 191; in Slovenia 218
gender and skills utilisation in Estonia 164–187; data and methods 169–173; employment segregation 166, 180, 181–183; factors: demographic, human capital, and employment 165, 170, **171–172**, 175, 177–178, 180, 181; gender disparity in skill use 166–168; gender gap statistics 168–169, **176**, **177**; gender wage gap 165–166, **168**, 168–169, 173–174, 175–181; governmental policy action 169, 182–183; regression and decomposition analysis 175–181; research questions 165–166, 173–175; task framework 164, 166
gender gap in retirement age and pension systems 248, 249, 250, 253
gender in part-time employment 121, 123–124, 135–136
Germany, occupational matrix of **62**, *78*
Global Labour Survey (GLS) database 28n2

Hiring and Firing Regulations (HFR) index 19, 23–26, 27
Hours Regulations (HR) index 23–26, 27

hours worked per capita *see* labour utilisation
Hungary: minimum wage effects 215, 216, 217; occupational matrix of **62**, *74*

ILO database 28n1
ILO EPLex indicator 28n2
immigration *see* migration
inclusive employment regimes 36
indicator-based databases for labour market regulations 10, 14, 17–20, 28n2
industrial relations 40, 285, 290–292, 296–297, 301
institutions *see* labour market institutions
International Social Survey Programme (ISSP) 91, 101, 109
International Standard Classification of Occupations (ISCO) 87n2
Italy, occupational matrix of **62**, *78*

job security rules/regulations *see* employment protection rules/regulations

labour force participation rate 310
Labour Market Efficiency (LME) index 28n2
labour market institutions: defined 1; list of xix; in Lithuania *see* return migration and skills utilisation in Lithuania; models of 309–310; old-age pensions *see* pension systems; role in part-time employment 127
labour market policies, and institutional determinants of employee training 40, **42**, **45**, 49, *49*, **52**
labour market regimes 34, 36–39, 47–48, 53–55, 261–262
labour market regulations 9–33; approaches, institutionalist and distortionist 9; descriptive database insights on reforms 10, 14–17; employment protection indicators, relation with labour utilisation measures 23–26; employment protection rules 10–11, 12–13; indicator-based database insights 10, 14, 17–20; labour utilisation in CEE countries 12–13, 20–22; measurement with databases 10, 14–20; reforms in CEE countries 14–17, *16*; *see also* employment protection rules/regulations
Labour Market Regulations (LMR) index 14, 28n2
labour unions *see* trade unions
labour utilisation: in CEE countries 20–22, **21–22**; defined, by OECD 2; employment protection indicators, relation with 23–26; and labour market regulation 12–13; labour productivity and utilisation of workers' skills 311; in Lithuania *see* return migration and skills utilisation in Lithuania; minimum wage effects on 232; of older workers and pension systems 239–241, 243–248; and part-time employment 117–118; precarious employment in Poland 144; unemployment benefit impact on 92–94
Labour Utilisation Framework (LUF) 60–61
LABREF database 14, 28n1
legislation *see* employment protection rules/regulations
Letter of Nine Labour Ministers 304
liberal transition regimes 34, 36–39, 53–55, 261
Lithuania: minimum wage effects 215, 220; *see also* return migration and skills utilisation in Lithuania
Lithuanian Labour Force Survey (LFS) 189, 195, 196, 197, 206

Mandated Costs of Worker Dismissal (MCWD) index 19, 23–26, 27
market employment regimes 36
media articles, text mining of 195, 196–197, 201–203, **204**, 205, 206
meritocracy, precarious employment in Poland 150–151
middle income trap 1, 205, 285
migration: from Bulgaria for employment 285, 295–296, 302, **303**; occupation-driven 65, 71–72, 81, 83; from and to Poland for employment 146, 285, 296, 300–301, 302, **303**; return to Lithuania *see* return migration and skills utilisation in Lithuania
minimum wage: in Bulgaria 285, 294–295; in CEE countries 220–221, 289; in Poland 147, 149, 285, 300
minimum wage in Slovenia 212–236; cross-country comparisons 219–221; data for analysis 221–222; effects on employment 212–215, 226–228, 228–230; effects on firm performance 213, 216–217, 227; effects on wage

distribution 212, 213, 215–216, 224–225; firm-level responses to minimum wage shocks 228–230; Minimum Wage Act 217–219; minimum-wage workers 222–223; spill-over effects 212, 213, 216, 225, 232; worker level analysis of minimum wage shocks 224–228
models: employment regimes 36; of labour market institutions 309–310; transition labour market regimes 34, 36–39, 47–48, 53–55, 261–262

NATLEX database 28n1
neo-corporatist model 309–310
neoliberal model 38, 148, 151, 263, 286, 297, 309–310
Netherlands, occupational matrix of **62**, *79*
Non-Accelerating Inflation Rate of Unemployment (NAIRUI) xix

occupational matrix 59–89; about skills utilisation 59–60; cross-country similarities and differences 65–72; methods and theoretical framework 61–65; in particular countries 72, *73–80*, 81; pay satisfaction in relation to 83–85; qualification mismatch and field of study mismatch 60–61; qualification mismatch in relation to 81–83
occupations: classifications (high-paid/low-paid and surplus/shortage) 60, 64, 65, **65–70**, 71–72; number of respondents in **63–64**
OECD: definition of labour utilisation 2; Job Strategy 28n1; Skills for Jobs database 64
old-age pension systems *see* pension systems
organisational spaces, in education systems and employee training 39

part-time employment 116–140; business cycle 126, **129**, 130, **131**, 135; CEE and Western Europe compared 116, 134; determinants of 118–121; determinants of, methodology and data 126–128; determinants of, results 128–134; development of, in CEE 121–126; employment protection legislation 119–120, 130, 134; gender specifics 121, 123–124, 135–136; labour market institutions, role of 127; labour utilisation and 117–118; taxation of labour 120, 133, 134; trade union strength 120, 128, 133, 134
patchwork capitalism 148
pay satisfaction, and occupational matrix 83–85, **84**
pension systems 237–259; in Czech Republic 241–242, 248–252; defined benefit and defined contribution systems 241, 248, 253–254; health and education of older workers 241–242; labour utilisation of older workers 239–241, 243–248; in Poland 241–242, 248, 252–254
Poland: Labour Code and employment contracts 147, 149–150, 156–157, 298–300; minimum wage effects 215, 217, 220; occupational matrix of **62**, *74*; pension systems in 241–242, 248, 252–254; *see also* collective bargaining; pension systems; precarious employment in Poland
political parties: precarious employment in Poland 149–150, 151, 155; and unemployment benefits 101, 108
Posting of Workers Directive 304
post-socialist transition regimes 34, 36–39, 48, 53–55
power resources thesis 99, 311
precarious employment in Poland 143–163; CATI PREWORK survey 151–152, 157–158, 159; drivers of 148–151; entrepreneurship 150–151, 156–158; institutional factors 144, 148, 149–150; junk contracts 151, 155; Labour Code and employment contracts 147, 149–150, 156–157; and labour utilisation 144; meaning for creatives, bricoleurs, and withdrawns 156–158; meaning for security and social status 153–155; meanings for young people 151–158; meritocracy 150–151; rise and perpetuation of 145–148; social agency and trade unions 144, 148, 149, 150–151, 155; social protests 143–144; socio-structural factors 148–149
Program of International Assessment of Adult Competencies (PIAAC) 165, 169–170, 174, 175

public works, and active labour market policy in Czech Republic **266**, 270, 273, *274*, 275, 277, 278

qualification mismatch, of skills 60–61, 81–83
qualification spaces, in education systems and employee training 39

relative deprivation 100
retirement *see* pension systems
return migration and skills utilisation in Lithuania 188–211; data and methodology 195–197; and labour market institutions 189, 194, 203, 204–205, 207–208; labour market performance of returnees 197–201; labour productivity and labour utilisation 191–193; media analysis 201–205; migration rates 190–191, 194; policy instruments 205; public employment service (PES) 189, 194, 198, 204–205, 207; text mining 195, 196–197, 201–203, **204**, 205, 206
Role of Government survey 91, 101, 109
Roma minorities 262, 266
Romania: minimum wage effects 215, 220, 221; occupational matrix of **62**, *75*
Russian Federation, occupational matrix of **62**, *75*

shortage occupations 64; *see also* occupations
skill development opportunities as employment quality 35
skills mismatch 60–61, 144, 149
skills utilisation, across countries and occupations 59–89, 311; in Estonia *see* gender and skills utilisation in Estonia; in Lithuania *see* return migration and skills utilisation in Lithuania; occupations *see* occupational matrix; occupations
Slovakia, occupational matrix of **62**, *76*
Slovenia *see* minimum wage in Slovenia
social protests 143–144
Spain, occupational matrix of **62**, *79*
subjective qualification mismatch, of skills 82
sub-protective transition regimes 34, 36–39, 48, 53–55, 261
subsidised workplaces, and active labour market policy in Czech Republic **266**, 270, 273, *274*, 278
surplus occupations 64; *see also* occupations
Sweden, occupational matrix of **62**, *80*

taxation of labour, and part-time employment 120, 133, 134
temporary employment *see* precarious employment in Poland
text mining 195, 196–197, 201–203, **204**, 205, 206
topic modelling 196–197, 202–203
trade union density: in Bulgaria 291, 292, 301; in CEE countries 128, 133, 134, 289, 310; in Poland 150, **298**; in Western European countries 41, 48
trade unions: in Bulgaria 292–294; in CEE compared with EU 310–311; in Poland 296–298
trade union strength: and collective bargaining 285, 286, 291–292; and institutional determinants of employee training 40, **42**, **45**, 48, *48*, **52**; in Lithuania 205; and part-time employment 120, 128, 133, 134; precarious employment in Poland 144, 148, 149, 150–151, 155
training programmes: and active labour market policy in Czech Republic **266**, 270, 272–273, 278; *see also* employee training
transition labour market regimes 34, 36–39, 47–48, 53–55, 261–262
tripartism 290–291, 296, 300

Ukraine, occupational matrix of **62**, *76*
underemployment, measurement of 87n1
unemployment: and emigration 191; long-term equilibrium rate of xix; *see also* active labour market policy (ALMP)
unemployment benefit generosity 94–95
unemployment benefits in CEE countries 90–115; about the study 90–91; construction of benefits system 91–92; data and methods 101–103; evolution of benefit schemes 95–99; impact on labour utilisation 92–94; measuring generosity 94–95; results 103–108;

societal expectations, theory and hypotheses 99–101; text mining in word cloud 205
unemployment trap 120
United Kingdom: minimum wage effects 216; occupational matrix of **62**, *80*
universalistic transition regimes 34, 36–39, 47, 48, 53–55, 261

valence voting theory 101, 110n11
vocational education 38–39

wage coordination 284–285, 296, 300, 301, 305
wage distribution, minimum wage effects 212, 213, 215–216, 224–225
wage gap: in CEE countries 220, 284, 289, 304–305; by gender in Estonia 165–166, **168**, 168–169, 173–174, 175–181
WageIndicator web survey 61–62, 82, 83
'wage penalty' phenomenon 60, 83, 86
withdrawn employees, and precarious employment in Poland 156–157, 158
word-cloud algorithms 196–197, 202–203, 205
Working Regulations (WR) index 19
World Bank: Doing Business, Rigidity of Hours index 29n7; Doing Business database 28n2; Ease of Doing Business database 29n8; Employing Workers Indicator 14

www.ingramcontent.com/pod-product-compliance
Lightning Source LLC
LaVergne TN
LVHW011112300926
849160LV00008B/357
9780367564230